MALT
WHISKY
YEARBOOK
2009

First published in Great Britain in 2008 by
MagDig Media Limited

ISBN 978-0-9552607-4-2

Translations by Hirschfeld Media.
www.hirschfeld.se

MagDig Media Limited
1 Brassey Road
Old Potts Way, Shrewsbury
Shropshire SY3 7FA
ENGLAND

E-mail: info@maltwhiskyyearbook.com
www.maltwhiskyyearbook.com

Contents

The editor, Ingvar Ronde (right) talking to Andrew Shand, Speyside distillery

Introduction

"How will you be able to write a new book about malt whisky every year? What can possibly have happened except for a few new bottlings being released?"

This was the common reaction I got when I decided three years ago to do the first Malt Whisky Yearbook. Well, I have just finished the fourth edition and I think even the most doubting have been convinced – there is no problem writing a Yearbook of malt whiskies, the problem is rather finding space for all that has happened during the year. At the moment optimism and exuberance abound in the whisky industry – demand is increasing, new distilleries are being built, mothballed distilleries are on stream again. But there are some clouds on the horizon. The economy is slowing down in many of the important export markets and the prices of grain and fuel are increasing rapidly. I do not envy the whisky CEOs in these times, especially when taking into consideration that they have to plan today for how the market will look in ten years' time. That is the torment and the beauty of producing whisky – it usually takes ten years before you have a product to sell and who knows if anyone will want to buy it then?

This and many other topics are scrutinized by some of the world's most distinguished whisky writers in this years' edition of Malt Whisky Yearbook:

If you ever had the dream of building your own whisky distillery, please read the article by *Gavin D Smith* first. It is not a task for the fainthearted. The whisky we like to drink is all a matter of taste but is it at all possible to be objective when you discuss taste? *David Stirk* gives us his views on the matter. Can we know for sure who were the first to make whisky? *Charles MacLean* has travelled into the dark ages to find the answer. According to *Dominic Roskrow* it is time to take malt whiskies produced in other parts of the world seriously. His enthusiastic report takes us to Tasmania, Sweden and Germany. Every year the big wigs of the whisky industry meet for the two day World Whiskies Conference. But what do they talk about? *Ian Buxton* was there to give us a unique and well-informed insight into the current trends. *Walter Schobert* spends most of the year on Islay and have many of the distillery people as his personal friends. Who better to profile this whisky paradise?

In Malt Whisky Yearbook 2009 you will also find the unique, detailed and much appreciated 164-page section on malt whisky distilleries which has been thoroughly revised and up-dated including numerous new pictures. There is a list of 120 of the best whisky shops in Europe with full details and a comprehensive list of more than 475 new bottlings during the year. The summary The Whisky Year That Was has been expanded, being warranted following an exciting and eventful year. A new feature this year is the tasting notes for the core expression of every working distillery in Scotland and Ireland prepared by Dominic Roskrow and David Stirk. Of course, how one perceives whisky is a very personal experience, but many readers have asked for comments from an experienced whisky nose since the first edition.

Thank you for buying Malt Whisky Yearbook 2009. We hope that you will have many enjoyable moments reading it and we can assure you that we will be back with a new edition in 2010.

Great care has been taken to ensure the accuracy of the information presented in this book. MagDig Media Ltd can, however, not be held liable for inaccuracies.

Malt Whisky Yearbook 2010 will be published in October 2009.
To make sure you will be able to order it directly, please register at
www.maltwhiskyyearbook.com.

Malt Whisky Yearbook has become a popular guide for the connoisseur but also the perfect gift for customers and co-workers alike.
To get a quote, contact the editor at
ingvar.ronde@magdig.com

Acknowledgments

First of all I wish to thank the writers who have shared their great specialist knowledge on the subject in a brilliant and entertaining way – Ian Buxton, Charles MacLean, Dominic Roskrow, Walter Schobert, Gavin D. Smith and David Stirk.

A special thanks goes to David and Dominic who put in a lot of effort nosing, tasting and writing notes for more than 100 different whiskies.

The following persons have also made important photographic or editorial contributions:

Stewart R Adamson, Tomo Akaike, Rob Allanson, Chris Allwood, Paul Aston, David Baker, Duncan Baldwin, Ian Bankier, Sonia Bastian, Keith Batt, Iain Baxter, Alex Bell, Lauren Beth, Etienne Bouillon, Stephen Bremner, Alex Brykin, Alexander Buchholz, Hamish Bunker, Bert Burger, Douglas Campbell, Ian Chapman, Margaret Mary Clarke, Frances Clotworthy, Michael Cockram, Yves Cosentino, Katherine Crisp, Jeremy Cunnington, Peter Currie, David Doig, Jean Donnay, Graeme Dunnet, Matt Edwards, Ralph Erenzo, Darryl Estrine, Joanna Fearnside, Robert Fleischmann, Robert Fleming, Thomas Gerber, Jess Graber, Alan Gray, Jan Groth, Ueli Hagen, Monika Haider, Anna Hall, Karen Hallgren, Diana Hamberger, Jay Harman, Michael Heads, Stuart Hendry, Holger Höhler, Anne Jack, Moritz Kallmeyer, Cara Laing, Ruedi Käser, Mari Laidlaw, Bill Lark, Patricia Lee, Aart van der Linde, Mark Littler, Iain Lochhead, Horst Lüning, Christine McCafferty, Iain McCallum, Stephen McCarthy, John MacDonald, Katrina Macdonald, Barbara McEwan, Frank McHardy, John MacLellan, Marie Macleod, Beth McMillan, Ian MacMillan, Grant MacPherson, Patrick Maguire, Dennis Malcolm, Brian Megson, Annabel Meikle, Jean Metzger, Michael Fraser Milne, Stephanie Mingam, Euan Mitchell, Henric Molin, Jemma Morris, Susan Morrison, Karen Murray, David Neave, Wendy Neave, Andrew Nelstrop, Stuart Nickerson, Jay Oddleifson, Donald R Outterson, Richard A Pelletier, Don Poffenroth, Nick Pollachi, Warren Preston, Anssi Pyysing, Greg Ramsay, Robert Ransom, Patrick Roberts, David Robertson, Colin Ross, Andrew Scott, Jill Scougall, Jacqui Seargeant, Sue Sellers, Abhishek Shahabadi, Andrew Shand, Euan Shand, Rubyna Sheikh, Sukhinder Singh, Alison Spowart, Verity Staniforth, Rory Steel, Thomas Sundblom, Lynne M Sutherland, Cameron Syme, Stephen Teeling, Julie Torrance, Gerry Tosh, Erkin Tuzmuhamedov, Lasse Vesterby, Alistair Walker, Andy Watts, Iain Weir, Brigitte Weutz, James Whelan, David Williamson, Cristina Wilkie, Allan Winchester, Patrick van Zuidam, Daniel and Ursula Zürcher

Thank you!

Ingvar Ronde
Editor

World Whiskies Conference

*It was clearly indicated at the third
World Whiskies Conference in April 2008
that not only whisky drinking but also whisky production
has become a global concern.
But what did the participants really say and talk about?
Who better to guide us than its promotor and
Conference Director Ian Buxton.*

Like a good Scotch Whisky, in its third year the World Whiskies Conference has begun to exhibit effervescent youth combined with a growing maturity. The Conference is starting to take on its own natural colour and develop a distinctive character. It's evolving nicely.

As regular readers of the Malt Whisky Year-book will know, I started the World Whiskies Conference in 2006 and act as the Conference Director. It's my job to recruit the speakers, trying always for a varied yet balanced programme; stroke and encourage the vitally important sponsors and even, if time permits, sell a few more delegate tickets: I like to think of myself as the Conference's Master Blender!

So this isn't an impartial report on the 2008 proceedings. Think of it rather as an inside view of an exclusive, senior-level, trade-only event that is rapidly gaining a reputation as the global whisky business summit. As whisky drinkers you're naturally concerned to eavesdrop on what was discussed and learn who was there.

All the heavy-weights were there

But to begin at the beginning: the Conference this year was a two day session, held on 15-16th April at the Radisson Hotel and Conference Centre in Glasgow. Delegates came from all parts of the industry and all over the world. We altered the programme slightly this year, grouping the most senior speakers into one plenary session on day one, then splitting into two tracks for sessions on a wider range of specialist topics.

Our presenters included Paul Walsh (CEO, Diageo); Dr Vijay Mallya (owner and Chairman of India's UB Group and Whyte & Mackay of Scotland); Tom Flocco (CEO, Beam Global); Dr Peter Cressy (President & CEO of DISCUS, the US trade association for the distilling industry); John Teeling (Chairman, Cooley Distillers); Kuni Himeno (MD, Suntory Europe) and Kenny Mackay (MD, Scottish Liqueur Centre). As we shall see, there were also a number of other important speakers and the audience went home happy, if slightly punch-drunk by the amount of material to be absorbed.
The opening session had aroused a lot of

*Paul Walsh - CEO of Diageo since 2000 and now also
the Chairman of the Scotch Whisky Association*

anticipation: little surprise, with Diageo's Paul Walsh on the same platform as Dr Vijay Mallya, the ebullient Chairman of India's largest distilling group and the new owner of Whyte & Mackay. Given the war of words (and lobbying) between the Scotch Whisky Association (SWA), of which Mr Walsh had recently been appointed Chairman, and the Indian government and industry, delegates were expecting a lively and provocative session.

They were not to be disappointed, though at first it looked as though the session was to end in anti-climax. Dr Mallya was nowhere to be found and the morning began with an empty chair on the podium! Fortunately, he was in the hotel finalising his speech with aides and arrived part way through Paul Walsh's presentation, his diamond ear-ring glittering provocatively as he made his way to the stage.

  Afterwards, delegates were divided: was the late arrival a deliberate snub to the Diageo chief; a piece of theatre or a genuine last-minute panic? Certainly, there seemed no ill-will between the two as they shared coffee at the break. But what did they have to say?

Chancellor Alistair Darling is not the most popular person in whisky circles these days.

Speaking as Chairman of the SWA, Paul Walsh's presentation was authoritative and unemotional, though that did not mean he avoided some hard or controversial issues. Though he began by noting the "real optimism" of the industry at large, typified by his own company's investment at Roseisle, he was immediately critical of the harsh duty rises announced in the UK budget just a few days previously.

"We were surprised and disappointed to hear the Chancellor's Budget this year. I think it is fair to say that we had a very constructive dialogue with Government until then but I'm unsure I can say the same now. Against this backdrop, the laws of unintended consequences come into play. One such consequence for example could be around investment in distilling in Scotland. If cider is to be treated so favourably in comparison to Scotch whisky, ironically perhaps a better investment could be orchards in Poland rather than distilleries we could build in Scotland?"

  For a normally diplomatic and reserved body as the SWA this is hard-hitting language. Much of the same was in store for the Indian Government. Having acknowledged positive changes at national level, Walsh then threw down a challenge to the individual Indian State Governments:

  "...challenges remain, particularly at State level where we must work to ensure the introduction of non-discriminatory tax treatment of domestic and imported products. If such steps are not taken, we will not hesitate to return to the WTO in the future to secure fair market access in line with international trade rules."

The themes of corporate social responsibility, sustainability and alcohol abuse were also candidly taken up, Walsh acknowledging that the industry could and should do more on all fronts. He called for distillers globally to show

  "...leadership and commitment in working with a wide range of partners to promote responsible attitudes to alcohol and to develop effective, evidence-based policy interventions."

  Finally, he turned to the new regulations on the labeling of Scotch Whisky, itself the subject of a major debate later in the Conference programme, and was harshly critical of the criticism, especially of the 'blended malt' category, observing that much of it was "misinformed, misleading, and comes from a narrow perspective."

Will Scotland and India come to terms?

Vijay Mallya had by this time arrived in the Conference hall, to my very considerable relief, and joined us on the platform. Following his colleague's excellently prepared presentation in 2007 (Dr Vijay Rekhi, President of United Spirits) we were expecting a sophisticated PowerPoint show, with embedded video, stylish graphics and startling statistics. In fact, I know Dr Mallya had such a presentation in his briefcase.

But once again he surprised us. Striding confidently to the lectern, without notes or slides, he gripped the delegates with a passionate and heartfelt address that surprised some; delighted others and perhaps caused just a few to think hard about their own position. Sadly, a full text of the speech doesn't exist – it was genuinely 'off the cuff', and all the more powerful for that.

Dr Vijay Mallya - dynamic owner and Chairman of United Breweries Group.

Many of his remarks were emollient. For example,

"(In India) it's not all one way traffic in that we want to shut you [international spirits producers] out. Companies need to look objectively at how to deal with government. Confrontation doesn't work in India, it gets our backs up." and "We in India not only welcome and acknowledge the Scotch whisky industry; we want to wholly cooperate with it. If that weren't the case, I wouldn't have invested £600m in Whyte & Mackay."

But more often he surprised. How many delegates, he wondered, realised that the Indian Constitution legally obliged the national Government to work for the introduction of Prohibition? Perhaps, he suggested, this explained at least in part the taxes on alcohol. From the platform I could see more than a few dropping jaws and muttered comments to neighbours. Dr Mallya then drew out the further significance of this point, which in his view had escaped the negotiators of the SWA:

"One of the directive principals enshrined in the Indian constitution is that the Government shall endeavour to introduce nationwide prohibition," he explained. "The same constitution of India also empowers every state government to tax, licence, restrict or permit the manufacture, distribution and sale of beverage alcohol in any manner of their choosing, over which the Indian federal government has absolutely no control. This is a constitutional provision."

"Yes, the Scotch whisky business lobbied hard and persuaded the Indian government to remove the additional customs duty and coming into line with WTO obligations," Mallya continued. "But those obligations start and end with the federal government of India. They do not apply to the state governments, who are constitutionally empowered."

"Be aware that it is not a simple open and shut case, where governments can be asked to fall in line with international duty structures. That is something that is not challengeable in any international court."

Finally, Dr Mallya brought up the question of flavoured whiskies. This has been discussed at the Conference previously, to some controversy, but he didn't shy away from this topic suggesting that younger consumers, drawn to vodka, would welcome the use of "natural additives" in their whisky. Not everyone agreed.

Breaking down stereotypes about Bourbon

So we enjoyed a lively morning, with a number of provocative questions following from the audience. Debate carried on over lunch, after which Tom Flocco, CEO of Beam Global took the chair.

He too surprised the delegates. During the lunch break the hall had been re-wired with an interactive voting system and Mr Flocco then ensured there was no opportunity for post-prandial snoozing by delegates by asking them a series of questions designed to break down stereotypes about Bourbon, his company's principal product.

In a very sophisticated presentation he dealt with some of the myths that surround bourbon and put the audience to the test.

"Bourbon is made by hillbillies, for hillbillies" was one example. The audience politely disagreed. But questions on Bourbon's ability to innovate confused delegates, who also weren't sure about the role of Scots pioneers in Bourbon's early days.

A display of premium Bourbons such as Maker's Mark, Booker's, Basil Hayden's, Knob Creek (named after Abraham Lincoln's boyhood home) and Baker's helped put Bourbon into a worldwide context of premiumisation and the move to ever more luxurious products and an early Jim Beam advertisement featuring a youthful Sean Connery caused a few delegates to sit up. And, at an educational level, even experienced whisky executives studied the chart on average maturation temperatures in Kentucky vs. Scotland with interest.

Two important case studies finished the day, with Michael Riley, Business Unit Director, Spirits for the Liquor Control Board of Ontario (LCBO) talking about the revitalisation of Canadian whisky in the LCBO stores.

Now the name Michael Riley may not mean much to you, but it does to people in the industry. As the LCBO's Business Unit Director Mr Riley buys more whisky (of all types) than any other person in the world. As local government controls all liquor distribution in the state of Ontario, the LCBO is said to be the largest single buying point for whisky anywhere on the planet. You may be very sure that few delegates took an extra break while he was speaking!

"Bourbon is made by hillbillies, for hillbillies" - a myth effectively laid to rest by Beam Global CEO, Tom Flocco (opposite page)

Global malt whisky consumption 1997-2012
('000s nine-litre cases)

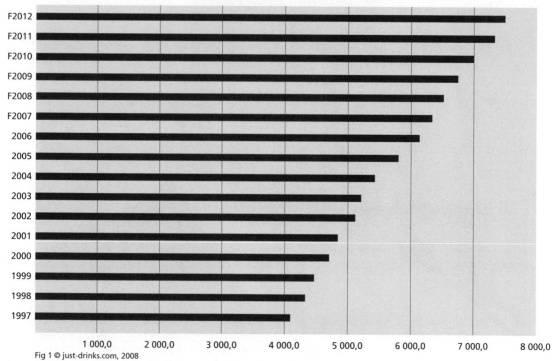

Fig 1 © just-drinks.com, 2008

Last up for the day were whisky writer and consultant Dave Broom, with Olly Wehring of industry newsletter *www.just-drinks.com* presenting a new report on single malts. Curiously, this attracted less debate than expected, perhaps because delegates were tired or perhaps because their conclusions – that single malt has a great future but that more education is needed – was insufficiently controversial to attract many questions.

If so, the industry would appear to have accepted the need for a greater investment in educational programmes which is good news for the consumer, especially in the so-called developing markets. Look out for more tasting and sampling opportunities, handsome literature and further growth in quality distillery visitor centres and mobile brand experiences (the Dewar's Academy being one such example).

However, the projection that single malt whisky sales would reach approximately 7.5 million 9 litre cases by 2012 sent everyone off to the Gala Dinner in good heart and represented a fitting high point to a busy first day (see Fig 1).

Patient Japanese whisky-makers

Delegates arrived suitably refreshed on the second day to be faced with a choice of presentations – the twin track approach meant that two presentations ran simultaneously. The idea is to offer better value and to give a greater number of speakers the opportunity to present to their peers.

On this occasion, one track focused mainly on Scotch whisky, with world whiskies being covered in the parallel session. Given that this is the Malt Whisky Yearbook I'll give most space in this review to the Scotch whisky track but must mention in particular two presentations from the alternative programme.

First of these was a fascinating and very detailed presentation by Kuni Himeno, Managing Director of Suntory Europe on "Japanese Whisky – European Sunrise" in which he was able to show the incredible achievements of the Japanese industry in Europe from a starting point at which Japanese whisky was, quite wrongly, scorned and laughed at and sales were negligible.

Many people would have given up at this point and returned to their home market. Not so the major Japanese producers. Mr Himeno showed how the Japanese industry has, slowly and patiently, built the reputation of their products to the point where they now win major awards and are penetrating the shelves of leading specialists and even some supermarkets.

The lesson of slow and patient sustained investment was not lost on those who attended this absorbing session – especially when they saw a chart demonstrating that sales of Yamazaki single malt in Europe had grown 2,300% (yes, 23 times) between 2003 and 2007. Perhaps some delegates recalled the UK car industry at this point!

The Indian whisky market is enormous, though as many readers will appreciate most Indian "whisky" being made from molasses, would not satisfy EU regulations and cannot be retailed in Europe. However, as Dr Mallya was at pains to point out, most of the Indian distilling industry had its roots during the period of British rule in India. "Perhaps," he said "you should have been more careful then about definitions!"

It's a fair point, if a painful for one for the UK industry, but the main Indian interest on day two was a presentation on packaging innovation given by UB Spirits' Alok Gupta.

In this very dynamic market the consumer appears ready to accept packaging innovation that would be rejected in Europe as 'not traditional' or gimmicky. Imagine, for example, getting your whisky in a TetraPack (like your milk or orange juice). Horrified? Then what about a pilfer-proof 'SmartPack', PET bottle or even a preformed cup?

All these packaging formats are seen in India and, according to Mr Gupta, have proved wildly popular with consumers. Given the impact of the Japanese invasion perhaps we should rethink. Has whisky regulation and tradition become too hide-bound for the good of the market? Such challenges will not go away.

The dynamism of non-traditional whisky markets was illustrated in a presentation by Euromonitor's Marlous Kuiper who reviewed whisk(e)y's place in the global spirits market. All types of whisky were holding their own in the global market and she forecast further exciting growth in India, South Africa, China and Russia. Looking to 2012 growth rates in terms of overall value may be seen on the chart below but again, alarmingly for the traditionalists, she emphasised flavourings as a key trend driving growth in other global spirit categories such as rum and vodka.

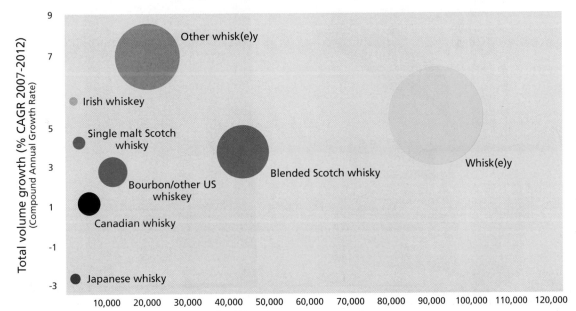

Whisk(e)y forecasts by type in 2012

Bubble denotes volume sales in 2012

© Euromonitor International

Different types of innovative whisky packaging from India

New Scotch regulations

But it's fair to say that, with a majority of delegates from Scotland, most chose to attend the sessions on the new Scotch Whisky regulations, presented by Glen Barclay, the SWA's Director of Legal Affairs and two subsequent debate and discussion sessions.

The new Scotch regulations have created a great deal of debate, much of it fairly late in the day and, at the time of writing, it would seem as if the regulations will pass into European law without significant changes. Barclay was at pains to point out the extensive consultation undertaken by the SWA and to emphasise, as Paul Walsh had done in the opening session that the motivation behind the changes was as much about consumer protection as it was for the industry's benefit.

The presentation illustrated a number of counterfeit whiskies (such as the wonderfully named "Glen Highland Green Blended Whisky", which for good measure also described itself as "Fine Single Pure Highland Malt Whisky") and allegedly misleading labels such as "Ardnave", a UK supermarket own-label which might be taken as the product of Ardnave distillery (if such a place existed) and "Glen Dornoch".

In his presentation, Barclay was at pains to defend the "blended malt" category, suggesting that there was no realistic alternative. "Vatted", he said, was hardly ever used (outside the industry, presumably), not understood by the consumer and "unattractive". "Pure Malt" was confusing and unclear. He was also critical of the critics, suggesting controversially at one point:

"It may also be significant that two sellers of blended malts described as 'Malt Scotch whisky' have complained that if they have to put the description 'Blended Malt Scotch' whisky on their labels, they will no longer be able to charge 'Single Malt' prices. If consumers know the truth about the product, will they, rightly or wrongly, not pay the price?"

It would seem that some in the audience at least were won over. Though the debate continues it appears that the process rolls on and that the new regulations will have passed into law, or at least be close to doing so, by the time that you read this.

The main part of the afternoon in this track was a more open and free-flowing debate in which delegates considered the possibility of a "Scotch Whisky Marketing Board" – a kind of industry-wide initiative to promote Scotch whisky generically. This attracted some support, especially from the smaller companies, and may be a topic that the Conference returns to in future years. A Working Party has been set up and, if this can be persuaded to come forward with workable proposals, it may be that you hear more of the idea.

The two days ended on a fun and upbeat note. "The Great Whisk(e)y Debate" is a consumer event, created for the US market in which Richard Paterson of Whyte & Mackay and Fred Noe III of Beam Brands debate the relative merits of Scotch vs. Bourbon and attempt to convince the audience of their point of view. Perhaps you've attended – if not, don't miss it if it comes to your town.

This was the first time this had been presented in the UK, or to a trade audience, the idea being to remind delegates of the importance of good education, combined with entertainment.

You will perhaps be delighted to know that the senior management of the global whisky industry enjoyed being showered with ice, exposed to indoor firecrackers and generally abused by the ebullient Richard Paterson, just as he does at whisky shows around the world to novice consumers.

Unfortunately, all photographs have been suppressed in the interests of the delegates' collective dignity!

Keeper of the Quaich and Liveryman of the Worshipful Company of Distillers, Ian Buxton is well-placed to write or talk about whisky, not least because he lives on the site of a former distillery!
Ian began work in the Scotch Whisky industry in 1987 and, since 1991, has run his own strategic marketing consultancy business. In addition, he regularly gives lectures, presentations and tastings on whisky and writes regular columns for Whisky Magazine, the Scottish Field website, and various other titles.
He is a co-author of the recent Eyewitness Companion to Whisky (Dorling Kindersley) and is currently working on a history of John Dewar & Sons and a history of Glenglassaugh Distillery.
He established the World Whiskies Conference in 2005 and, with Neil Wilson, also established Classic Expressions to reprint facsimile editions of rare whisky classics.

The Fathers of Whisky

*We are still uncertain when and where
whisky distillation began, though what we can be certain of
is that it all probably started much earlier than previously thought.
Follow Charles Maclean into the dark ages on his quest
to find the Fathers of Whisky.*

*Did the art of whisky distilling come into being
here, in Tipperary in the 6th century?*

My original brief for this article was 'Unsung Heroes of the Whisky Industry'. I made a list, cleared it with the editor and started work.

I got no farther than the 'unsung heroes of pre-history', so engrossed did I become, peering into the Celtic twilight! Some of my heroes you will have heard of, but I hope there are others with whom you are unfamiliar. And I hope you will agree with me that their contribution to the history of whisky is not inconsiderable. You will have to wait until next year for the next batch of heroes!

St. Ruadan of Lothra (d.584)

Let me start with someone you may not have heard of. Certainly, I hadn't until he was brought to my attention by a friend, Graham Martin, a retired professor of French from the University of Edinburgh, who now spends much of his leisure time researching the so-called 'Dark Ages'. While he was translating the Lives of the Irish Saints from Latin, he came upon the following passage:

"There were three times fifty monks in the monastery of Lothra with Saint Ruadan, to whom all-powerful God gave sustenance without any labour except prayer and kneeling. For there was a cask in the 'curia' of the monastery, whose sap gave a sufficiency to the aforesaid monks and their guests. For the sap of this same sweet tree was powerful, and sufficed to all who tasted it as much for food as for drink. When they heard about this, the monks from all over Ireland ran away from their monasteries to go to the place in which they had heard so much divine grace was to be found. For there the monks and their guests tasted nothing other than the sap of the aforesaid tree and its flavours, which had the savour of wine' [from 'The Invention of Whiskey' (Edinburgh, 2008)].

So what, you might say? But then Graham explained: a) that the Latin *arbor* stands not only for 'tree', but for 'wood' and therefore 'cask', b) *curia* can mean both a 'courtyard' (outside) and a 'courthouse' (indoors), and c) that in several versions of the tale when the liquid is described as 'dripping' from the tree, the verb *stillare* is used (i.e. 'distilled')… So the story might be read as a coded account of a novel kind of drink that made all the monks joyful – i.e. a distilled spirit of wine. To my knowledge, nobody has made this connection before.

Is it possible that St. Ruadan - a contemporary of St. Columba (521-597); a hero who was reputed to be seven feet tall, and is numbered among the 'Twelve Apostles of Erin' - was distilling in his monastery of Lothra, in County Tipperary in the 6th century?

Well, it's certainly possible. From as far back as the 5th century, Ireland had trade links with Gaul, Northern Spain, Greece, Syria and Egypt. It is highly likely that the art of distilling was known by the early Christians in the Middle East, inherited from their Coptic antecedents and used for ritual purposes. Might Irish monks have returned with the secrets during 'The Age of Saints'?

The earliest written record of distilling in Ireland comes from the *Red Book of Ossory*, thought to have been compiled by an Irish bishop, who was appointed in 1316:

"Simple aqua vitae is to be made in the following manner: take choice one year old wine, and rather of a red than of a thick sort, strong and not sweet, and place it in a pot, closing the mouth well with a clepsydra[1) made of wood, and having a linen cloth rolled round it; out of which pot there is to issue a cavalis[2) leading to another vessel having a worm. This latter vessel

St Finian preaches to his monks at Clonard.
It was here that St Ruadhan was educated

is to be kept filled with cold water, frequently renewed when it grows warm and the water foams through the cavalis. The pot with the wine having been placed previously on the fire, distil it with a slow fire until you have from it one half of the quantity of wine that you put in."

[1] This is clearly a plug, but a clepsydra is a water clock!
[2] I cannot make sense of cavalis from my Latin dictionary. We would call it a lyne arm.

Michael Scot (1175 – c.1232)

"That other there, his flanks extremely spare, was Michael Scot, a man who certainly knew how the game of magic fraud was played."
– Dante The Divine Comedy: Inferno (canto XX.115-117)

Michael Scot was one of the leading scholars of his day – notwithstanding the fact that by Dante's day he had become a 'wizard', languishing among magicians and soothsayers in the eighth circle of Hell.

He was born in Scotland, either in the Borders or Fife, studied in Durham, then at Oxford and Paris, and taught in Toledo, Bologna, Padua (where he instructed Leonardo Fibonacci (1170-1250), 'the most talented mathematician of the middle Ages') and Palermo, where he entered the service of Emperor Frederick II as Court Astrologer. In 1223 Pope Honorius III urged Stephen Langton, Cardinal Archbishop of Canterbury during the reign of King John (and the man behind Magna Carta), to confer an English benefice upon him, and himself nominated Scot Archbishop of Cashel in Ireland, an apointment he refused to take up.

A mathematician, an alchemist, an astrologer, a physician, a theologian, a linguist; at the instigation of the Emperor he produced a fresh translation of Aristotle's works, and the Arabic commentaries on them. He also translated the works of Avicenna and Averroes, the 'Fathers of Western Medicine'.

Scot certainly knew the secrets of distilling, indeed, his text Lumen Luminum ['Light Illuminated', c.1225] supplies the first description of the technical terms of distilling in Western Europe:

The ruins of Melrose Abbey where Michael Scot is buried.

Hec omnia unum terendo et pone curcurbita cum alembico et quod distillaverit [literally "all these things brought together are made one [in a] retort with an alembic and that which will have been distilled"]

Did he return to Scotland with these secrets? Well, he is buried in Melrose Abbey, where there is a monument to him, having prophesied his own death by a stone hitting his head. According to legend, after he had had this vision he wore a metal helmet. Unfortunately, he took it off in church one day and received the blow from 'on high'. Calmly he sorted through his affairs and died the next day.

The Clan MacBeatha (after 1300)

In Gaelic society professions and crafts were the preserve of specific families, passed down from generation to generation. The most familiar example is the MacCrimmons, pipers to the Macleod chiefs.

Members of the MacBeatha family (the name literally translates as 'Son of Life'; it also appears as MacBeth, McVey, and, in its anglicised

Kilchoman Cross (sometimes known as the Beaton Cross) in the Kilchoman churchyard.

form, Beaton) were Scotland's hereditary olamhs or physicians. They practised medicine in the classical Gaelic tradition from at least the early 14th century. Such medicine was based on a mixture of native herbal lore and Latin or Greek medical tracts, many of them translations from Arabic. Over the centuries, members of Clan MacBeatha amassed a large medical library – many fragments of which are still extant – containing Gaelic translations of Classical medical writers, including Avicenna, Averroes and Hippocrates. As we have seen, these authors were familiar with distillation.

Tradition has it that the MacBeatha family arrived in Scotland around 1300 from "O'Cahanes country otherwise known as Colerane" in Ulster, in the marriage train of the lady Agnes (in some sources her name is given as Margaret or Áine), a daughter of Cú-maige nan Gall Ó Catháin, one of the great barons of Ulster. She was to marry Angus Og MacDonald, Lord of Islay, and their son became the 1st Lord of the Isles.

The MacBeathas were not alone. Also in the marriage train came "140 Irish fighting men, one for each surname in her father's territory", among them the founders of the Scottish families Munro, Rose, Dingwall, Dunbar, Maclinen and MacGilleglas. According to another tradition, she invited Irish gentlemen and artisans of talent to the island, because the Lordship needed, and could afford, their services. The MacBeathas were granted lands at Kilchoman on Islay.

Time and place fit neatly with more solid historical evidence. The first record of a MacBeatha doctor in Scotland is from around 1302, when Angus Og sent Patrick MacBeth to his friend King Robert I ('The Bruce'). He cured the king, when other physicians had failed and his descendants became 'principal physicians' (*Medicus Regis*) to the royal house: one was granted lands in Easter Ross, another was given the Island of Jura by Robert II in 1386. The first named MacBeatha on Islay is Fergus Beaton, in 1408. The presence of the family in the Kilchoman area of Islay is confirmed by the 'Beaton Cross' cross, dating from the second half of the 14th century (still standing in Kilchoman kirkyard), and by later charters.

Maybe these 'learned physicians' brought the secrets of distilling with them from Ireland, and perhaps it was they who began to distil from ale rather than wine – grapes being in short supply on Islay!

King James IV

Surgeons), with a monopoly for the manufacture of aqua vitae. The first and most famous mention of distilled spirits appears in the Exchequer Rolls of 1494;

"Eight bolls of malt to Friar John Cor wherewith to make aqua vitae": the first written reference to spirits in Scotland, and made from malted barley! Forby (as we say in Scotland!), the King had been campaigning in Islay to subdue John, 4th (and last) Lord of the Isles, and it is generally accepted that he encountered aqua vitae while he was there.

Was the King interested in the liquid solely for use in medical, scientific and alchemical experiments? Between 1494 and 1512 the Exchequer Rolls record fifteen separate instances where aqua vitae was purchased; most uses are clearly 'scientific', but one hints at recreational consumption:

'Item to ane man brocht aqua vitae and glasses fra Edinburgh to Striveling [i.e Stirling]. 41s; Item that nicht to the King to play at the cartis with the Abbot of Tungland. Lib 6, 12s.'

King James IV (1473 - 1513)

When James came to the throne in 1488 there was little evidence of recreational consumption of spirits in Britain. Yet the renaissance King's procurement of aqua vitae, detailed famously in his Exchequer's accounts, surely marks him as an unsung hero in the development of the dram.

As befitted a Renaissance monarch, King James was fascinated by medicine and science. A contemporary described him as "well learned in the airt of medicyn and ane singular chirugiane [i.e. surgeon]" He could draw teeth, set a broken leg, apply leeches, and in 1496 supported the foundation of the first medical faculty in Britain, at Aberdeen University. In 1506 he granted a charter to the Guild of Surgeon Barbers of Edinburgh (now the Royal College of

John Damian, Abbot of Tongland (dates unknown)

Maister Damian doesn't really deserve a place in the Pantheon of 'Whisky Fathers', but his story is so good that I cannot resist giving him a section for himself!

John Damian, alchemist (or conjurer), physician (or quack), failed inventor; Italian, French, or perhaps Dutch, arrived in Scotland in the early 1500s, possibly from Nottingham Castle – where a 'John a'Dammys' operated a laboratory – but perhaps from France (he was referred to at Court as 'the French leich' – i.e. 'leech', or doctor)…

William Dunbar, Court poet – and the grea-

Stirling Castle where John Damian
made his attempt to fly.

King James V

test of Scotland's makars – described Damian as a "Turk who murdered a monk in Italy and assumed both his habit and profession"! Although unpopular with the Court, 'Maister' John soon succeeded in ingratiating himself with the King, who created him Abbot of Tongland (in Galloway, Southern Scotland) in 1504. It is possible that it was from him that

James developed his passion for alchemy. The Exchequer Rolls reveal that the King erected at Stirling a furnace for conducting alchemical experiments, and continued during the rest of his reign to expend considerable sums of money in support of Damian's attempts to convert base metal into gold. Bishop Lesley observed, "Maister John caused the king believe, that he by multiplying and utheris his inventions sold [should] make fine gold of uther metal, quhilk science he callit the Quintassence, whereupon the king made great cost, but all in vain." Others, less polite, called him simply 'the imposter' or 'an unprincipled adventurer'!

A popular English text of the day, familiar to both King and Abbot, was *The Quinte Essense or the Fifth Being*; that is to say Man's Heaven, which contains the following passage:
"[In a] distillatorie of glass with a hoole aboue in the head, [the liquor was condensed and distilled again and again] unto a thousand times, so … it schal be a medicine incorruptible almost as heauene aboue and of the nature of heauene. And when ye opene the hoole, if ther come out of passynge hevenly swete flauour that alle men that come yn naturally draw therto, thanne ye have ure quinta essencia, and ellis sele the vessel and putte it to the fier agen till ye haue it."

The most famous story about John Damian concerns his attempt to fly. An embassy was returning to France from Stirling, and the Abbot undertook to fly on ahead of them, jumping off the walls of Stirling Castle with Icarus-like wings attached. Not surprisingly, the entire Court turned out to watch. Bishop Lesley reported: "And to that effect he causit mak ane pair of wingis of fedderis quilkis fessinit upoun him, he flew of the Castil wall of Striveling, but shortlie he fell to the ground and brak his thee bane: but the weyt thairof be assyvit to that thair was sum hen fedderis in the wingis quilk yarnit and covet the mydding and not the skyis". [in other words, he put it about that the reason for his failure was that he had used hen's feathers in his false wings, and that 'hens aspire more to the midden than the skies'!].

William Dunbar composed a waspish poem entitled: Ane Ballat of the False Friar of Tongland: How He Fell into the Myre Flying to Turkiland!

But were the King and his chum bibbing aqua vitae in their chamber at 'Striveling' Castle? The Exchequer Roll entries quoted at the end of the last section suggest that they might be indulging while playing at 'cartis', but we really don't know.

Were spirits being enjoyed socially by this time? On the one hand, the convivial use of aqua vitae in monasteries was well established - for semi-medicinal purposes, and specifically to assist in the recuperation of patients after minor surgery and 'leeching' (i.e. blood-letting,

which men in holy orders had to endure three or four times a year, in order to balance the humours in the body). On the other hand, following the vainglorious death of James IV on Flodden Field in 1513, there are no more references in the royal account books to the purchasing of aqua vitae.

Other mentions of whisky/aqua vitae during the 16th century are few, but there is a telling account of a royal hunt on the 'Braes o' Mar' (i.e. Braemar, near present day Royal Lochnagar Distillery) in 1531, where the eighteen year old James V and his mother and other noblesse were entertained by the Earl of Atholl with "all manner of meats, drinks, and delicacies that were to be gotten, at that time, in all Scotland, either in burgh or land; that is to say, all kinds of drink, as ale, beer, wine, both white and Claret, Malvesy, Muskadel and Alicante, Hippocras aquavitae.'
'Hippocras' was both a contemporary medical tonic and an intoxicant, compounded from aqua vitae and assorted spices, strained trough a 'Hippocras Sieve' and named after the Classical patron of Physicians.

Maybe here at last is proof of aqua vitae/uisge beatha's move from laboratory to dining-room – or at least to picnic table! However, I can't help but think that, as soon as the taste and pleasant effects of whisky were experienced – by physicians and their patients, monks and their supplicants, alchemists and their guests in closeted castle chambers, farmers on cold winter nights – the drinking of it will have been endemic, in Scotland and Ireland, and anywhere else where spirits were known.

Charles MacLean has spent the past twenty-five years researching and writing about Scotch whisky and is one of the leading authorities.
*He spends his time sharing his knowledge around the world, in articles and publications, lectures and tastings, and on TV and radio. His first book (*Scotch Whisky*) was published in 1993 and since then he has published nine books on the subject, his most recent being* Charles MacLean's Whisky Tales*, published in 2006. He was elected a Keeper of the Quaich in 1992, in 1997* Malt Whisky *won the Glenfiddich Award and in 2003* A Liquid History *won 'Best Drinks Book' in the James Beard Awards. His* Whiskypedia *is due to be published early in 2009.*

So you want to build a Whisky Distillery?

*There are probably quite a few
Malt Whisky Yearbook readers who have nourished
a dream of building their own distillery. After having read this article,
it will hopefully stay just like that - a dream.
Gavin Smith has met with some of those who are in the middle of the
process and it is clearly not an occupation for the fainthearted.*

Scotch whisky is currently one of the hottest drinks on the planet; a fact confirmed by record export figures for 2008 and increasing output from most of the major distillers. But at the opposite end of the scale, the last few years have seen a welcome growth in 'start-up' distilling ventures that are never likely to trouble the balance sheets of Diageo, Pernod Ricard, William Grant and their like.

Because of the prescriptive definitions of what can be termed 'Scotch whisky' there is less innovation in terms of product in Scotland than in the USA, where there are currently no fewer than 28 'craft distilleries' which make whisky/whiskey. Some operate along very traditional lines, while others are notably innovative, producing, for example, fruit-flavoured whiskey and whiskey distilled with an infusion of hops in a manner that would have the Scotch Whisky Association reaching for the smelling salts!

As we shall see, many of the trials and tribulations associated with starting up a small distillery transcend national boundaries, but given that there are many trials and tribulations, why would anyone want to begin distilling whisky in the first place?

Distillers in need of a challenge

Some of the recent Scottish ventures, such as *Glengyle in Campbeltown* and *Port Charlotte on Islay* are the work of established, local distillers, namely J&A Mitchell & Co Ltd of Springbank fame and Mark Reynier and his team at Bruichladdich. Glengyle has an annual capacity of 750,000 litres, and when opening for business in 2004 it was the first 'new' distillery to be established in the once thriving whisky centre of Campbeltown for 125 years, though it is really the revival of a distillery that closed in 1925.

Similarly, Port Charlotte, due to open

around 2010, may be seen as the revival of the old Lochindaal distillery, which shut its doors in 1929. A new, eco-friendly distilling plant is being installed in one of the original Lochindaal warehouses, and with a potential capacity of 1.2 million litres per annum, this is a significantly larger operation than many similar developments.

When asked why he is setting up a second distillery, Mark Reynier replies "Why not? We already have the machinery, all the distilling plant, we have the buildings and we have the site. Production at Bruichladdich is set to increase towards capacity, and we can distil more styles and different tunes. It's intriguing."

In cases such as Glengyle and Lochindaal, expertise, resources and chains of supply are already in place, which, theoretically, gives those operations a better likelihood of financial success than some of their counterparts.

Aberdeenshire-based Duncan Taylor & Co Ltd is primarily an independent bottler, and under the auspices of *Huntly Distillers Ltd*, the firm is currently creating a new distillery in a former creamery. Managing director Euan Shand says "I'm creating my own distillery out of necessity. It is nearly impossible to get new-fill spirit from distillers to lay down, mature and release under an independent label. There is also no mature stock available on the market from brokers that meets our requirements for quality of spirit and character."

When it comes to *Daftmill distillery*, established by the Cuthbert family of farmers in Fife during 2005, a strong interest in Scotch whisky combined with redundant, traditional agricultural buildings led brothers Francis and Ian to develop a small distillery to add value to their existing farming business.

Meanwhile, at Aultbea, in the far north-west Scottish Highlands, John and Frances Clotworthy have established the ultimate 'boutique' distillery in the shape of *Loch Ewe*, situated next to their Dromchork Lodge Hotel. As Frances Clotworthy explains;

"Drumchork Lodge Hotel had been awarded numerous UK and worldwide accolades in recognition of the work we were doing to raise awareness of malt whisky. There was only one thing left which we could not do, so it seemed a natural progression to produce our own whisky. Apart from anything else, the distillery provides a lot of interest and good publicity for the hotel."

The right location is crucial

So having made the decision to distil whisky, what are the principal factors that determine where you start to distil it? Of all the elements that influence distillery development, location is surely the most significant.

In the case of Glengyle and Port Charlotte distilleries, proximity to the company's existing businesses was obviously a major factor in determining location, while Loch Ewe had, of necessity, to be close to Drumchork Lodge Hotel.

On Islay, Anthony Wills established *Kilchoman distillery* in 2005, and he says "Islay was always my preference because of the increased interest and demand for Islay malts worldwide and also because I knew Islay as my wife's family had owned an estate there since the 1930s. Rockside Farm was chosen for the distillery site because it had ideal buildings and was the best farm on Islay for growing malting barley, which we wanted to use for the production of our whisky."

As has already been noted, in the USA there is greater flexibility in terms of production processes than there is with 'Scotch whisky,' and when it comes to location, Bill Owens, president of the American Distilling Institute, suggests "Open up next to a micro-brewery to give yourself access to wash."

Jess Graber of *Stranahan's Colorado Whiskey*, which began producing an all-malt whiskey during the spring of 2003 in Denver, says;

"Locating next to a craft brewery was a primary consideration, though that relationship has changed and we are now trucking in our wash from Oskar Blues Brewery."

Whatever the choice of location, obtaining official permission to create a new distillery and a licence to operate can be major hurdles to overcome, depending, in part, on the location in question and whether there are already buildings on the site. In the case of Glengyle, Director of Production Frank McHardy says "We had no problems obtaining planning permission for the re-use of the buildings as a distillery. As far as we know, the authorities were pleased to see another distillery created within Campbeltown."

Similarly, at Drumchork Lodge Hotel, Frances Clotworthy says "We had no problem with planning because essentially we were 'repairing' an existing eyesore of a shed."

Glengyle in Campbeltown and Daftmill in the Lowlands – two examples of distilleries that have been established in recent years.

Jess Graber of Stranahan's in Colorado (left) is happy with the newly formed cooperation with Dale Katechis, founder of Oskar Blues Brewery

Ralph Erenzo (left) and Brian Lee decided to do almost everything on their own when starting Tuthilltown Spirits in New York State

However, when it came to obtaining a licence to distil in the manner they wanted, matters were very different. "From initial inquiries, Customs intimated that we could go ahead with a distillery," explains Clotworthy, "but it must be in the same format as every other distillery in the country. As the overall whisky-making process is the same throughout Scotland, would you travel an extra couple of days on remote roads to get to the north-west to see the same distilling which you could see at numerous locations around Speyside or Islay? Our distillery had to be different."

During research, Frances Clotworthy discovered that old legislation relating to the minimum size of stills had never been repealed, which meant, in effect, that it would be perfectly legal to operate an extremely small still along the lines favoured by illicit whisky-makers during the 19th century.

"Customs consistently denied my application," recalls Clotworthy, "so I then contacted local Member of Parliament Charles Kennedy and told him of my findings via the law. Finally, three years later, we got the licence we wanted and 15 minutes after that the loophole was closed!"

A forthright Euan Shand of Huntly Distillers Ltd declares "Planning and bureaucracy come hand in hand. Put it like this, it still isn't over despite having planning and building warrants. I'm afraid that the powers that be are out of control. I certainly would never consider a venture such as this again. It entirely consumes your life, just appeasing faceless bureaucrats."

When asked about the greatest challenges he faces in creating Port Charlotte distillery, Mark Reynier immediately answers "Dealing with the authorities."

Overcoming 'red tape' is not restricted to the UK, however, and Jess Graber of Stranahan's in Colorado answers "Educating the local bureaucracy and then educating the consumer," when asked the same question. "Federal and state licenses were methodical but relatively simple to obtain," he explains, "but the local building and planning were excruciating and prohibitive. Their fears stemmed from ignorance of the process and it took a great deal of education for them to understand we wouldn't burn the town down!"

Tuthilltown Spirits is located in Gardiner, New York State, and produces Bourbon, rye and single malt whiskeys. Co-founder Ralph Erenzo says "We are one of twelve distilleries in New York State, but all the others are

John and Frances Clotworthy began Scotlands smallest whisky distillery at their Drumchork Lodge Hotel

Good raw materials such as barley and water are, of course, essential if you want to succeed with your distillery

fruit brandy distillers on wineries. We are the first and only whiskey producer in the State since Prohibition. It took two years to get through the licensing process at Federal then State level. The State liquor authority is totally unused to dealing with small distillery issues and so every single issue is major and takes review, and usually ends up in a 'no' till we argue it through and get our legislative representatives involved.

"Unlike Scotland, there are no regulations about building conversion, except in the case of local zoning regulations, with which we complied. In the meanwhile we converted the buildings, built out the facility, taught ourselves how to make whiskey and vodka. We did an end run around zoning regulations by licensing the site as a winery, then adding the distillery. In New York a winery is considered a farm use, and farming is a use by right, while a distillery is an 'accessory use' to a farm. We ended up dropping our winery license and nary a word was heard!"

Securing barley and water

More bureaucratic difficulties may be encountered in relation to the abstraction of water, and a guaranteed supply of pure water is very high on every distiller's list of priorities. In these times when 'health and safety' legislation and environmental consciousness are high on everybody's agenda, the provision of a water supply is one of the issues that can cause significant headaches for start-up distillers.

In Scotland, water-related matters come under the remit of the Scottish Environment Protection Agency (SEPA), and despite making less than 600 litres of spirit per year, Loch Ewe distillery encountered difficulties with the Agency. According to Frances Clotworthy, "Initially, water was not a problem as we intended to draw it straight from the loch to the rear of the distillery. Unfortunately, SEPA contacted us and advised that this was not acceptable. Because you consume whisky it is regarded as a food, so all raw materials used must be to European standards. We were not allowed to use untreated water for our product so had to comply with their regulations and use water from the tap. Previously, during whisky tastings in the hotel's Uisge Beatha Lounge, we had identified problems due to the smell of chlorine from the water masking the aroma of the malt. We had to install a filtration system to remove the chlorine from the water, so this has to be utilised for the distillery also."

Problems relating to water supply are less acute in the USA, as Ralph Erenzo of Tuthilltown Spirits at Gardiner in New York State notes. "Unlike Scotland, there are no regulations about water source, apart from it being potable," he says. "Water did not affect our choice of location. We drilled a well and use our own water."

If a viable, local water supply is as vital today as it has always been for distilling purposes, the same cannot necessarily be said about malting barley. In these days of centralised, industrial-scale maltings, the proximity of the distillery to supplies of good barley is no longer relevant in many cases. However, as Anthony Wills indicates, above, it was a factor in the location of Kilchoman, which operates its own floor maltings, while at Daftmill all the barley used for distilling is grown on the family farm.

John and Frances Clotworthy experienced difficulties in obtaining barley in sufficiently small quantities for their bijou Loch Ewe venture, with Frances saying "Throughout our search for malted barley, Simpson's of Berwick-upon-Tweed was the only company who would sell the barley to us in the form we required. The problem was not with obtaining the barley but with delivery, so we just go to Berwick and pick it up ourselves."

In large-scale distilling, the maximisation of spirit yield is often a crucial factor in the choice of barley varieties, but perhaps craft distillers do not need to pay such attention to quantity and are able to focus more on quality?

"Maximising spirit yield is not as important for us as for the bigger distilleries," agrees Anthony Wills, "but it had to be carefully monitored to make sure we got the best we could. We currently use Optic and Oxbridge, and 35 per cent of our barley is grown and malted at the distillery and the balance bought from Port Ellen Maltings. We keep them separate in the production and when matured we will release two expressions of Kilchoman. The extra cost of malting our own barley is actually minimal."

Frank McHardy makes the point that "All the malted barley used at Glengyle is made on the Springbank malting floors." However he insists that "Malting on traditional floors significantly adds to the cost, but by doing this we are in the unique position of carrying out the whole production process in Campbeltown."

If the raw materials are important, then so too are the casks into which spirit is finally filled. The necessity of using good 'wood' is of particular significance in the case of small-scale distillers whose every cask is likely to be open to scrutiny as it progresses through the process of maturation.

The pressures of expanding production in the Scotch whisky industry means that the best casks are now at a premium, but as Anthony Wills notes, "As a small production unit getting hold of good quality casks hasn't been a problem. Jim Swan, our consultant, sources all our casks requirements and we buy fresh Bourbon from Buffalo Trace and fresh oloroso direct from Spain. A small proportion of Kilchoman spirit is also filled into carefully selected refill Bourbons."

Francis Cuthbert of Daftmill observes that "Getting good wood is definitely much harder now than when we started up and it is more expensive as well. The majority of our casks are first-fill Bourbons, mainly from Heaven Hill."

Theoretically, one of the advantages of being small and flexible is that it is possible to fill some spirit into a variety of casks and monitor their maturation closely in a way a larger distiller cannot, but Wills says "We are tending to follow a very traditional maturation programme with the majority filled into Bourbon and Sherry, although we are filling a few 30-litre casks and will look at a few very carefully selected casks for finishing."

Francis Cuthbert makes the point that "We are not being very experimental at all. With such a small stock you don't want to take any risks with quality."

*Kilchoman Distillery on Islay (top left), Glengyle distillery in Campbeltown (top right)
and Loch Ewe Distillery at The Drumchork Lodge Hotel in Aultbea in the Scottish Highlands*

To build new or refurbish

Interestingly, none of the recent batch of small-scale, start-up Scottish distillers has opted to construct premises from scratch, preferring to adapt existing buildings.

When asked whether utilising existing structures at Port Charlotte distillery helps to reduce costs, Mark Reynier replies "Not much, but they look better. Ours were built in 1905 and are beautiful!"

Francis Cuthbert adds "Repairing the old buildings probably cost more than building a brand new one, especially when you consider the added problems of getting all the equipment in and fitted and complying with modern fire and 'health and safety' regulations."

Euan Shand notes that "Its actually as expensive to rebuild, but the end product is so much better than a breeze block, harled building."

Apart from the cost of creating suitable premises, the new distiller's principal expense is inevitably equipment, and the price of copper and many other materials has risen significantly during the past couple of years in the UK. Additionally, many craftsmen now have lengthy waiting lists due to the expansion of so many larger distilleries.

"Equipment took up half our budget for start up," says Tuthilltown Spirits' Ralph Erenzo, while Anthony Wills of Kilchoman notes "Thirty per cent of the capital required for the project was taken up with purchasing equipment. The stills, mash tun, four washbacks and boiler were new and the rest was second-hand. Forsyth's of Rothes built the stills, mash tun and washbacks and when we had the work done there wasn't a long lead time."

Frances Clotworthy of Loch Ewe recalls that "We began the project with £50,000. The quotes for the stills, casks and building were horrendous, and to me seemed ludicrous. Eventually, I contacted some whisky enthusiast builders, removed the word distillery from other essential quotes and looked to mainland Europe for the equipment. We completed the basics under budget."

Euan Shand's new distillery at Huntly in Aberdeenshire is incurring higher costs than some others because of its environmentally-friendly credentials. "We plan to use a woodchip/biomass process and space heating, along with rain water harvesting," he says. "This adds around £1 million to the project."

Both Glengyle and Port Charlotte were able to make significant savings by purchasing second-hand stills. In the case of Glengyle, a pair of pot stills from the small Ben Wyvis operation, which once operated within Invergordon grain distillery, were purchased and subsequently adapted, along with a spirit safe and spirit receivers. "The ex-Ben Wyvis stills were a real bargain," says Frank McHardy, "having been lightly used at Invergordon distillery."

Going one better, the Bruichladdich team purchased the entire Inverleven malt whisky unit for Port Charlotte distillery out of Dumbarton grain distillery following its closure in 2003, and subsequently transported it to Bruichladdich on barges.

Euan Shand of Duncan Taylor has decided to make his new distillery environmentally-friendly

Mark Reynier was not content with saving only one distillery from oblivion; Bruichladdich. He decided to recreate the old Port Charlotte distillery.

How to learn distilling

Having obtained permission to distil whisky and created a distillery in which to do it, there remains the vital matter of having the ability to create good spirit. In the cases of Glengyle and Port Charlotte, this is obviously not an issue, since both are associated with existing distilling operations.

Others, however, have to either learn for themselves, or employ people with the necessary skills. Francis Cuthbert of Daftmill attended the 'Whisky School' at Bladnoch distillery, and also called upon the expert help of Ron Gibson, of Carrick Engineering Services, and whisky industry consultants Jim Swan and Harry Riffkind.

Anthony Wills of Kilchoman says "I employed consultants to build and design the equipment lay out. Jim Swan is our production and cask maturation consultant and I employed Malcolm Rennie as distillery manager. He had spent eight years prior to joining Kilchoman

as a stillman at Ardbeg. Gavin Douglas, his assistant, worked for two years at Bowmore as a mashman prior to joining us. I act as cover for both Malcolm and Gavin when they are on holiday and I'm a fully trained stillman/mashman."

Frances Clotworthy says "Local people in Wester Ross have a great knowledge of illicit distilling and there is no end of them willing to tell of their experiences in days gone by. A great source for distilling secrets is one of our neighbours who (allegedly) made the best whisky in the area. Her name is Kay Mathieson. John also attended the 'Whisky School' at Bladnoch. The three day course was invaluable."

Ralph Erenzo of Tuthilltown Spirits says "We taught ourselves distilling. We researched, emailed, worked on the web, and visited distillers. I made two research trips to Europe to visit a grappa distillery in northern Italy and several Cognac distillers in France and absinthe distilleries in the Jura. It was moderately difficult to get the theory of what was happening inside the still and columns, but once it clicked it was much easier. Working at a seminar with the actual equipment helped, as did material and advice from the distillery designers and fabricators Christian Carl.

"But mainly it was Brian and me constantly reading, phoning, visiting and emailing. Most of the information out there is useless for beginners and small distillers, and what the big guys are doing is irrelevant for the most part due to the scale. There's no 'manual' for starting a craft distillery in the US and as it's been over 80 years since a small distilling industry existed in the US the only guys who knew anything of any real value were the big boys who were not interested in talking to two novice wannabees. We experimented constantly and are still doing so."

Show me the money

Inevitably, financial considerations are crucial to a start-up distillery project, and in the USA Bill Owens, president of the American Distilling Institute, says "When someone comes to me to ask about starting up a distillery the first thing I tell them is not to give up the day job! You're likely to have between $250,000 to $1 million negative cash flow for the first three years until you start to make a profit. Can you deal with that?"

Already operating successful distilling enterprises, as in the case of Glengyle and Port Charlotte may ease some of the pressure, though, as Mark Reynier notes "Port Charlotte will still be expected to make a profit before it's been running for too long. It is business after all, not a charity."

For the Cuthbert family at Daftmill, profitable farming and quarrying ventures have bankrolled the distillery's creation and initial operation, but for other distillers, putting a financial package in place can be a steep mountain to climb.

Jess Graber of Stranahan's Colorado Whiskey says "I brought in investors to provide for about 25 per cent of the project. The rest was financed by savings and my local bank, where I mortgaged my house. It was necessary to borrow enough to make payments until sales began."

"Raising the funds to kick start the project was the single most challenging factor," declares Anthony Wills. "This took me the best part of four years to achieve, and having raised £1million, after a year I had to raise a further £1.5million. We are now fully funded. The distillery is financed by private investors and a grant from the local enterprise company, but it will take between 10 and 15 years before a proper return will be realised.

"The increased costs now of malt, energy and just about everything else have impacted on our cash flow, but we have investors who are fully committed and additional finance is available if required."

On the subject of increasing costs, Euan Shand of Huntly Distillers Ltd insists that "The changing economy is affecting the plans greatly. If the whole process had not become protracted by bureaucrats we would have saved around £500,000."

Earning sufficient income is obviously crucial to the success or failure of any commercial activity, but few other 'manufacturing' businesses have the sort of lead-in times associated with malt whisky. In Scotland there is a legal minimum maturation period of three years to begin with, and few distillers, large or small, have such a cavalier attitude to the long term reputation of their brand name that they will sell whisky before it reaches its optimum level of maturation.

Large-scale distillers always have the option of selling some young spirit for blending purposes, but, ideally, the small-scale distiller needs to hold on to the spirit he makes in order to realise its full potential value. Meanwhile, the bills keep arriving in the mail.

Some micro-distillers are in more urgent need of creating cash-flow than others, and Francis Cuthbert of Daftmill says "The age when we bottle our whisky will depend purely on quality. We will either bottle it when we feel it is ready or when we have run out of money, whichever comes first!"

In more serious vein he notes that "It's going to be a premium product selling at a premium price, so it must be good. We set out to produce a typical Lowland whisky, something like Rosebank or St Magdalene."

The single malt whisky from Glengyle will be marketed as Kilkerran, and this is another 'long haul' distillery, with Frank McHardy noting that "The entry level for Kilkerran is likely to be at 12 years old, in April 2016. However, we may release limited quantities as a 'work in progress' before then, to allow consumers to see how it is maturing."

Until then, Kilkerran is earning its keep in a modest way and getting its name into the public consciousness, with Frank McHardy observing that "We produce Mitchell's Kilkerran blend, which contains grain whisky, Springbank, Longrow and some Kilkerran malt."

Meanwhile, across on Islay, in order to help pay those bills, Kilchoman sells miniature bottles of its 'new make' spirit and operates a visitor centre, complete with shop, café and distillery tours. "Selling the new spirit is about a combination of raising awareness of Kilchoman and receiving income," explains Anthony Wills.

"Our first whisky will be released in 2009 as a three-year-old and it is the intention to do small releases each year thereafter. Our consultant Jim Swan is confident our whisky will be very attractive as young, aged malt."

Issues of ageing are less relevant to John and Frances Clotworthy, whose Loch Ewe distillery has had an income source virtually from day one. "Loch Ewe single malt is distilled using essentially illicit methods," notes Frances Clotworthy, "therefore it is ready to consume as it comes off the still, as was done in the last century. The clearach has been distilled relatively quickly due to the small volume of mash, therefore it has not had time to become harsh or tainted, so is palatable immediately. We do rack the spirit into casks, but have been surprised at the number of people requesting bottles of the 'white' whisky."

"A tour with tasting costs £5.00 per person and many people purchase a 100ml gift boxed bottle as a keepsake. These bottles are also available by mail order. In addition we sell 50cl pottery jugs at £75.00."

Having spirit for sale from the commencement of distilling is part of most North American craft distillers' business plans, and Bill Owens says "I suggest turning out gin initially to get cash flow until the whiskey matures."

Ralph Erenzo of Tuthilltown Spirits declares "The sale of unaged or short-aged spirits is what kept us (and many other start up distilleries) alive. It is naive to start up a distillery unless you have very, very deep pockets to reach into – either yours or some angel's. It is imperative to make money right away."

While waiting for these casks to mature, Kilchoman have been selling miniature bottles of their new make spirit in the visitor centre

In Scotland, Euan Shand's Huntly Distillers Ltd has embraced the same business model, and a column still as well as copper pot stills are being installed in the company's new distillery.

"Not only are we going to produce single malt but we are also going to distil single grain for our blends and neutral alcohol for some of our other drinks products," declares Shand. "Column still distillation has always interested me as I haven't been involved in it before. However, I have tasted and have in my stock some amazing grain whisky. I believe we have a great future in grain spirit, and blends will still be a part of our portfolio."

Regarding the single malt output of Huntly distillery, he considers that "We will be having annual releases from three years onwards, with a peaty version at six years and quarter cask versions at eight years. We believe the optimum age will be around 10 to 12 years, though this will be monitored very closely."

Marketing on small means

As every good businessman appreciates, no matter how wonderful the product, it is only successful if people know about it and purchase it, so marketing strategies would seem to be an important element of start-up distilling ventures.

However, Jess Graber of Stranahan's in Colorado points out that "Marketing budgets are always difficult to define for craft distilleries and often overlooked. In theory, the more you spend, the more you will get noticed, but it is always difficult to know how well 'ad dollars' work. Stranahan's has focused on trade shows, tastings, and promotional events."

Tuthilltown Spirits' Ralph Erenzo notes that "I think we have spent a total of maybe $10,000 over the last four years on advertising and marketing. The rest resulted and continues to come from my personal efforts."

Frances Clotworthy says of Loch Ewe that "We have always marketed ourselves and the hotel at whisky fairs around the world, and in addition we regularly advertise in whisky magazines in various countries. As we are running both the hotel and distillery, it is becoming a bit of a problem to find the time to attend these shows. We actually class these shows as our holidays, so the expenditure is offset."

According to Anthony Wills, "The marketing of Kilchoman is via our website and attending whisky fairs in a number of key markets. We have now stopped selling casks and are offering the chance to purchase six bottles of our 5-year-old, which will be bottled in 2011. This is limited to 1,540 cases. The marketing budget will become significantly more important as we get close to launching our first bottling in May 2009. The intention is to hold a launch party at the distillery for press and journalists, as well as appointed distributors in key markets."

Not everyone takes the view that conventional marketing is important, however, with Wills' Islay neighbour Mark Reynier declaring in characteristically maverick style "We aren't going to do any marketing for Port Charlotte. We don't spend any money on it at Bruichladdich, so why should we bother at Port Charlotte?"

Clearly, there are many intrepid small-scale distillers and would-be distillers with varying views on how to go about the great adventure of starting up and running a whisk(e)y distillery, and who are prepared to ignore Bill Owens' advice not to give up the day job. In an era of ever-increasing corporate conformity the world of whisk(e)y needs entrepreneurs who are prepared to break the mould and do things their way. We should all celebrate and support their brave, entrepreneurial efforts.

Gavin D Smith is one of Scotland's leading whisky writers and Contributing Editor to www.whisky-pages.com. He hosts whisky talks and tastings and produces feature material for a wide range of specialist and general interest publications. He is the author of some 20 books, ten on the subject of whisky. These include Whisky, Wit & Wisdom, The A-Z of Whisky, Worts, Worms & Washbacks, The Secret Still *and* The Whisky Men. *His most recent publications are* Ardbeg: A Peaty Provenance *and* Goodness Nose *(with Richard Paterson). He lives on the Fife coast in Scotland.*

Classifying Whisky

Is there an objective approach?

*Many of us want to organise and classify
what is around us, it is in our nature. This is of course true
for tasting whiskies as well and that's all fine when you keep your
tasting notes to yourself, but once you start comparing with others
the trouble begins. David Stirk has taken a look at different tools
and their advantages and disadvantages.*

Photo: © Whyte & Mackay

Science and whisky. One is a subject I was rather good at at school, the other is something I rather enjoy now (and I still enjoy whisky too – you know what I mean). My point is they're not the same thing; I know people like to claim distilling is a science, and granted, there is definitely Science behind it but sometimes, in fact too often, science shoves its inquisitive nose into fields that are clearly marked 'Scientists keep off the grass'.

Two areas in particular where science leaks into the whisky world is the appreciation and classification of whisky. Science should leave appreciation alone (for example, a mathematician recently created a formula to explain why we like certain faces over others – the devil makes work for idle hands) but is there room for science in the classification of whisky and do we even need to classify whisky? Isn't it good enough to simply say this comes from the Lowlands, or Highlands etc? To answer this question let me repeat two overheard conversations heard a long time ago in a specialist whisky shop;

Shopper: *"I would like to buy a bottle of whisky for a friend."*
Shopkeeper: *"Ok, what does your friend usually drink?"*
Shopper: *"I believe he is partial to peaty Islay whiskies."*
Shopkeeper: *"OK, well how about a bottle of Bunnahabhain."*

Second overheard conversation;

Shopper: *"I would like to buy a bottle of whisky but do not like the smoky whiskies from the Isle of Islay."*
Shopkeeper: *"How about a bottle of Talisker from the Isle of Skye?"*

Ok, so this is simply a bit of shopkeeper ignorance but it highlights one simple problem (there are many) we have with classifying by region; not all Islay whiskies are peated and not all whiskies made elsewhere are unpeated. The problem in classifying whisky (and I am going to concentrate on single malt Scotch Whisky for the purpose of this article) is best demonstrated by some lines (this is not scientific, understood). The range of flavours in most alcohol drinks is often not very great (below):

I will be quick to point out to all of the Bourbon drinkers that I adore Bourbon but it is a fact that there are not sweeping ranges in flavour from one bourbon to the next. And, If I have offended any vodka drinkers, I'm not going to apologise.

The problem with the above is that the flavours don't go from right to left or left to right; in other words there aren't two dominant flavours such as fruity and oaky with all of the other flavours somewhere in the middle.

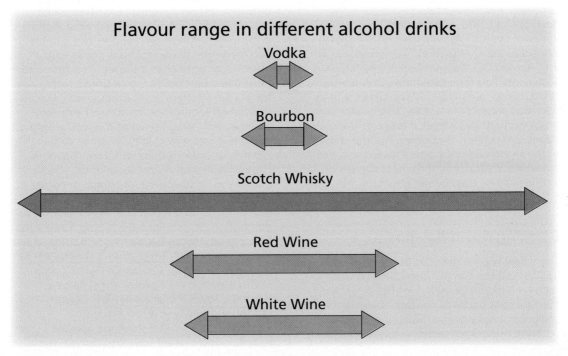

Flavour range in different alcohol drinks
Vodka

Bourbon

Scotch Whisky

Red Wine

White Wine

If I was to use the line diagram to properly attribute flavour profiles for malt whisky it would look something more like this:

feinty, woody, sulphury & winey. There was an additional wheel for flavour and mouth-feel broken down into nine categories: sweet, sour,

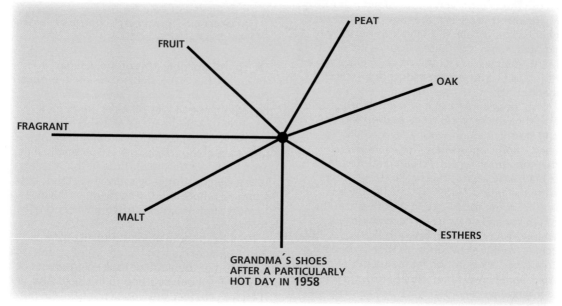

PEAT

FRUIT

OAK

FRAGRANT

MALT

ESTHERS

GRANDMA'S SHOES
AFTER A PARTICULARLY
HOT DAY IN 1958

The last one is a bit far fetched as 1958 was a rather cold year, but you get the point; classifying whisky is a difficult and complicated business. In fact it is deemed so complex that 'experts' (sometimes in teams) have sat around big tables and come up with wheels and graphs and all sorts of tools scientists use to confuse each other. The first such scientific approach was the *Pentland's Whisky Wheel* developed in 1979 by Pentland's Scotch Whisky Research Institute (now known as the Scotch Whisky Research Institute). The wheel was an attempt to place flavours commonly found in Scotch into fourteen categories; primary taste, feints, cereal, aldehydic, estery, sweet, woody, oily, sour, sulphury and stale. There were two problems with this wheel; it was confusing and about as much fun as cleaning out the stables of the world's largest horse. This is harsh, yet enjoyable, criticism, as the wheel was never intended to be used by the public.

Breaking down flavours

The wheel was re-invented, sorry, developed, by Charles MacLean, Dr James Swan and Dr Jennifer Newton (sounds a lot like Scientists to me – except Charles of course). The new wheel broke commonly found flavours into eight separate categories: cereal, estery, floral, peaty,

salty, bitter, warming, cooling, prickly, viscous and cloying. If you are using a panel of tasters this wheel is brilliant for guiding tasters into a consensus of opinion

It is quite easy to be critical of flavour wheels as they are confusing and seriously not fun. However, they do fulfil an excellent function in that they can help you decide between certain flavours; I am often asked (usually by non-whisky drinkers) what is the difference between peat and smoke and tar and medicinal flavours. This is not as easy a question to answer as it sounds. The first, and most important point, is that unlike taste, flavours are memories. In other words, I could put something in your mouth and although you may not recognise what it is, you would know if it was sweet, salty, bitter or sour. Flavour, or smell, is quite different. Flavours trigger memories. So for some of us, vanilla means vanilla flavoured ice cream, or coffee means coffee flavoured sweets. And this is really where the problem begins in flavour description. So someone describing a whisky as being 'peaty' to an Eskimo is going to have as hard a problem trying to dissect the flavour as someone telling an Amazonian what cola is.

This is where the flavour wheel helps as it breaks down the levels of each flavour (although the wheel is not exhaustive – thankfully). So when someone asks me to break down peaty flavours I can use the

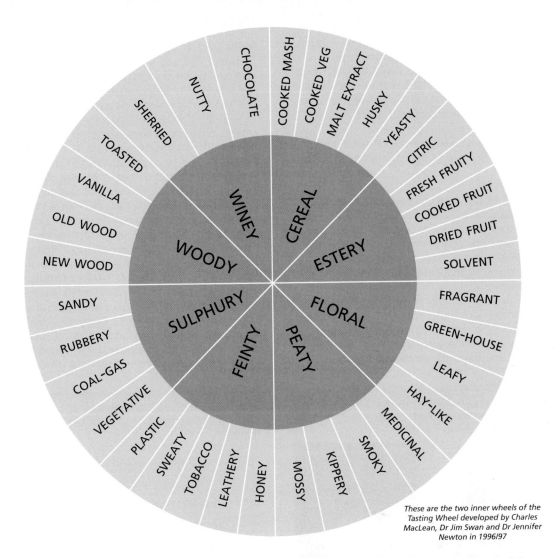

The labels on the tasting wheel (outer ring, clockwise from top): CHOCOLATE, COOKED MASH, COOKED VEG, MALT EXTRACT, HUSKY, YEASTY, CITRIC, FRESH FRUITY, COOKED FRUIT, DRIED FRUIT, SOLVENT, FRAGRANT, GREEN-HOUSE, LEAFY, HAY-LIKE, MEDICINAL, SMOKY, KIPPERY, MOSSY, HONEY, LEATHERY, TOBACCO, SWEATY, PLASTIC, VEGETATIVE, COAL-GAS, RUBBERY, SANDY, NEW WOOD, OLD WOOD, VANILLA, TOASTED, SHERRIED, NUTTY

Inner ring: WINEY, CEREAL, WOODY, ESTERY, SULPHURY, FLORAL, FEINTY, PEATY

These are the two inner wheels of the Tasting Wheel developed by Charles MacLean, Dr Jim Swan and Dr Jennifer Newton in 1996/97

wheel to break it down into four categories; medicinal, smoky, kippery and mossy. Now they say 'but what exactly is "medicinal"?' The wheel then breaks each sub category further, so for medicinal it suggests TCP, iodine, sea-spray, carbolic, tar, menthol etc. Hopefully, the interested parties will be able to relate to at least one of the sub-sub-categories (if the Eskimo is still having difficulties, try lighting a cigar and then slap him across the face with a fish).

The system is not perfect as it is a bit long-winded and assumes a lot of flavour memories in the interested party. But, as far as being helpful to a tasting panel, there is nothing else that comes close. This brings me onto another point, and one that is widely debated by those with too much time. Whilst working for a magazine that was interested solely in

whisky, I had a letter that complained of the whisky tastings being 'subjective' and not 'objective'. At first I laughed at the suggestion, and to be honest I still am. My mother, who despises whisky making her the best person to ask, suggested that it was possible to have an objective tasting:

"Is this whisky?"
"Yes."
"Objective complete."

I am being incredulous but if someone really pressed me on the question I would have to answer 'why would you want an objective tasting? For what purpose would it serve?' A while back there was a great argument in whisky corners about whether or not there was salt in whisky. Apparently, according to a scientist (who clearly had nothing better to do), there is no salt (not a trace of Sodium Chloride) in whisky but does that really matter? I smell and taste salt in a great many whiskies (I remember a particular Bowmore that I presented to a group and was asked, seriously, by one of the group at what stage the distiller had added the salt). In an objective scientific experiment it was discovered there is no salt in whisky - but I really don't care if it is physically or scientifically in the whisky or not. So what could be the point of objectively trying to taste whiskies?

I am digressing here but enjoying it, so let me pose another question: Why do we need research into where the flavours come from in whisky? Isn't this really slaying the golden goose? You can already buy powder that when mixed with alcohol will, it states on the packaging, taste like whisky – and there was only one group of people responsible for innovations like that – scientists, quite possibly the ones who endlessly study the chemical compounds within whisky trying to identify what it is and more importantly, for them, where it came from. At what point do we stop researching into the origin of flavours within whisky? Is it when the bar man asks you whether you would like the strawberry, vanilla or chocolate whisky?

David Wishart´s approach

Right, back to the classification of whisky. Dr David Wishart, a sort of scientist but not one to slay the golden goose, fully realised the subjectivity of whisky tasting but also realised that there was potential correlation with tasting notes. For instance, Glen Ord is often described by writers as being malty, Royal Lochnagar is often grassy, Loch Lomond often oily and so on. What Wishart did, and I commend him on his patience, was trawl through Baltic Forests' worth of tasting notes and correlate them; he has, after all, a PhD in classification methodology. His book "Whisky Classified" is therefore not a startling or revelationary read (it was not meant to be) but allows you to gain a fair and unbiased insight into what a whisky may taste like (Wishart also kindly steers you towards other whiskies that are similar in flavour to whichever one takes your fancy). Using 12 categories (body, sweetness, smoky, medicinal, tobacco, honey, spicy, winey, nutty, malty, fruity & floral) Wishart scores each category out of four and then clusters together whiskies that taste similar. Due to his approach of not relying on one taster, Wishart's book is perhaps the most dependable and trustworthy book on the market.

Flavour profile of Lagavulin according to *Whisky Classified* by David Wishart

Feature	Profile
●●●●	Body
●	Sweetness
●●●●	Smoky
●●●●	Medicinal
●	Tobacco
	Honey
●	Spicy
●●	Winey
●	Nutty
●	Malty
●	Fruity
	Floral

The next attempt at classifying whisky was Phillip Hills' "*The Scotch Whisky Directory*" which was out of date before being published due to the numerous take-overs and buyouts that occurred at the time within the industry. In his Directory, Hills uses tasting notes from arguably the four biggest names who work within the Scotch Whisky industry; Jim McEwan (a Director of Bruichladdich), Richard Paterson (Master Blender Whyte & Mackay), David Robertson (previous Master Distiller Macallan) & David Stewart (Master Blender Wm Grant & Sons). As if these four leviathans didn't have enough whisky to taste in their day jobs, Hills asked them to all blind taste identical whiskies scoring against fifteen categories; floral, fruity, vanilla, caramel, nutty, sweet, smoky, cereal, aldehydic, woody, resinous, sulphurous, sour, soapy & musty. Hills then scores each whisky out of five for quality and adds a short conclusion.

This approach is very easy to criticise, and I like things that are easy. First and foremost it is confusing; how many ordinary drinkers will have a clue what are aldehydic, resinous or musty flavours (and many won't understand sulphury – rotten eggs or something like that)? Secondly the bars are very confusing to non-scientific brains; it just looks like some sort of high school maths text and this coupled with the five star scoring system makes the book very difficult to follow. There is also no categorisation of the whiskies tasted leaving a reader to think that because one whisky has a big number in one bar chart, they might taste the same as another whisky with a similarly high score. For example, Ardbeg 10yo gets a six for floral flavours – so does Ben Nevis 10yo. Difficult to link these two whiskies. And don't get me started on the five star scoring system – too late.

There is a big problem with scores; the whisky industry (and wine industry – thank you Mr Parker) hates scores and scoring. The problem is how do you give points that are not totally biased towards your preferred flavour profile(s)? The answer is you cannot. I remember one industry exec who was lambasting a certain whisky book for consistently scoring his whisky low resulting in poor sales where the book was a best-seller. The problem with his whisky was that it was not aged in heavily sherried casks and it was not peaty. And I'm glad it wasn't. What a dull world the whisky world would be if all of the whiskies were heavily sherried and heavily peated.

Jim McEwan of Bruichladdich, whose tasting notes were used by Phillip Hills in his "The Scotch Whisky Directory"

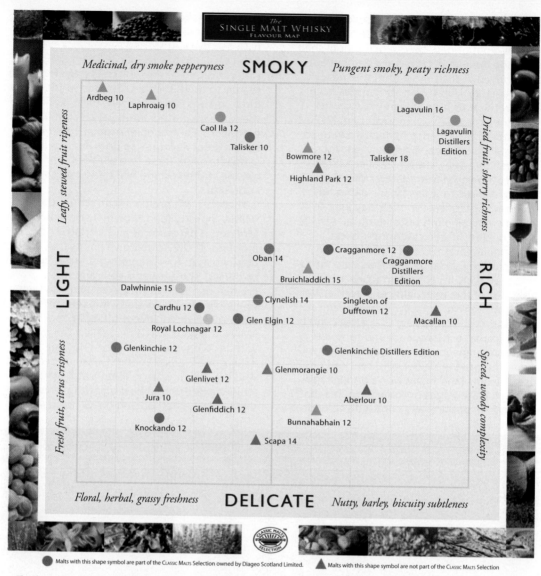

The Single Malt Whisky Flavour Map

SMOKY

Medicinal, dry smoke pepperyness — *Pungent smoky, peaty richness*

LIGHT — RICH

Leafy, stewed fruit ripeness — *Dried fruit, sherry richness*

Fresh fruit, citrus crispness — *Spiced, woody complexity*

Floral, herbal, grassy freshness — DELICATE — *Nutty, barley, biscuity subtleness*

Ardbeg 10
Laphroaig 10
Caol Ila 12
Talisker 10
Lagavulin 16
Lagavulin Distillers Edition
Bowmore 12
Talisker 18
Highland Park 12
Oban 14
Cragganmore 12
Cragganmore Distillers Edition
Bruichladdich 15
Dalwhinnie 15
Clynelish 14
Singleton of Dufftown 12
Cardhu 12
Glen Elgin 12
Royal Lochnagar 12
Macallan 10
Glenkinchie 12
Glenkinchie Distillers Edition
Glenmorangie 10
Glenlivet 12
Jura 10
Aberlour 10
Glenfiddich 12
Bunnahabhain 12
Knockando 12
Scapa 14

Malts with this shape symbol are part of the CLASSIC MALTS Selection owned by Diageo Scotland Limited. ▲ Malts with this shape symbol are not part of the CLASSIC MALTS Selection

The Flavour Map has been prepared and endorsed by the independent whisky expert, Dave Broom, together with Diageo Scotland Limited. In addition to the names of individual distilleries listed on the Flavour Map, the Classic Malts words, the Quaich device, the Flavour Map device and associated logos are trademarks. A PDF version of the Flavour Map can be downloaded on www.malts.com.

The trouble with whisky writers (and food and drink critics), is that they are all biased; myself included. The most famous whisky writer in modern times was Michael Jackson and he was continually berated for his high scores for certain whiskies. Why? Because he liked those whiskies. I can't help being drawn towards the fairly big whiskies with broad flavours (Like Highland Park, Redbreast, Glenfarclas, Mortlach, Springbank and so on) – thus if I was scoring or recommending whiskies, I can't help myself. Scores rarely accommodate nuances, subtleties and difference of opinion. And when you remember that around 90% of all whisky drunk is blended and most of that is not peated or aged in sherry casks, how can it be that a malt showing lots of distillery character (in other words not masked by peat or sherry) gets a low score? Because scores are personal and very biased it is actually an arrogance to print them as it is the author stating: 'This whisky is better than that whisky. Why? How dare you ask! Because I say so!'

Mapping makes it easier

Diageo put their might into the classification ring and came up with their own *Flavour Map* concentrating on four flavours; smoky, rich, delicate & light. By Diageo's own admissions this is a simplified approach making it actually very easy to use and is easily adopted for a web blog or private notes. What Diageo have achieved is to remove most of the complications you get with flavour wheels and bar charts by having four simple quadrants to flag each whisky. The real beauty of this system, is that at a glance you can cluster whiskies and very easily agree or disagree with someone's plotting. Remembering the shopkeeper already mentioned, this map carefully plotted would prevent such erroneous advice being given out.

Having spent some time analysing the map, it is clear that Diageo are really onto something. I doubt it will become an industry standard but, readily available, we may well see a few of these replicated on several websites and in future books. The Flavour Map does assume a few things however; firstly, it assumes a whisky cannot be smoky and delicate at the same time (a few Ardmores I have tasted could fall into this category) and it also assumes that a complex whisky is a rich whisky. Having said that, it is so easy to use that you find yourself wanting to plot everything you've ever tasted and then continually move them as you argue with yourself.

So is there a best way to classify whisky? The cliché answer is of course your own personal way, but as most drinkers are not going to systematically sit down and plan a method and then taste whiskies from every distillery (or are you?), then one of the above attempts will

fit the bill. I like Wishart's book as I know it is unbiased and does not cloud your judgement with nonsense stars or scores. Should it be the definitive way to classify whisky? I hope there is never such a thing – too much power in one person's hands (just look at the poor wine industry clambering over themselves to try and impress Robert Parker). Instead I hope that it is a subject that is broached every now and again and that no two books come to the same conclusion.

Footnote:
It would not be fair to be so critical of these attempts at classification without also looking at my own attempt within *"The Malt Whisky Guide"*. I divided all of the whiskies I tasted into seven categories ranging from light to medium-heavy. The aim was to allow readers to be able to choose a whisky that may fit their preferred flavour profile. There were no scores and no flavour profiles to stick to so anyone hoping to find the best whisky was going to have to do their own homework. It is of course only one person's opinion and is therefore flawed but it is certainly simple and was a lot of hard work. Why doesn't anyone believe me when I tell them that?!

David Stirk was born in Ripon in 1976. By his mid-twenties he had visited most of Scotland's distilleries and contributed to Whisky Magazine *before writing the* Malt Whisky Guide *(GW Publishing, 2002) and* The Distilleries of Campbeltown *(Neil Wilson Publishing, 2005). He is now involved in bottling single malt whiskies (www.creativewhisky.co.uk).*

Big whiskies with broad flavours are among David's own favourites; for example Springbank, Glenfarclas och Highland Park.

Islay
Whisky Treasure Island as seen from the inside

This windswept island on the west coast of Scotland may be remote, but with its eight distilleries, it is centre of single malts and a pilgrimage to the island is the highlight for many whisky enthusiasts. For others, it is a new home. Walter Schobert was one of those that stayed permanently and tells the story about the island and its liquid gold.

Maybe somebody else should write this article. One who is not living on this island which lies just off the Scottish west coast and only has the population of a village. It is also home to a world-class and world-significant industry. As a whisky writer one is part of this industry, in the same way as someone living in Islay is a part of the village. This intimacy creates problems that are not always obvious to the casual visitor.

If you live here, you hear many things that are not destined for the ears of a journalist. You meet the managers officially, but you also see them after work in the local pub, at a ceilidh or a family party. Or you meet the wife of a manager when she is shopping at the Co-op in Bowmore and she tells you news which certainly has not passed through the owner's PR-department. Or maybe you see the stillman at the filling station and he lets you know that once again people will be made redundant. In Islay nothing remains a secret for long. But if you, as a journalist, can make use of the news: that's another story.

When researching for this article I went to Mickey Heads to ask him about new developments in Ardbeg. After our conversation he offered, quite mysteriously, to show me something but only if I would promise him not to write about it. Behind the Cafeteria in Ardbeg is a small sample room where Mickey let me nose a new expression, something really special, an Ardbeg with half the ppm of phenols than usual. Of course I promised to keep silent – just to find the announcement of a new Ardbeg expression for September on a Norwegian website a few days later. Its name would be Blasda and it has only half the ppm of the ordinary Ardbeg.

Two years ago I suffered what can only be called a journalistic super disaster. It was one of those quiet evenings after work which I sometimes spend with Jim McEwan of Bruichladdich to enjoy a nice cigar and to have what in Islay is called a blether, a conversation covering mostly banalities but sometimes becomes very significant, even existential. All of a sudden Jim asked: "Do you know that we will build a new distillery in Port Charlotte?" I knew that the company owns the warehouses of the old Loch Indaal Distillery which is derelict since 1929 and Jim pointed out that they wanted to use one of the warehouses to install the equipment of the also derelict Inverleven Distillery in Dumbarton to create a distillery with a glass roof and

Mickey Heads, Distillery Manager at Ardbeg

Jim McEwan - the whisky designer of Bruichladdich

distill under the stars. He even pulled detailed building plans out of his desk, and went on talking and dreaming of the future. At the end I had to promise not to talk about our conversation and of course not to write about the news. I kept my mouth shut and didn't write even a line in the next issue of my newsletter WhiskyWatch. No mention of a new distillery in Port Charlotte, as promised. Two days later I got a press release from Bruichladdich with the sensational announcement of a new distillery...

An island in the centre of global economy

Those are the troubles of a whisky writer living in Islay - and these problems of intimacy and loyalty are part of a phenomenon which fascinate me even after ten years on the island: the clash between the big wide world and the small intimate island with its small community or, to use modern language, the coexistence of globality and locality. Everyone coming to the island is captivated by how friendly and open-minded the people are towards visitors and maybe this open-mindedness of the Ilich (to use the plural of Ileach, the name of someone living in Islay in Gaelic) is due to the fact that they have been dependent on whisky for a very long time and the other fact, that this whisky doesn't, in most cases anyway, belong to them but rather to global companies.

This however does not alter the fact that they are immensely proud of it. They know how much sought after Islay whisky is, and they see that people from all parts of the world are coming to Islay to see where and how their favourite drink is made. Even those who are not directly involved in the production are therefore depending on whisky: the shops where the tourists buy food and souvenirs, the hotels and B&Bs where they find accommodation and learn about the excellent produce Islay has to offer; the finest beef, the best lamb, scallops of an unparalleled quality.
   The people of Islay of course know which incredibly high contribution they make to the British economy: 3,500 inhabitants generating half a billion in taxes. No wonder they are angry about the outrageous high prices they have to pay for their journey on the (state owned!) ferry and they cannot understand why the roads are in such a poor condition. And sometimes they certainly wish that those who own the distilleries where they work would

be closer to the island. He who wants to see the negative as well as the positive sides of globalization should come to Islay. This small island is in the centre of the world economy!

It's important to always bear in mind to whom the Islay distilleries belong, where the money earned is going and where the decisions to hire or to fire staff are made. These are the same people who decide where to mature the spirits, on the island or abroad, and whether or not a new expression will be released. More often than not, these people do not live on Islay, which is again a problem for a journalist living here because the workforce in the distillery and even its manager are the last to be told by headquarters of new expressions.
   On Islay you can find all the global players in the industry with the exception of number 2, Pernod Ricard. Two years ago, together with Fortune Brands, they bought Allied Domecq, but missed the opportunity to acquire Laphroaig at the same time.

But let us see who owns which distillery in the same geographical order a visitor, taking the ferry from Kennacraig to Port Ellen, would discover them. The first to come into sight after approximately 90 minutes travel on the ship (weather permitting) is Ardbeg, until 1998 owned by Allied just like Laphroaig. The distillery was treated like an unwanted child, and was eventually sold to Glenmorangie. They transformed a Cinderella into a beauty queen and developed Ardbeg malt into a great brand with a huge and very loyal following of costumers and the distillery itself into a tourist attraction with a great visitor centre and an excellent restaurant. The family which owned Glenmorangie all of a sudden wanted to sell their company, which means that Ardbeg now belongs to French luxury giant LVMH, Louis Vuitton Moët Hennessy.

A few yards further down the road lies Laga-vulin, a distillery which in the 80s belonged to the biggest Scottish whisky concern at the time, DCL (Distillers Company Limited) before they became the victim of a very hostile takeover by Guinness. They went through a series of more takeovers, mergers and new company names and finally became Diageo, a public limited company, registered in London. Lagavulin therefore belongs to its shareholders.
   Close by is Laphroaig which, when the Allied-imperium was divided, went to Fortune Brands whose most famous whisk(e)y brand is Jim

A view from the Caol Ila still room towards Jura

Beam and who concentrate their spirit interest under the name of Beam Global.

You pass the Port Ellen Maltings with the Diageo sign and after 10 miles you enter into Bowmore, the capital of the island with the distillery right in the centre. It lies on the shores of Loch Indaal like an enormous cruise ship, white washed and spotless. Bowmore Distillery belongs to Morrison Bowmore, but the Scottish firm is since 1994 wholly owned by the Japanese giant Suntory.

On the east coast are Bunnahabhain and Caol Ila, the latter being a part of Diageo whereas Bunnahabhain is licensed to a Scottish company, Burn Stewart, which in turn was bought some years ago by CL Financial, a consortium from far away Trinidad and Tobago.

Slowly we fill the white spots on the world map especially when we take the short boat trip from Port Askaig where Caol Ila and Bunnahabhain are, to Jura, the neighbouring island. Jura has only one distillery and the license is held by an old Scottish firm, Whyte & Mackay. This company has experienced quite an impressive amount of owners during the years with proprietors first in USA, then Germany, then South Africa and since a year ago India through United Breweries. The Master Blender though has always remained the same, the one and only Richard Paterson.

Anthony Wills, founder and owner of Kilchoman distillery

The two independents

Back on Islay we find two distilleries that are not owned by foreign (sorry England) companies, but by people not only from Scotland but from the island itself. People who don't have to report to bosses in Tokyo, New York, Paris and who decide for themselves which cask they want to bottle.

The first is Bruichladdich, which share not only the same foundation year with Bunnahabhain (1881) but also the tradition of using only lightly peated malt and therefore produce soft and mellow whiskies. Bunnahabhain was somewhat neglected by the then owners but it could carry on distilling. Bruichladdich on the other hand was closed and mothballed for five sad years at the end of the 1990s. Then came a group of enthusiasts headed by Mark Reynier, a former London wine merchant, his business partner Simon Coughlin and Jim McEwan, former manager of Bowmore and pronounced they had bought the distillery and wanted to open it again during the Islay Festival of Malt and Music 2001. Phoenix rose from the ashes and today Bruichladdich plays the role of the maverick showing the multinational Scottish whisky industry new ways of producing whisky. Their belief is that only deindustrialization will guarantee the integrity, quality and consistency of malt whisky in the future.

Kilchoman, today the most westerly distillery in Islay, is a maverick too, starting three years ago and therefore at the end of this year celebrating the proud moment when spirit transfers into whisky. Kilchoman is owned by a small group of shareholders, amongst them Mark French, the farmer of Rockside where the distillery was built, and Anthony Wills, managing director, married to a lassie from Islay and of course living on the island. Kilchoman competes with Edradour for the title of the smallest distillery in Scotland and is a true farmhouse distillery getting everything it needs for production from the surrounding farm: water, barley and peat which is also bought from Port Ellen Maltings. Today Kilchoman makes two different kinds of spirits which will, once bottled, also bear different names.

The bid question of course is: is it damaging to Islay and its whisky distilleries that most of them are in foreign ownership? This is not a question with a simple answer; on the one hand it is a fact that for the first time in decades all managers are natives, born and

Peat burning at Laphroaig

Mull of Oa on southern Islay

bred in Islay, some of them even went to school together. On the other hand nobody has forgotten the shock which hit Islay when Jim Beam came to the island for the first time and closed down Bruichladdich. More than 40 people lost their jobs and looking back most Ileachs agree that this was the beginning of depression and despair, and that nobody could see a future for the island. This paralysis came to an end when Ardbeg and Bruichladdich reopened and were revitalized. Bruichladdich today employs a workforce of more than 40 – many of them part of the old team - and they are the biggest employer on the island, mainly because they also have a bottling facility.

Caring for the environment

It´s no exaggeration to state that the years since then, since 2001, have been boom years. Islay is blooming and for the first time in many years the population is actually growing (with 500 in five years). Young people are coming to live here, sometimes Ilich who were forced to look for jobs elsewhere, new businesses are opening, a second ferry offers more crossings, more tourists are visiting. And the production of Islay´s liquid gold is increasing – no wonder that all distillery managers show just pure satisfaction. They can produce more, offer new jobs and they can make urgently needed investments. For instance, by installing new, high-efficiency boilers which are good for the environment and bring with them less oil consumption. Islay and the whisky industry still depend on oil, a big problem when the prices are the highest in Europe.

Everyone on the island understands the importance of caring for the environment and are aware of the effects global warming can bring to the island and its main industry. Everyone who is engaged in whisky production knows exactly how careful they have to be with resources like energy, water and peat.

At the moment, no one sees a realistic alternative to oil. Islay has plenty of wind but the RSPB (Royal Society for the Protection of the Birds) which has huge reserves on the island, argue that the turbines are a threat to the birds. People on the island who depend on the tourists for their living and are not that keen on wind power either are well aware that visitors are annoyed by seeing landscapes destroyed by the white asparagus stems.

Surrounded by water, energy generated by tidal waves could be the way forward. Since a few years ago there is a small power station in the sea making use of the tide but the energy generated by it could not flow into the grid due to very old and very weak cables. Especially the tide in the fast flowing waters of the sound of Islay could be useful.

Another option is biomass. Diageo has just announced plans to invest £69 million for the installation of a bio-energy system in Cameron-bridge distillery and its new distillery in Ros-eisle is designed to be carbon-neutral. Diageo is the biggest producer of whisky in Islay and owns the Port Ellen Ellen Maltings where almost all the malt for the Islay (and Tobermory and Jura) distilleries is made. The maltings will get a new kiln and it will certainly be more energy efficient. At the moment they need 3,000 tons of peat every year, used, of course, not for heating but to aromatize the crop.

The new Port Charlotte distillery will also be "green" – but Mark Reynier of Bruichladdich knows that it could be difficult to achieve. He just received, finally, the planning permission but still has no permission to use the distillery once it has been built. SEPA (Scottish Energy Protection Agency) foresees problems with the water, the supply and the effluents. But Reynier says he feels no pressure, he is looking to find old documents showing how the old Loch Indaal distillery worked – and thinks of compensation. Instead of oil, why not perhaps use the waste heat for the nearby school? Bowmore on the other side of Loch Indaal is proud to use the waste hot water since many years back to heat the local swimming pool next door.

A bright future

All these ideas and innovations make people on the island see the future in bright colours. The universal optimism within the Scottish whisky industry can be found everywhere in Islay. The peated malts are trendy, in fact no category of whisky has grown quicker than Islay and there is no sign of change. But there is also room for new options in the shape of a second maturation, introduced at one time by Glenmorangie but perfected by the good

Eddie MacAffer, new Distillery Manager at Bowmore

John MacLellan, Distillery Manager at Bunnahabhain

John Campbell, Distillery Manager at Laphroaig

production and more staff. Ardbeg on the south coast is working seven days a week – more than ever, but there are no plans for further expansion. The news is that manager Mickey Heads got the money to build a new warehouse which now means that everything destined to be bottled as Ardbeg Single Malt will remain to mature on the island, a decision welcomed by those who believe that the environment where a cask is warehoused influences the character of its content. That is why the same people cannot understand why Diageo removed all maturing Lagavulin from Islay and shipped it to the mainland.

Lagavulin is the place where rationalization and efficiency are king and where today only one man per shift is working supervising a computer which effectively is producing the whisky. Now the last step has been taken with the whisky being matured more efficiently elsewhere. Of course distillery manager Graham Logie and more so his bosses on the mainland deny that this will have a negative effect on a whisky considered by many as one of the greatest that Islay and Scotland have to offer. It will take another 16 years to see whether the taste of the whisky has changed.

The fact that Jim Beam bought Laphroaig and would come back to Islay after the disaster they caused with Bruichladdich was not good news for many people who were afraid of a new blow. But even they are quiet after the first years with the new owner. Manager John Campbell had a new boiler installed and he finally has new facilities to cater to the many (350,000!) members of the "Friends of Laphroaig". Campbell also enjoys the triumph of being the only one of the managers of the foreign-owned distilleries to welcome his CEO to the distillery, even though Tom Flocco's intention was not to see his jewel on the remote Hebridean island but to meet HRH Prince Charles who made another visit to his favourite distillery. The first trip some years ago cost him his pilot's license when he hit the sand instead of the runway.

people from Bruichladdich who are creating more and more new whiskies with new types of casks. And this seems only to be the beginning: Bruichladdich today makes (at least) nine different new makes. In the future there will be many more: malt from barley from single farms (24 are already contracted), from different yeasts, malts matured in different places in a warehouse...

The whole of the island is set on expansion. All distilleries are working at full capacity and have increased their output massively. Once again we make a round trip, to see what is going on, and this time the start is in the west. Kilchoman is making 95,000 litres annually, more is simply not possible – and not wanted; small is beautiful. Bruichladdich is now near a million litres, all destined for single malt and the building of the new Port Charlotte distillery lies ahead.

Bunnahabhain, as mentioned long neglected, is on the way to discover its potential, both as a distillery and as a brand. The manager John MacLellan has the money to renovate; to fix the roofs, to distill more spirit, and can finally see that the sales people are doing more for his matured whisky than before with the 18 and 25 year olds as well as the single cask bottling. "Black Bottle", the blend which has its home in Bunnahabhain and the favorite drink of many Ilich, had a relaunch. Caol Ila was the work horse of the Diaego distilleries and continues on with the job, with again increased

New opportunities for visitors

There is another issue John Campbell is happy about: next year he will be able to offer visitors two different tours, the normal, "tourist" tour and a new one which is aimed at more experienced visitors. He knows that not every visitor to a distillery is a tourist coming more or less by chance and wanting to see for the first time how whisky is made. On the contrary, many people coming to Islay are almost experts who know a lot about whisky, sometimes even more then the young guides who do it as a summer job. These visitors get frustrated when what they are told is that whisky in Scotland is distilled twice in pot stills. They know all these things; what they want to see and to hear is what makes one distillery different from the next.

This is the way Bowmore has been doing it for a while. Everybody understands that these tours are more expensive than the normal ones, but if the visitors are guided by Eddie MacAffer, the manager himself with 40 years of experience, taking them to one of the warehouses to open up a cask or two, they feel it is worth the money. And if they, by the end of the tour, are offered an extensive tasting with many expressions, they leave the place happy and satisfied. Maybe the other distilleries will follow Bowmore (which offers some accommodation too) and, soon, Laphroaig. Even Bruichladdich (which, in the shape of the "Academy", has the most intense "education") should consider offering a second kind of tour.

Is this the only wish? No negative observations, no criticism? Of course many have fears that the good times could come to an end that people would walk away from Islay whisky to prefer other whiskies and that the tourists would discover other places to go. And sometimes there is a feeling that Islay could become the victim of its own success. That the whiskymakers could forget what this success is based on and that the quality Islay is famous for could be compromised by increasing the production.

Grant Carmichael has known Islay for more than 40 years during which he was, until his retirement, manager for Caol Ila, for Port Ellen Distillery (the closing was one of his hardest jobs), and for Lagavulin. He believes there is no need to point to certain things and he is of course loyal and would never bite the hand which has fed him during his working days. But he says the only thing which could endanger

Grant Carmichael - an Islay veteran

Islay's success is the success itself, if trying to keep up with the demand results in an inferior whisky.

It is therefore a pleasure to see that Grant Carmichael's successors as distillery managers are united in one thing: to maintain the quality, integrity and consistency of their whiskies. Of course Mickey Heads and Jim McEwan are in rather different positions: Jim is his own boss at Bruichladdich and can pursue his visions and dreams whereas Mickey has to exercise what his bosses in Paris and Glasgow want him to do. But I´m sure he would rather quit the job than do things he could not agree with.

And both insist that they have one thing in common: the knowledge that they are caretakers of a great past and that it´s their responsibility to save everything that made this past possible for a great future.

Walter Schobert got interested in whisky already in the sixties. Since then he has written several books on the subject; Malt Whisky Guide – Führer zu den Quellen, The Glenmorangie Trail, Single Malt Note Book, Scotch Whisky – Wasser des Lebens *and* Das Whisky-Lexikon. *Since 1997 he is also the publisher of the newsletter* Schobert´s Whisky Watch. *Walter has been living on Islay temporarily since 1997 and moved there permanently in 2007*

Cooking with Whisky

*Cooking with whisky is not a new innovation.
The perfect marriage between haggis and a nip of whisky,
for example, has been known for a long time. The new innovations
come from making more exciting combinations and selecting a
special single malt for a special dish. We went to the
Amber restaurant in Edinburgh to see if chef
David Neave could bring us up to date.*

In this contemporary fast-moving world a novelty is, by definition, anything that is not older than three months. Based on that, we cannot say that the combination of whisky and food is a novelty. In fact there are some people today who state that whisky cuisine has become unfashionable. This must come as a surprise to all those whisky drinkers out there who have not had the opportunity of experiencing their first encounter with whisky and food.

When I confront David Neave, chef at award winning restaurant Amber at Scotch Whisky Experience in Edinburgh, with this statement he is adamant

"We are just at the beginning of starting to understand the infinite whisky and food combinations".

And he is of course right. The innovators and early adopters, to use marketing gibberish, of whisky cuisine have already moved on to something else. That is the point in being an early adopter - you always have to find something new, always be at the cutting edge.

But those of us who belong to the groups which clever marketeers call Early and Late Majority are a little slower. We need time to struggle with our preconceptions, and to mentally adjust our taste buds before experiencing these new combinations. That is why many of us are newcomers to matching whisky and food.

Not a new concept

The concept of whisky dinners is not as new as one might think. In his excellent book *A Taste of Whisky*, Hans Offringa mentions a dinner at Pennsylvania State University that was held in the late 1980s when Michael Jackson selected the whiskies. But of course long before that, a nip of whisky was added to the Scottish national dish haggis. In the late nineties some of the first books about whisky and food appeared and the French whisky expert Martine Nouet stood at the forefront and continued to write about pairing whisky and food in, among other publications, Whisky Magazine. Since then, whisky dinners have become commonplace in connection with many whisky festivals.

David Neave, with 40 years of experience and practice at restaurants in France and London, has been on board since Amber opened their doors in late 2003. His daughter Wendy, who is the Events & Hospitality Manager of the restaurant, has also been there since the start. Amber is a part of Scotch Whisky Experience in Edinburgh which is the most visited whisky venue in the world attracting over 250.000 visitors per year. The SWE, which until recently was known as Scotch Whisky Heritage, is collectively owned by a number of Scottish distillers

Chef David Neave, Amber Restaurant

so it was quite obvious that Amber would also lead the whisky and food movement.

The cuisine at Amber is definitely Scottish but David has modified what he calls the "high energy" dishes to meet with contemporary demands. This does not, however, mean serving dots and spots on the plate but rather make the food lighter and less fat. Many parts of the Scottish cuisine has roots in the French method of preparing food, a heritage that goes back centuries. But nowadays David feels that the Scottish cuisine has been overly influenced by foreign cuisine and the traditions have become lost.

"Amber´s ambition, David says, is to serve world class food at the standard of a world class drink - whisky".

Whisky is not an ingredient in every dish at Amber, far from it. Every evening there are a couple of dishes in which whisky has been used while cooking but you always have the possibility of ordering a malt whisky to accompany the meal as well. With a selection of more than 300 malt whiskies, it would prove an almost impossible task for most of the visitors to select which whisky goes with which food but there is help to be had. As the ubiquitous wine sommelier in every gourmet restaurant worth its name, a whisky sommelier helps with choices at Amber. He (or she) will help you select the perfect dram to the venison or the smoked salmon. Or he may suggest an ice cold Dalwhinnie with your crème brulé!

Seafood and Islay malt - a perfect match

The Amber dining room

When I ask if visitors aren´t sometimes intimidated by the fact that they are entering a"whisky restaurant" Wendy tells me that it is quite the opposite. First of all Amber is not a whisky restaurant but a Scottish restaurant. Local produce is sourced from the glens and the mountains and from the rivers and the seas and Scotch whisky obviously has its natural place as one of the ingredients. Contrary to my conception, she tells that 90% of the guests have whisky with their food, often suggested by the sommelier and many times the whisky is a topic of conversation when people dine. And if less experienced guests wish a lighter introduction to whisky and food, they can always try the popular Scottish Tapas for lunch - a small haggis, smoked salmon or a game paté served with a whisky on the side.

Different ways to add the flavour

But if we for a moment leave whisky served on the side with the meal behind and focus on whisky as a part of cooking - how does David go about creating the ultimate combination?

Well first of all, do not expect to find all the different notes in your favourite malt when it is a part of the dish. As David explains, once the alcohol has burnt off, there is always the one flavour that becomes evident in the food no matter how many flavours you discover when nosing a glass. Sometimes the result can even be very surprising to an experienced chef like David and it takes a lot of experimenting to find the perfect marriage.

One such successful combination is Islay whisky and seafood, where the peat in the whisky combines beautifully with for example scallops. Another is venison that goes very well with a sherried Speyside like Mortlach. In both cases one can add a couple of table spoons to the sauce with excellent results.

But what about marinating in whisky I ask. Wouldn´t that be the perfect way to use the spirit? David hesitates; "I have found that when marinating, the whisky might dominate the flavours. A flambée is much better but not as a showpiece just before serving. The alcohol has to burn off and the flavours have to marry." And if the successful Islay/seafood connection already is routine for some of you, why not try a Highland Park with a vegetarian dish? The earthiness of this Orcadian malt goes especially well with root vegetables, says David.

Whisky and sushi?

I am curious to know if it would be possible to use whisky in other ethnic cuisines. Wouldn´t it be great to have a Chinese evening at the Amber? David isn´t as thrilled as I am.

"I think it would be difficult to match for example Italian or Asian food with whisky, at least as an ingredient, but served on the side it can be perfect with certain Italian desserts".

But not everyone agrees with David when it comes to matching whisky with ethnic cuisines. Whisky with sushi for example, has many followers who claim that the sweet and sour flavours of rice and vinegar and the intense saltiness of the soy sauce go very well with especially Japanese whisky. And Richard Whittington, the food consultant who created the recipes for Diageo´s Whisky & Food part of www.malts.com, suggests whiskies for several oriental dishes like crispy duck spring roll (Cragganmore), garam masala prawns (Glenkinchie) and chicken satay (Glen Elgin). And Diageo is by the way not the only producer of malt whisky that strongly supports the combination of whisky and food which, by the way, goes hand in hand with their commitment for "responsible drinking".

On their new website, Glenmorangie have commissioned chef Alejandro Sanchez to create dishes that go well with each of the distillery's expressions. Not only can one download the recipes, but Glenmorangie also go to great lengths explaining why a certain malt can be successfully paired with certain flavours in the dish.

But just as I´m about to leave the subject of whisky and "foreign" cuisines, David comes up with an idea of having a whisky/soda based drink to go with Indian food and this is when it strikes me that there is nothing traditional or preconceived when it comes to how malt whisky is treated at the Amber. True, they serve traditional Scottish cusisine but David and his team are not bound by any rules of what goes and what doesn´t. It is a question of trial and error that knows no boundaries.

For example, when they discovered that normal rice didn´t go well with whisky or Scottish dishes for that matter they invented a barley risotto. The same base in the whisky as in the risotto - as simple as that! Served with venison sausage and Ayrshire bacon it is an absolute hit!

David is always on a quest for new combinations of whisky and food. When I leave him his thoughts revolve around finding combinations of autumnal notes, of mushrooms and truffles. "When I do, he says, it will be a breakthrough and a whole new world of taste will open up."

The Scotch Whisky Experience

The Scotch Whisky Experience is a five star visitor attraction and an absolute must for whisky devotees visiting the city. This unique, interactive visitor centre dedicated to the history of Scotch is situated in the heart of the city with Edinburgh castle as its nearest neighbour. An impressive whisky shop with more than 300 different single malts, grain and blended whiskies to choose from can be found here.

The Scotch Whisky Experience will undertake a £2 million expansion during autumn 2008. The expansion will among other things turn the famous barrel ride, which takes you through the whisky making process, into a new, truly unique and exclusive feature.

www.whisky-heritage.co.uk

Malt Whisky Yearbook
Whisky Dinner

To help you prepare your very own Whisky Dinner, here are three recipes which David was kind enough to share with us.

Scallops and seaweed with Islay whisky

I use Islay hand dived scallops for this – not scallops that have been gathered by a dredger, which destroys the seabed. This recipe also uses clams from the beach, and pearls of barley to relate back to the origins of whisky itself.

Ingredients

8 large west coast scallops (cleaned and trimmed)
16 surf clams
seaweed
2 oz pearl barley
flesh from 1 small uncooked lobster
ground white pepper
2 oz unsalted butter
Islay whisky

✓ Wash and cook the barley for about 20 minutes, drain and set aside.

✓ Cook the surf clams in a little water for two minutes. Separate the clams from the liquid, setting aside the liquid for later use.

✓ Melt the butter in a pan, place the scallops in one at a time, turning each after 30 seconds.

✓ Add the lobster, sliced very thinly.

✓ Add the whisky allowing it to flame and then quickly add the seaweed, surf clams, liquid and the barley.

✓ Season with white pepper and serve.

Duck breast with whisky and Orange marmalade

Ingredients

breast of duck
25 ml West Coast malt whisky
butter & oil
25 oz orange marmalade

✓ Melt butter in a pan, add oil.

✓ Place duck breast skin down and cook till coloured.

✓ Place on a tray and cook in the oven at 180°.

✓ Cook the juice left in the pan with the orange marmalade and the whisky.

✓ Serve with seasonal vegetables and potatoes.

Cranachan

Ingredients

60 g of medium oatmeal
150 g of raspberries
4 tablespoons of malt whisky
4 tablespoons of runny Scottish honey
600 mls of double cream

✓ Scatter the oatmeal onto a baking tray and toast in a low oven or under the grill until they become golden brown. Do stand and watch this because they can easily and quickly burn.

✓ Whip the double cream until a stiff mixture forms.

✓ Stir in the honey and the whisky and mix well.

✓ Fold in 50 g of the toasted oatmeal then fold in 100 g of the raspberries.

✓ Spoon the mixture into glasses or individual serving dishes.

✓ Gently scatter the remaining oatmeal and raspberries on the top of each dish.

The rise and rise of New World Whiskies

*Is the world of whisky set
for its own version of New World Wines?
With shortages of Scotch coupled with an ever-improving
quality of whisky from elsewhere in the world, this may
well be the case. Dominic Roskrow reports.*

About 25 years ago a revolution shook the world of wine to its core. Countries once derided for their poor quality wine turned the traditional and staid markets on their head, bringing freshness, excitement and youth to a new generation of drinkers. Eventually it brought fine quality, too, and now the likes of Australia, South Africa and New Zealand compare favourably to 'old world wines.'

Could the same thing happen to whisky? It could be argued that it already is. Japan's success in both the single malt and blended categories at the 2008 World Whisky Awards were proof, should any more be needed, that Japan has gate-crashed the old world whisky party where Scotland, America, Ireland and Canada were the only worthy guests. Japan is actually a special case, having had a long and inconsistent gestation period. But now there is the very real prospect of a genuine 'New World' movement of whisky. Countries as diverse as India, Wales, South Africa, Belgium, and France are not only making whisky, but they're putting a unique spin on it, and raising the stakes in terms of quality.

There are two principle reasons for this. Firstly, demand from the emerging markets in South East Asia, India and China have made supplies of Scotch whisky scarce, and in some territories bottles of Scottish whisky have all but been sucked out, leaving a vacuum for a home-produced whisky to fill. Secondly, the standard of whisky in a number of countries across the world has risen sufficiently to attract the interest of enthusiasts in 'Old World' whisky markets. Some whisky – albeit a trickle so far – has made it across international borders. Whisky writers have started to take notice. And some world whiskies have started to pick up medals at the world's most important and influential whisky competitions.

Focus on three regions

Some perspective here. Unlike the situation when the wine revolution happened, New World Whisky is at a very early stage, and the nature of the beast dictates that it will be some years before we're regularly picking up a European malt or South American malt-bourbon hybrid. Nevertheless, the signs are there, and three regions in particular are not only now making good whisky, but unusual and nationally-distinctive ones, too: Sweden, the German-speaking parts of Central Europe, and Australia, and in particular, Tasmania.

Mackmyra Distillery, north of Stockholm, is one of those happy feel-good stories. It started as a whisky-fuelled late night holiday conversation just over 10 years ago.

Charring the casks at
Mackmyra distillery

It's resulted in a multi-million Euro business which is making waves across the world. Mackmyra Swedish malt whisky is starting to win converts even in Scotland, and is picking up accolades at the world's most prestigious drinks competitions.

And if you think that outstanding Swedish whisky is about as likely as a successful Swiss sailing team, check out who the winners of the last two America's Cup was, and then read what leading whisky writer Jim Murray has to say about Mackmyra. He's chosen its whiskies for awards two years in a row.

Mackmyra is based in an old industrial town of the same name 90 minutes north of Stockholm and now employs about 30 people – not bad for a company formed by eight Swedish engineering friends during a skiing holiday to Salen in March 1998. The company developed gradually, involving enthusiasts sourced from the internet to help make decisions on what style of whisky to make, and evolving experimental distillations on an ever-increasing scale.

On the face of it the Mackmyra emulates Scottish malt production. The copper stills are imported from Scotland and a traditional double distillation process is employed.

Mackmyra, though, tastes nothing like anything produced in Scotland. Scandinavian tweaks have given Sweden a flavour all of its own, and it will be fascinating to watch whether the country's new distillery, opened in the middle of 2008, produces a similar malt. At the heart of the operation was an early decision to use only Swedish products. The team moved in to an old industrial premises that had previously served time as an ironworks and a dairy in the region known as Mackmyra – mosquito swamp in Swedish. Swedish oak and barley are used in the process. So why so different? There are a number of explanations for Mackmyra's distinctive and oft-acquired taste.

The oak itself seem to impart different flavours to the whisky, aided by the fact that at least some of the casks are made of virgin oak and many of the casks used are smaller than those normally employed in Scotland. Perhaps the biggest difference though, comes from the drying process. Mackmyra uses peat but its properties are significantly different from Scottish peat. It has been formed over centuries but for much of that time it would have been under sea water, so it imparts a saltier and more bitter taste. To counterbalance

Drying the malt with juniper adds to the Mackmyra character

this Mackmyra also uses the traditional Swedish method of smoking food, using juniper leaves. Mackmyra's maturation process, too, is breaking new ground, though whether this will impact on flavour remains to be seen. The malt is still quite young. Nevertheless, as an ongoing experiment it's a fascinating one.

At the heart of it is the decision by the distillery to offer customers buying their own cask a choice of places to store it. In all Mackmyra has four places where its warehouse are laid down, varying from a cool inland disused mine (one of the strangest and most atmospheric maturing areas in the world), an island in the heart of Stockholm and a seaside location on the West Coast. As with pretty much all things to do with the distillery, the choice of East, West, North or South came about through a mixture of natural evolution and people power.

"Originally we matured the whisky close to the distillery but when we offered casks for sale we noticed a large number of requests from the south," says managing director Magnus Dandanell. "This is the region in Sweden traditionally associated with food and drink. It meant people were having to travel a long way to visit their cask so we came up with the idea of storing some casks in the south. "But then we had some complaints from people in Gothenburg, which is Sweden's second city. They felt that they should have been next to be considered for storing casks, so we found somewhere on the West Coast too." It will be seen in time what, if anything, location offers to flavour, but Mackmyra is now well and truly part of the debate.

Casks aside, though, the strange and unique mix of Swedish influences have made for astounding results. Early bottlings under the names Preludium and Privus were to varying degrees oily, earthy, young and grungey, the whisky equivalent of a Nirvana album: hit and miss with the odd gem in the ranks. In some cases the balance was lost and the fruitiness squeezed out. But undoubtedly the bottles improved over the months and years and by the time the distillery launched its first whisky proper, First Edition, in mid 2008, the distillery had hit its stride. First Edition has a rich orange liqueur flavour, bordering on a sweet medicinal note, and it is very different and very good.

Most importantly the Swedish distillery is giving every impression that it is painting new shapes on the whisky world's canvas and taking it into new and very attractive regions indeed.

Australian distillers harvest success

On the other side of the world, the distilleries of Australia have thus far taken a more conventional route and reproduced a style of single malt that would be recognizable to a Scotch drinker. To this point, too, there has been relatively little to concern the Scots. But this, too, might be set to change. For a starter, the Australians take their whisky very seriously. Here is a new country proud of the fact it has thrown away old world shackles and free to do what the hell it likes with the rules of whisky within Australian law which still requires malt whisky to be made from malt barley and aged for a minimum of 2 years. And to their shame there have been one or two unscrupulous producers who have tried to dispense with such trivialities as copper and oak, made neutral grain spirit and infused it with glorified teabags containing spices and oak shavings.

But they are vastly in the minority and have been closed down by Australia's federal authorities. Conscious that any corner cutting and compromise in quality will be at best dismissed in serious whisky markets and at worse ridiculed, the serious Australian distilleries, a number of which are clustered on the verdant and river-rich island of Tasmania, have stringently adopted the rules imported from Scotland and Europe.

And in the last year Australian malt whisky has fully come in to its own. In his 2008 Whisky Bible Jim Murray concluded his section on Australian whisky with the words 'Congratulations. Australia has entered the ranks of serious whisky distilling nations.' You betcha. Judging from the green fruit-rich cask samples on offer at Whisky Live New Zealand, whisky spring's arrived in Australia. Others on the international stage are noticing too. Great Southern Distilling Company's first release single malt Limeburners was awarded a medal at the 2008 London Wine and Spirits Show. Lark Distillery of Tasmania won medals at the 2007 London Wine and Spirit Show, and Sullivan's Cove won medals at the San Francisco Spirits show.

Further awards will surely follow. It's 17 years since Lark owner Bill Lark pioneered Australian whisky and started making malt, and several other distilleries have followed, particularly on the South East coast isle of Tasmania. Newer distilleries such as Nant have not only been able to follow in Lark's footsteps but have employed Bill Lark in a consultative role,

Bill Lark, the father of modern whisky making in Australia, with his wife Lyn and daughter Kristy

The Cellar Door (visitor centre) at Great Southern Distilling Company

David Baker, founder and owner of Bakery Hill distillery

A spectacular view from the Atrium Lounge Bar at Nant distillery

giving the region a cohesion and identity that will grow stronger in the future. Tellingly, a distillery delegation from Tasmania travelled with a Tasmanian government official to Whisky Live in New Zealand, emphasizing the growing importance malt whisky could have on the island's future.

According to Lark Distillery owner Bill Lark, this is just a starting point.

"We have been distilling malt whisky since 1992 and since then five more distilleries have commenced production in Tasmania and another four or five distilleries throughout mainland Australia," he says.

"They are all at various stages of production and maturation. But with the wonderful accolades we are getting around the world we are receiving an increasing number of calls from people wanting to be part of this industry. We feel part of the New World of whisky because of the wonderful reception our whiskies are having. The world market for whisky is also becoming far more sophisticated and open to exploring new whiskies."

Australia is, of course, a long way from the heart of whisky's traditional old world, and given Australia's relative youth it's unlikely to get the world to sit up and take notice by trying to match and better Scottish single malt. But it has two factors in its favour: one, that geography and climate of Australia will give it the opportunity to develop a malt that matches the quality of Scotch but has a taste profile all its own; and two, that the whisky axis is moving from its traditional and old Euro-centric base and moving south and eastwards towards Australasia.

The first requires something of a balancing act. For credibility's sake the general feeling in Australia is that the strict rules governing Scotch should be adhered to. But at the same time in order to carve out a unique place for Australian whisky its distillers need to find ways of breaking away from the old world straitjacket.

Undoubtedly geographical location is starting to influence the overall flavour and give Australian malts a distinctive characteristic of their own.

"Australia is definitely in a unique position to develop its own taste profile," says David Baker of the Bakery Hill Distillery in mainland Victoria.

"The most important difference we have to Scotland is the climate. Higher daily ambient temperatures ensure a more speedy maturation without the negative effects

associated with unduly high temperatures that might over-cook the spirit. Geographically with a huge coast line there is ample room for distilleries to establish near the coast and to take advantage of its salt characteristics or to go further inland to gain a more full bodied flavour."

Baker is ideally placed to know. While Lark is producing one or two malts that are at the top of their game and Sullivan Cove's six year old cask strength malt is a world monster and would hold its own in any company, Bakery Hill has been the country's most consistent producer. More than that, the distillery backs up Baker's claim to geographical variety by producing rich, fruity and full Speyside offerings and some quite amazing peated offerings.

As with Sweden the jury is out as to whether an inland or seaside location is affecting flavour to any great degree – the evidence would seem thin at this stage – but of more interest is the question of ambient temperature and maturation. This is an area where Australia can stay strictly within the rules but motor down a new track. Some American micro-distillers are successfully 'bourboning' single malt, so what's to stop Australia finding its own niche somewhere between the old Scottish way and the new American one?

Australian whiskies gaining respect

What makes the future so exciting for the distilleries of Australia and perhaps eventually New Zealand is that while they still have a long way to go before they can truly be said to match the great malts of Scotland, they also come 'baggage free' and open up the possibility of creating a new generation of malt whisky enthusiasts. Part of that opportunity might result from the second of the two trends that work in Australia's favour – the movement of whisky's epicentre from central Europe to emerging markets in South East Asia, India and China.

Cameron Syme is a director of the Great Southern Distilling Company in Western Australia and chair of the Australian Distillers' Association Inc. He believes that the first hurdle – to be taken seriously in the home market – has been safely negotiated, and that while Australian whisky is starting from a very low base, it's moving in the right direction.

"There has definitely been an increased

interest in the last two to seven years and this has no doubt been helped by a number of Australian whiskies performing very well in international spirit competitions," he says. "Here we have recently released Limeburners First Release Single Malt which has sold for up to $500 AUD a bottle, so good luck if you can get it but ther just isn't enough to go round. We were even offered $1,000 AUD for a bottle of our first release, which we had to turn down as we had already allocated the entire release. To me this consumer recognition is the best recognition there is that we are making quality single malt."

"For this reason there is little room for most of us to think about export markets but looking forward I believe these emerging markets are important for our future. It's the premium quality that is attracting the interest and Australian distilleries are already making premium single malt whisky.

"There is no reason why we should not be able to build a substantial whisky industry. We have premium quality water and malt and a very clean environment which should add up to a premium quality product. I believe we have to have a high standard of production to ensure there is consistent quality and to make sure people are comparing apples with apples. As long as the standard is consistent we should be fine." David Baker agrees. He reckons Australians' have plenty to look forward to in the world of whisky.

"The notion of malts being consumed by middle-aged males is being challenged by younger drinkers and an increasing number of women," he says. "Brand loyalties are being questioned and consumers are looking far wider for their malts. If the malt is of good quality then the customer will actively seek it out and enjoy it. So for us emerging countries the future for distilling is very rosy indeed."

The message from Australia at present is clear, then. If Australia continues to make whisky to the highest standard and let it take its natural course, it'll develop its own unique personality and carve out new markets for itself. This being Australia, though, the potential for innovation isn't being ignored. Experimentation in America hasn't gone unnoticed in Tasmania, for instance.

"This is an interesting topic and one in which I think the Australian and New Zealand industries should probably keep an open mind on," says Bill Lark. "When we started making whisky we had a view to produce a malt whisky true to the traditional notion of a single malt whisky, albeit an Australian one. Having said that, look at the United States, which has an emerging whiskey market other than bourbons. I was quite surprised when I went there by some of the outstanding whiskies being produced in 'new' styles but that are finding great favour with the traditional malt whisky market."

The country's wine story proves that experimental whisky and quality needn't be mutually exclusive. Watch this space.

Experiments with different grains

Back in the Northern Hemisphere there are plenty of distilleries operating outside Scotland which are set to contribute in the continent's whisky future. In Austria, Germany, and Switzerland distilleries are already experimenting with a range of grains and with variations of malts.

Distilleries such as Weidenauer Distillery (oats, spelt wheat) and Waldviertler Roggenhof (malted barley, malted rye, rye) in Austria are taking whisky in to new exciting regions while in Switzerland Swissky from Brennerei-Zentrum Bauernhof and the malts from Whisky Castle at Elfingen prove that European malt can give some Scottish malts a run for their money. Germany, Austria and Switzerland are all offering considerable grounds for excitement and optimism in the future.

Johann Haider from Waldviertler Roggenhof distillery in Austria

The still room at SLYRS distillery in Germany

In Germany, for instance Slyrs in Bavaria has produced a young but very promising single malt. It's not particularly sophisticated and there is a degree of flabbiness about its overall structure, but a healthy mix of honey and fruit suggest that with time its highly drinkable characteristics will be decorated by more spice, oak and depth. Meanwhile Blaue Maus – Blue Mouse - is almost literally adding colour and variety to the market place, and starting to tick the right buttons when it comes to top-notch production techniques.

Meanwhile over in the west of Germany, in a picturesque tree-covered region known as the German Highlands and just a few kilometers from Limburg, arguably the world's biggest whisky festival and certainly one of the best, lies Brennerei Hoehler. Here in a small room off a courtyard Holger Hoehler is experimenting with malts made from malt beer, German altbeer and a range of other grains. Under the name Whessky, a reference to the region the whisky comes from, a whole range of unusual and exciting flavours are emerging, including a strange wheat-malt-bourbon hybrid by the name of Hessicher whisky.

The empty shelves in the shop are testament to the demand locally for Hoehler's whiskies and prove that the seeds have been planted here of a vibrant and dynamic distinctly different whisky.

In Austria, too, distilleries are breaking new ground. The country's oldest distillery is Waldviertler Roggenhof, which has now attracted more than 50,000 visitors. Here the whisky-making process is again unique. Grains including rye and barley are used and they are roasted to different degrees, releasing nougat, caramel and chocolate characteristics. The spirit itself is the result of quadruple distillation, and the process is ingenuously turned on its head, with unwanted fats, oils and impurities removed at the start of the process rather than

Holger Hoehler from Brennerei Hoehler in Germany

the end – so that 'the cut' is made in the first distillation.

The distillery's trying to be different in other ways too. The facilities there have been expanded to include a children's play area, an interactive whisky experience complete with video, and a somewhat hippie-ish series of Celtic tree circles embracing the four elements of earth, air, fire and water.

Over in Switzerland the country's oldest distillery Holle will this year celebrate the 10th anniversary of its decision to start making whisky after a change in Switzerland's alcohol laws allowed it to do so. Holle is the brainchild of Ernst Bader, a retired dairy farmer who for many years distilled fruits and thought he'd chance his arm at whisky. He was bought a bottle to find out exactly what it was.

But from such modest beginnings whisky has boomed and it's now the distillery's main focus. As with other distilleries making fruit liqueurs in all three countries, traditional and heritage suggest whisky won't take over completely – but the potential to grow further is great.

From Stockholm to Hobart, New World whisky is taking shape, guaranteeing us whisky lovers years of future exploration and adventure. In Switzerland Ruedi Kaesar of the Whisky Castle at Elfingen perhaps sums it up best.

"Of course it is possible for distillers such as us to open new markets for whisky," he says. "It is like wine – the difference between old world and new world. We want to be the leaders of the new world of whisky."

Dominic Roskrow is a freelance whisky writer and former editor of Whisky Magazine, which he edited for four years. He writes regularly for Whisky Magazine and Malt Advocate, has columns in magazines in America, China and Ireland and has contributed to leading drinks titles such as Harpers Food & Wine, Imbibe, Decanter and Morning Advocate. He is the business development director for The Whisky Shop chain, and his business is based at the company's shop in Norwich. He has been writing about drinks for 15 years and is the author of Whiskies: From Confused to Connoisseur *published by Harper Collins, and the new* Collins Gems Whisky, *published in 2009. He is currently working on updating Michael Jackson's* Companion to Whisky, *for publicaton in March 2010. He lives in Norfolk, home of England's first malt*

Ruedi Käser from Whisky Castle in Switzerland

Malt distilleries
of Scotland and Ireland

127 Scottish and Irish distilleries are described in detail on the following pages.

Most are active, while some are mothballed, decommissioned or demolished. Some of the latter can be considered 'active' as their whisky is still bottled and sold.

Long since closed distilleries from which whisky is very rare or practically unobtainable are described at the end together with four new and upcoming distilleries.

Japanese malt whisky distilleries and distilleries in other countries are covered on pp. 204-235.

Explanations

Owner:
Name of the owning company, sometimes with the parent company within brackets.

Region/district:
There are four formal malt whisky regions in Scotland today; the Highlands, the Lowlands, Islay and Campbeltown. Where useful we mention a location within a region e.g. Speyside, Orkney, Northern Highlands etc.

Founded:
The year in which the distillery was founded is usually considered as when construction began. The year is rarely the same year in which the distillery was licensed.

Status:
The status of the distillery's production. Active, mothballed (temporarily closed), closed (but most of the equipment still present), dismantled (the equipment is gone but part of or all of the buildings remain even if they are used for other purposes) and demolished.

Visitor centre:
The letters (vc) after status indicate that the distillery has a visitor centre. Many distilleries accept visitors despite not having a visitor centre. It can be worthwhile making an enquiry.

Address:
The distillery's address.

Tel:
This is generally to the visitor centre, but can also be to the main office.

website:
The distillery's (or in some cases the owner's) website.

Capacity:
The current production capacity expressed in litres of pure alcohol (LPA).

History:
The chronology focuses on the official history of the distillery and independent bottlings are only listed in exceptional cases. They can be found in the text bodies instead.

Tasting notes: NEW FEATURE
For all the Scottish and Irish distilleries that are not permanently closed we present tasting notes of what, in most cases, can be called the core expression (mainly their best selling 10 or 12 year old).

We have tried to provide notes for official bottlings but in those cases where we have not been able to obtain them, we have turned to independent bottlers.

The whiskies have been tasted by *Dominic Roskrow* (DR) and *David Stirk* (DS), well-known whisky profiles and contributors to Malt Whisky Yearbook over three years now. We have strived to have both gentlemen's comments for each distillery but in a few cases, only one of them has been able to provide notes.

The notes have been prepared especially for Malt Whisky Yearbook 2009.

Brief distillery glossary

A number of terms occur throughout the distillery directory and are briefly explained here. We can recommend for example *A to Z of Whisky* by Gavin D Smith for more detailed explanations.

Blended malt
A type of whisky where two or more single malts are blended together. The term was introduced a few years ago by SWA to replace the previous term vatted malt. The term is controversial as those who oppose the use of it are of the opinion that it can be confused with 'blended whisky' where malt and grain is blended.

Cask strength
It has become increasingly common in recent times to bottle malt whisky straight from the cask without reducing the alcohol contents to 40, 43 or 46%. A cask strength can be anything between 40 to 65% depending on how long the cask has been matured.

Chill-filtering
A method used for removing unwanted particles and, especially used to prevent the whisky from appearing turbid when water is added. Some producers believe that flavour is affected and therefore avoid chill-filtering.

Continuous still
A type of still used when making grain whisky. The still allows for continuous distillation and re-distillation. Can also be called column still, patent still or Coffey still.

Cooling
The spirit vapours from the stills are cooled into liquids usually by a shell and tube condenser, but an older method (worm tubs) is still in use at some distilleries.

Dark grains
The draff and pot ale from the distillation process is used for making fodder pellets, so-called dark grains.

Drum maltings
The malting method used on all major malting sites today.

Dunnage warehouse
Also called traditional warehouse. The walls are made of stone and the floors of earth. The casks (up to three) are piled on top of each other.

Floor maltings
The traditional method of malting the barley on large wooden floors. This method is only used by a handful of distilleries today.

Lyne arm
The lyne arm leads the spirit vapours from the wash or spirit still to the condenser. The angle of the lyne arm has great significance for reflux and the final character of the whisky.

Mash tun
The procedure after the malt has been milled into grist is called the mashing. The mash tun is usually made of cast iron or stainless steel, but can sometimes be made of wood. The grist is mixed with hot water in order to release the sugars in the barley. The result is the wort which is drawn off through a perforated floor into the underback. The mashed grains in the mash tun are called draff and are then used for making animal feed.

Pagoda roof
A roof shaped as a pagoda which was built over the kiln to lead the smoke away from the drying peat. The pagoda roof was invented by the famous architect Charles Doig. These days pagoda roofs provide mainly aesthetical value as the majority of distilleries usually buy their malt elsewhere.

Peat
A soil layer consisting of plants which have mouldered. Used as fuel in drying the green malts when a more or less peaty whisky is to be produced. In other cases the kiln is usually heated by oil or gas.

PPM
Abbreviation for Parts Per Million. This is used to show the amount of phenols in the peated malt. Peated Islay whisky usually uses malt with 40-60 ppm, which is reduced to 10-20 ppm in the new make spirit.

Purifier
A device used in conjunction with the lyne arm which cools heavier alcohols and lead them back to the still. A handful of distilleries use this technique to make a lighter and cleaner spirit.

Racked warehouse
A modern warehouse with temperature control and built-in shelves. Casks can be stored up to a height of 12.

Reflux
When the heavier vapours in the still are cooled and fall back into the still as liquids. The amount of reflux obtained depends on the shape of the still and the angle of the lyne arm. A distillation process with high reflux gives a lighter, more delicate spirit while a small amount of reflux gives a more robust and flavour-rich whisky.

Saladin box
A method of malting barley which replaced floor maltings. It was invented by the Frenchman Charles Saladin in the late 19th century and was introduced in Scottish distilleries in the 1950s. The only distillery using the method today is Tamdhu.

Shell and tube condenser
The most common method for cooling the spirit vapours. It is a wide copper tube attached to the lyne arm of the still. Cold water is led through a number of smaller copper pipes and cools the surrounding vapours.

Spirit still
The second still, usually a little smaller that the wash still. The low wines are collected in the spirit still for redistilling. Alcohol increases to 64-68% and unwanted impurities disappear. It is only the middle fraction of the distillate (the cut) which is utilized.

Vatted malt
See blended malt.

Washback
Large tubs of stainless steel or wood in which fermentation takes place. Yeast is added to the worts and the sugars change into alcohol. The result is a wash with an alcoholic content of 6-8% which is then used for distillation.

Wash still
The first and usually largest of the stills. The wash is heated to the boiling point and the alcohol is vaporized. The spirit vapours are cooled in a condenser and the result is low wines with an alcohol content of c 21%.

Worm tub
An older method for cooling the spirit vapours in connection with distilling. This method is still used in approximately ten distilleries. The worm tub consists of a long, spiral-shaped copper pipe which is submerged in water in a large wooden tub, usually outdoors. The spirit vapours are led through the copper spiral so they can condense.

Aberfeldy

Owner:
John Dewar & Sons
(Bacardi)

Region/district:
Eastern Highlands

Founded: 1896

Status: Active (vc)

Capacity: 3 500 000 litres

Address: Aberfeldy, Perthshire PH15 2EB

Tel: 01887 822010 (vc)

website: www.dewarswow.com

History:
1896 – John and Tommy Dewar embark on the construction of the distillery a stone's throw from the old Pitilie distillery which was active from 1825 to 1867. Their objective is to produce a single malt for their blended whisky - White Label.

1898 – Production starts in November.

1917-19 – The distillery closes.

1925 – Distillers Company Limited (DCL) takes over.

1930 – Operations are transferred to Scottish Malt Distillers (SMD).

1972 – Reconstruction takes place, the floor maltings is closed and the two stills are increased to four.

1991 – The first official bottling is a 15 year old in the Flora & Fauna series.

1998 – Bacardi buys John Dewar & Sons from Diageo at a price of £1,150 million. Five malt distilleries and Bombay Sapphire Gin are included in the purchase.

2000 – A visitor centre opens and a 25 year old is released to commemorate.

2005 – A 21 year old is launched in October, replacing the 25 year old.

Aberfeldy 12 year old

DR – The nose is a mix of fresh and clean barley, honey and a hint of smoke. The honey carries through to the palate and the pleasant finish is shaped by a touch of smoke and peppery spice.

DS – Apples, honey and caramel with a hint of champagne on the nose. The palate is sweet and firm with some herbal, vanilla flavours and the finish is sugary.

Before Bacardi bought Aberfeldy in 1998, few people had encountered a single malt from the distillery. This was a whisky that the previous owners, Diageo, did not spend any effort on at all. Neither are sales booming under new ownership, in fact, it is selling only 6,000 cases per year which puts it in the range of brands like Edradour, Tamnavulin and Tobermory. But Bacardi has been keener to promote Aberfeldy recently not least because they wish to associate it with the blend where it is the key malt, namely Dewars White Label. Even if sales have been flat for a couple of years, White Label is still uncontested in US as the premier blended Scotch. In 2008 a novel marketing move was tried at various airports with the Whisky Challenge where travellers got a chance to blind taste Dewars and two unspecified competitors.

A seven day week and shorter fermentation time has increased capacity (and current production) to 3.5 million litres and three new stillmen were employed in the beginning of 2008. The equipment consists of a stainless steel mash tun, eight washbacks made of Siberian larch, two stainless steel washbacks placed outdoors and two pairs of stills. There are six warehouses on site though they are no longer used for storage. Instead the spirit is tankered to Stirling for filling on casks (mostly ex-bourbon) and maturation. A new pot ale plant has recently been built to take care of residues from the distilling.

A lavish, ground-breaking visitor centre, Dewar´s World of Whisky, was opened in 2000. It now receives some 40,000 visitors annually.

There are currently only two official bottlings; a 12 year old and a 21 year old.

Independent bottlings have been very rare in recent years.

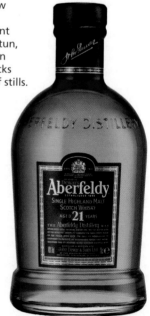

21 years old

Aberlour

Owner:
Chivas Brothers Ltd
(Pernod Ricard)

Region/district:
Speyside

Founded: 1826

Status: Active (vc)

Capacity: 3 500 000 litres

Address: Aberlour, Banffshire AB38 9PJ

Tel: 01340 881249

website: www.aberlour.com

History:

1826 – James Gordon and Peter Weir found the first Aberlour Distillery.

1827 – Peter Weir withdraws and James Gordon continues alone.

1879 – A fire devastates most of the distillery. The local banker James Fleming constructs a new distillery a few kilometres upstream the Spey river.

1892 – The distillery is sold to Robert Thorne & Sons Ltd who expands it.

1898 – Another fire rages and almost totally destroys the distillery. The architect Charles Doig is called in to design the new facilities.

1921 – Robert Thorne & Sons Ltd sells Aberlour to W. H. Holt & Sons, a brewery near Manchester.

1945 – S. Campbell & Sons Ltd buys the distillery.

1962 – Aberlour terminates floor malting.

1973 – Number of stills increased from two to four.

1975 – Pernod Ricard buys Campbell Distilleries.

2000 – Aberlour a´bunadh is launched. A limited 30 year old cask strength is released.

2001 – Pernod Ricard buys Chivas Brothers from Seagrams and merges Chivas Brothers and Campbell Distilleries under the brand Chivas Brothers.

2002 – A new, modernized visitor centre is inaugurated in August.

2008 – The 18 year old is introduced also outside France.

Aberlour 12 year old

DR – The nose combines horse chestnut casing then sweet melon and fresh spearmint, the taste is beautifully fresh and clean, with mint and gentle fruit.

DS – Rich dried fruits and spices with star of anise on the nose. Citrusy and rich-caramel flavours in the mouth with a fruity, sherried finish.

Of the 13 active distilleries owned by Pernod Ricard, two have an exceptionally stronger position as single malts than the others – Glenlivet (obviously) and Aberlour. The latter currently occupies place 7 on the top list with 2.3 million bottles sold in 2006. A few years ago it was even among the top four. Aberlour is a big seller in especially France and is neck and neck with Glenfiddich as the most sold single malt in the country. France has for many years now been the most important export market for Scotch whisky when it comes to sheer volume. In terms of value, USA is the biggest market. The volume has increased by 30% in the last ten years and one has to look to markets in South America and Asia to find a greater rate of increase. It is even said that more Scotch is sold in France in a month than cognac in a year.

The distillery is equipped with one semi-lauter mash tun, six stainless steel washbacks and two pairs of stills. There are six racked warehouses on site with a total of 27,000 casks and about half of the production is used for single malts.

The core range of Aberlour includes a *10 year old* (sherry/bourbon), a *12 year old Double Cask Matured*, a *16 year old Double Cask matured* and *a'bunadh* of which there are 23 batches launched up to and including spring 2008. A new expression in spring 2008 was the *18 year old*; previously sold exclusively in France. In France, a *10 year old Sherry Cask Finish* and the *15 year Cuvée Marie d'Ecosse* are available. Two 'exclusives' are available for the duty free market – *12 year old sherry matured* and *15 year old double cask matured*. A very limited expression in 2008 was the Aberlour *31 year old*, a single cask reserved for French travel retail.

Recent independent bottlings include a 17 year old from Blackadder, an 18 year old from Cadenhead and three bottlings by Douglas Laing, the oldest a 21 year old.

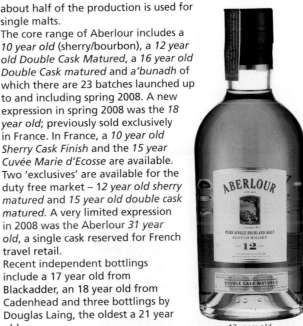

12 years old

Allt-a-Bhainne

Owner: **Region/district:**
Chivas Brothers Ltd   Speyside
(Pernod Ricard)

Founded: **Status:**   **Capacity:**
1975   Active   4 500 000 litres

Address: Glenrinnes, Dufftown,
Banffshire AB55 4DB

Tel: **website:**
01542 783200   -

History:
1975 – The distillery is founded by Chivas Brothers, a subsidiary to Seagrams, in order to secure malt whisky for their blended whiskies. The total cost amounts to £2.7 million.

1989 – Production has doubled.

2001 – Pernod Ricard takes over Chivas Brothers from Seagrams.

2002 – Mothballed in October.

2005 – Production restarts in May.

Deerstalker 12 year old

DR – Autumn fields and damp hay on the nose, a richer, sweeter earth and heathery taste on the palate and a gentle rounded finish.

DS – Pine and anise on the nose with biscuit and lemon grass. Sweet and perfumed on the palate. Sugary and spiky with a medium, sweet finish.

Allt-a-Bhainne distillery is a glowing example of how quickly changes take place in the whisky industry. Constructed as recently as 1975, Allt-a-Bhainne was closed in autumn 2002 just a few months after a new boiler had been installed. The reason was overproduction in the receding whisky market. The following year it was advertised for sale. Another two years later it was recommissioned since sales figures for Chivas Regal (in which Allt-A-Bhainne is a component) took a great leap forward and now the distillery is producing at full capacity. Sales of Scotch whisky continue to increase and this year the sister distillery Braeval has also been recommissioned.

Allt-a-Bhainne's equipment consists of a 7-roller Buhler mill (as Porteus and Boby mills were hard to obtain when the distillery was built), a stainless steel mash tun, eight stainless steel washbacks and two pairs of stills. The wash stills are of the traditional broad-necked versions but the two spirit stills have rather unusual, long necks with parallel sides which increase reflux and thus produce a lighter spirit. The whisky is not filled on casks on site but transported by lorry to a facility in Keith.

Allt-a-Bhainne is normally closed for visitors but Chivas Bros took a new, promising initiative when they made it possible to book a guided tour here and at Longmorn during 8 Sundays in autumn 2008. Hopefully this opportunity will continue. Both Braeval and Allt-a-Bhainne are located in a remote and beautiful part of the Highlands between Dufftown and Tomintoul and it only takes 20 minutes to drive between the two.

There are no official bottlings of Allt-a-Bhainne and according to Chivas Brothers there are no plans for any either. Independent bottlings can be found though in the shape of Deerstalker 12 year old from Aberko. Recently there was also a 15 year old from Cadenhead and an 11 year old from Douglas Laing.

Deerstalker 12 year old

Ardbeg distillery

Ardbeg

Owner: Glenmorangie Co (Moët Hennessy)

Region/district: The Islay

Founded: 1815

Status: Active (vc)

Capacity: 1 000 000 litres

Address: Port Ellen, Islay, Argyll PA42 7EA

Tel: 01496 302244 (vc)

website: www.ardbeg.com

History:

1794 – First record of a distillery at Ardbeg. It was founded by Alexander Stewart.

1798 – The MacDougalls, later to become licensees of Ardbeg, are active on the site through Duncan MacDougall.

1815 – The current distillery is founded by John MacDougall, son of Duncan MacDougall.

1853 – Alexander MacDougall, John's son, dies and sisters Margaret and Flora MacDougall, assisted by Colin Hay, continue the running of the distillery. Colin Hay takes over the licence when the sisters die.

1888 – Colin Elliot Hay and Alexander Wilson Gray Buchanan renew their license.

1900 – Colin Hay's son takes over the license.

1959 – Ardbeg Distillery Ltd is founded.

1973 – Hiram Walker and Distillers Company Ltd jointly purchase the distillery for £300 000 through Ardbeg Distillery Trust.

1974 – Widely considered as the last vintage of 'old, peaty' Ardbeg. Malt which has not been produced in the distillery's own maltings is used in increasingly larger shares after this year.

1977 – Hiram Walker assumes single control of the distillery. Ardbeg closes its maltings.

1979 – Kildalton, a less peated malt, is produced over a number of years.

Ardbeg and its two neighbours, Laphroaig and Lagavulin, are side by side in the south part of Islay which is called Kildalton and their peated whisky is in high demand everywhere in the world. They may seem similar, but there are great differences between the three. Ardbeg's capacity is considerably less than half of the others. Whilst Laphroaig and Lagavulin have been producing more or less without interruption since WWII, Ardbeg was closed 1981-1989 and was only in production for a few months per year between 1989-1996. This means problems for the owners as the demand of Ardbeg has increased in recent years and the question is if demand eventually will outstrip supply with so small amounts, of at least older expressions, in the warehouses. Production has increased since 2007 from 12 to 13 mashes per week. Ardbeg used to buy all their malt from Port Ellen maltings on Islay but with the increased production at Diageo's own two Islay distilleries, 20% of requirements now come from the mainland. The specification of Ardbeg's malt is 55 ppm which gives c 23 ppm in the finished spirit

The distillery is equipped with a stainless steel mash tun, six washbacks made of Oregon pine and one pair of stills. In the spirit still, installed as recently as in 2001, lies a large part of the secret of Ardbeg's taste; compared to neighbours Laphroaig and Lagavulin the peatiness is supplemented by a fruitiness which gives Ardbeg its own, very special style. The character is achieved by a purifier attached to the spirit still and increasing the reflux.

Some refurbishings were recently announced by the owners with both the distillery and visitor centre being upgraded and a new warehouse will also be built.

In 2005 Ardbeg Very Young appeared, the first step towards a new 10 year old based on the spirit distilled since Glenmorangie took over in 1997 and in August 2008 the "new" 10 year old finally appeared. A cask strength version called Rennaissance was launched a few months prior to this and at the same time they also launched a limited Committee bottling called Corryvreckan, no age statement but made up from 12 year old bourbon casks and some younger French oak casks. The lightly peated Blasda (8 ppm and unaged) and Mor II (4.5 litre bottle) were another two new releases in autumn. Ardbeg's core range consists of 10 year old, Uigeadail, Lord of the Isles (not many left) and Airigh Nam Beist 1990 (bottled in 2006).

Independent bottlings have become quite rare but two 14 year olds (1993 and 1994) were released by Cadenheads this year.

History (continued):

1981 – The distillery closes in March.

1987 – Allied Lyons takes over Hiram Walker and thereby Ardbeg.

1989 – Production is restored with Iain Henderson as Manager. All malt is taken from Port Ellen.

1996 – The distillery closes in July and Allied Distillers decides to put it up for sale during the autumn.

1997 – Glenmorangie plc buys the distillery for £7 million (whereof £5.5 million is for whisky in storage). On stream from 25th June. Ardbeg 17 years old and Provenance are launched

1998 – A new visitor centre opens.

2000 – Ardbeg 10 years is introduced. The Ardbeg Committee (a worldwide forum for Ardbeg fans) is launched and has 30 000 members after a few years.

2001 – Lord of the Isles 25 years and Ardbeg 1977 are launched.

2002 – Ardbeg Committee Reserve and Ardbeg 1974 are launched.

2003 – Uigeadail is launched.

2004 – Very Young Ardbeg (6 years) and a limited edition of Ardbeg Kildalton (1300 bottles) are launched. The latter is a non-peated cask strength from 1980.

2005 – Serendipity is launched.

2006 – Ardbeg 1965 and Still Young are launched. Distillery Manager Stuart Thomson leaves Ardbeg after nine years. Almost There (9 years old) and Airigh Nam Beist are released.

2007 – Michael Heads becomes the new distillery manager. Ardbeg Mor, a 10 year old in 4.5 litre bottles is released.

2008 – The new 10 year old, Corryvreckan, Rennaisance, Blasda and Mor II are released.

Ardbeg 10 year old

DR – Intense smoke and tar on the nose but with some distinctive sweet lemon notes, a mouth-coating palate with honeyed but firey peat, completely balanced and impressive, and a long smoke tail at the finish.

DS – Sweet peat smoke with apples in syrup on the nose. Strong, spiky peat with a searing hot hit of salt and pepper. Long, peppery finish.

Renaissance

Blasda

Ardbeg Mór (4.5 litre)

10 years old

Corryvreckan

Ardmore

Owner:
Beam Global
Spirits & Wine

Region/district:
Highland

Founded: 1898   **Status:** Active

Capacity:
5 100 000 litres

Address: Kennethmont,
Aberdeenshire AB54 4NH

Tel:
01464 831213

website:
www.ardmorewhisky.com

History:

1898 – Adam Teacher, son of William Teacher, starts the construction of Ardmore Distillery which eventually becomes William Teacher & Sons´ first distillery. Adam Teacher passes away before it is completed.

1955 – Stills are increased from two to four.

1973 – A visitor centre is constructed.

1974 – Another four stills are added, increasing the total to eight.

1976 – Allied Breweries takes over William Teacher & Sons and thereby also Ardmore. The own maltings (Saladin box) is terminated.

1999 – A 12 year old is released to commemorate the distillery's 100th anniversary. A 21 year old is launched in a limited edition.

2002 – Ardmore is one of the last distilleries to abandon direct heating (by coal) of the stills in favour of indirect heating through steam.

2005 – Jim Beam Brands becomes new owner when they take over some 20 spirits and wine brands from Allied Domecq for five billion dollars.

2007 – Ardmore Traditional Cask is launched.

Ardmore Traditional

DR – Unique and remarkable mix of burnt meat savouriness on the nose, and a delicatessen of flavours on the palate, smoked vanilla, burnt fruit and a distinctive and highly addictive sweet and savoury mix towards the peated finish

DS – Burnt toffee and caramel with spiky peat on the nose. Sweet and mushy with sweet peat flavours and some fruitiness in the earthy finish.

Ardmore, an anonymous distillery in Aberdeenshire, struck gold in 2005 when it became part of American Beam Global with Laphroaig. Annual production was approximately 3 million litres before Beam acquired it from Allied Domecq. A couple of years later capacity has reached over 5 million litres and, above all, Ardmore has its own place on the single malt shelves. Ardmore Traditional was launched in 2007; first matured in ex-bourbon barrels it received a second maturation on quarter casks (similar to Laphroaig). It was first released as a duty free whisky but in March 2008 it was also released onto the US market. The new owners will not stop at this; a visitor centre is under development and will be opened in 2009.

A few miles to the north lies a distillery which could be considered as sister distillery of Ardmore during the past 50 years; Glendronach. The two had the same owner in 1960, William Teacher & Sons, the whisky from both distilleries at the time having long since been a part of Teacher´s blended whisky. After the millennium, Ardmore and Glendronach were the last distilleries to use open coalfires to heat the stills. In 2003 Ardmore converted to steam and was followed two years later by Glendronach. Ardmore is equipped with a cast-iron mash tun, 14 washbacks made of Douglas fir and four pairs of stills. Ardmore has regularly used malt with a phenol level of 12-14 ppm. An unpeated version called Ardlair is produced for a few weeks each year, but is used exclusively by other companies as a blending malt.

The current range is just the *Traditional* but Ardmore fans can look forward to some goodies in 2009. A *25 year old* will be launched as a duty free exclusive while a *30 year old* will be released on the American market.

Several independent bottlers have taken up Ardmore during the years but lately they have been more scarce. The most recent was a 13 year old released by Signatory in 2006.

Ardmore Traditional Cask

Arran

Owner:
Isle of Arran Distillers

Region/district:
Islands (Arran)

Founded: **Status:** **Capacity:**
1993 Active (vc) 750 000 litres

Address: Lochranza, Isle of Arran KA27 8HJ

Tel: **website:**
01770 830264 www.arranwhisky.com

History:
1993 – Harold Currie founds the distillery.

1995 – Production starts in full on 17th August.

1996 – A 1 year old is released with the text '1 year old spirit' on the label as it is not, in legal terms, whisky.

1997 – A visitor centre is opened by Her Majesty the Queen.

1998 – The first release is a 3 year old (1 000 bottles).

1999 – The Arran 4 years old is released.

2002 – Single Cask 1995 is launched.

2003 – Single Cask 1997, non-chill filtered and Calvados finish is launched.

2004 – Cognac finish, Marsala finish, Port finish and Arran First Distillation 1995 are launched.

2005 – Arran 1996 is launched (6 000 bottles). Two more finishes are launched - Chateau Margaux and Grand Cru Champagne.

2006 – After an unofficial launch in 2005, Arran 10 years old is released as well as a couple of new wood finishes.

2007 – Arran is named Scottish Distiller of the Year by Whisky Magazine. Four new wood finishes and Gordon´s Dram are released.

2008 – The first 12 year old is released as well as four new wood finishes.

Arran 10 year old

DR – Creamy barley, toffee and citrus notes on the nose then creamy, full and chunky fruit centre. The finish is rich and full.

DS – Honey, malt and biscuit on the nose. A malty, honeyed palate – not a robust whisky but flavourful. The finish is biscuity and sweet

---

The only distillery on Arran (and the first legal since 1837) has one of the most picturesque locations in the whole of Scotland, situated just outside the beautiful village of Lochranza and surrounded on three sides by towering mountains. A pair of breeding Golden Eagles are visible from the distillery's courtyard.

The lauter mash tun, the four Oregon pine washbacks and the two stills all stand in one room which makes the production easily overviewed by the 60,000 annual visitors to the distillery. Arran used to buy ready grist from the mainland but as of 2008 a mill has been installed and now they grind the malted barley themselves.

One dunnage warehouse holds 3,000 casks and a new, racked warehouse completed in summer 2007 has a capacity of a similar number which means that the whisky temporarily stored at Springbank now has moved back home and to another warehouse on the mainland. The capacity is 750,000 litres but current production only amounts to just over 150,000.

Of that, 8-10,000 litres has for the last couple of years been a peated version with a phenol content of 12ppm.

The core range of Arran consists of *10 year old*, *100 Proof* and *Robert Burns*. The latter is a single malt usually bottled as a 5 year old. Limited editions include yearly bottlings of single casks, either sherry matured or bourbon matured. Since last year, the number of wood finishes has been limited to around four each year. The 2008 expressions are *Sassicaia, Moscatel, Madeira* and *St. Emilion*. Furthermore, the first *12 year old* Arran was released in October 2008 and there has also been the release of a *Robert Burns Malt 1998 Vintage* to celebrate the 250th Anniversary of the great Scottish poet who was born on the 25 of January 1759.

Independent bottlings are not that common but both Cadenhead and Douglas Laing have recently released bottlings from 1995 and 1996.

12 years old

Auchentoshan

Owner: **Region/district:**
Morrison Bowmore   Lowlands
(Suntory)

Founded: **Status:**   **Capacity:**
1823   Active (vc)   1 750 000 litres

Address: Dalmuir, Clydebank, Glasgow G81 4SJ

Tel: **website:**
01389 878561   www.auchentoshan.com

History:

1800 – First mention of the distillery Duntocher, which may be identical to Auchentoshan.

1823 – An official license is obtained by the owner Mr. Thorne.

1903 – The distillery is purchased by John Maclachlan.

1923 – G. & J. Maclachlan goes bankrupt and a new company, Maclachlans Ltd is formed.

1941 – The distillery is severely damaged by a German bomb raid and reconstruction does not commence until 1948.

1960 – Maclachlans Ltd is purchased by the brewery J. & R. Tennant Brewers.

1969 – Auchentoshan is bought by Eadie Cairns Ltd who who starts major modernizations.

1984 – Stanley P. Morrison, eventually becoming Morrison Bowmore, becomes new owner.

1994 – Suntory buys Morrison Bowmore.

2000 – A cask strength 31 year old is launched in a limited edition.

2002 – Auchentoshan Three Wood is launched in May.

2004 – More than a £1 million is spent on a new, refurbished visitor centre. The oldest Auchentoshan ever, 42 years, is released.

2006 – Auchentoshan 18 year old is released.

2007 – A 40 year old and a 1976 30 years old are released.

2008 – New packaging as well as new expressions - Classic, 18 year old and 1988.

Auchentoshan 12 year old

DR – Toffee, rose water and Milk Chocolate Crisp on the nose, grape and crisp apple on the palate before a spicy fruity interplay in a lengthy finish.

DS – Sweet straw and icing sugar on the nose with heavy sherry notes. Sweet and sherried – slightly bitter with grape skin flavours in the aftertaste.

Most of the famous brands have in recent years overhauled their ranges of whiskies – both in terms of expressions and bottle design. This year it was the turn of Auchentoshan; in May a completely new look appeared on all bottles and a couple of new expressions were launched. The 10 year old was discontinued and the bourbon-matured Classic and an 18 year old were added to the line. Investments were also made in a redevelopment of the visitor centre and a brand new website was launched whereby visitors could enter a competition to win a 50 year old Auchentoshan.

Auchentoshan is the only triple distilled whisky in Scotland (except for Hazelburn, produced at Springbank distillery). The distillery is equipped with a semi-lauter mash tun, four Oregon pine washbacks which have been doubled in size and three stills. There are another four washbacks which are not in use at the moment. The spirit matures in three dunnage and two racked warehouses which currently house 18,000 hogsheads. Contrary to virtually all other Scottish distilleries, Auchentoshan is not running at full capacity. A five-day week with two shifts produces 850,000 litres which is about half of maximum output.

Even if Auchentoshan sales have been steady at the same level in recent years, the brand has made a nice advance in total sales during the last decade increasing from 120,000 bottles to 340,000 bottles, of which 85% of are exported.

The core range of Auchentoshan is *Classic, 12 years, Three Wood, 18 years* and *21 years. Select* (no age statement) has been moved to the duty free range. Apart from *Auchentoshan 1957*, bottled in summer 2007, recent limited editions include a *16 year old bourbon matured* cask strength and *Auchentoshan 1988*, a Bordeaux finish exclusive for the duty free market. Recent independent bottlings include a 9 year by Duncan Taylor, a 17 year old by Douglas Laing and an 18 year old from 1990 released by Cadenheads.

Auchentoshan Classic

Auchroisk

Owner: **Region/district:**
Diageo   Speyside

Founded: **Status:**   **Capacity:**
1974   Active   3 580 000 litres

Address: Mulben, Banffshire AB55 6XS

Tel: **website:**
01542 885000   www.malts.com

History:
1972 – Building of the distillery commences by Justerini and Brooks (which, together with W. A. Gilbey, made up the group IDV) in order to produce blending whisky. In February the same year IDV is purchased by the brewery Watney Mann which, in July, merges into Grand Metropolitan.

1974 – The distillery is completed and despite the intention of producing malt for blending the first year's production is sold 12 years later as single malt thanks to the high quality.

1986 – The first whisky is marketed under the name Singleton.

1997 – Grand Metropolitan and Guinness merge into the conglomerate Diageo. Simultaneously, the subsidiaries United Distillers (to Guinness) and International Distillers & Vintners (to Grand Metropolitan) form the new company United Distillers & Vintners (UDV).

2001 – The name Singleton is abandoned and the whisky is now marketed under the name of Auchroisk in the Flora & Fauna series.

2003 – Apart from the 10 year old in the Flora & Fauna series, a 28 year old from 1974, the distillery's first year, is launched in the Rare Malt series.

Auchroisk 10 year old

DR – Young and zesty and citrusy on the nose, warming tangerine and citrus fruits and a touch of salt on the palate, medium long malty finish.

DS – Malt loaf with raisins and vanilla on the nose. The palate is oily and sweet with fortified wine flavours. A long, oily finish.

Between Keith and Craigellachie lies Auchroisk, a distillery which is probably unknown to most people. Built as late as in 1974 by Justerini & Brooks, its purpose was to produce malt whisky for their main blend J&B. Despite this, the company's master blender Jim Milne wanted to launch it as a single malt, though he was not completely satisfied with its style if it was to be a stand-alone malt. He decided that the bourbon-matured single malt should have an extra year on sherry casks which changed everything. In 1986, a 12 year old was launched as Singleton as Auchroisk was considered too difficult to pronounce. Moreover, Milne was the man who created the legendary version of J&B called Ultima – a blend of 116 malts and 12 grain whiskies.

Justerini & Brooks were meticulous when they chose the location of the distillery. The water in Dories Well was a determining factor once large tankers with water had been driven to Glen Spey distillery for large-scale distillation tests. The spring and grounds was acquired for a staggering £5 million – £50 million in today's money. Auchroisk is a fairly large distillery with one stainless steel mash tun, eight stainless steel wash-backs and four pairs of stills. Fermentation in the wash-backs can often be quite vigorous and to prevent overflow most distilleries have rotating blades to keep away the wash. At Auchroisk however, each wash-back is equipped with four stainless steel bars containing a fibre-based solution to prevent frothing. The storage facilities at Auchroisk are huge with a capacity of 265,000 casks which is enough to offer storage to other distilleries as well. The core range consists of a *10 year old Flora & Fauna* under the name Auchroisk. Independent bottlings occur now and then. Some of the more recent are an 18 year old released by Blackadder and a really old one from 1975 by Douglas Laing.

Flora & Fauna
10 years old

Aultmore

Owner:
John Dewar & Sons
(Bacardi)

Region/district:
Speyside

Founded: **Status:** **Capacity:**
1896 Active 2 900 000 litres

Address: Keith, Banffshire AB55 6QY

Tel: **website:**
01542 881800 -

History:
1896 – Alexander Edward, owner of Benrinnes and co-founder of Craigellachie Distillery builds Aultmore.

1897 – Production starts.

1898 – Production is doubled; the company Oban & Aultmore Glenlivet Distilleries Ltd manages Aultmore.

1923 – Alexander Edward sells Aultmore for £20,000 to John Dewar & Sons.

1925 – Dewar's becomes part of Distillers Company Limited (DCL).

1930 – The administration is transferred to Scottish Malt Distillers (SMD).

1971 – The stills are increased from two to four.

1991 – UDV launches a 12-year old Aultmore in the Flora & Fauna series.

1996 – A 21 year old cask strength is marketed as a Rare Malt.

1998 – Diageo sells Dewar's and Bombay Gin to Bacardi for £1 150 million.

2004 – A new official bottling is launched (12 years old).

Aultmore 12 year old

DR – Orange blossom and flowers on the nose, lemon and lime Starburst on the palate, with late sherbet spicy and drying and more-ish finish. Altogether, zesty and very pleasant.

DS – Fresh and crisp on the nose with a herbal, green tea aroma. The palate is soft and sweet with oatmeal and malt flavours which linger on the finish.

In the 1960s and 70s nearly 50 distilleries were refurbished by owners Scottish Malt Distillers (part of today's Diageo), which unfortunately led to many losing much of their original 19th century character when transformed into efficient production plants instead. This also happened to Aultmore, located three miles west of Keith, which today looks rather industrial.

For the first year or so, the plant was powered by a water wheel but this was replaced in 1898, as production increased, by an Abernethy 10 horsepower steam engine. It was in use round the clock until 1969 when electricity was introduced. The steam engine can still be seen on display in the distillery lobby. Since 2008 production has been running seven days a week, as at the other of the distilleries of the Dewar's group, which means full capacity of 2,9 million litres. They are operating with one Steinecker full lauter mash tun, six washbacks and two pairs of stills. The still house control system has also been modernised in 2008. All the warehouses were demolished in 1996, in fact Dewar's no longer have any maturation capacity at any of the distilleries. Instead the company has redeveloped its headquarters at Westthorn in Glasgow where they have built another five warehouses. A new site at Pontiel has been bought with plans for a new maturation centre to be opened in 2009/2010.

Aultmore has its place in history when it comes to using distillation by-products. Together with Imperial distillery they were pioneers in the creation of dark grains made of pot ale and draff which then was used as fodder for livestock. Most of the output is used above all, in Dewar's blended whiskies but a *12 year old* official bottling appeared on the market in 2004. An Inverarity 10 years old, which was in fact Aultmore, was released as independently bottled by Loch Fyne Whiskies in Inverarity, Argyll. An 18 year old (1989) came from Blackadder in 2008 as did an 11 year old from Cadenhead.

12 years old

Balblair

Owner:
Inver House Distillers
(Thai Beverages plc)

Region/district:
Northern Highlands

Founded: 1790 **Status:** Active **Capacity:** 1 330 000 litres

Address: Edderton, Tain, Ross-shire IV19 1LB

Tel: 01862 821273 **website:** www.balblair.com

History:
1790 – The distillery is founded by John Ross.

1824 – The son Andrew Ross starts taking over, but moves to Brora after a couple of years and John Ross takes over again.

1836 – The founder John Ross dies and Andrew Ross takes over with the help of his sons.

1872 – New buildings replace the old.

1873 – Andrew Ross dies and his son James takes over.

1894 – Balnagowan Estate signs a new lease for 60 years with Alexander Cowan. He builds a new distillery, a few kilometres from the old.

1911 – Cowan is forced to cease payments and the distillery closes. The staff sell out the whole stock in the 20-year period until 1932.

1941 – Balnagowan Estate goes bankrupt and the distillery is put up for sale.

1948 – The lawyer Robert Cumming from Keith buys Balblair for £48 000.

1949 – Production restarts.

1970 – Cumming sells Balblair to Hiram Walker. A third still is installed.

1988 – Allied Distillers become new owners through the merger between Hiram Walker and Allied Vintners.

1996 – Allied Domecq sells the distillery to Inver House Distillers.

2000 – Balblair Elements and the first version of Balblair 33 years are launched.

2001 – Thai company Pacific Spirits (part of the Great Oriole Group) takes over Inver House.

2004 – Balblair 38 years is launched.

2005 – 12 year old Peaty Cask, 1979 (26 years) and 1970 (35 years) are launched.

2006 – InverHouse changes owners when International Beverage Holdings acquires Pacific Spirits UK.

2007 – Three new vintages replace the entire former range.

2008 – Vintage 1975 is released.

Balblair 1997

DR – Crystal clear and clean barley and vanilla nose, vanilla ice cream and soft yellow melon on the palate, and a gentle oakiness towards the finish.

DS – Juniper berries with sherry notes and hazelnuts on the nose. The palate is sweeter than expected, earthy, oily and complex and the apple turnover in the finish is sublime.

Inver House Distillers have been very much in the spotlight this past year with Balblair without hesitation receiving the most attention. Last year a bold step was taken and the entire range of bottlings with age statements was replaced with vintages. This was a clever decision as the brand got a fresh start and the first three vintages were very well received.

The distillery, or at least the name, is one of the oldest in Scotland but it has been rebuilt and resurrected in the same area at least three times. The attractive buildings we see today with a great view across Dornoch Firth were initially constructed around the mid 1890s.

The equipment at Balblair consists of a stainless steel mash tun, six Oregon pine washbacks and one pair of stills. There is actually a third still but it has not been used since 1969. The spirit is matured in eight dunnage warehouses with a capacity of 26 000 casks. Some 12-15% of the production is bottled as single malt which is filled and stored on site. Currently, a six day week is in place with 17 mashes per week. The water is drawn from Ault Dreag more than 4 miles from the distillery and is pumped to a tank, equipped with a copper filter, on the other side of the road.

In February 2007 the old expressions were all discontinued and replaced by three vintages - *1979, 1989* and *1997*. All three had been matured in first or secondfill bourbon casks. The 1979 sold out quickly and was replaced by 3,000 bottles from *1975*, this time from second filled sherry butts. 2008 also saw the launch of a *1986 duty free exclusive* and a *1985 single cask* for Maison du Whisky in Paris. Another vintage to look forward to is the 1969 matured in sherry casks. Independent bottlings have recently become rarer. Cadenheads recently released an 18 year old.

Balblair 1975

Balmenach

Owner:
Inver House Distillers
(Thai Beverages plc)

Region/district:
Speyside

Founded: 1824　**Status:** Active　**Capacity:** 1 800 000 litres

Address: Cromdale, Moray PH26 3PF

Tel: 01479 872569　**website:** www.inverhouse.com

History:

1824 – The distillery is licensed to James MacGregor who operated a small farm distillery by the name Balminoch for decades.

1897 – Balmenach Glenlivet Distillery Company is founded.

1922 – The MacGregor family sells to a consortium consisting of MacDonald Green, Peter Dawson and James Watson.

1925 – The consortium becomes part of Distillers Company Limited (DCL).

1930 – Production is transferred to Scottish Malt Distillers (SMD).

1941 – The distillery closes.

1947 – The distillery reopens.

1962 – The number of stills is increased to six.

1964 – Floor maltings is replaced by Saladin box.

1992 – The first official bottling is a 12 year old.

1993 – The distillery is mothballed in May.

1997 – Inver House Distillers buys Balmenach from United Distillers.

1998 – Production recommences.

2001 – Thai company Pacific Spirits (part of Great Oriole Group) takes over Inver House at the price of £56 million. The new owners launch a 27 and a 28 year old.

2002 – To commemorate the Queen's Golden Jubilee a limited edition of 800 bottles of 25-year old Balmenach is launched.

2006 – International Beverage Holdings acquires Pacific Spirits UK.

Deerstalker 18 year old

DR – Herb and hay on the nose, strange but beguiling mix of vegetable roots, earthy peat and savoury hors d'oeuvres on the palate, and a satisfying finish.

DS – Sweet and creamy sherry flavours on the heavily spiced nose. Sweet and full-bodied palate with oak and heavy spice. Long aftertaste with rich sherry and nut flavours.

The owner of Balmenach, InverHouse, was established already in 1964 as a subsidiary of the American company Publicker Industries. A decade of good years were followed by a decade of recession. The Scottish management felt increasingly abandoned by the American owners and managed to make a management buy-out in 1988. They took over a number of brands, but no production resources. Garnheath distillery, established in 1964 had been closed and Bladnoch had been both bought and sold again. Consequently, the new owners embarked on acquiring distilleries with Knockdhu as the first (1988) and Balmenach (1997) as the fifth and final.

The distillery is equipped with a mash tun made of cast iron, six wooden washbacks and three pairs of stills. A traditional feature still remains - a worm tub with a 94 metres long worm used for cooling the spirit vapours. The three dunnage warehouses have space for 14,000 casks but only the spirit destined for sale as single malt is stored there. The rest is sent away for central storage in Airdrie.

We are still waiting for an official bottling of Balmenach from the current owner. When they took over from United Distillers there was no maturing whisky included in the deal, so they had to start from scratch. This means that their oldest whisky will be around 10 years old, so with luck, we may soon be about to see the first InverHouse-produced Balmenach on the shelves.

The only "official" bottling so far is the *12 year old Flora & Fauna* from the previous owners and this is now becoming increasingly difficult to find. A few limited releases have also been made - *27* and *28 years Highland Selection* and a *25 year* commemoration bottle on the occasion of the Queen's Golden Jubilee.

There are however other Balmenach on the market. One is produced by an independent company called Aberko in Glasgow under the name Deerstalker 18 years. Two other recent releases came from Ian MacLeod (18 years) and Cadenheads (19 years).

Deerstalker 18 years

Balvenie

Owner:	**Region/district:**
William Grant & Sons	Speyside
Founded: **Status:**	**Capacity:**
1892 Active (vc)	6 200 000 litres

Address: Dufftown, Keith,
Banffshire AB55 4DH

Tel:	**website:**
01340 820373	www.thebalvenie.com

History:
1892 – William Grant rebuilds Balvenie New House to Balvenie Distillery (Glen Gordon was the name originally intended). Part of the equipment is brought in from Lagavulin and Glen Albyn.

1893 – The first distillation is made in May.

1955 – The distillery is modernized.

1957 – The two stills are increased by another two.

1965 – Two new stills are installed.

1971 – Another two stills are installed and eight stills are now running.

1973 – The first official bottling.

1982 – Founder's Reserve, in an eye-catching Cognac-reminiscent bottle, is launched.

1990 – A new distillery, Kininvie, is opened on the premises.

1996 – Two vintage bottlings and a port wood finish are launched.

2001 – The Balvenie Islay Cask, with 17 years in bourbon casks and six months in Islay casks, is released.

2002 – Balvenie releases 83 bottles of a 50 year old that has been in sherry casks since January 1952. Recommended price £6 000 a bottle.

2004 – The Balvenie Thirty is released to commemorate Malt Master David Stewart's 30th anniversary at Balvenie.

2005 – The Balvenie Rum Wood Finish 14 years old is released.

2006 – The Balvenie New Wood 17 years old, Roasted Malt 14 years old and Portwood 1993 are released.

2007 – Vintage Cask 1974 and Sherry Oak 17 years old are released.

2008 – Signature, Vintage 1976, Balvenie Rose and Rum Cask 17 year old are released.

Balvenie is one of the top selling malts and has occupied place number 9 on the ranking list for the last few years. But the owners apparently anticipate a growing demand. In February 2008 two new stills and an additional five washbacks made of stainless steel were installed. The total equipment now consists of 14 washbacks (the previous nine made of Oregon pine), five wash stills and six spirit stills. This gives the distillery an impressive capacity of 6.2 million litres.

Balvenie is also unique in having both its own floor maltings and a cooperage. The floor maltings supply less than 10% of the malt needs. Both bourbon and sherry casks, stored in dunnage, racked or palletised warehouses are used. The distillery opened up for visitors only recently, but instead of catering to the masses, a quality tour for smaller groups is on offer.

The "old" Balvenie 10 year old was discontinued a year ago and replaced by more of the popular *Doublewood 12 years old*. *Portwood 21 years* is also included in the core range.

The latest of numerous limited editions are *Signature*, a 12 year old to mark the Master Blender David Stewart's 45th year in the whisky industry, *Balvenie Vintage 1976*, *Balvenie Rose*, a 16 year old with one year of finishing in Port pipes, a *Single Cask 1970* exclusive for France and finally the *Balvenie Rum Cask 17 years old*. The last one has been maturing first in American oak before spending a second period in rum casks.

The other distillery on the premises of Balvenie, Kininvie built in 1990, is used for producing malt whisky for Grant's blends and also makes up the major part of Monkey Shoulder, a vatted malt released in 2005. The distillery has one mash tun (located at Balvenie), nine Douglas fir washbacks, three wash stills and six spirit stills. The capacity is 4,4 million litres. The *17 year old Hazelwood Reserve*, the first official bottling of Kininvie (except for a very limited release in August 2006) was launched at Heathrow's Terminal 5 in February 2008. There are no independent bottlings of Balvenie.

The Balvenie Signature

The Balvenie Doublewood 12 year old

DR – Red fruits and berries, a hint of smoke on the nose, on the palate mouth filling, rich and fruity and, surprisingly, with a peat presence. Lots of sherry and some toffee in the finish.

DS – A sherried and malty nose with rich honey and fruitcake. The most honeyed palate there is with rich spice and fruit. The finish is akin to a honey liqueur.

Ben Nevis

Owner:
Ben Nevis Distillery Ltd
(Nikka, Asahi Breweries)

Region/district:
Western Highlands

Founded:
1825

Status:
Active (vc)

Capacity:
2 000 000 litres

Address: Lochy Bridge, Fort William PH33 6TJ

Tel:
01397 702476

website:
www.bennevisdistillery.com

History:

1825 – The distillery is founded by 'Long' John McDonald.

1856 – Long John dies and his son Donald P. McDonald takes over.

1878 – Demand is so great that another distillery, Nevis Distillery, is built nearby.

1908 – Both distilleries merge into one.

1941 – D. P. McDonald & Sons sells the distillery to Ben Nevis Distillery Ltd headed by the Canadian millionaire Joseph W. Hobbs. He has already bought Bruichladdich, Glenesk and Glenury Royal and he opens Lochside in 1957.

1955 – Hobbs installs a Coffey still which makes it possible to produce both grain and malt whisky.

1964 – Joseph Hobbs dies.

1978 – Production is stopped.

1981 – Joseph Hobbs Jr sells the distillery back to Long John Distillers and Whitbread.

1984 – After restoration and reconstruction totalling £2 million, Ben Nevis opens up again.

1986 – The distillery closes again.

1989 – Whitbread sells the distillery to Nikka Whisky Distilling Company Ltd.

1990 – The distillery opens up again.

1991 – A visitor centre is inaugurated.

1996 – Ben Nevis 10 years old is launched.

2006 – A 13 year old port finish is released.

Ben Nevis 10 year old

DR – Grape skins, over-ripe pear on the nose, baked apple and liquorice roots on the palate, pleasant malty finish.

DS – Pine nuts with a malty sweetness on the nose. The palate is full of bittersweet bread and nut flavours – warm dough. The finish is short and yeasty.

For more than two decades, Ben Nevis distillery was owned by one of the more eccentric whisky personalities of the 1900s, Joseph Hobbs from America. He installed a patent still at Ben Nevis in 1955 (and three years later he did the same at Lochside distillery) so as to be able to produce both malt whisky and grain whisky at the same distillery. Proof of this duality appeared in 2002 when the blend Dew of Ben Nevis 40 years was released. It also had the added name 'Blended at Birth' since the new make malt and grain whiskies were blended and left to mature for 40 years. Hobbs was also elected chairman of Independent Scotch Whisky Association in 1952 which was founded because "the existing associations were unduly influenced by a particular cartel or group whose aim was to drive the independent out of business and capture all markets". This is interesting to compare with today's "battle" between independent producers and SWA.

Ben Nevis is equipped with one lauter mash tun, eight stainless steel washbacks and two pairs of stills. A combination of bourbon and sherry casks are used for maturation.

Ben Nevis became the second distillery (following Tomatin) to be acquired by Japanese interests, namely by Nikka Whisky Co. founded by Masataka Taketsuru who spent some time in Scotland in the 1920s to learn the art of whisky distilling.

Since 1996 the core of the range has been a *10 year old*. Some one-off bottlings have appeared with regular intervals such as the *13 year old Port finish* released in 2006 and the *1992 single cask* released in 2007. There have also been some interesting *26 year olds*, the first released in the early nineties and the last, distilled in 1975, a couple of years ago.

Recent independent bottlings include one 11 year old distilled in 1996 from Douglas Laing and one 1990 Duncan Taylor.

10 years old

BenRiach

Owner: **Region/district:**
Benriach Distillery Co   Speyside

Founded: **Status:**   **Capacity:**
1897   Active   2 800 000 litres

Address: Longmorn, Elgin, Morayshire IV30 8SJ

Tel: **website:**
01343 862888   www.benriachdistillery.co.uk

History:

1897 – John Duff & Co founds the distillery.

1899 – John Duff gets into financial trouble and pawns his company. Finally, the bank sells Benriach to the Longmorn Distilleries Company.

1903 – The distillery is mothballed. The maltings is kept running to supply the 'sister' distillery Longmorn with malt.

1965 – The distillery is reopened by the new owners, The Glenlivet Distillers Ltd.

1978 – Seagram Distillers plc takes over ownership.

1983 – Seagrams starts producing a peated Benriach.

1985 – The number of stills is increased from two to four.

1994 – The first official bottling is a 10 year old.

1999 – The maltings is decommissioned.

2001 – Pernod Ricard takes over Chivas Brothers.

2002 – The distillery is mothballed in October.

2004 – A South African group, Intra Trading, buys Benriach together with the former Director at Burn Stewart, Billy Walker. The price is £5.4 million which also includes 5,000 casks aged between 3-34 years.

2004 – Standard (no age), Curiositas (10 years, quite peaty), and 12, 16 and 20 year olds are released.

2005 – Four different vintages are released in limited editions - 1966, 1970, 1978 och 1984.

2006 – Sixteen new releases, among them a 25 year old, a 30 year old and 8 different vintages.

2007 – A 40 year old and three new heavily peated expressions are released.

2008 – New expressions include a peated Madeira finish, a 15 year old Sauternes finish and nine single casks. Benriach Distillery Co buys Glendronach distillery from Chivas Brothers.

BenRiach 12 year old

DR – Almost defines a Speyside nose, with honey and mixed fruits calling for attention. The palate is full, rounded sweet, clean and fruity, with plenty of malty notes, the finish satisfying and warming.

DS – Sweet, spicy with heather and pine notes on the nose. Malty with nutmeg, cloves and again heather on the palate. A short finish with a heather after-taste.

Last year BenRiach owners could report that the floor maltings, not in use since 1999, were to be functioning in early 2008. This was delayed, however, and it is now hoped that this will happen by the end of 2008 instead. Ten tonnes per week, corresponding to around 10% of annual needs, will be produced as both peated and unpeated malt and this will put BenRiach in the exclusive club of Scottish distilleries working their own malting floors.

The distillery is equipped with a traditional cast iron mash tun, eight washbacks made of stainless steel and two pairs of stills. The annual production of this independent distillery has increased from year to year and has now reached 1.8 million litres. The five dunnage warehouses currently contain 25,000 casks. They also have some older casks (1966-2002) stored at Chivas Brothers' warehouses in Keith.

The Far East with Japan and, foremost, Taiwan have become an increasingly important market for BenRiach and no less than seven new expressions during 2008 were earmarked exclusively for the two countries.

The core range of BenRiach is *Heart of Speyside* (no age), *12, 16* and *20 years old* in what the distillery themselves call classical Speyside style and *Curiositas 10yo, Authenticus 21yo* and the three *12 year olds* named *Fumosus* - heavily peated whiskies with different finishes and launched 2007 as the peated varieties. A new addition is *Maderensis Fumosus*, 13 year old with a Madeira finish. Four different *15 year olds* with different finishes were supplemented in 2008 with a *16 year old Sauternes finish*. According to tradition, the distillery also launched a batch (the fifth) of no less than nine different *single casks* ranging from *1976 to 1994* in 2008. Some old BenRiachs of between *25-40 years* of age complete the range.

Independent bottlings are becoming rare. One of the latest was a 23 year old from 1984 by Speciality Drinks. Younger expressions came from Duncan Taylor (11 years) and Ian MacLeod (14 years).

16 year old Sauternes

Benrinnes

Owner:
Diageo

Region/district:
Speyside

Founded: Status: Capacity:
1826 Active 2 540 000 litres

Address: Aberlour, Banffshire AB38 9NN

Tel:
01340 872600

website:
www.malts.com

History:

1826 – The first Benrinnes distillery is built at Whitehouse Farm by Peter McKenzie.

1829 – A flood destroys the distillery.

1834 – A new distillery, Lyne of Ruthrie, is constructed a few kilometres from the first one. The owner John Innes files for bankruptcy and William Smith & Company takes over.

1864 – William Smith & Company goes bankrupt and David Edward becomes the new owner.

1896 – Benrinnes is ravaged by fire which prompts major refurbishment and rebuilding including electrification. David Edward dies and his son Alexander Edward takes over. Alexander also founds the distilleries Dallas Dhu, Aultmore and Craigellachie and purchases Oban.

1922 – John Dewar & Sons takes over ownership.

1925 – John Dewar & Sons becomes part of Distillers Company Limited (DCL).

1930 – DCL transfers management and operations to Scottish Malt Distillers (SMD).

1955/56 – The distillery is completely rebuilt.

1964 – Floor maltings is replaced by a Saladin box.

1966 – The number of stills doubles to six.

1984 – The Saladin box is taken out of service and the malt is purchased centrally.

1991 – The first official bottling from Benrinnes is a 15 year old in the Flora & Fauna series.

1996 – United Distillers releases a 21 year old cask strength in their Rare Malts series.

Benrinnes 15 year old
DS – Heavily sherried nose with figs in syrup. Rich and sweet in the mouth like a dark rum. Sweet and rich throughout with figs on the finish.

When travelling to the southern parts of Speyside, a famous view is often present; that of the mountain Ben Rinnes. Even if it is only 840 metres high, the surrounding, low topography makes it well visible. No less than five distilleries draw their water from Ben Rinnes - Aberlour, Allt-a-Bhainne, Dailuaine, Glenfarclas and Benrinnes - but only the latter can be said to rest on the very slopes of the mountain, at an elevation of 200 metres.

The distillery is equipped with a stainless steel lauter mash tun, eight wash backs made of larch and six stills. Worm tub is used for condensation. Instead of running the stills in three pairs, they are grouped three and three resulting in a partial triple distillation similar to that of Springbank.

This is how it works; the heads from the No. 1 wash still goes to one receiver and the tails to another. The heads are then sent as part of the charge to spirit still No. 2 while the tails are distilled together once more with fore-shots and feints from the previous distillation. This takes place in spirit still No. 1 which acts as an intermediate spirit still. After this, the middle cut (now distilled twice) from number one spirit still flows to the second receiver to become part of the charge together with the heads from the wash still and fore-shots and feints from the previous distillation. The charge goes into the second spirit still and one part will, after this, have been distilled three times and one part twice - hence a partial triple distillation, similar to that of Springbank.

The lion part of Benrinnes is used in blended whiskies, especially A & A Crawford but also in J&B and Johnnie Walker. The only official bottling is a *Flora & Fauna 15 years old*. Apart from that, independent bottlings are pretty rare. A couple of the most recent are a 12 year old from Cadenheads and an 11 year old Tokay-finish from 1996 by Ian MacLeod.

Flora & Fauna 15 years old

Benromach

Owner:	**Region/district:**
Gordon & MacPhail	Speyside
Founded: **Status:**	**Capacity:**
1898 Active (vc)	500 000 litres

Address: Invererne Road, Forres,
Morayshire IV36 3EB

Tel:	**website:**
01309 675968	www.benromach.com

History:

1898 – Benromach Distillery Company starts the distillery. Duncan McCallum is one of the owners.

1909 – The distillery operates under the name Forres Distillery for a few years.

1911 – London-based Harvey McNair & Co buys the distillery.

1919 – A well-known brewer from Alloa, John Joseph Calder, buys Benromach but immediately sells it to recently founded Benromach Distillery Ltd owned by several breweries.

1931 – Benromach is mothballed.

1937 – The distillery reopens.

1938 – Joseph Hobbs buys Benromach through Associated Scottish Distillers and sells it on to National Distillers of America (NDA).

1953 – NDA sells Benromach to Distillers Company Limited (DCL).

1966 – The distillery is refurbished .

1968 – Floor maltings is abolished.

1983 – Benromach is mothballed in March.

1993 – Gordon & McPhail buys Benromach from United Distillers.

1998 – The distillery is once again in operation. A limited edition 17 year old is released to commemorate this and the 100th anniversary of the distillery.

1999 – A visitor centre is opened.

2004 – The first bottle distilled by the new owners is released under the name 'Benromach Traditional' in May. Other novelties (although distilled in UD times) include a 21 year Tokaji finish and a Vintage 1969.

2005 – A Port Wood finish (22 years old) and a Vintage 1968 are released together with the Benromach Classic 55 years.

2006 – Benromach Organic is released.

2007 – Peat Smoke, the first heavily peated whisky from the distillery, is released.

2008 – Benromach Origins Golden Promise is released.

When the independent bottler Gordon & MacPhail in Elgin bought Benromach Distillery in 1993, they were determined to produce a whisky which reminded of old time Speyside, i. e. with a distinct but not too powerful touch of phenols. So instead of buying malted barley with 1-2 ppm which most distilleries do today, their specification is around 12 ppm. It took the new owners five years before the distillery was operational again.

Benromach is the smallest working distillery in Speyside. Only two people are employed in the production, working a five-day week. Although it has the capacity to produce 500,000 litres per annum, the current output is approximately 200,000 litres. There is a filling store on site and some of the production is stored in the three warehouses while the rest is taken to the owners' facilities in Elgin

The core range of Benromach consists of *Traditional* (around 6 years old), *21 years old, 25 years old, Cask Strength 1981* and *Vintage 1968*. There is also *Organic*, the first single malt to be fully certified organic by the Soil Association and first launched in 2006, and last year's *Peatsmoke* produced using barley peated to 55 ppm. For several years now, many producers have focused on how to enhance the spirits once it has been distilled, mainly by wood finishing. This year Benromach starts at the other end, namely with the raw material and the distillation process. In a series called *Origins*, they will highlight how differences in the process produces different whiskies. The first expression, *Batch 1*, is made using Golden Promise barley and matured in first and second fill sherry casks. Limited editions include *Marsala Wood Finish* (replacing last years Sassicaia) and *Benromach Classic 55 years*. Celebrating Benromach's involvement in the 07-08 Clipper Round the World Yacht Race, the distillery has also launched three single sherry casks named *Benromach Lat 53°, Lat 55°* and *Lat 57°*.

Origins Batch 1

Benromach Traditional

DR – Mandarin and honey on the nose, an intriguing flip-flop of a taste, with young citrusy barley battling it out with some peat and wood. It ends all square at the finish.

DS – Honey and straw with a hint of smoke on the nose. Sweet and floral on the palate with quite a strong phenolic hit which lingers into the smoky finish.

Bladnoch

Owner:
Co-ordinated
Development Services

Region/district:
Lowlands

Founded: 1817
Status: Active (vc)
Capacity: 100 000 litres

Address: Bladnoch, Wigtown,
Wigtonshire DG8 9AB

Tel: 01988 402605
website: www.bladnoch.co.uk

History:

1817 – Brothers Thomas and John McClelland found the distillery.

1825 – The McClelland brothers obtain a licence.

1878 – John McClelland's son Charlie reconstructs and refurbishes the distillery.

1905 – Production stops.

1911 – Dunville & Co. from Ireland buys T. & A. McClelland Ltd for £10,775. Production is intermittent until 1936.

1937 – Dunville & Co. is liquidated and Bladnoch is wound up. Ross & Coulter from Glasgow buys the distillery some time after the war. The equipment is dismantled and shipped to Sweden.

1956 – A. B. Grant (Bladnoch Distillery Ltd.) takes over and restarts production with four new stills.

1964 – McGown and Cameron becomes new owners.

1966 – The number of stills is increased from two to four.

1973 – Inver House Distillers buys Bladnoch.

1983 – Arthur Bell and Sons take over.

1985 – Guiness Group buys Arthur Bell & Sons which, from 1989, are included in United Distillers.

1988 – A visitor centre is built.

1993 – United Distillers mothballs Bladnoch in June.

1994 – Raymond Armstrong from Northern Ireland buys Bladnoch in October.

2000 – Production commences in December.

2003 – The first bottles from Raymond Armstrong are launched, a 15 year old cask strength from UD casks.

2004 – New varieties follow suit: e. g. 13 year olds 40% and 55%.

2008 – First release of whisky produced after the take-over in 2000 - three 6 year olds.

Bladnoch 6 year old - lightly peated

DR – Korma chicken tin and butter with traces of pepper on the nose, dark spicy chili chocolate and prickly smoke on the palate, oil and pepper finish.

DS – Strong malt and cheddar cheese flavours on the nose. Again slightly cheesey with a hard hit of bitter earth and oak in the long finish.

Bladnoch is the southernmost of the Scottish distilleries and lies almost isolated down at Wigtown Bay. Despite this 27,000 visitors a year find their way to it. It was mothballed by the owner, United Distillers, in 1993 and then sold to Raymond Armstrong, a builder from Northern Ireland. One of the clauses in the sales was that it was not to be used as a distillery and Armstrong's intention was to make it into a holiday home. But in 2000, after lobbying from the local community and Armstrong, Diageo gave permission for Bladnoch to produce 100,000 litres of alcohol per year.

The distillery is equipped with a stainless steel semi-lauter mash tun, six washbacks made of Oregon pine and one pair of stills. Unusually enough, both stills were originally wash stills. There used to be two pairs of stills and when the spirit stills were due for replacement, they decided not to renew them but to turn one of the wash stills into a spirit still. The whisky is mainly matured in ex-bourbon casks in one of the 11 warehouses where 3,000 casks are currently stored.

Up until recently, all official bottlings were from the previous owner's production. They included 13 to 16 year olds with the Beltie and the Sheep labels. One of the more recent bottlings was a 15 year old rum finish and in 2007 an 18 year old was released. As most people had expected a first release from stock distilled under the current ownership to be an 8 year old, there was much surprise when Raymond Armstrong released not one but three 6 year olds in April 2008. A bourbon matured, a sherry matured and one lightly peated from a bourbon barrel – all at cask strength. One should probably not expect any further releases in the foreseeable future. It will most likely take at least a couple of years before the "new" Bladnoch becomes a regular on the shelves. Recent independent bottlings include a 15 year old from 1992 by Douglas Laing.

6 year old sherry matured

Blair Athol

Owner:		Region/district:
Diageo		Eastern Highlands
Founded:	**Status:**	**Capacity:**
1798	Active (vc)	2 500 000 litres

Address: Perth Road, Pitlochry,
Perthshire PH16 5LY

Tel:	website:
01796 482003	www.malts.com

History:
1798 – John Stewart and Robert Robertson found Aldour Distillery, the predecessor to Blair Athol. The name is taken from the adjacent river Allt Dour.

1825 – The distillery is expanded by Robert Robertson and takes the name Blair Athol Distillery.

1826 – The Duke of Atholl leases the distillery to Alexander Connacher & Co.

1832 – The distillery closes.

1860 – Elizabeth Connacher runs the distillery.

1882 – Peter Mackenzie & Company Distillers Ltd of Edinburgh (future founders of Dufftown Distillery) buys Blair Athol and expands it.

1932 – The distillery is mothballed.

1933 – Arthur Bell & Sons takes over by acquiring Peter Mackenzie & Company.

1949 – Production restarts.

1973 – Stills are expanded from two to four.

1985 – Guinness Group buys Arthur Bell & Sons.

1987 – A visitor centre is built.

2003 – A 27 year old cask strength from 1975 is launched in Diageo's Rare Malts series.

Blair Athol 12 year old
DR – The nose is rich and full, with orange and citrus fruit. The palate, too, is big and chunky, with some tannin and spice in the mix, and with water, parma violet notes.

DS – Stewed fruits and cider on the nose. Rich and fruity on the palate with raisins and cinnamon. Dry, fruity finish that lingers.

Blair Athol malt was used for blended whisky already in the mid 1800s and the connection with Bell's blended Scotch is probably as old as that. However it was not until the 1930s that Arthur Bell & Sons acquired the distillery which is now considered the spiritual home of Bell's.

The distillery is equipped with a semi-lauter mash tun, four washbacks of stainless steel and four of larch, and two pairs of stills. The wooden washbacks, half the size of the stainless steel ones, are 75 years old and were brought in from Mortlach. The No. 2 wash still was renewed in January 2007 and all the stills are heated using North Sea gas. Except for three weeks in April/May, the distillery is running seven days a week giving a production of 2.5 million litres of spirit. The malt is brought in from Diageo's own Roseisle maltings.

The part of the spirit which goes into Bell's (90-95%) is matured mainly in bourbon casks while the rest is matured in sherry casks.

Blair Athol is one of a select few active distilleries founded in the 18th century but most of the buildings date back to 1825. Despite its name, the distillery is not situated in Blair Atholl but rather a few miles south in Pitlochry, very near to Edradour.

The village of Blair Atholl itself deserves a visit. Here one finds Blair Castle with its roots in the 13th century. This is Britain's most visited private house and home to the 11th Duke of Atholl and the Atholl Highlanders, the sole remaining private army in Europe.

Official bottlings are scarce. Except for the 12 year old Flora & Fauna there is a 27 year old Rare Malts released in 2003 and it may still be possible to obtain an 18 year old bottling from 1998 commemorating the bi-centenary of the distillery.

Independent bottlings are rarely encountered. Among the most recent are a couple from Douglas Laing - 12 and 18 years old.

Flora & Fauna 12 years old

Bowmore

Owner:
Morrison Bowmore
Distillers (Suntory)

Region/district:
Islay

Founded: 1779
Status: Active (vc)
Capacity: 2 000 000 litres

Address: School Street, Bowmore, Islay,
Argyll PA43 7GS

Tel: 01496 810441
website: www.bowmore.com

History:

1779 – Bowmore Distillery is founded by John Simpson and becomes the oldest Islay distillery.

1837 – The distillery is sold to James and William Mutter of Glasgow.

1892 – After additional construction, the distillery is sold to Bowmore Distillery Company Ltd, a consortium of English businessmen.

1925 – J. B. Sheriff and Company takes over.

1929 – Distillers Company Limited (DCL) takes over.

1950 – William Grigor & Son takes over.

1963 – Stanley P. Morrison buys the distillery for £117,000 and forms Morrison Bowmore Distillers Ltd.

1989 – Japanese Suntory buys a 35% stake in Morrison Bowmore.

1993 – The famous, legendary Black Bowmore is launched. The recommended price is £100 (today it is at least ten times that if it can be found). Another two versions are released 1994 and 1995.

1994 – Suntory now controls all of Morrison Bowmore.

1995 – Bowmore is nominated 'Distiller of the Year' in the International Wine and Spirits competition.

With the review of the entire range of whiskies that took place a year ago, Bowmore made a deliberate move to get away from the bulk sales and supermarket segment and into the more lucrative travel retail. This means that they will not be part of the price war battled out on Tesco and Asda shelves but rather aim at less price-sensitive duty free customers instead. 60% of sales come from this segment already.

Bowmore is one of few Scottish distilleries with its own malting floor with as much as 40% of the malt requirement produced in-house. The distillery has a stainless steel semi-lauter mash tun, six washbacks of Oregon pine and two pairs of stills. The spirit stills are filled to 90% of capacity in the distillation which gives a heavier spirit than, for example Caol Ila which fills them to roughly 50%. This, on the other hand, is compensated by the upwards-tilting lyne arm on the spirit stills at Bowmore which increases the reflux and allows for more light flavourings to remain in the spirit. 27,000 casks are stored in two dunnage and one racked warehouse. The 12 men in the production work three shifts five days a week which, for 2008, resulted in 12 mashes per week i. e. 1.6 million litres per year. Eddie MacAffer, who acted as a temporary manager last year has now been formally appointed distillery manager.

Sales increased by 10% last year to nearly 1.7 million bottles and Bowmore is number two among Islay single malts after Laphroaig.

The range of Bowmore is divided into core domestic markets and travel retail. The former includes *Legend* (no age), *12 years, Darkest 15 years, 18 years* and *25 yeas*. The duty free line-up contains *Surf, Enigma, Mariner* (15 years old), *17 year old* and *Cask Strength. Black Bowmore*, the legendary vintage from 1964 that was first bottled in 1993, also saw a return last year. This year´s limited highlight is *White Bottle*, also distilled in 1964 and matured on bourbon barrels for 43 years. Look out for a 44 year old Red Bottle next year! A total of 732 bottles of White Bottle are for sale. If one wishes to go for a more affordable bottling, look for the *1992 Vintage*, a 16 year old with a finish in Bordeaux wine casks. Last year saw the release of a similar bottling, a *1991 Vintage* (16 year old) Port matured. There are also a number of recent independent bottlings; several vintages from Duncan Taylor, the oldest from 1982, a 25 year old from Douglas Laing and a 15 year old from Cadenhead.

1996 – A Bowmore 1957 (38 years) is bottled at 40,1% but is not released until 2000.

1999 – Bowmore Darkest with three years finish on oloroso barrels is launched. A Claret cask strength is also released in 12,000 bottles.

2000 – Bowmore Dusk with two years finish in Bordeaux barrels is launched.

2001 – Bowmore Dawn with two years finish on port pipes is launched. A bottle from 1890 is sold at an auction in Glasgow and brings in £14,300 which is a new world record. The Manager Jim McEwan moves to Bruichladdich.

2002 – A 37 year old Bowmore from 1964 and matured in fino casks is launched in a limited edition of 300 bottles (recommended price £1,500).

2003 – Another two expressions complete the wood trilogy which started with 1964 Fino - 1964 Bourbon and 1964 Oloroso.

2004 – Morrison Bowmore buys one of the most outstanding collections of Bowmore Single Malt from the private collector Hans Sommer. It totals more than 200 bottles and includes a number of Black Bowmore.

2005 – Bowmore 1989 Bourbon (16 years) and 1971 (34 years) are launched.

2006 – Bowmore 1990 Oloroso (16 years) and 1968 (37 years) are launched. A new and up-graded visitor centre is opened.

2007 – Dusk and Dawn disappear from the range and an 18 year old is introduced. New packaging for the whole range. 1991 (16yo) Port and Black Bottle are released.

2008 – White Bottle and a 1992 Vintage with Bourdeaux finish are launched.

Bowmore 12 year old

DR – Rich peat and seaweed and the merest hint of characteristic palma violets on the nose, smoked fish in butter, menthol cough sweets and lemon on the palate, sweet peat in the finish.

DS – Fresh peat with a hint of fruity sweet-ness on the nose. Sweet and peaty, perfumed and oily on the palate with a fruity, yet smoky finish.

25 years old   White Bowmore   1992 Bourdeaux finish

12 years old   15 years old Darkest   18 years old

Braeval

Owner:
Chivas Brothers Ltd
(Pernod Ricard)

Region/district:
Speyside

Founded: **Status:**
1973 Active

Capacity:
3 800 000 litres

Address: Chapeltown of Glenlivet,
Ballindalloch, Banffshire AB37 9JS

Tel:
01542 783042

website:
-

History:
1973 – The Chivas and Glenlivet Group founds
Braes of Glenlivet, the name which will be used
for the first 20 years. The Glenlivet, Tomintoul
and Tamnavulin are the only other distilleries
situated in the Livet Glen valley. Production
starts in October.

1975 – Three stills are increased to five.

1978 – Five stills are further expanded to six.

1994 – The distillery changes name to Braeval.

2001 – Pernod Ricard takes over Chivas Brothers.

2002 – Braeval is mothballed in October.

2008 – The distillery starts producing again in
July.

Deerstalker 10 year old

DR – Grass and violin bow on the nose, zippy
sherbet and citrus fruit on the palate, with a
clean and refreshing finish.

DS – Apple skin and melon balls on the
green nose. Green and appley on the palate
– bittersweet with a malty-fresh finish and
herbal aftertaste.

In 2005, Allt-a-Bhainne was the distillery chosen among four
mothballed distilleries owned by Chivas Bros to be recommissioned. In July 2008, it was the turn of its sister distillery Braeval
to be reinstated as a working distillery. Braeval is situated in a
very remote part of the Highlands and there are no signs showing the way to it. A mile south of Tamnavulin on the B9008 lays
the small hamlet Auchnarrow. If one follows the narrow road
towards Chapeltown and continues to where the road ends, a
very impressive and surprisingly handsome distillery appears.
The sight is unexpected bearing in mind that it was constructed
in the seventies as a working distillery. The surroundings are
breathtaking and the grazing sheep around the buildings add
to the pastoral idyll.

Braeval had only been mothballed for six
years so not much work had to be done
in order to start production once again.
A new boiler was installed and an upgrade of still venting and control systems
was made. The distillery is equipped with
a stainless steel mash tun (the largest in
the Chivas group together with the one
at Allt-a-Bhainne), fifteen washbacks
made of stainless steel and six stills.
There used to be four pairs but now
each of the two wash stills serve two
spirit stills.

With Braeval distilling again,
Dalwhinnie now has lost its claim of
being the highest situated working
distillery in Scotland.

Official bottlings of Braeval do not
exist and independent bottlings are
also difficult to find. Despite this,
Braeval is obtainable albeit under
a different name. Aberko Ltd, a
small spirits company in Glasgow
has acquired the rights to the name
Deerstalker which was established
already in 1880. There are four
versions of Deerstalker with the
10 and 15 years old consisting of
Braeval whisky.

Deerstalker 10 year old

Bruichladdich distillery

Bruichladdich

Owner: **Region/district:**
Bruichladdich Distillery Co   Islay

Founded: **Status:**   **Capacity:**
1881   Active (vc)   1 500 000 litres

Address: Bruichladdich, Islay, Argyll PA49 7UN

Tel: **website:**
01496 850221   www.bruichladdich.com

History:

1881 – Barnett Harvey builds the distillery with money left by his brother William III to his three sons William IV, Robert and John Gourlay. The Harvey family already owns the distilleries Yoker and Dundashill.

1886 – Bruichladdich Distillery Company Ltd is founded and reconstruction commences.

1889 – William Harvey becomes Manager and remains on that post until his death in 1937.

1929 – Temporary closure.

1936 – The distillery reopens.

1938 – Joseph Hobbs, Hatim Attari and Alexander Tolmie purchase the distillery for £23 000 through the company Train & McIntyre.

1938 – Operations are moved to Associated Scottish Distillers.

1952 – The distillery is sold to Ross & Coulter from Glasgow.

1960 – A. B. Grant buys Ross & Coulter.

1961 – Own maltings ceases and malt is brought in from Port Ellen.

1968 – Invergordon Distillers take over.

1975 – The number of stills increases to four.

1983 – Temporary closure.

Mark Reynier and his fellow owners could rejoice at increased profits of no less than 58% to £831,000 when the books were closed in 2007. Many have become aware of Bruichladdich's success and according to Reynier at least four offers for the distillery have been received this past year, all of which were rejected. At present sales are running at 35,000 cases per year which gives them a ranking around 25 on the sales' list. The goal is to reach 60,000 cases by 2012.

The distillery is equipped with a cast iron, open mash tun, six washbacks of Oregon pine and two pairs of stills. All casks are stored either at Bruichladdich or at the old Port Charlotte site. The yearly production at Bruichladdich is 700 000 litres, half of its capacity. All whisky produced at the distillery is based on Scottish barley and Bruichladdich have experimented with both organic and the old variety bere barley. Nowadays the malt comes from Baird's in Inverness.

There are three main lines in Bruichladdich's production; lightly peated Bruichladdich, moderately peated Port Charlotte and the heavily peated Octomore. In addition to these, experiments with triple-distilled (Trestarig) and quadruple distilled (Perilous) spirit have been made. Bruichladdich usually present a number of bottlings each year but 2008 was unusual in that the first *Octomore* (131ppm) was launched as a 5 year old as well as the first *Bruichladdich 2001* from the new owners' own production. In an attempt to show the full repertoire of Bruichladdich, the Multi Vintage Trilogy was also introduced whereby Jim McEwan mixes several vintages, different types of casks and varying peating levels. The three selected were the previously released lightly peated *Rocks* and moderately peated *Waves* and the new, heavily peated *Peat*. Add a new Port Charlotte, *PC7* (40 ppm), three new in the *Links* series, the *Golder Still* from 1984, a *21 year old* and no less than seven *16 year olds* with a finishing (or enhancement as Bruichladdich themselves prefer to say) in various Grand Cru Bourdeaux casks and the picture is almost complete. Finally, one now has the opportunity to compare two sherry-matured expressions from the same year (*1998*) - one *Manzanilla* and one *Oloroso*. This makes over 20 new expressions in just six months!

Apart from all these new releases, there is the previous core range of Bruichladdich 10, 12, 15, 17 and *20 years old*. Earlier limited releases include *Infinity, 3D, The Forty, Blacker Still, Redder Still* and *Legacy* - a series with quite old bottlings. In summer 2008, Bruichladdich finally received all the necessary planning permission for the new Port Charlotte distillery which will be built on the site of the Old Lochindaal distillery.

History (continued):

1993 – Whyte & Mackay buys Invergordon Distillers.

1995 – The distillery is mothballed in January.

1998 – In production again for a few months, and then mothballed.

2000 – After several years of attempts, Murray McDavid buys the distillery from JBB Greater Europe (previously Whyte & Mackay Group) for £6.5 million. 1.4 million litres of whisky from 1964 and younger is included in the purchase.

2001 – Jim McEwan from Bowmore becomes Production Director. The first distillation (Port Charlotte) is on 29th May and the first distillation of Bruichladdich starts in July. In September the owners' first bottlings from the old casks are released, 10, 15 and 20 years old.

2002 – The world's most heavily peated whisky is produced on 23rd October when Octomore (80ppm) is distilled.

2003 – Bruichladdich becomes the only distillery on Islay bottling on-site. It is awarded Distillery of the Year for the second time and launches the golf series, Links, 14 years old.

2004 – Second edition of the 20 year old (nick-named Flirtation) and 3D, also called The Peat Proposal, are launched.

2005 – Several new expressions are launched - the second edition of 3D, Infinity (a mix of 1989, 1990, 1991 and Port Charlotte), Rocks, Legacy Series IV, The Yellow Submarine and The Twenty 'Islands'.

2006 – Included in a number of new releases in autumn is the first official bottling of Port Charlotte; PC5.

2007 – New releases include Redder Still, Legacy 6, two new Links, PC6 and an 18 year old.

2008 – More than 20 new expressions including the first Octomore, Bruichladdich 2001, PC7, Golder Still and two sherry matured from 1998.

Peat   Rocks   1998 Manzanilla

Port Charlotte PC7

21 year old

Bruichladdich 12 year old

DR – Very welcoming mix of melon, grape and pear on the nose, and over-ripe peach, soft melon and other sweet fruits on the palate, with a delightful clean and fresh finish.

DS – Sweet and fruity on the nose with icing sugar and tangerine peel. Round and pleasant on the palate it is again fruity and slightly buttery. The long finish is creamy with a hint of spice.

Port Charlotte PC6

DR – Peat with the volume turned up, intense smoke and soot. On the palate quite stunning mix of candy sweets in intense barbecue smoke, with a long sweet and sooty finish that will delight Islay fans.

DS – Icing and fruit cake with champagne sorbet on the nose. Smoked meat flavours on the palate with a thunderous hit of peat and salt. Long, smoky, cheesy finish.

Links Torrey Pines

Bunnahabhain

Owner: Burn Stewart Distillers (CL Financial)

Region/district: Islay

Founded: 1881   **Status:** Active (vc)   **Capacity:** 2 500 000 litres

Address: Port Askaig, Islay, Argyll PA46 7RP

Tel: 01496 840646   **website:** www.bunnahabhain.com

History:

1881 – William Robertson of Robertson & Baxter, founds the distillery together with the brothers William and James Greenless. The Greenless brothers co-founded the Islay Distillers Company Ltd in 1879 with James Ford.

1883 – Production starts in earnest in January.

1887 – Islay Distillers Company Ltd merges with William Grant & Co. in order to form Highland Distilleries Company Limited.

1930 – The distillery closes.

1937 – The distillery reopens.

1963 – The two stills are augmented by two more.

1982 – The distillery closes.

1984 – The distillery reopens. A 21 year old is released to commemorate the 100th anniversary of Bunnahabhain.

1999 – Edrington takes over Highland Distilleries and mothballs Bunnahabhain but allows for a few weeks of production a year.

2001 – A 35 year old from 1965 is released in a limited edition of 594 bottles during Islay Whisky Festival.

2002 – As in the previous year, Islay Whisky Festival features another Bunnahabhain – 1966, a 35 year old in sherry casks and limited to 401 bottles. Auld Acquaintance 1968 (33 years, 2002 bottles) is launched at the Islay Jazz Festival. It is also named Hogmanay (after the Scottish New Year) as it was filled on 31st December 1968.

2003 – In April Edrington sells Bunnahabhain and Black Bottle to Burn Stewart Distilleries (C. L. World Brands) at the princely sum of £10 million. A 40 year old from 1963, matured in sherry casks, is launched.

2004 – The distillery experimented in the late 90s with a peated whisky and the first limited edition sample is a 6 year old cask strength called Moine.

2005 – Three limited editions are released - 34 years old, 18 years old and 25 years old.

2006 – 14 year old Pedro Ximenez and 35 years old are launched.

Bunnahabhain 12 year old

DR – Ginger and barley candy on the nose, then sweet and sour mix on the palate, lots of sweetness but with a distinctive savoury and earthy undertow.

DS – A sweet, smoky and scented nose with hints of sherry. Delicate smoke and touches of oakiness are on the palate and the finish is peaty and malty.

The demand for heavily peated single malt from Islay has increased dramatically in recent years. That creates a problem for the owner of Bunnahabhain, Burn Stewart Distillers. Their respected blend Black Bottle is reputed to contain malt whisky from every distillery on Islay but at least Lagavulin have not sold to Burn Stewart for a long time and will eventually have to be replaced by Bunnahabhain. That is why, in recent years, 200,000 litres of a special, peated variety (38 ppm) has been distilled as Bunnahabhain's whisky is traditionally made of virtually unpeated malt. This share will increase in 2008. The total production of Bunnahabhain will also increase from 1.7 to 2.0 million litres.

The distillery has a stainless steel mash tun, six wash backs made of Oregon pine and two pairs of stills. The spirit destined for single malt bottling and for Black Bottle is stored on site in six dunnage and one racked warehouse (totally 21,000 casks) while the rest is shipped to other sites for maturation.

When distillery owners occasionally mention specific investments it is often things like new stills or a new visitor centre that catch attention. What is rarely mentioned is refurbishing and replacement of less spectacular, but vital equipment. The owners of Bunnahabhain have invested large sums in this type of refurbishment recently. Last year approx. £700,000 was spent on, among other items, two new boilers. The old boilers were over 40 years old. A similar sum will be spent this year and will include investment in the draff handling equipment, condenser replacement and new compressed air equipment.

The core range consists of *12 years old*, *18 years old* and *25 years old*. A limited edition of a *21 year old* from 1986 was released during the Islay festival.

Several independent bottlers have also released Bunnahabhain. Some of the more recent are Duncan Taylor 1970 and an 18 year old from Ian MacLeod

18 years old

Bushmills

Owner: Diageo

Region/district: N Ireland (Co. Antrim)

Founded: 1784

Status: Active (vc)

Capacity: 3 000 000 litres

Address: 2 Distillery Road, Bushmills, Co. Antrim BT57 8XH

Tel: 028 20731521

website: www.bushmills.com

History:

1608 – James I issues Sir Thomas Philips a licence for whiskey distilling.

1784 – The distillery is formally registered.

1885 – Fire destroys part of the distillery.

1890 – S.S. Bushmills, the distillery's own steamship, makes its maiden voyage across the Atlantic to deliver whiskey to America and then heads on to Singapore, China and Japan.

1923 – The distillery is acquired by Belfast wine and spirit merchant Samuel Wilson Boyd. Anticipating the end of US prohibition, he gears Bushmills up for expansion and increases production.

1939-1945 – No distilling during the war. The distillery is partly converted to accommodate American servicemen.

1972 – Bushmills joins Irish Distillers Group which was formed in 1966. Floor maltings ceases.

1987 – Pernod Ricard acquires Irish Distillers.

1996 – Bushmills 16 years old is launched.

2005 – Bushmills is sold to Diageo at a price tag of €295.5 million as a result of Pernod Ricard's acquisition of Allied Domecq.

2007 – The 40 year old cast iron mash tun is replaced by a new stainless steel one at a cost of £1.4m.

2008 – Celebration to mark the 400th anniversary of the original license to distil granted to the area in 1608.

Bushmills 10 year old

DR – Autumn orchard of over-ripe apples on the nose, soft red apples and pear on the palate, soft sweetie finish.

DS – Dried citrus fruit with apricot and peach on the nose. Malty sweet with herbal barley flavours and bubblegum. A tasty, fruity finish.

When Diageo took over Bushmills distillery from Pernod Ricard three years ago, sales volumes had been flat for over 10 years. The new owners set a goal to reach 1 million cases by the end of 2012. This is an admirably bold aim, considering that current sales are 400,000 cases per year. To achieve the goal, major investments (£6 million) have been made in both marketing and in the distillery itself. A new lauter mash tun was installed in 2007, a new (10th) still is scheduled for September 2008 and a new maturation warehouse (the 11th) is also being built. When taking over, Diageo increased the production rate to five days a week and since 2008 they have implemented a seven-day week. This has tripled the production in just 2.5 years. Bushmills uses two kinds of malt, one unpeated and one slightly peated. The distillery uses triple distillation, which is the traditional Irish way, contrary to Cooley which uses double distillation. They have four wash stills and five spirit stills and the whiskey is matured and bottled on site.

Bushmills' core range of single malts consists of a *10 year old*, a *16 year old Triple Wood* with a finish in port pipes for 6-9 months and a *21 year old* finished in Madeira casks for two years. There is also a *12 year old Distillery Reserve* which is sold exclusively at the distillery. There used to be several single casks as well but they have all been discontinued. Black Bush and Bushmills Original are the two main blended whiskeys in the range. To celebrate the 400th anniversary, a Bushmills 1608 Anniversary Edition was launched. The malt whiskey part was distilled using a proportion of crystal malt (malted barley which has been dried at a high temperature whilst the grains are still moist, thus partly converting the grain's starch into sugars and caramelising them). This special ingredient gives the blend distinct toffee/chocolatey notes. The grain whiskey used for Bushmills blended whiskeys is bought from Midleton distillery in Cork which is owned by arch rival Pernod Ricard. Bushmills is the only working distillery in Ireland open to the public and it receives more than 100,000 visitors per year.

16 years old

Caol Ila

Owner:
Diageo

Region/district:
Islay

Founded: 1846
Status: Active (vc)
Capacity: 3 650 000 litres

Address: Port Askaig, Islay, Argyll PA46 7RL

Tel: 01496 302760
website: www.malts.com

History:

1846 – Hector Henderson founds Caol Ila.

1852 – Henderson, Lamont & Co. is subjected to financial difficulties and Henderson is forced to sell Caol Ila to Norman Buchanan.

1863 – Norman Buchanan encounters financial troubles and sells to the blending company Bulloch, Lade & Co. from Glasgow.

1879 – The distillery is rebuilt and expanded.

1920 – Bulloch, Lade & Co. is liquidated and the distillery is taken over by Caol Ila Distillery.

1927 – DCL becomes sole owners.

1930 – DCL transfers administration to Scottish Malt Distillers (SMD). The distillery closes.

1937 – Operations recommence.

1972 – All the buildings, except for the warehouses, are demolished and rebuilt.

1974 – The renovation, which totals £1 million, is complete and six new stills are installed.

1999 – Experiments with a completely unpeated malt are performed.

2002 – The first official bottlings since Flora & Fauna/Rare Malt appear; 12 years, 18 years and Cask Strength (c. 10 years).

2003 – A 25 year old cask strength is released.

2005 – A 25 year old Special Release is launched.

2006 – Unpeated 8 year old and 1993 Moscatel finish are released.

2007 – The second edition of the unpeated 8 year old is released.

2008 – The third edition of unpeated 8 year old is released.

Caol Ila 12 year old

DR – Barbecued fish and seaweed on the nose, oily bacon-fat, squeezed lemon and sweet smoke on the palate, immensely satisfying citrusy seaside barbecue of a finish.

DS – Sweet toasted tar and peat on the nose. The peatiness and maltiness are immediate on the palate and continue into the after-taste which is slightly burnt.

Water supplies can at times be problematic for distilleries and especially so on Islay. But there are further differences between the distilleries on the island; The Kildalton trio (Ardbeg, Lagavulin and Laphroaig) are better endowed than the others as their water is acquired from springs situated at high elevations, around 450 metres. The springs on the northern part of the island are at lower levels and subjected to draughts. Caol Ila belongs to those which may encounter problems. In 1997 they had to close for several weeks due to water shortage and in 2008 the same thing happened when the Western isles experienced their warmest and driest spring for years.

Apart from that Caol Ila is a distillery which has been much in fashion in recent years since Diageo decided in 2002 to bring it out of Lagavulin's shadow by a number of new expressions. Caol Ila, which is running at full capacity, has as its main task to produce malt for Johnnie Walker and around 5% of the production is today reserved for single malt.

The distillery is equipped with a cast iron mash tun, eight washbacks made of Oregon pine and three pairs of stills in a still room with a beautiful view of Jura across the Sound of Islay. There is a three-floored warehouse on site but today's production is sent by lorry to the mainland for filling and maturation. The whisky from Caol Ila is peated but low phenol trials started already in the 1980's. The result of the trials, destined for blended whisky, is that unpeated Caol Ila has been produced annually ever since, with the exception of 2006 and 2007, due to the high demand for peated whisky. The unpeated Caol Ila (Highland) was bottled for the first time in 2006.

The core range consists of *12 and 18 years old* and *Cask Strength*. Limited editions have included *25 years old* and a *1993 Distiller's Edition Moscatel finish*. The third edition of the *unpeated 8 year old* was released in autumn 2008.

Recent independent bottlings include a 32 year old from Signatory, a 17 year old from Single Malts of Scotland, a 17 year old from Cadenheads, a Duncan Taylor 1981 and two from Ian MacLeod (15 and 24 years).

8 years old unpeated

Caperdonich

Owner:	**Region/district:**
Chivas Brothers	Speyside
(Pernod Ricard)	

Founded:	**Status:**	**Capacity:**
1897	Mothballed	2 200 000 litres

Address: Rothes, Aberlour, Banffshire AB38 7BN

Tel:	**website:**
01542 783000	-

History:
1897 – The distillery is founded by James Grant and is named Glen Grant Number 2 Distillery after the neighbouring sister distillery Glen Grant.

1902 – The Pattison crash shakes the industry and the distillery closes.

1965 – It reopens with The Glenlivet & Glen Grant Distilleries as owners. According to law two distilleries cannot bear the same name so it is changed to Caperdonich.

1967 – The number of stills are increased from two to four.

1977 – Seagrams buys The Glenlivet Distilleries Ltd (the new, shortened name) and forms Chivas and Glenlivet Group. Longmorn, Benriach, Glen Grant and The Glenlivet are also included in the deal.

2001 – Pernod Ricard and Diageo take over Seagram Spirits & Wine, the Chivas Group becomes part of Pernod Ricard.

2002 – The distillery is mothballed.

2005 – A 16 year old from 1988 is launched.

Caperdonich 16 year old 55,8%

DS – Lemony and earthy with icing sugar on the nose. Sweet and fruity on the palate. Dry. Long, hot finish and again very dry.

Of the three distilleries that Pernod Ricard mothballed in 2002, two have been resurrected; Allt-a-Bhainne and Braeval. The third, Caperdonich was put up for sale in 2003 but nothing much has happened since then. Even though most of the equipment remains in place, some of it has been dismantled and sent to other distilleries in the group. The condensers for example, have all been removed. Since Caperdonich's capacity is considerably smaller than its two siblings, it is doubtful whether the current owners will start it up again.

Caperdonich was founded under the name Glen Grant No 2 in 1897, at a time when the whisky industry went into one of its greatest crises which culminated in the Pattison crash. The demand for Scotch had grown disproportionately but production and investments with borrowed money increased even more and it was more or less obvious that the bubble would eventually burst. Several distilleries had to close and it was the turn of Caperdonich five years after its inception. It was not reopened until 1965 and investment was made in another two pot stills and the very latest in modern technology enabling the whole process to be controlled by two men only. The old pipe which was used for transporting spirit from Caperdonich to neighbouring Glen Grant for filling was not used after 1902 but was not removed until the 1980s.

The distillery is equipped with a cast iron mash tun, eight wash backs made of stainless steel and two pairs of stills. The stills are, in common with Glen Grant, equipped with purifiers which give a light and rather elegant whisky. Almost all the production was used to different blended whiskies, e. g. 100 Pipers, Chivas Regal and Passport. The only official bottling ever launched was a 16 year old cask strength released in 2005.

There are, however, more to be found among independent bottlings. Some more recent are a 27 year old from Cadenheads and two 40 year olds from Douglas Laing and Duncan Taylor.

16 years old

Cardhu

Owner:
Diageo

Region/district:
Speyside

Founded: 1824

Status: Active (vc)

Capacity: 2 390 000 litres

Address: Knockando, Aberlour, Moray AB38 7RY

Tel: 01340 872555 (vc)

website: www.malts.com

History:

1811 – The whisky smuggler John Cumming founds an illicit distillery.

1824 – John Cumming applies for and obtains a licence for Cardhu Distillery.

1846 – John Cumming dies and his son Lewis takes over.

1872 – Lewis dies and his wife Elizabeth takes over.

1884 – A new distillery is built to replace the old.

1893 – John Walker & Sons purchases Cardhu for £20,500 but the Cumming family continues operations. The whisky changes name from Cardow to Cardhu.

1908 – The name reverts to Cardow.

1930 – Administration is transferred to Scottish Malt Distillers (SMD).

1960-61 – Reconstruction and expansion of stills from four to six.

1981 – The name changes to Cardhu once again.

1998 – A visitor centre is constructed.

2002 – The popularity of Cardhu leads to supply problems for Diageo. They decide to change Cardhu single malt to a vatted malt with contributions from other distilleries in it.

2003 – The whisky industry protests sharply against Diageo's plans. Diageo negotiates a compromise with Scotch Whisky Association.

2004 – Diageo withdraws Cardhu Pure Malt.

2005 – The 12 year old Cardhu Single Malt is relaunched and a 22 year old is released.

Cardhu 12 year old

DR – Honeycomb and chocolate Crunchie bar on the nose, fluffy over-ripe apples, toffee, boiled sweets on the palate, delightful clean and crisp finish.

DS – A spicy and floral nose coupled with a honeyness that is also on the spicy palate. The finish is also honeyed and lingers.

The whisky from Cardhu distillery has enjoyed a solid reputation for more than 100 years. When the legendary Alfred Barnard visited the distillery in 1885, he was received by the founder's daughter-in-law Elisabeth Cumming a. k. a. "The Queen of the Whisky Trade". Barnard was so impressed by her and the whisky that he wrote "…(the whisky) is of the thickest and richest description, and admirably adapted for blending purposes." It is currently the owner's, Diageo, most sold single malt and number six in the world with 3.3 million bottles a year. Diageo used to divide their brands into three groups; First global priority brands which contains the eight largest, among them Johnnie Walker and J&B. Second is local priority brands which comprises 30 brands with a dominating position in a single market or at least in a region and that is where Cardhu fits in with its stronghold in above all Spain (at least 75% of the production is sold in Spain). The final category is category brands with, e. g. , Classic Malts Selection.

Cardhu distillery's location is unrivalled; on a small hill with a view over Ben Rinnes and with Knockando and Tamdhu as its closest neighbours. The distillery is one of Diageo's smallest and is equipped with one stainless steel full lauter mash tun, eight washbacks made of Scottish larch and three pairs of stills. In common with so many other distilleries these days, Cardhu has increased production and is working a seven day week. Some 30% of output is bottled as single malt while the rest is an important ingredient in Johnnie Walker.

The core range consists of the *12 year old* and a *22 year old Special Release* which was released for the Spanish and French markets in 2005. In October 2006, a *Special Cask Reserve* with no age statement was released in Spain.

The only independent bottling is a 27 year old from Signatory which appeared in 1999.

22 years old

Clynelish

Owner:		Region/district:
Diageo		Northern Highlands
Founded:	**Status:**	**Capacity:**
1967	Active (vc)	4 200 000 litres

Address: Brora, Sutherland KW9 6LR

Tel:	website:
01408 623003 (vc)	www.malts.com

History:

1819 – The 1st Duke of Sutherland, founds a distillery called Clynelish Distillery.

1827 – The first licensed distiller, James Harper, files for bankruptcy and John Matheson takes over.

1834 – Andrew Ross takes over the license.

1846 – George Lawson & Sons takes over.

1896 – James Ainslie & Heilbron takes over.

1912 – James Ainslie & Co. narrowly escapes bankruptcy and Distillers Company Limited (DCL) takes over together with James Risk.

1916 – John Walker & Sons buys a stake of James Risk's stocks.

1925 – DCL buys out Risk.

1931 – The distillery is mothballed.

1939 – Production restarts.

1960 – The distillery becomes electrified.

1967 – A new distillery is built adjacent to the first one, it is also named Clynelish and both operate in parallel from August.

1968 – 'Old' Clynelish is mothballed in August.

1969 – 'Old' Clynelish is reopened as Brora and starts using a very peaty malt.

1983 – Brora is closed in March.

2002 – A 14 year old is released.

2006 – A Distiller's Edition 1991 finished in Oloroso casks is released.

Clynelish 14 year old

DR – Fresh green fruit and unripe melon on the nose, sweet almost fizzy lemon sherbet on the palate, a wispy hint of peat and pepper, and satisfying and balanced finish.

DS – Sweet rubber and mustard married with tar and alcohol. The palate also has a hint of mustard the goes long into the peppery finish.

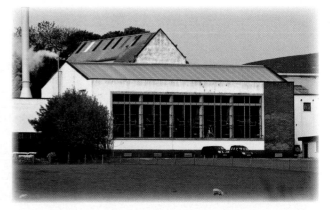

The first Clynelish distillery, which in more modern days became known as Brora, was built by one of the most infamous people in Scottish history, the 1st Duke of Sutherland. At the beginning of 1800 he owned the biggest private estate in Europe covering a huge part of northern Scotland. He found that he could make more money from the land by grazing sheep on it rather than leasing it to peasants, therefore he simply forced 15,000 farmers from their lands. Some of them moved to the coast while others emigrated to America. His actions became known as the Highland Clearances. Dunrobin Castle, home to the earls and dukes of Sutherland since the 13th century is open to the public and is only a couple of miles south of the distillery. On the top of Beinn a' Bhragaidh is a 100ft statue of the 1st Duke of Sutherland. It was erected in 1834 and can be seen from many miles away.

In 1967 a new distillery was built adjacent to the first one. This was also called Clynelish and they both operated parallel until 1983 when the old distillery closed. Note, however, that for the last 14 years the old Clynelish was renamed Brora. The old buildings are still there but only the warehouses are used for maturation of Clynelish. Mashtun, washback and the two old stills are intact in the old stillhouse although not in the best of shape due to holes in the roof.

The distillery we today call Clynelish lies on the other side of the small road and is a modern creation made of glass, steel and concrete. It is equipped with a cast iron mash tun, eight wooden washbacks, two stainless steel washbacks installed in 2008 and three pairs of stills. Since January 2008 a seven-day working week enables the production of 4.2 million litres. The spirit from Clynelish is stored in its own warehouses or in the old warehouses of Brora. The whisky is much less peated than Brora .

Official bottlings include a *14 year old* and a *Distiller's Edition 1991*. The first distillery shop exclusive, a *cask strength*, was released in 2008. A recent independent bottling is a 36 year old from 1971 by Douglas Laing.

Brora

1991 Distiller's Edition

Cooley

Owner:
Cooley Distillery plc

Region/district:
Ireland (County Louth)

Founded: **Status:**
1987 Active

Capacity:
3 250 000 litres

Address: Riverstown, Cooley, Co. Louth

Tel: **website:**
+353 (0)42 9376102 www.cooleywhiskey.com

History:
1987 – John Teeling purchases Ceimici Teo Distillery in Dundalk. Previously it has produced spirits in column stills (e. g. vodka) and is now renamed Cooley Distillery.

1988 – Willie McCarter acquires part of A. A. Watt Distillery and the brand Tyrconnell and merges with Teeling. Teeling simultaneously buys decommissioned Locke's Kilbeggan Distillery which will be used for storage of whiskey from Cooley.

1989 – A pair of pot stills is installed for production of both malt and grain whiskey.

1992 – Locke's Single Malt, without age statement, is launched as the first single malt from the distillery. Cooley encounters financial troubles and Pernod Ricard, via Irish Distillers, offers to purchase the company for £24.5 million.

1994 – The Competition Authority establishes that Irish Distillers cannot acquire Cooley as they then would be dominating the Irish whiskey market.

1995 – Finances improve and production resumes.

1996 – Connemara is launched.

2000 – Locke's 8 year old single malt is launched.

2003 – The Connemara 12 year old is launched.

2006 – Five Connemara Single Casks from 1992 are released.

2007 – Kilbeggan distillery is reopened.

Connemara 12 year old

DR – Soft fruit and tarry peat on the nose, then fluffy red apples, toffee and smoke intriguingly mixed into an unusual and very enticing whole. Smoke in the finish.

DS – Fresh, melon and apple on the nose with aniseed and herbs. A mix of tropical fruit, mild peat and herbs swims about on the palate into the long, lingering finish.

Cooley distillery

The old Locke's distillery (now Kilbeggan)

Last year was an exciting one for the owners of Cooley distillery when they opened their second distillery, or, perhaps more appropriately, reopened, because Kilbeggan distillery was first opened in 1757 and stopped production in 1957. Actually the owners were already quite familiar with the site as they had bought the old Locke distillery (as Kilbeggan was sometimes called) back in 1988 to serve as a maturation place for their Cooley whiskey. Currently only the second distillation is performed at Kilbeggan; mashing, fermenting and first distillation is all conducted at Cooley. However, efforts are underway to source a matching pot still to enable a full distillation process on site

Cooley distillery is currently also investing in new bottling and labelling equipment, another new warehouse is to be built and maintenance work on both grain and malt distilleries is planned.

Around 95% of production is exported and the distillery also has the capacity to produce 10 million litres of grain whiskey a year. The range of single malts from Cooley has come to be quite extensive; *Locke's 8 years old, Tyrconnell with no age* and *1992 single cask* and *Connemara with no age, 12 years old* and *Cask Strength.* The experimental wood finishes of Tyrconnel from last year (*port, madeira* and *sherry*) are now a part of the core range. The Connemara brand comes peated but recently distillery manager Noel Sweeney has been experimenting with some heavier peated malt, the result of which will be seen in a couple of years. Another special Connemara will be sherry finished and will be released in early 2009.

A number of blended whiskeys are also produced: Inishowen (lightly peated), Kilbeggan and Millar's Special Reserve. A 15 year old Kilbeggan was released in 2007 and a single grain called Greenore 8 years was very successful and has sold out. A limited edition of a 15 year old Greenore has also been released.

Tyrconnell no age

Cragganmore

Owner:		Region/district:
Diageo		Speyside
Founded:	**Status:**	**Capacity:**
1869	Active (vc)	1 520 000 litres

Address: Ballindalloch, Moray AB37 9AB

Tel:	website:
01479 874700	www.malts.com

History:

1869 – John Smith, who already runs Ballindalloch and Glenfarclas Distilleries, founds Cragganmore.

1886 – John Smith dies and his brother George takes over operations.

1893 – John's son Gordon, at 21, is old enough to assume responsibility for operations.

1901 – The distillery is refurbished and modernized with help of the famous architect Charles Doig.

1912 – Gordon Smith dies and his widow Mary Jane supervises operations.

1917 – The distillery closes.

1918 – The distillery reopens and Mary Jane installs electric lighting.

1923 – The distillery is sold to the newly formed Cragganmore Distillery Co. where Mackie & Co. and Peter Mackie share half ownership. The remaining half is owned by Sir George Macpherson-Grant and Ballindalloch Estate.

1927 – White Horse Distillers is bought by DCL who thus obtains 50% of Cragganmore.

1964 – The number of stills is increased from two to four.

1965 – DCL buys the remainder of Cragganmore.

1988 – Cragganmore 12 years becomes one of six selected for United Distillers' Classic Malts.

1998 – Cragganmore Distillers Edition Double Matured (port) is launched for the first time.

2002 – A visitor centre opens in May.

2006 – A 17 year old from 1988 is released.

Cragganmore 12 year old

DR – The nose has honey, soft fruits and sweet spring meadow notes and is very inviting, and on the palate soft barley, summer fruits and a sweetness lead up to an almost tangy finish.

DS – Soft and buttery at first with a hint of mild, perfumed smoke. A spicy palate carries on the short but sweet finish.

Cragganmore has led a comparatively quiet life despite having being selected in 1988 as one of the original six Classic malts by its owners Diageo. Of the original six this is the least visited distillery with just a few hundred visitors finding their way there annually. Talisker, on the other hand, receives almost 40,000 visitors. Sales figures are not impressive either, - around 350,000 bottles compared to its Skye sibling which sells 1.1 million. If sales are low, reputation is high, not least among blenders who have always appreciated whisky from Cragganmore. The main part of production is used as an ingredient in Old Parr blended whisky and also in White Horse. The distillery is equipped with a stainless steel full-lauter mash tun which was installed in 1997. As Cragganmore receives visitors, Diageo decided to decorate the tun with Oregon pine and put the old tun's copper dome on top to make it look more traditional. In addition to the tun there are six washbacks made of Oregon pine and two pairs of stills. The stills look odd with their flat tops and there are many theories as to why they have this shape. Some claim the roof was too low when they were originally installed whilst others say this was a novelty of the era. One thing is for sure, the owners would not dare to change this as the shape, combined with the worm tubs, is one of the things that give the whisky its character. Part of the production matures in three dunnage warehouses on site after having been filled on casks at Diageo's huge facility in Cambus.

The core range is made up of a *12 year old* and a *Distiller's Edition*. There has also been five limited bottlings since 2000 – a *14 year old* destined for 'Friends of Classic Malts', a *1973 29 year old*, a *10 year old cask strength* in 2004, a *1993 Bodega Cask* the same year and, finally, a *17 year old* released in 2006. Recent independent bottlings include a Duncan Taylor from 1990, a 15 year old from Cadenheads and a 22 year old (1985) from Single Malts of Scotland.

12 years old

Craigellachie

Owner:
John Dewar & Sons
(Bacardi)

Region/district:
Speyside

Founded:
1891

Status:
Active

Capacity:
3 600 000 litres

Address: Aberlour, Banffshire AB38 9ST

Tel:
01340 872971

website:
-

History:

1891 – The distillery is built by Craigellachie–Glenlivet Distillery Company which has Alexander Edward and Peter Mackie as part-owners. The famous Charles Doig is the architect.

1898 – Production does not start until this year.

1916 – Mackie & Company Distillers Ltd takes over.

1924 – Peter Mackie dies and Mackie & Company changes name to White Horse Distillers.

1927 – White Horse Distillers are bought by Distillers Company Limited (DCL).

1930 – Administration is transferred to Scottish Malt Distillers (SMD), a subsidiary of DCL.

1964 – Refurbishing takes place and two new stills are bought, increasing the number to four.

1998 – United Distillers & Vintners (UDV) sells Craigellachie, together with Aberfeldy, Brackla and Aultmore and the blending company John Dewar & Sons to Bacardi Martini.

2004 – The first bottlings from the new owners are a new 14 year old which replaces UDV's Flora & Fauna and a 21 year old cask strength from 1982 produced for Craigellachie Hotel.

Craigellachie 14 year old

DR – Intriguing and deep mix of light fruits on the nose, a spicy bite then clean and smooth mouth feel, and a soft finish.

DS – Mild spice with vanilla and honeycomb on the nose. More honey on the palate with malt and fruit flavours. The finish is short but sweet.

Craigellachie is a working distillery and visitors are not catered for. This is perhaps in order as there is a lot of competition in the area with visitor's centre destinations such as Speyside Cooperage just outside Craigellachie village, the Macallan distillery and visitor centre across the River Spey and the Craigellachie Hotel with its (still) famous whisky bar. Another famous landmark in the vicinity is the magnificent Craigellachie Bridge, designed and built by Thomas Telford in 1815 and the oldest surviving iron bridge in Scotland.

During virtually all of Craigellachie's lifetime it has produced malt whisky for blends, first White Horse and more recently Dewar's. Malted barley is bought from Glenesk maltings and the distillery has a very modern Steinecker full lauter mash tun installed in 2001 which replaced the old open cast iron mash tun. There are also eight washbacks made of larch wood and two pairs of stills. Since 2008 a seven-day working week is in place at the distillery which means that it is now producing at full capacity, 3.6 million litres. Neither filling of casks nor maturation takes place on site and all spirit is tankered away to the Dewar's site outside Glasgow.

The distillery is not easily missed as it sits just north of Craigellachie village by the A491. Especially at night it is a stunning sight to see the large copper stills lit by spotlights through the glazed curtain walls.

Bacardi launched a *14 year old* in 2004 and this is, so far, the only official bottling. Recent independent bottlings include an 11 year old (1996) from Douglas Laing and a 1994 from Berry Brothers.

14 years old

Dailuaine

Owner:		Region/district:
Diageo		Speyside

Founded:	Status:	Capacity:
1852	Active	3 370 000 litres

Address: Carron, Banffshire AB38 7RE

Tel:	website:
01340 872500	www.malts.com

History:

1852 – The distillery is founded by William Mackenzie.

1865 – William Mackenzie dies and his widow leases the distillery to James Fleming, a banker from Aberlour.

1879 – William Mackenzie's son forms Mackenzie and Company with Fleming.

1884 – Rebuilding transforms the distillery into one of the largest in the Highlands.

1889 – Charles Doig builds his and Scotland's first pagoda roof on Dailuaine.

1891 – Dailuaine-Glenlivet Distillery Ltd is founded.

1898 – Dailuaine-Glenlivet Distillery Ltd merges with Talisker Distillery Ltd and forms Dailuaine-Talisker Distilleries Ltd. Imperial Distillery, built by Thomas Mackenzie the previous year, and a grain distillery in Aberdeen are also incorporated.

1915 – Thomas Mackenzie dies without heirs.

1916 – Dailuaine-Talisker Company Ltd is bought by the previous customers John Dewar & Sons, John Walker & Sons and James Buchanan & Co.

1917 – A fire rages and the pagoda roof collapses. The distillery is forced to close.

1920 – The distillery reopens.

1925 – Distillers Company Limited (DCL) takes over.

1960 – Refurbishing. The stills increase from four to six and a Saladin box replaces the floor maltings.

1965 – Indirect still heating through steam is installed.

1983 – On-site maltings is closed down and malt is purchased centrally.

1991 – The first official bottling, a 16 year old, is launched in the Flora & Fauna series.

1996 – A 22 year old cask strength from 1973 is launched as a Rare Malt.

1997 – A cask strength version of the 16 year old is launched.

2000 – A 17 year old Manager's Dram matured in sherry casks is launched.

Dailuaine was one of many Speyside distilleries that used the railway system to transport barley, coal and casks of whisky. Strathspey Railway had reached the village of Carron, less than a mile from the distillery by 1863, but it took another 42 years until the distillery obtained its own station. The crew at the distillery included an engine driver, a fireman and a railway man who were employed full time to operate the steam locomotive, a so called "puggie". The last of the engines, Dailuaine No. 1, was taken out of service in 1967 when the railway was closed. For a period of time it could be found at Strathspey Railway Museum in Boat of Garten but Diageo reclaimed the locomotive in the 1990s and it is now at Aberfeldy distillery. Apart from distilling whisky which principally becomes a part of Johnnie Walker, Dailuaine has also become an "environmental hub" to seven distilleries nearby. A dark grains plant, built in 1960, processes draff and pot ale into cattle feed. The capacity of the plant is 900 tonnes per week. There is also an effluent treatment plant which treats wastewater using various filters. The effluent is discharged into the river when the BOD level (biological oxygen demand) is less than 20 ppm.

The distillery is equipped with a stainless steel full-lauter mash tun installed in 1993, eight washbacks made of larch and three pairs of stills. There are also some magnificent granite warehouses but they are no longer used for storing whisky. Instead the spirit is tankered away to Cambus for filling and then to the Diageo warehouses in Blackrange. Except for a *16 year old* in the Flora & Fauna series, only a couple of limited versions have been released by the owners.

Independent bottlings are rare but there have been a couple of interesting ones recently; a 34 year old from 1973 by Douglas Laing and an 11 year old with a Tokay-finish from Ian MacLeod.

Flora & Fauna 16 years old

Dailuaine 16 year old

DS – Heavy chocolate and syrup flavours on the nose with cheese-cake notes. The palate is soft at first with a burst of sherry and raisins in Cointreau. An aggressive finish.

Dalmore

Owner:
Whyte & Mackay Ltd
(United Spirits)

Region/district:
Northern Highlands

Founded: 1839

Status: Active (vc)

Capacity: 4 200 000 litres

Address: Alness, Ross-shire IV17 0UT

Tel: 01349 882362

website: www.thedalmore.com

History:

1839 – Alexander Matheson founds the distillery and lets it to the Sunderland family.

1867 – The brothers Charles, Andrew and Alexander Mackenzie run the distillery.

1874 – The number of stills is increased to four.

1886 – Alexander Matheson dies.

1891 – Sir Kenneth Matheson sells the distillery for £14,500 to the Mackenzie brothers.

1917 – The Royal Navy moves in to start manufacturing of American mines.

1920 – The Royal Navy moves out and leaves behind a distillery damaged by an explosion.

1922 – The distillery is in production again. Andrew Mackenzie and the Royal Navy disagree on compensation for the damages.

1956 – Floor malting is replaced by Saladin box.

1960 – Mackenzie Brothers (Dalmore) Ltd merges with Whyte & Mackay and forms the company Dalmore-Whyte & Mackay Ltd.

1966 – The number of stills is increased from four to eight.

1982 – The Saladin box is abandoned.

1990 – American Brands buys Whyte & Mackay.

1996 – Whyte & Mackay changes name to JBB (Greater Europe).

2001 – Through management buy-out, JBB (Greater Europe) is bought from Fortune Brands and changes name to Kyndal Spirits.

2002 – A 62 year old Dalmore is sold at McTear's auction for £25,877.50 and becomes the world's so far most expensive bottle of whisky. Kyndal Spirits changes name to Whyte & Mackay.

2004 – A new visitor centre opens.

2005 – Black Pearl, with six months on Madeira barrels, is launched.

2007 – United Spirits buys Whyte & Mackay. 15 year old, 1973 Cabernet Sauvignon and a 40 year old are released.

2008 – 1263 King Alexander III and Vintage 1974 are released.

Dalmore 12 year old

DR – Orange jelly and squidgy fruit on the nose, an impressive full confectionery and fruit salad taste on the softest of peat beds, and a wonderful and warming finish.

DS – Cherries with fruitcake and hints of marzipan on the nose. The palate is softer and quite oily-rich. Bitter fruitcake dominates and continues onto the finish.

With a stunning view across the Cromarthy Firth over to the Black Isle, lies Dalmore distillery. Not only is it the biggest distillery in the Whyte & Mackay group but by far also the most renowned.

The distillery is equipped with a semi-lauter mash tun, eight washbacks made of Oregon Pine and four pairs of stills. Four of these stills were installed in the sixties and are considerably bigger than the old ones. The still room is divided into two parts with the small stream from where the water is taken flowing underneath the floor. The spirit stills have water jackets, a peculiar device that cannot be seen anywhere else. This allows cold water to circulate between the reflux bowl and the neck of the stills, thus increasing the reflux. This construction has been present since Dalmore was built and one of the present water jackets dates back to 1874. The owners have been running the distillery at near full capacity for eight years now, which means 22 mashes per week and 3.6 million litres per annum. Two weeks per year a heavily peated spirit is produced. The usual strains of barley are used but once in a while, master blender Richard Paterson orders an experimental run using Golden Promise, Halcyon or similar. 200 casks a week are filled on site with the rest going straight to the adjacent Invergordon grain distillery.

The core range consists of a *12 year old*, a *15 year old* and *Gran Reserva* (which replaced the previous Cigar Malt). Limited editions released in 2007 included *1973 Cabernet Sauvignon* (33 years old) and the *40 year old* with two additional maturations (Oloroso and Amoroso sherry). Two new limited expressions were released in 2008 - *1263 King Alexander III* and *Vintage 1974*.

Independent bottlings are not commonly found. Among the latest are a Duncan Taylor 1990 and a 1995 (12 years) from Ian MacLeod.

1263 King Alexander III

Dalwhinnie

Owner:		Region/district:
Diageo		Speyside

Founded:	Status:	Capacity:
1897	Active (vc)	2 200 000 litres

Address: Dalwhinnie, Inverness-shire PH19 1AB

Tel:	website:
01540 672219 (vc)	www.malts.com

History:

1897 – John Grant, George Sellar and Alexander Mackenzie from Kingussie commence building the facilities. The first name is Strathspey and the construction work amounts to £10,000.

1898 – Production starts in February. The owners encounter financial troubles after a few months and John Somerville & Co and A P Blyth & Sons take over in November and change the name to Dalwhinnie. The architect Charles Doig is called in to make some improvements.

1905 – America's largest distillers, Cook & Bernheimer in New York, buys Dalwhinnie for £1,250 at an auction. This marks the first time a foreign company takes ownership of a Scottish distillery. The administration of Dalwhinnie is placed in the newly formed company James Munro & Sons.

1919 – Macdonald Greenlees & Willliams Ltd headed by Sir James Calder buys Dalwhinnie.

1926 – Macdonald Greenlees & Williams Ltd is bought by Distillers Company Ltd (DCL) which licences Dalwhinnie to James Buchanan & Co.

1930 – Operations are transferred to Scottish Malt Distilleries (SMD).

1934 – The distillery is closed after a fire in February.

1938 – The distillery opens again.

1968 – The maltings is decommissioned.

1986 – A complete refurbishing takes place.

1987 – Dalwhinnie 15 years becomes one of selected six in United Distillers' Classic Malts.

1991 – A visitor centre is constructed.

1992 – The distillery closes and goes through a major refurbishment costing £3.2 million.

1995 – The distillery opens in March.

1998 – Dalwhinnie Distillers Edition 1980 (oloroso) is introduced for the first time. The other five in The Classic Malts, each with a different finish, are also introduced as Distillers Editions for the first time.

2002 – A 36 year old is released.

2003 – A 29 year old is released.

2006 – A 20 year old is released.

Dalwhinnie 15 year old

DR – Full honey and sweet peat on the nose, a rich creamy mouthfeel and a delicious honey and exotic fruits mix all layered on soft peat foundations.

DS – A light and grassy nose with hints of heathery-sweetness. Light palate with malty flavours. Warming and slightly oaky finish.

Dalwhinnie distillery is beautifully situated in the Grampian mountains at the northern end of Loch Ericht, the tenth largest loch in Scotland but draws its water from Allt an t'Sluic in the mountains northwest of the distillery. This is in fact one of the sources of the mighty Spey river. It is one of the highest situated distilleries in Scotland and the village also experiences the coldest average annual temperature of 6°C.

The distillery is equipped with a full-lauter mash tun, six wooden washbacks and just the one pair of stills. From the stills, the lyne arms lead out through the roofs to the wooden wormtubs outside. Dalwhinnie is one of few distilleries still using worm tubs where the spirit condenses in a long copper spiral submerged in cool water. Dalwhinnie did in fact use modern shell and tube condensers during a period in the eighties, but reverted to worm tubs as they found the character of the whisky changed.

In common with the recent trend at many other distilleries, Dalwhinnie has since February 2008 speeded up production to full capacity. That means 15 mashes/week instead of 10, resulting in 2.2 million litres per year. Two racked warehouses are able to store approximately 5,000 casks.

Dalwhinnie was licensed to James Buchanan & Co in 1926 and the malt has since been a vital part of Diageo's Buchanan blended Scotch. This is still evident by the sign on the distillery wall and many of the 22,000 annual visitors come from South America where Buchanan's De Luxe have many followers. Diageo have done a good job in positioning Dalwhinnie on the market, and the whisky is among the top 15 most sold single malts worldwide.

The core range is made up of a 15 year old and a *Distiller's Edition*. Some older versions have also been released in recent years. It is very difficult to find an independently bottled Dalwhinnie.

15 years old

Deanston

Owner:
Burn Stewart Distillers
(C L Financial)

Region/district:
Eastern Highlands

Founded: **Status:** **Capacity:**
1965 Active 3 000 000 litres

Address: Deanston, Perthshire FK16 6AG

Tel: **website:**
01786 841422 www.burnstewartdistillers.com

History:
1965 – A weavery from 1785 is transformed into Deanston Distillery by James Finlay & Co. and Brodie Hepburn Ltd (Deanston Distillery Co.). Brodie Hepburn also runs Tullibardine Distillery.

1966 – Production commences in October.

1971 – The first single malt is named Old Bannockburn.

1972 – Invergordon Distillers takes over.

1974 – The first single malt bearing the name Deanston is produced.

1982 – The distillery closes.

1990 – Burn Stewart Distillers from Glasgow buys the distillery for £2.1 million.

1991 – The distillery resumes production.

1999 – C L Financial buys an 18% stake of Burn Stewart.

2002 – C L Financial acquires the remaining stake.

2006 – Deanston 30 years old is released.

Deanston 12 year old

DR – Light and delicate nose with lemon and floral notes. The palate is sweet with lemon and orange notes, and the vanilla notes towards the finish make this a dessert of a malt.

DS – Weak grape juice with pine needles on the nose. Liqueurish on the palate with hints of sour fruits and berries. Minty and spicy on the finish.

Deanston is one of six surviving distilleries in Perthshire, a region where, at one time, there were 140 active distilleries Very little single malt distilled at Deanston reaches the market. Instead the whisky finds its way mainly into the blend Scottish Leader which is the owners', Burn Stewart Distillers, big seller. This blend has steadily sold around five million bottles a year for the latest five years which gives the brand a place just below the top thirty. There are now even a couple of vatted malt versions of Scottish Leader which appeared last year. The European version of the blend is called Supreme and has no age statement but is typically 3 years old. Taiwanese versions are much older with some over 20 years.

Much restoration work has been going on at Deanston the past few years. Firstly the offices were refurbished to better accommodate (trade) visitors. The distillery was closed between January and March 2008 in order to replace the bases of both wash stills and was re-opened at the beginning of April. Despite this Deanston intends to increase production to 2,4 m litres as they will operate 24/7 with no summer closedown period. The equipment consists of a cast iron mash tun with an open top, eight stainless steel washbacks and two pairs of stills. There are two warehouses, one modern racked and one listed building from the old mill which altogether can contain 45,000 casks with the oldest dating back to 1971. A dam and a turbine make it unique in being the only Scottish distillery that is self-sustaining with electricity.

At the moment there are only two official bottlings from Deanston, the 12 year old and the 30 year old which was released in 2006. A new version of the 12 year old with higher alcohol content (46% instead of 40%) was released in September 2008. Independent bottlings are not easy to come by. One recent is an 11 year old released by Douglas Laing in 2006.

12 years old

Dufftown

Owner:
Diageo

Region/district:
Speyside

Founded: 1896   **Status:** Active   **Capacity:** 4 120 000 litres

Address: Dufftown, Keith, Banffshire AB55 4BR

Tel: 01340 822100   **website:** www.malts.com

History:
1895 – Peter Mackenzie, Richard Stackpole, John Symon and Charles MacPherson build the distillery Dufftown-Glenlivet in an old mill.

1896 – Production starts in November.

1897 – The distillery is owned by P. Mackenzie & Co., who also owns Blair Athol in Pitlochry.

1933 – P. Mackenzie & Co. is bought by Arthur Bell & Sons for £56 000.

1968 – The floor maltings is discontinued and malt is bought from outside suppliers. The number of stills is increased from two to four.

1974 – The number of stills is increased from four to six.

1979 – The stills are increased by a further two, to eight.

1985 – Guinness buys Arthur Bell & Sons.

1997 – Guinness and Grand Metropolitan merge to form Diageo.

2006 – The Singleton of Dufftown is launched as a special duty free bottling.

Singleton of Dufftown

DR – Honeycomb and tinned peach and apricot in syrup on the nose, sharp and spicy clean barley on the palate, with some bitter orange notes towards the finish.

DS – A malty, sherried nose with heavy spices and mulled wine notes. A heavy, mouth coating whisky – very oily and full of sherry flavours. Oily, hot finish.

Dufftown distillery was built by the wine merchant Peter Mackenzie and his name still lives on in a blended whisky launched by Diageo in Taiwan in 2005 – The Real Mackenzie. Dufftown distillery itself is a giant in terms of production. It is in fact the biggest of all Diageo's 27 working distilleries Dufftown has also one of the biggest mash tuns in the industry, with a capacity of no less than 13 tonnes. It is a full lauter model and was installed in 1979. There are twelve stainless steel wash backs (more than any other in the Diageo group) which replaced old, wooden ones in 1998 when the distillery closed for four months for refurbishing. Throughout the years stills have been added and it is a bit of a mystery how all have managed to fit into such small premises. The still-house with its three pairs of stills must be one of Scotland's most cramped. Despite the huge capacity of four million litres per year, very little finds its way into single malt bottles. In fact 98% goes into Diageo's blends, especially Bell's.

Dufftown was the sixth distillery to be built in Dufftown, known by many as the Malt Whisky Capital in Scotland. At first the distillery was to be called Pittyvaich but the owners changed their minds. Almost 80 years later a neighbouring distillery was built and named Pittyvaich. It was almost a copy of Dufftown but was later forced to close and has now been demolished. The only official bottling of Dufftown used to be the *15 year old* in the Flora & Fauna series. In 2006, however, Diageo launched a special duty free version called *Singleton of Dufftown* (cf. Singleton of Glen Ord that appeared just before). Compared to the 15 year old, Singleton contains a larger share of ex-sherry European oak casks. Independent bottlings turn up now and then. A couple of the most recent are a 30 year old from 1977 by Douglas Laing and a Zinfandel finish from 1997 by Murray McDavid.

The Singleton of Dufftown

Edradour

Owner:
Signatory Vintage
Scotch Whisky Co. Ltd

Region/district:
Eastern Highlands

Founded: 1825

Status: Active (vc)

Visitor centre: 90 000 litres

Address: Pitlochry, Perthshire PH16 5JP

Tel: 01796 472095

website: www.edradour.com

History:

1825 – This is probably the year when a distillery called Glenforres is founded by farmers in Perthshire.

1837 – The first year Edradour is mentioned.

1841 – The farmers form a proprietary company, John MacGlashan & Co.

1886 – The American company J. G. Turney & Sons acquires Edradour through its subsidiary William Whitely & Co.

1922 – William Whiteley buys the distillery in order to produce its own blended whiskies, among them King's Ransom and House of Lords. The distillery is renamed Glenforres-Glenlivet.

1975 – Pernod Ricard buys Campbell Distilleries.

1982 – Campbell Distilleries (Pernod Ricard) buys Edradour and builds a visitors' centre.

1986 – Edradour's first single malt (10 years) is released.

2002 – Edradour is bought by Andrew Symington from Signatory Vintage Scotch Whisky for £5.4 million (£3 million consists of stocks). The product range is expanded in autumn with a 10 year old and a 13 year old cask strength. Iain Henderson, Distillery Manager at Laphroaig, becomes Director of Operations at Edradour.

2003 – A 30 year old and a 10 year old that are non chill-filtered are released. As an experiment a heavily peated variety (50ppm) is also distilled.

2004 – A number of wood finishes (port, sauternes, burgundy and chardonnay) are launched as cask strength.

2006 – James McGowan becomes the new distillery manager. The first bottling of peated Ballechin is released.

2007 – A Madeira matured Ballechin is released.

2008 – A Ballechin matured in port pipes and a 10 year old Edradour with a Sauternes finish are released.

Edradour distillery produces 90,000 litres every year which is considerably less than a major distillery produces in a week. But this does not trouble the owners, the independent bottler Signatory. On the contrary, its craftman-like production and small size helps it to be one of the most visited distilleries in Scotland with around 90,000 visitors travelling to it each year. Andrew Symington, the owner of Signatory Vintage Scotch Whisky, acquired Edradour from Pernod Ricard in July 2002. Today with all the visitors, the distillery is responsible for 80% of the profits in the group. When Pernod Ricard owned the distillery, three quarters of the production went into different blended whiskies, e. g. House of Lords and Clan Campbell. Today all of it is reserved for single malts. Edradour operates an open cast iron mash tun, two Oregon pine washbacks and one pair of stills. In 2007/2008 the Signatory operations moved from Edinburgh to Edradour after a new bottling plant and a bonded warehouse were built on the premises.

The core expression is the *10 year old*. A large number of single casks, vintages and wood finishes have been released in addition to this. A series of wood finishes in 50 cl bottles was commenced in 2004. Most have been around 10-11 years but older versions have also been launched.

The most recent was a *10 year old* from 1997 with a *Sauternes finish*. Older versions have also been released earlier; *1985 Ch d`Yquem, 1983 Pedro Ximinez* and *1983 Port*. Another release for 2008 was a *single sherry cask from 1994* bottled in a decanter.

An exciting experiment, inspired by Iain Henderson, the former distillery manager, commenced in 2003 with the first distilling of a heavily peated (no less than 50 ppm) malt. The first bottling of *Ballechin*, as it is called, appeared on the market in 2006. It was fully matured for 3 years and 5 months in a red *burgundy* cask. The next expression was a *Madeira-matured* in 2007 and in May 2008 came the third, matured in *port pipes* for almost six years. The idea is to launch one new expression every year until it reaches 10 years.

10 years old

Edradour 10 year old

DR – Delightful mix of citrus lime fruits and gentle spearmint on the nose, soft fruits, honey, vanilla and gentle peat with a lingering and pleasant finish.

DS – Scented soap with dried fruit and mothballs on the nose. Thick and sweet with a soap sud taste mixed with sherry and fruit flavours on the finish.

Fettercairn

Owner:
Whyte & Mackay Ltd
(United Spirits)

Region/district:
Eastern Highlands

Founded: **Status:** **Capacity:**
1824 Active (vc) 2 300 000 litres

Address: Fettercairn, Laurencekirk,
Kincardineshire AB30 1YB

Tel: **website:**
01561 340205 www.whyteandmackay.co.uk

History:

1824 – Sir Alexander Ramsay, owner of Fasque Estate, founds the distillery.

1825 – The first licensee is James Stewart & Co.

1830 – Sir Alexander Ramsay sells Fasque Estate and the distillery to Sir John Gladstone.

1887 – A fire erupts and the distillery is forced to close for repairs.

1890 – Thomas Gladstone dies and his son John Robert takes over. The distillery reopens after the fire.

1912 – The company is close to liquidation and John Gladstone buys out the other investors.

1926 –The distillery is mothballed.

1939 – The distillery is bought by Associated Scottish Distillers Ltd. Production restarts.

1960 – The maltings discontinues.

1966 – The stills are increased from two to four.

1971 – The distillery is bought by Tomintoul-Glenlivet Distillery Co. Ltd owned by W. & S. Strong & Co. and Hay & McLeod & Co.

1973 – Tomintoul-Glenlivet Distillery Co. Ltd is bought by Whyte & Mackay Distillers Ltd.

1974 – The mega group of companies Lonrho buys Whyte & Mackay.

1988 – Lonrho sells to Brent Walker Group plc.

1989 – A visitor centre opens.

1990 – American Brands Inc. buys Whyte & Mackay for £160 million.

1996 – Whyte & Mackay and Jim Beam Brands merge to become JBB Worldwide.

2001 – Kyndal Spirits, a company formed by managers at Whyte & Mackay, buys Whyte & Mackay from JBB Worldwide.

2002 – The whisky undergoes a major makeover including new bottle, new packaging and the name which is changed from Old Fettercairn to Fettercairn 1824.

2003 – Kyndal Spirits changes name to Whyte & Mackay.

2007 – United Spirits buys Whyte & Mackay. A 23 year old single cask is released.

Of the four malt distilleries owned by Whyte & Mackay, there are two which are much less famous, namely Tamnavulin and Fettercairn. The latter is situated between Dundee and Aberdeen, in a part of Scotland with few distilleries, and only has Glencadam as its neighbour. The founder of the distillery, Alexander Ramsay, had 15 years earlier built Fasque house which is situated close to the distillery. Ramsay had to make over both distillery and estate to John Gladstone already in 1830 due to financial difficulties. John Gladstone was the father of William Gladstone who eventually became Prime Minister and Fasque house belonged to the Gladstone family until late 2007 when it was put up for sale.

Fettercairn distillery is equipped with a mash tun made of cast iron, eight washbacks made of Douglas fir and two pairs of stills. One feature makes it unique among Scottish distilleries: cooling water is allowed to trickle along the spirit still necks and is collected at the base for circulation towards the top again in order to increase reflux and thereby produce a lighter and cleaner spirit. A similar installation can be found at Dalmore distillery but each spirit still has a water jacket which circulates cold water between the reflux bowl and the neck of the stills. It is difficult to ascertain which distillery was first with this innovation, but according to Drew Sinclair, ex manager of Dalmore, they inspired Fettercairn.

The core range of Fettercairn simply consists of a *12 year old*. Some older, limited versions exist such as *Stillmans Dram 26* and *30 years* respectively. There are also two casks of *15 year old* Fettercairn that visitors can bottle when visiting the distillery.

Independent bottlings are very rare but turn up occasionally. Scott's Selection 1989, Douglas Laing 1991 (13 years) and a 25 year old Part Nan Angelen (Swedish Vin & Sprit) released in 2003 are among the more recent.

Fettercairn 1824 12 year old

DR – The nose is quite light, and honeyed, the palate oily, artichoke, nutty and with some clean barley. The finish is short with a hint of ginger.

DS – A spicy, malty and woody nose overshadowed by a sweeter, malty palate. There is oakiness in the finish which is short but pleasantly nutty.

12 years old

Glenallachie

Owner:
Chivas Brothers
(Pernod Ricard)

Region/district:
Speyside

Founded: 1967
Status: Active
Capacity: 3 000 000 litres

Address: Aberlour, Banffshire AB38 9LR

Tel: 01542 783042
website: -

History:
1967 – The distillery is founded by Mackinlay, McPherson & Co. a subsidiary of Scottish & Newcastle Breweries Ltd. William Delmé Evans is architect.

1985 – Scottish & Newcastle Breweries Ltd sells Charles Mackinlay Ltd to Invergordon Distillers which acquires both Glenallachie and Isle of Jura.

1987 – The distillery is decommisioned.

1989 – Campbell Distillers (Pernod Ricard) buys the distillery, increases the number of stills from two to four and takes up production again.

2005 – The first official bottling for many years becomes a Cask Strength Edition from 1989.

Glenallachie 16 year old 56,7%

DS – Intense sherry with raisins and brown sugar on the nose. The palate is powerful with sherry and coffee liqueur flavours. Long finish with a coffee aftertaste.

Just outside Aberlour in the shadow of Ben Rinnes, from where the distillery obtains its water, lays Glenallachie. It is constructed by the famous architect William Delmé Evans with the purpose of functioning as a gravity fed distillery. This means that a flow of liquids run naturally through the distillery at different levels as opposed to requiring pump action. Delmé Evans had plans for such a distillery already in 1940 but it took until 1967 before he could realise them.

The distillery, with a semi-lauter mash tun, six stainless steel washbacks and two pairs of stills, has five employees and is operating at full capacity which equals an annual production of three million litres of alcohol. The spirit is filled into bourbon casks and matured in 12 racked and two palletised warehouses. Until a few years ago, Glenallachie was unique in Scotland for using so called Ramsden heaters for their wash stills. They were large single copper pans with copper steam coils though they have now been replaced by steam pans and stainless steel radiators.

Wastewater treatment is increasingly becoming an issue to distillery owners in Scotland and large sums are invested annually in new systems. A new plant from German Wehrle Umwelt GmbH was tested at Glenallachie in summer 2007. The trial runs were successful and a Membrane Bioreactor, integrated with the distillery's earlier equipment, which can handle 144 m^3 of wastewater per day, is now installed.

Currently the only official bottling is a *16 year old cask strength* matured in first fill oloroso casks and released in 2005. Independent bottlings have also been scarce even if single versions have appeared in the Netherlands and Germany. Duncan Taylor recently released a bottling distilled in 1995 and Balmoral Hotel in Edinburgh launched a 12 year old Glenallachie as their own single malt in 2004.

1989 16 years old

Glenburgie

Owner:		Region/district:
Chivas Brothers (Pernod Ricard)		Speyside

Founded:	Status:	Capacity:
1810	Active	4 200 000 litres

Address: Glenburgie, Forres, Morayshire IV36 2QY

Tel:	website:
01343 850258	-

History:

1810 – William Paul founds Kilnflat Distillery. Official production starts in 1829.

1870 – Kilnflat distillery closes.

1878 – The distillery reopens under the name Glenburgie-Glenlivet, Charles Hay is licensee.

1884 – Alexander Fraser & Co. takes over.

1925 – Alexander Fraser & Co. goes bankrupt and the receiver Donald Mustad assumes control of operations.

1927 – James & George Stodart Ltd buys the distillery which by this time is inactive.

1930 – Hiram Walker buys 60% of James & George Stodart Ltd.

1936 – Hiram Walker buys Glenburgie Distillery in October. Production restarts.

1958 – Lomond stills are installed producing a single malt, Glencraig. Floor malting ceases.

1981 – The Lomond stills are replaced by conventional stills.

1987 – Allied Lyons buys Hiram Walker.

2002 – A 15 year old is released.

2004 – A £4.3 million refurbishment and reconstruction takes place.

2005 – Chivas Brothers (Pernod Ricard) become new owners through the acquisition of Allied Domecq.

2006 – The number of stills are increased from four to six in May.

Glenburgie 10 year old G&M

DR – Classic sherry, barley and prickly wood on the nose, sweet and gentle red berry on the palate, and a warming mouth-filling soft and pleasant finish.

DS – Rich with raisins and sherry notes on the nose. Hint of burnt rubber. Again sweet and slightly sulphury. Raisins and fruit-cake on the finish.

Glenburgie distillery lies a few kilometres from the main road between Elgin and Forres. A few years ago it was a rather antiquated distillery with a capacity of only 2 million litres, but now it is on the cutting edge when it comes to production and technology. It all started in autumn 2003 when former owners Allied Domecq invested £4.3 million on refurbishment which included a new lauter mashtun and twelve stainless steel wash backs. At the same time space for two new stills was made but none were installed at that time. In combination with shorter fermentation time, the capacity suddenly increased to 2.8 million litres. Pernod Ricard took over in 2005 and the year after two new stills increased the capacity to more than 4 million litres which makes it the third biggest in the group after Glenlivet and Miltonduff. This capacity enhancement is necessary as Glenburgie is one of the most important ingredients in the Ballantine blend.

After several years of standstill, it seems that Ballantines is now on the move again. Pushed by a giant marketing campaign launched by Pernod Ricard last year, sales of Ballantines grew 22% during 2007 to 5.9 million cases and second place was taken from J & B.

With a little luck a single malt from Glenburgie named Glencraig can still be found on the market. It came into being by Hiram Walker's experimenting with Lomond stills in the fifties. Glenburgie's first Lomond still was a small model, originating in Dumbarton. It was replaced in 1958 by a pair of full-size Lomond stills and it is the make from these stills that received the name Glencraig.

A new version of the *15 year old cask strength* Glenburgie appeared in early 2008. Independent bottlings are rare. One recent is a Duncan Taylor from 1996.

Gordon & MacPhail Glenburgie 10 years old

Glencadam

Owner:
Angus Dundee Distillers

Region/district:
Eastern Highlands

Founded: 1825
Status: Active
Capacity: 1 400 000 litres

Address: Brechin, Angus DD9 7PA

Tel: 01356 622217
website: www.angusdundee.co.uk

History:

1825 – George Cooper founds the distillery.

1827 – David Scott takes over.

1837 – The distillery is sold by David Scott.

1852 – Alexander Miln Thompson becomes the owner.

1857 – Glencadam Distillery Company is formed.

1891 – The blending company Gilmour, Thompson & Co Ltd takes over.

1954 – Hiram Walker takes over.

1959 – Refurbishing and modernization of the distillery.

1987 – Allied Lyons buys Hiram Walker Gooderham & Worts.

1994 – Allied Lyons changes name to Allied Domecq.

2000 – The distillery is mothballed.

2003 – Allied Domecq sells the distillery to Angus Dundee Distillers.

2005 – The new owner releases a 15 year old.

2008 – A re-designed 15 year old and a new 10 year old are introduced.

Glencadam 15 year old

DR – Very delicate nose with pineapple notes, with water a touch of grapefruit and wispy smoke. On the palate exotic fruits, cocoa powder, pineapple and a touch of smoke. The finish is attractive, full and warming.

DS – A rich and herbal nose with vanilla and fudge. The palate is full of toffee and caramel flavours and the finish is rich and sweet.

GRIST MILL

Glencadam was the second distillery that London-based Angus Dundee Distillers bought after Tomintoul which they acquired from Whyte & Mackay three years previously. While Tomintoul lies in a remote part of the Highlands, Glencadam has a more urban location just outside the medieval town of Brechin, 35 kilometres northeast of Dundee. Brechin, today with a population of 7,000, used to be a seat of religion and learning with a 13th century cathedral.

The distillery had been mothballed for three years but was in perfect condition and when Allied closed it they took care to do it so that a quick restart would be possible. The stills were running two months after Angus Dundee´s acquisition and Brechin once again had a functioning whisky distillery (North Port was closed permanently in 1983 and was replaced by a supermarket.)

Glencadam operates at full capacity (1.4 million litres) and uses a stainless steel mash tun, six stainless steel washbacks and one pair of stills. The wash still is heated by an external heat exchanger (employing the same technique as Glenburgie and Miltonduff) while the spirit still uses a steam kettle. The lye pipes of both stills ascend 15 degrees adding to the reflux and giving a light and mellow spirit. Maturation takes place in bourbon casks and there are nine dunnage warehouses and two racked on the site. A large blending centre was completed in October 2006 to cater for the owner's range of blended whiskies and the centre has recently (June 2008) been extended.

An eagerly awaited official bottling of Glencadam from the new owners appeared in 2005 when a 15 year old was released. In November 2008 the package of the 15 year old was re-designed but also the whisky itself. It is now bottled at 46% without chill-filtration. And while they were at it, the owners also introduced a brand new expression, the 10 year old.

10 years old

Glendronach

Owner:
Benriach Distillery Co

Region/district:
Speyside

Founded: 1826
Status: Active (vc)
Capacity: 1 300 000 litres

Address: Forgue, Aberdeenshire AB54 6DB

Tel: 01466 730202
website: -

History:
1826 – The distillery is founded by a consortium. James Allardes is one of the owners.

1837 – The major part of the distillery is destroyed in a fire.

1852 – Walter Scott (from Teaninich) takes over.

1887 – Walter Scott dies and Glendronach is taken over by a consortium from Leith.

1920 – Charles Grant, son of the founder of Glenfiddich Distillery, William Grant, buys Glendronach for £9 000 and starts production three months later.

1960 – William Teacher & Sons buys the distillery.

1966-67 – The number of stills is increased from two to four.

1976 – A visitor centre is opened.

1976 – Allied Breweries takes over William Teacher & Sons.

1991 – Glendronach is one of a select few in Caledonian Malts, launched by Allied Distillers.

1996 – The distillery is mothballed.

2002 – Production is resumed on 14th May.

2005 – Glendronach 33 years old is launched. The distillery closes for six months to rebuild from coal to indirect firing by steam. Reopens in September. Chivas Brothers (Pernod Ricard) becomes new owner through the acquisition of Allied Domecq.

2008 – Pernod Ricard sells the distillery to the owners of BenRiach distillery.

Glendronach Original 12 year old

DR – Full blood orange and tangerine nose with a smoky underlay on the nose and sweet peat wrapped a winey barley centre and a surprisingly soft and fruity finish to conclude a tour de force of a whisky.

DS – Grassy, earthy and crème fraiche on the nose. Sweet and soft and creamy on the palate – liqueurish and slightly spicy in the warming finish.

The recent speculations over Pernod Ricard's true intentions with Glendronach ended in summer 2008 when it was announced that it was up for sale. Whilst the average capacity for a distillery in the Pernod Ricard group is 3.5 million litres, Glendronach plays in a totally different league at around 1 million litres. Nor is this a brand with a high profile but rather competing with dozens of other Speysiders instead. Independent bottler Duncan Taylor was interested in Glendronach a couple of years ago, but the owners of BenRiach Distillery headed by Billy Walker became the final buyers. The price is estimated at around £15 million.

The mash tun at Glendronach is a cast iron traditional infusion version. There are eight washbacks made of Oregon pine and two pairs of stills. There is a special venting system for extraction of carbon dioxide in the washbacks. Maturation takes place in both dunnage and racked warehouses. There are also malting floors that are still intact although they have not been in use since 1996. Glendronach was the last Scottish distillery to fire the stills with coal. This old process continued until September 2005 when indirect heating using steam coils replaced it. Whisky from the coal-fired stills will be available for another 10 years or so and it remains to be seen how the character of the whisky will have changed by then. Although known for maturing predominantly in sherry casks, since reopening in 2002 the whole production has been on bourbon casks so it is quite possible that character changes may be accentuated as the years pass.

Glendronach has been a vital part of the Teachers blend since the late 19th century but with Pernod Ricard as new owners it has increasingly been part of Chivas Regal and, to some extent, Ballantines.

The official bottling is *Original 12 years Double Matured* with 12 years on sherry butts but with a final finish of 6 months on bourbon casks. Recent limited editions have included a *33 year old* and a *Vintage 1968*. Independent bottlings of Glendronach are almost impossible to find.

Original 12 years old

Glendullan

Owner:
Diageo

Region/district:
Speyside

Founded: 1897

Status: Active

Capacity: 3 360 000 litres

Address: Dufftown, Keith, Banffshire AB55 4DJ

Tel: 01340 822100

website: www.malts.com

History:

1896-97 – William Williams & Sons, a blending company with Three Stars and Strahdon among their brands, founds the distillery.

1902 – Glendullan is delivered to the Royal Court and becomes the favourite whisky of Edward VII.

1919 – Macdonald Greenlees buys a share of the company and Macdonald Greenlees & Williams Distillers is formed.

1926 – Distillers Company Limited (DCL) buys Glendullan.

1930 – Glendullan is transferred to Scottish Malt Distillers (SMD).

1962 – Major refurbishing and reconstruction.

1972 – A brand new distillery, accommodating six stills, is constructed next to the old one and both operate simultaneously during a few years.

1985 – The oldest of the two distilleries is mothballed.

1995 – The first launch of Glendullan in the Rare Malts series becomes a 22 year old from 1972.

2005 – A 26 year old from 1978 is launched in the Rare Malts series.

2007 – Singleton of Glendullan is launched in USA.

Glendullan 12 year old

DR – The nose has a mix of fruits including grapefruit melon and even banana, the taste is more-ish, with the citrus and melon notes coming through. Warm and pleasant finish.

DS – Strong sherry notes on the nose with prune juice and oak. The palate is sweet with strong sherry flavours and malty. A fine finish with some oakiness in the aftertaste.

Even though they are number 1 in the spirits business, Diageo cannot afford to market all of their brands globally. Especially with 27 distilleries in their portfolio, the costs would simply be too large. This is why three of the more obscure varieties were selected and launched as 12 year olds under the name Singleton. All were targeted with their own market in mind - Glen Ord for Asia, Dufftown for Europe (mainly duty free) and the last one to be released was Singleton of Glendullan. This was meant to become Diageo´s treat for the US whisky enthusiasts and was test-launched in April 2007 in Chicago and New Jersey. After one year and much praise it was rolled out across the country in spring 2008.

Glendullan is one of the largest distilleries in the Diageo group with one stainless steel mash tun, eight washbacks made of larch and three pairs of stills. It is one of the original seven distilleries of Dufftown and the last of them to open. However the distillery that opened in 1896 is not the one distilling today; a new Glendullan was built in 1972 next to the old one. The two were operated in parallel for a few years until 1985 when the old distillery closed. It is now used as a workshop for Diageo´s a malt distillery engineering team. The old distillery was equipped with one pair of stills with a capacity of 1 million litres a year. During the 13 years when they were both distilling, the whisky from the two was vatted together before bottling.

The core range consists of the *12 year old* in the Distillery Malts (Flora & Fauna) series and the recently released *Singleton of Glendullan* for the US market.

Independent bottlings are rare. The latest is a 1993 Rioja finish from Murray McDavid but a couple of bottlings from Douglas Laing a few years ago are worth naming. They are interesting as they were distilled in the old still house in the early 1970s.

The old distillery

The Singleton of Glendullan

Glen Elgin

Owner:		Region/district:
Diageo		Speyside

Founded:	Status:	Capacity:
1898	Active	1 830 000 litres

Address: Longmorn, Morayshire IV30 3SL

Tel:	website:
01343 862100	www.malts.com

History:
1898 – The bankers William Simpson (former manager of Glenfarclas distillery) and James Carle found Glen Elgin. The famous Charles Doig is called in as architect.

1900 – Production starts in May but the distillery closes just five months later.

1901 – In February, the distillery is auctioned for £4,000 to the Glen Elgin-Glenlivet Distillery Co. and is mothballed.

1904 – Production restarts.

1905 – Production ceases.

1906 – The wine producer J. J. Blanche & Co. buys the distillery for £7,000 and production resumes.

1929 – J. J. Blanche dies and the distillery is put up for sale again.

1930 – Scottish Malt Distillers (SMD) buys it and the license goes to White Horse Distillers.

1964 – Expansion from two to six stills plus other refurbishing takes place.

1992 – The distillery closes for refurbishing and installation of new stills.

1995 – Production resumes in September.

2001 – A 12 year old is launched in the Flora & Fauna series.

2002 – The Flora & Fauna series malt is replaced by a Hidden Malt 12 years.

2003 – A 32 year old cask strength from 1971 is released.

2008 – A 16 year old is launched as a Special Release.

Glen Elgin 12 year old

DR – Ginger, crystallised barley sweet and a complex array of fruit on the nose, a beautiful balanced taste with light fruit, sweet spice and a zesty freshness and mouth filling finish.

DS – Soft honey, heather and malt on the nose with some fruitiness. The palate is much sweeter and quite delicate. An appealing finish with honey lozenge in the aftertaste.

Just a few miles south of Elgin along the A941 lies the small village of Fogwatt. It takes a mere minute to drive through it which is why it is easy to miss Glen Elgin distillery which also happens to lie in a side street. The whisky blenders have, however, never overlooked the whisky from Glen Elgin. They have always considered it to be top class and the main part of production has always found its way into various blended whiskies, especially White Horse. This classic brand from the end of the 1800s has entered into a downward spiral in recent years and fallen from place 14 to 21 on the sales list, despite still selling almost nine million bottles per year.

The distillery is equipped with a Steinecker full lauter mash tun, six washbacks made of larch and three pairs of rather small stills. It practises a balanced distillation meaning that each wash back provides six individual charges for the wash stills. It then takes two distillations in a wash still to charge one spirit still which ends up in one of three low wines & feints receiver. This means that in one shift nine separate still charges have to be managed. Spirit from the new production is stored at Glenlossie and Auchroisk while the older production is stored in dunnage warehouses on site. Despite its small size, it has a great capacity for storing malted barley. The 36 malt bins hold 400 tonnes, more than the three other distilleries in the Elgin group (Glenlossie, Linkwood, Mannochmore) hold together.

In 2001 Glen Elgin was launched as a part of the Flora & Fauna series but was replaced the year after by a new *12 year old* in what was then called "Hidden Malts". Three limited editions have also been released – a *19 year old* in 2000, a *32 year old* in 2003 and finally a *16 year old* was launched in autumn 2008.

Recent independent bottlings include a 16 year old from 1991 released by Douglas Laing.

16 years old

Glenfarclas

Owner:
J. & G. Grant

Region/district:
Speyside

Founded: 1836
Status: Active (vc)
Capacity: 3 000 000 litres

Address: Ballindalloch, Banffshire AB37 9BD

Tel: 01807 500257
website: www.glenfarclas.co.uk

History:

1836 – Robert Hay founds the distillery on the original site since 1797.

1865 – Robert Hay passes away and John Grant and his son George buy the distillery for £511.19s on 8th June. They lease it to John Smith at The Glenlivet Distillery.

1870 – John Smith resigns in order to start Cragganmore and J. & G. Grant Ltd takes over.

1889 – John Grant dies and George Grant takes over.

1890 – George Grant dies and his widow Barbara takes over the license while sons John and George control operations.

1895 – John and George Grant take over and form The Glenfarclas-Glenlivet Distillery Co. Ltd with the infamous Pattison, Elder & Co.

1898 – Pattison becomes bankrupt. Glenfarclas encounters financial problems after a major overhaul of the distillery but survives by mortgaging and selling stored whisky to R. I. Cameron, a whisky broker from Elgin.

Glenfarclas is the second oldest family-owned malt distillery in Scotland and the Grant family has followed a conscious line since 1865 saying no to wood finishes, restricting sales to independent bottlers and preferring sherry butts for maturation despite the tenfold higher price for these rather than bourbon casks.

The distillery is equipped with a semi-lauter mash tun which measures ten metres in diameter, twelve stainless steel washbacks and three pairs of stills. There are 28 dunnage warehouses on site which hold 52,000 casks. All the stills at Glenfarclas are directly fired by North Sea gas, which is rather unusual. The risk with directly heated stills is that solid particles sink to the bottom where they burn, stick and risk adding unwanted flavour to the whisky. In order to prevent this from happening a device called a rummager is used on the wash stills. It is a kind of copper chain which rotates at the bottom of the still. Glenfarclas' production has increased during 2008 and the silent season was also busy when a new yeast tank and a new pot ale evaporator tank were installed and the shoulders of two of the stills replaced.

Glenfarclas was one of the first distilleries to open a visitor centre. "The Ship's Room", where each tour is ended with a dram is unique and very beautiful. The decorations were taken from an ocean liner, the "Empress of Australia" which had a colourful history from 1913 to 1952.

Glenfarclas have a number of expressions in their core range; *10, 12, 15, 21, 25* and *30 years old*. Furthermore, there is *Glenfarclas 105*, one of the first cask strength in the business and limited editions of *40* and *50 years old*. A limited edition of the 105 is due for release soon and this time it is a *40 year old*. 105 in the name relates to the old way of measuring spirit strength called proof which was abandoned in Europe in 1980 and replaced by today's system; percentage of alcohol. 105 is 5 overproof indicating a strength of 60%.

Last year, Glenfarclas presented a unique collection of bottlings called *Family Casks*. No less than 43 single casks from 43 different years were launched at once. To add to the uniqueness it turned out that this was an unbroken series of vintages from 1952 to 1994. Some of these have now sold out and in spring 2008 new bottlings were released from some of the years (1952, 1957, 1960, 1967 and 1969) and a third release is already planned for (1959, 1961, 1962, 1978, 1979 and 1987).

History (continued):

1914 – John Grant leaves due to ill health and George continues alone.

1948 – The Grant family celebrates the distillery's 100th anniversary, a century of active licensing. It is 9 years late, as the actual anniversary coincided with WW2.

1949 – George Grant senior dies and sons George Scott and John Peter inherit the distillery.

1960 – Stills are increased from two to four.

1968 – Glenfarclas is first to launch a cask-strength single malt. It is later named Glenfarclas 105.

1972 – Floor maltings is abandoned and malt is purchased centrally.

1973 – A visitor centre is opened.

1976 – Enlargement from four stills to six.

2001 – Glenfarclas launches its first Flower of Scotland gift tin which becomes a great success and increases sales by 30%.

2002 – George S Grant dies and is succeeded as company chairman by his son John L S Grant

2003 – Two new gift tins are released (10 years old and 105 cask strength).

2005 – A 50 year old is released to commemorate the bi-centenary of John Grant's birth.

2006 – Ten new vintages are released.

2007 – Family Casks, a series of single cask bottlings from 43 consecutive years, is released.

2008 – New releases in the Family Cask range. Glenfarclas 105 40 years old is released.

12 years old

105 Cask Strength

Glenfarclas 10 year old

DR – Creamy sherry and bitter oranges on the nose, rich fruit cake and red berries on the palate with a pleasant spice and barley interplay and long and warming finish.

DS – Lots of malt and sherry notes on the nose that continue on the palate with an added creaminess – full bodied. The finish is long and sweet.

The Family Casks 1969

10 years old

The Family Casks 1952

Glenfiddich

Owner:
William Grant & Sons

Region/district:
Speyside

Founded: 1886

Status: Active (vc)

Capacity: 10 000 000 litres

Address: Dufftown, Keith, Banffshire AB55 4DH

Tel:
01340 820373 (vc)

website:
www.glenfiddich.com

History:

1886 – The distillery is founded by William Grant, 47 years old, who had learned the trade at Mortlach Distillery. The equipment is bought from Mrs. Cummings of Cardow Distillery. The construction totals £800.

1887 – The first distilling takes place on Christmas Day.

1892 – William Grant builds Balvenie.

1898 – The blending company Pattisons, largest customer to Glenfiddich, files for bankruptcy and Grant decides to blend their own whisky. Standfast becomes one of their major brands.

1903 – William Grant & Sons is formed.

1957 – The famous, three-cornered bottle is introduced.

1958 – The floor maltings is closed.

1963 – Glennfiddich becomes the first whisky to be marketed as single malt in the UK and the rest of the world.

1964 – A version of Standfast's three-cornered bottle is launched for Glenfiddich in green glass.

1969 – Glenfiddich becomes the first distillery in Scotland to open a visitor centre.

1974 – 16 new stills are installed.

2001 – 1965 Vintage Reserve is launched in a limited edition of 480 bottles. Glenfiddich 1937 is bottled (61 bottles).

In 2007 a campaign was launched that would make Glenfiddich the first single malt ever to reach one million cases sold in a year. The campaign, with a budget of £23 million was called "Every year counts" and the goal was meant to be achieved in 18 months. During 2007, 927,000 cases were sold and it remains to be seen if the goal will be achieved at the end of 2008. Everything at Glenfiddich is huge; two large full lauter mash tuns, at least 24 washbacks made of Douglas Fir (six new were installed in 2008, some of them to replace older ones), one still house with five wash stills and eight spirit stills and a second with five wash stills and ten spirit stills. The casks are stored in 43 warehouses – dunnage, racked and palletised – which can accommodate in total 800,000 casks! Add on top of this in-house cooperage, coppersmiths and bottling line. The only on-site facility missing is maltings but some of the malted barley produced at sister distillery Balvenie is used.

The Glenfiddich single malt is not the only mega brand of William Grant & Sons. They also hold fifth place on the list of most sold blended Scotch - Grant's. This famous whisky has seen a steady increase the last decade and in order to secure malt whisky for future blending as well as freeing up Glenfiddich and Balvenie for branded single malt, the owners set up a new distillery in record time at their huge grain distillery complex at Girvan. The £10 million investment was announced in spring 2007 and in October the first spirit was distilled at Ailsa Bay distillery. The new distillery has four pairs of stills and they are now looking to increase warehouse capacity as well. The most recent malt whisky was produced at Girvan back in 1975 when Ladyburn distillery closed.

Glenfiddich's core range consists of *Special Reserve 12 years*, *Caoran Reserve 12 years*, *Solera Reserve 15 years*, *Ancient Reserve 18 years*, *Gran Reserva 21 years* and *Glenfiddich 30 years old*. Recent limited bottlings include *Glenfiddich Private Vintage 1973* (177 bottles) launched at Heathrow's Terminal 5 in March 2008. Another is a new vatting (the fifth since 2000) of the *40 year old* (600 bottles) in honour of whisky writer Michael Jackson, who passed away in 2007. Finally this year's *Vintage Reserve*, a sherry cask from 1977, was released in October.

History (continued):

2002 – Glenfiddich Gran Reserva 21 years old, finished in Cuban rum casks is launched. Sales in the US are not possible due to the trade embargo between the US and Cuba. Caoran Reserve 12 years, an attempt to recreate the peaty Glenfiddich produced during the war years, is launched. Glenfiddich Rare Collection 1937 (61 bottles) is launched at a recommended price of £10,000 each and becomes the oldest Scotch whisky on the market.

2003 – 1973 Vintage Reserve (440 bottles) is launched.

2004 – 1991 Vintage Reserve (13 years) and 1972 Vintage Reserve (519 bottles) are launched.

2005 – Circa £1.7 million is invested in a new visitor centre.

2006 – 1973 Vintage Reserve, 33 years (861 bottles) and 12 year old Toasted Oak are released.

2007 – 1976 Vintage Reserve, 31 years is released in September.

2008 – 1977 Vintage Reserve is released.

Glenfiddich Special Reserve 12 year old

DR – Classic rich fruit and peerless clean barley nose, fruit bowl and sharp malt palate and pleasant and warming lengthy finish.

DS – A green nose with sweet heather honey notes. The palate is wave upon wave of soft honey and a hint of spice. A short and bittersweet finish.

Solera Reserve 15 years old   Ancient Reserve 18 years old   Glenfiddich 30 years old

Special Reserve 12 years old   Caoran Reserve 12 years old   1977 Vintage Reserve

Glen Garioch

Owner:
Morrison Bowmore
(Suntory)

Region/district:
Eastern Highlands

Founded: 1797
Status: Active (vc)
Capacity: 1 000 000 litres

Address: Oldmeldrum, Inverurie,
Aberdeenshire AB51 0ES

Tel: 01651 873450
website: www.glengarioch.com

History:

1797 – The distiller Thomas Simpson founds Glen Garioch.

1837 – The distillery is bought by John Manson & Co., owner of Strathmeldrum Distillery.

1884 – The distillery is bought by J. G. Thompson.

1908 – Glengarioch Distillery Company, owned by William Sanderson, buys the distillery.

1933 – Sanderson & Son merges with the gin maker Booth's Distilleries Ltd.

1937 – Booth's Distilleries Ltd is acquired by Distillers Company Limited (DCL).

1943 – Glen Garioch is transferred to Scottish Malt Distillers (SMD).

1968 – Glen Garioch is decommissioned.

1970 – Sold to Stanley P. Morrison Ltd.

1973 – Reconstruction and production starts again. A more peaty whisky is produced.

1978 – Stills are increased from two to four.

1982 – Becomes the first distillery to use gas from the North Sea for heating.

1994 – Suntory controls all of Morrison Bowmore Distillers Ltd.

1995 – The distillery is mothballed in October.

1997 – The distillery reopens in August.

2004 – 336 bottles of the oldest ever Glen Garioch is released, a 46 year old from 1958.

2005 – 15 year old Bordeaux Cask Finish is launched. A visitor centre opens in October.

2006 – An 8 year old is released.

Glen Garioch 12 year old

DR – Fresh clean and fruity on the nose, and a pleasant mix of clean malt and rich berry fruits on the palate. The finish is short but more-ish.

DS – Sherry and malt with herbal notes on the nose. Sweet and chewy with a bittersweet, burnt rubber flavour and a herbal finish.

Glen Garioch was an important ingredient in VAT69 in the early 20th century, the famous blend that was born already in 1882. The brand had been established by William Sanderson and his company also held a 50% stake in Glen Garioch. The demand for his blended Scotch increased rapidly and in 1921 Sanderson persuaded his co-directors to buy the remaining 50% of the distillery, which they did, in spite of Prohibition in America which had begun the previous year. Sanderson thought it would not last long, which was a fatal misjudgement. Prohibition did not come to an end until 1933 by which time Sanderson was broke and had to sell his beloved distillery.

Glen Garioch belongs to a small but well composed group of distilleries representing the Highlands, Auchentoshan the Lowlands and Bowmore Islay. The distilleries are owned by Morrison Bowmore which in their turn have been owned by Japanese Suntory since 1995.

Glen Garioch is equipped with a full lauter mash tun, eight stainless steel washbacks and one pair of stills. The spirit is tankered to Glasgow, filled on casks and returned to be stored in the distillery´s four warehouses. Capacity is only 1 million litres but production has increased steadily during recent years and stands at 700,000 litres in 2008. The old cooperage was turned into a visitor centre in 2006. The malting floors have not been in use since 1979 though they are in perfect condition. The owners are explicitly interested in starting the maltings again but have not taken any firm decisions yet.

Around 250,000 bottles are sold each year with the majority of them going to Taiwan and Japan.

The core range consists of *8, 12, 15* and *21 years old*. The 8 year old was released in 2006 and marks the first bottling from the new production started in 1997. Limited editions include the *16 year old Bordeaux Cask Finish*, the rare *46 year old* from 1958 and *Highland Tradition* reserved for the duty free market. Recent independent bottlings include a 1988 from Duncan Taylor and a 12 year old from Douglas Laing.

15 years old

Glenglassaugh

Owner:
Glenglassaugh Distillery Co
(Scaent Group)

Region/district:
Speyside

Founded: **Status:** **Capacity:**
1875 Active 1 000 000 litres

Address: Portsoy, Banffshire AB45 2SQ

Tel: **website:**
- www.glenglassaugh.com

History:

1873-75 – The distillery is founded by Glenglassaugh Distillery Company. The total cost is £10,000.

1887 – Alexander Morrison embarks on renovation work including new stills and other equipment.

1892 – Alexander Morrison, the sole survivor of the original founders, sells the distillery to one of his customers, Robertson & Baxter. They in turn sell it on to Highland Distilleries Company for £15,000.

1908 – The distillery closes.

1931 – The distillery reopens.

1936 – The distillery closes.

1957-59 – Substantial reconstruction, including acquisition of new stills, takes place. Own maltings are abandoned and the malt is bought from Tamdhu Distillery instead.

1960 – The distillery reopens.

1986 – Glenglassaugh is mothballed in November.

2005 – A 22 year old is released.

2006 – Three limited editions are released - 19 years old, 38 years old and 44 years old.

2008 – The Distillery is bought by the Scaent Group for £5m.

Glenglassaugh 30 year old

DR – Rich orange and plum on the nose, after time sweet cocoa. Briefly fruit sherbet on the palate then rounded pineapple candy held together by a sharp oak and tannin burst. The finish is gentle, pleasant and fruity.

DS – Rich, stewed fruits (mandarins in syrup) on the nose. Sweet, fruity and spicy on the palate with a long aftertaste and fruity finish.

In February 2008 the number of mothballed distilleries in Scotland was reduced yet again by one when Edrington sold Glenglassaugh to the Scaent Group with its headquarter in Amsterdam. The Scaent Group, originally founded in Sweden in 2003, is primarily concerned with the energy market in 12 countries, but they have also diversified into real estate, publishing and telecommunications. Acquisition cost £5 million and with help from Barclays bank the buyers intend to invest another £2 million in bringing the distillery back to life. The plan is to start distilling already by the end of 2008 and to open up the distillery to visitors in the second quarter of 2009. Stuart Nickerson, who used to work at Highland Park, Glenfiddich and, in fact, Glenglassaugh was appointed Managing Director of Glenglassaugh Distillery Company. For the daily running of operations at the distillery, Graham Eunson, manager at Glenmorangie since 1998, has been chosen.

A number of releases from existing stocks (the first probably by the end of 2008) are planned with the help of the well-known author and whisky consultant Ian Buxton who will be developing the brand strategy. The distillery will have an annual capacity of 1 million litres.

The history of Glenglassaugh spans short periods of production interspersed with longer periods of inactivity. After the latest refurbishment, the distillery produced malt for the blending industry for 26 years before it was mothballed in 1986. The equipment consists of a cast iron mash tun, six stainless steel washbacks and one pair of stills.

The first official bottling since closure came in 1998 when Highland Distillers released a Glenglassaugh from *1973*. In 2005/2006 Edrington released four limited expressions - *19, 22, 38* and *44 year old*. Some of the more recent independent bottlings are from 2005 and include a 27 year old from Douglas Laing, a 38 year old from Signatory and a 40 year old from Murray McDavid.

*Gordon & MacPhail
Glenglassaugh 1986 (bottled 2000)*

Glengoyne

Owner:
Ian Macleod Distillers

Region/district:
Southern Highlands

Founded: 1833
Status: Active (vc)
Capacity: 1 100 000 litres

Address: Dumgoyne by Killearn,
Glasgow G63 9LB

Tel: 01360 550254 (vc)
website: www.glengoyne.com

History:

1833 – The distillery is licensed under the name Burnfoot Distilleries by the Edmonstone family.

1851 – George Connell is replaced as licensee by John MacLelland.

1867 – Archibald C. McLelland takes over.

1876 – Lang Brothers buys the distillery and changes the name to Glenguin.

1905 – The name changes to Glengoyne.

1910 – Own floor maltings ceases.

1965-66 – Robertson & Baxter takes over Lang Brothers and the distillery is refurbished. The stills are increased from two to three.

2001 – Glengoyne Scottish Oak Finish (16 years old) is launched as the first single malt stored in Scottish oak casks.

2003 – Ian MacLeod Distillers Ltd buys the distillery plus the brand Langs from the Edrington Group for £7.2 million.

2004 – A 12 year old cask strength is released.

2005 – Relaunch of Scottish Oak Finish (15 years old). Limited editions of a 19 year old, a 32 year old and a 37 year old cask strength are launched.

2006 – Nine "choices" from Stillmen, Mashmen and Manager are released. The 10 and 17 year olds are relaunched.

2007 – A new version of the 21 year old, two Warehousemen´s Choice, Vintage 1972 and two single casks are released.

2008 – A 16 year old shiraz cask finish and a 40 year old are released.

Glengoyne 10 year old

DR – Uncluttered crystal ginger barley on the nose, full clean and crisp malt on the palate, with a rich sorbet-clean finish. Sweet, full and pleasant.

DS – A spicy, heathery nose with brandy notes and a mild whiff of coconut. Soft and sweet on the palate with a hint of nutty flavours that continue into the bittersweet finish.

Glengoyne, owned by Ian Macleod Distillers, a family-owned blending and bottling company, is the southernmost of the Highland distilleries. In style though the malt reminisces more of a Lowland, fresh and clean although with a malty flavour. A reason for this could be that the stills are run very slowly. Glengoyne obtains 4-5 litres of spirit per minute compared to the 12-15 litres of many other distillerys.

The distillery is equipped with a traditional mash tun, six Oregon pine washbacks, one wash still and two spirit stills. It is possible that once Glengoyne practised triple distillation. It is also probable that the whisky produced during one period was smoked (possibly until the mid sixties) even if today it is unpeated and marketed as such. The reason we cannot be certain is that the company records were completely destroyed in a fire in the 1980s. Production has increased since 2007 and this year it will be around 960,000 litres. The spirit is stored in five dunnage warehouses and the company shares huge bottling plants at Broxburn together with J & G Grant, owner of Glenfarclas Distillery.

The high quality visitor centre receives some 40,000 visitors annually who are offered the opportuny of cask tasting and creating their own whisky blend.

The core range consists of 10, 12 (cask strength), 17 and 21 years old. Several limited releases have been made the last couple of years chosen by the stillmen, mashmen, warehousemen and the manager Robbie Hughes.

In October 2007 two single casks aged 20 and 14 years respectively were released as well as an un-aged expression called Burnfoot (the original name of the distillery). Burnfoot is a travel retail exclusive and the owners have developed a five year strategy to strengthen their prominence in duty free outlets. New releases for 2008 are a 16 year old shiraz cask finish and the oldest Glengoyne still in the warehouse, a 40 year old. Independent bottlings are not that common.

16 year old
Shiraz finish

Glen Grant distillery

Glen Grant

Owner:
Campari Group

Region/district:
Speyside

Founded: **Status:** **Capacity:**
1840   Active (vc) 5 900 000 litres

Address: Elgin Road, Rothes,
Banffshire AB38 7BS

Tel:
01340 832118

website:
www.glengrant.com

History:

1840 – The brothers James and John Grant, managers of Dandelaith Distillery, found the distillery.

1861 – The distillery becomes the first to install electric lighting.

1864 – John Grant dies.

1872 – James Grant passes away and the distillery is inherited by his son, James junior (Major James Grant).

1897 – James Grant decides to build another distillery across the road; it is named Glen Grant No. 2.

1902 – Glen Grant No. 2 is mothballed.

1931 – Major Grant dies and is succeeded by his grandson Major Douglas Mackessack.

1953 – J. & J. Grant merges with George & J. G. Smith who runs Glenlivet distillery, forming The Glenlivet & Glen Grant Distillers Ltd.

1961 – Armando Giovinetti and Douglas Mackessak found a friendship that eventually leads to Glen Grant becoming the most sold malt whisky in Italy.

1965 – Glen Grant No. 2 is back in production, but renamed Caperdonich.

Glen Grant is somewhat of an enigma. It is among the top five single malts in the world regarding sales but does not get talked about as often as Glenfiddich, Glenlivet and Macallan. One reason could be that in the past Glen Grant have not released spectacular, limited expressions as other distillery's have. Previous owners (Seagrams and Pernod Ricard) have regarded the distillery to be more or less the work-horse. However, under new ownership things are beginning to change even if sales during 2007 were a disappointment, 312,000 cases (-22%). Campari presented new packaging last year for the two youngest expressions and have repeated this in 2008 with the 10 year old. Even more interesting are the special releases which now have started to appear beginning with a 15 year old single cask in autumn 2007. Also, 71 casks between 15 and 35 years old have been bought back for special releases.

The distillery is equipped with semi-lauter mash tun, ten Oregon pine washbacks and four pairs of stills. The stills are somewhat peculiar in that they have vertical sides at the base of the neck and are all fitted with purifiers. This gives an increased reflux and creates a light and pale whisky. Since last year production has increased to 5.8 million litres which is more or less capacity. The idea now is to increase production in a big way: 8 new stills would double the capacity to 12 million litres. This development is dependant on an animal feed plant being refitted as a power generating plant but everything could be in place by 2010.

Bourbon casks are used for maturation and the share of sherry butts is less than 10%, mostly used for the 10 year old. A new addition is red wine casks from Sardinia used for both finishing and to fill with new make. So far very little has been stored on-site as Chivas still owns most of the warehouses. In August 2008 however, Glen Grant bought 11 warehouses in Rothes from Chivas to hold 60,000 casks. During autumn 2008 on-site filling re-commenced. A reconstruction of the visitor centre took place in late 2007 at a cost of £500,000 with The Major's Coachmans House being converted into a new visitor centre.

Some 50% of the production goes into blended whisky, especially Chivas Regal. The Glen Grant core range of single malts consists of a *5 year old* (number one malt in Italy), a *10 year old* and a *no age statement*. Recent, limited editions include a *16 year old* and a *27 year old*, both at cask strength. Independent bottlings are frequent. Some of the most recent include a 31 year old by Douglas Laing, a 14 year old by Cadenheads, a 34 year old from Single Malts of Scotland and a 1969 released by Duncan Taylor.

History (continued):

1972 – The Glenlivet & Glen Grant Distillers merges with Hill Thompson & Co. and Longmorn-Glenlivet Ltd to form The Glenlivet Distillers. The drum maltings ceases.

1973 – Stills are increased from four to six.

1977 – The Chivas & Glenlivet Group (Seagrams) buys Glen Grant Distillery. Stills are increased from six to ten.

2001 – Pernod Ricard and Diageo buy Seagrams Spirits and Wine; with Pernod acquiring the Chivas Group.

2006 – Campari buys Glen Grant for €115 million in a deal that includes the acquisition of Old Smuggler and Braemar for another €15 million.

2007 – The entire range is re-packaged and re-launched and a 15 year old single cask is released. Reconstruction of the visitor centre.

2008 – Two limited cask strengths - a 16 year old and a 27 year old - are released.

Glen Grant 10 year old

DR – Sweet banana and toffee, vanilla and pear on the nose, sweet barley, crystallised pineapple on the palate with a touch of honey and finally a cinnamon and spice note at the finish.

DS – An earthy, boiled sweet nose. The palate is creamy and bittersweet – light and delicate. The finish is also light and quite elegant.

The new visitor centre

The Major's spirit safe in the garden.

James Grant - The Major

10 years old   5 years old   unaged

Glen Keith

Owner:
Chivas Brothers
(Pernod Ricard)

Region/district:
Speyside

Founded: 1957
Status: Mothballed
Capacity: 3 500 000 litres

Address: Station Road, Keith,
Banffshire AB55 3BU

Tel: 01542 783042
website: -

History:
1957 – The Distillery is founded by Chivas Brothers (Seagrams).

1958 – Production starts.

1970 – The first gas-fuelled still in Scotland is installed, the number of stills increases from three to five.

1976 – Own maltings (Saladin box) ceases.

1983 – A sixth still is installed.

1994 – The first official bottling, a 10 year old, is released as part of Seagram's Heritage Selection.

2000 – The distillery is mothballed.

2001 – Pernod Ricard takes over Chivas Brothers from Seagrams.

Glen Keith 10 year old
DS – Soft heather and honey on the nose with a hint of banana. The palate is quite flat and light and the finish is soft and smooth with a honeyed aftertaste.

When Glen Keith was built in the late 1950s on the site of the old Mill of Keith corn mill, the decision was made to triple distil the spirit. This is perhaps not a unique decision, but rather an unusual one for a distillery outside of the Lowlands. Practising triple distillation results in a lighter and cleaner spirit and this was exactly what Sam Bronfman, the owner of Seagrams wanted. Seagrams was at this time the parent company of Chivas Brothers and Sam Bronfman had long since dreamed of a new blended Scotch which could compete with Cutty Sark on the American market. The style would be light to fit the American customers and the whisky was named 100 Pipers when it was launched in the mid sixties. 100 Pipers still exists and is currently one of the ten most sold blended Scotch with main markets in Thailand, India and Spain.

Triple distillation was abandoned in the early 70s but innovation did not cease. Some heavily peated whiskies were made (later released as Craigduff and Glenisla although some sources claim these were made at nearby Strathisla), malt whisky was distilled using a column still, new strains of yeast were tried out in the process and microprocessors were installed to control mashing, milling and distilling.

Glen Keith has not been producing since 2000 and there is no sign of the owners, Chivas Brothers, opening up again. All the equipment is however still there; one stainless steel, infusion mash tun, nine washbacks made of Oregon pine and three pairs of stills visible through the large windows. Today Glen Keith is mainly used as a filling-store for neighbour Strathisla which pumps in the new make through pipes but is also used by other distilleries within the group. The distillery accommodates a technical centre and the laboratory from Miltonduff was moved there when Allieds' distilleries were taken over.

The official *10 year old* is difficult to obtain nowadays but there are independent bottlings. The latest is a 13 year old from 1995 released by Ian MacLeod.

10 years old

Glenkinchie

Owner: Diageo

Region/district: Lowlands

Founded: 1837

Status: Active (vc)

Capacity: 1 750 000 litres

Address: Pencaitland, Tranent, East Lothian EH34 5ET

Tel: 01875 342004

website: www.malts.com

History:

1825 – A distillery known as Milton is founded by John and George Rate.

1837 – The Rate brothers are registered as licensees of a distillery named Glenkinchie.

1840 – James Gray takes over operations.

1852 – John Rate is once again licensee.

1853 – John Rate sells the distillery to a farmer Christie who converts it to a sawmill.

1881 – The buildings are bought by a consortium from Edinburgh made up of wine merchants, whisky blenders and brewers.

1890 – Glenkinchie Distillery Company is founded with Major James Gray as General Manager. Reconstruction and refurbishment is on-going for the next few years.

1914 – Glenkinchie forms Scottish Malt Distillers (SMD) with four other lowland distilleries.

1925 – Distillers Company Limited buys SMD.

1939-45 – Glenkinchie is one of few distilleries allowed to maintain production during the war.

1968 – Floor maltings is decommissioned.

1969 – The maltings is converted into a museum.

1988 – Glenkinchie 10 years becomes one of selected six in the Classic Malt series.

1998 – A Distiller's Edition with amontillado finish is launched.

2007 – A 12 year old and a 20 year old cask strength are released.

Glenkinchie 12 year old

DR – The nose is light and flowery, with wet meadow notes and cucumber, the palate is pure barley with a touch of star anise spice and an earthy note.

DS – A powerful heather and honey nose with brown sugar. Soft sherry and spice comes through on the heavy palate and a rather sticky after-taste

---

Glenkinchie can boast of having one of the largest wash stills (30,963 litres) in the industry and in spring 2008 it was time it was replaced. Some distilleries rebuilt in the 1960s and 1970s had large panoramic windows in their still houses, as temperatures should not become too warm. The windows also facilitate replacement of equipment. Glenkinchie did not have such windows so the only way of replacing the stills was to remove the roof to bring out the old still and install the new one. Almost all Scottish distilleries receive their new stills from Forsyth's in Rothes. Not Diageo though, who have their own coppersmiths in Alloa north of Edinburgh. 25 staff have been working under high pressure recently to produce 14 new copper stills for the new distillery in Roseisle. It takes six weeks to produce one still.

Glenkinchie is just 20 kilometres east of Edinburgh which means that the visitor centre is well-visited (40,000 vistors a year). The whisky is also sometimes called the Edinburgh malt. By the time Glenkinchie was founded in 1837, 115 licensed distilleries were recorded in the Lowlands but now only five remain producing malt whisky today (Auchentoshan, Bladnoch, Daftmill and Ailsa Bay being the others). Glenkinchie is equipped with a lauter mash tun, six wooden washbacks and one pair of stills. Worm tubs are used for cooling the spirits but these are unusually enough made from cast iron rather than wood.

The core range consist of a *12 year old* (which used to be a 10 year old) and a *Distiller's Edition 14 years old* since 2007. Autumn 2007 it also appeared for the first time in the Special Release series as a *20 year old* cask strength. Independent bottlings are extremely rare.

20 year old cask strength

Glenlivet

Owner:
Chivas Brothers
(Pernod Ricard)

Region/district:
Speyside

Founded: **Status:** **Capacity:**
1824   Active (vc)   5 800 000 litres

Address: Ballindalloch, Banffshire AB37 9DB

Tel:
01340 821720 (vc)

website:
www.theglenlivet.com

History:
1817 – George Smith inherits the farm distillery Upper Drummin from his father Andrew Smith who has been distilling on the site since 1774.

1840 – George Smith buys Delnabo farm near Tomintoul and leases Cairngorm Distillery. His son William takes over operations at Upper Drummin.

1845 – George Smith leases three other farms, one of which is situated on the river Livet and is called Minmore.

1846 – William Smith develops tuberculosis and his brother John Gordon moves back home to assist his father. Sales of Smith's Glenlivet increases steadily and neither Upper Drummin nor Cairngorm Distillery can meet demand.

1858 – George Smith buys Minmore farm, which he has leased for some time, and obtains permission from the Duke of Gordon to build a distillery.

1859 – Upper Drummin and Cairngorm close and all equipment is brought to Minmore which is renamed The Glenlivet Distillery.

1864 – George Smith cooperates with the whisky agent Andrew P. Usher and exports the whisky with great success.

Most of the large producers presented plans to enhance capacity already in 2007 and in some cases (William Grant) they have already managed to start up the facilities. The reason behind this is of course the increased demand for malt whisky. Pernod Ricard announced similar plans in February 2008, having started talks with Moray Council about expansion of Glenlivet comprising no less than six new stills, one full lauter mash tun and eight new washbacks. This should be completed some time during 2009 if everything goes according to plan. An old malt barn will be upgraded to a still house for the new stills. The owners have not mentioned anything about the new capacity, but the added equipment will probably put Glenlivet in the vicinity of Glenfiddich in terms of production (10 million litres).

In 2006 Glenlivet could report a record-breaking sales of over 500,000 cases which makes it number two in the world just in front of Macallan, but number one in the USA, Mexico and Hungary and in strong expansion in Taiwan, Japan and other Asian markets. The long-term goal is to challenge Glenfiddich for the top spot, an impressive goal indeed. Sales in 2007 increased by 16% to 613,000 cases.

Despite being a large distillery, the production at Glenlivet is run by few employees. The reason for this is that casks are never filled on site. Instead they are sent to Chivas bonded warehouses in Keith for filling. Nor are there any warehousemen at the distillery; they are assisted by a central team which alternates between the different distilleries in the group. 62,000 casks are stored on-site in both dunnage and racked warehouses. The rest is stored at other distilleries. The current equipment consists of a stainless steel mashtun, eight washbacks made of Oregon pine and four pairs of stills.

Glenlivet's core range is the *12 year old*, matured in bourbon casks, the *French Oak 15 years* (with 6-9 months finish in new Limousin Oak casks) and the *18 year old* (matured in ex-sherry casks). Limited editions include the re-launched *21 year old Archive*, *1969 Cellar Collection* and *Glenlivet XXV*, a 25-year old which has spent its last two years on oloroso casks, launched in spring 2007.

Three expressions are earmarked for the Duty Free market: *First Fill Sherry Cask 12 years old*, *15 years old* and *Nadurra* (16 years old and non-chill filtered). A *cask strength version of Nadurra* was released in the U.S. in 2006. Among the independents, Berry Brothers recently released a Glenlivet from 1971 and Duncan Taylor presented two old bottlings from 1968 and 1970.

History (continued):

1871 – George Smith dies and his son John Gordon takes over.

1880 – John Gordon Smith applies for and is granted sole rights to the name The Glenlivet. Only Glenlivet Distillery may thus use the name. All distilleries wishing to use Glenlivet in their names must from now hyphenate it with their brand names.

1890 – A fire breaks out and some of the buildings are replaced.

1896 – Another two stills are installed.

1901 – John Gordon Smith dies.

1904 – John Gordon's nephew George Smith Grant takes over.

1921 – Captain Bill Smith Grant, son of George Smith Grant, takes over.

1953 – George & J. G. Smith Ltd merges with J. & J. Grant of Glen Grant Distillery and forms the company Glenlivet & Glen Grant Distillers Ltd.

1966 – Floor maltings closes.

1970 – Glenlivet & Glen Grant Distillers Ltd merges with Longmorn-Glenlivet Distilleries Ltd and Hill Thomson & Co. Ltd to form The Glenlivet Distillers Ltd.

1978 – Seagrams buys The Glenlivet Distillers Ltd. A visitor centre opens.

1996/97 – The visitor centre is expanded, and a multimedia facility installed.

2000 – French Oak 12 years and American Oak 12 years are launched

2001 – Pernod Ricard and Diageo buy Seagram Spirits & Wine. Pernod Ricard thereby gain control of the Chivas group.

2004 – This year sees a lavish relaunch of Glenlivet, the objective is to overtake Glenfiddich as number one on the sales lists. French Oak 15 years replaces the previous 12 year old.

2005 – Two new duty-free versions are introduced – The Glenlivet 12 year old First Fill and Nadurra, a 16 year old non chill-filtered matured in first-fill bourbon casks. The 1972 Cellar Collection (2,015 bottles) is launched.

2006 – Nadurra 16 year old cask strength and 1969 Cellar Collection are released. Glenlivet sells more than 500,000 cases for the first time in one year.

2007 – Glenlivet XXV is released.

Glenlivet XXV

Nadurra cask strength

1969 Cellar Collection

Glenlivet 12 year old

DR – Freshly chopped apple, rhubarb and crisp barley on the nose, soft rounded and beautiful mouth feel with green fruit and gooseberries and a delicate, rounded and medium long finish.

DS – Floral and malty on the nose with vanilla and soft fruits. The palate is bittersweet and creamy with a hint of fudge. The finish is long and nutty.

12 years old

18 years old

*15 years old
French Oak Reserve*

Glenlossie

Owner:
Diageo

Region/district:
Speyside

Founded: 1876
Status: Active
Capacity: 2 140 000 litres

Address: Birnie, Elgin, Morayshire IV30 8SS

Tel: 01343 862000
website: www.malts.com

History:
1876 – John Duff, former manager at Glendronach Distillery, founds the distillery. Alexander Grigor Allan (to become part-owner of Talisker Distillery), the whisky trader George Thomson and Charles Shirres (both will co-found Longmorn Distillery some 20 years later with John Duff) and H. Mackay are also involved in the company.

1895 – The company Glenlossie-Glenlivet Distillery Co. is formed. Alexander Grigor Allan passes away.

1896 – John Duff becomes more involved in Longmorn and Mackay takes over management of Glenlossie.

1919 – Distillers Company Limited (DCL) takes over the company.

1929 – A fire breaks out and causes considerable damage.

1930 – DCL transfers operations to Scottish Malt Distillers (SMD).

1962 – Stills are increased from four to six.

1971 – Another distillery, Mannochmore, is constructed by SMD on the premises. A dark grains plant is installed.

1990 – A 10 year old is launched in the Flora & Fauna series.

Glenlossie 10 year old

DS – A fresh, herbal and grassy nose with sweet mint notes. Chewy in the mouth with sweet caramel and bitter chocolate flavours. A long finish with a herbal aftertaste.

Even if Glenlossie is counted in among the mid-sized distilleries in terms of production capacity, other parts of the facilities are more large-scale. Glenlossie Bonds for example comprises ten warehouses which together house no less than 200,000 casks from many different distilleries within Diageo. The dark grains plant on the site, which transforms draff and pot ale to cattle fodder as pellets, receives almost 3,000 tonnes of draff each year. Similar facilities within Diageo are to be found at Dailuaine distillery and Pittyvaich where the distillery has closed but the dark grains processing continues.

The blender's list from 1974 categorizes malt and grain whiskies according to the characteristics appropriate to a blended whisky. Glenlossie, relatively anonymous for the average single malt buyer, steps into the limelight in this list as it is rated 'top class', i. e. among the 12 top single malts. Glenlossie malt whisky has been a part of the Haig blend for many years.

The distillery is equipped with a stainless steel mash tun installed in 1992, eight washbacks made of larch and three pairs of stills. The spirit stills are also equipped with purifiers between the lyne arms and the condensers to increase the reflux which gives a light and clean spirit. The workforce used to alternate between Glenlossie and its sister distillery Mannochmore with each of them being in production for half a year at a time. With the increasing demand for whisky this has changed into both distilleries producing 12 months a year since 2007.

The only official bottling available today is a *10 year old* in the Distillery Malts (Flora & Fauna) series.

Glenlossie's high quality has, however, inspired several independent bottlers. The two most recent are a 20 year old from 1988 released by Blackadder and 14 year old port finish from Cadenheads.

Flora & Fauna 10 years old

Glenmorangie distillery

Glenmorangie

Owner:
The Glenmorangie Co
(Moët Hennessy)

Region/district:
Northern Highlands

Founded: 1843
Status: Active (vc)
Capacity: 4 000 000 litres

Address: Tain, Ross-shire IV19 1BR

Tel: 01862 892477 (vc)
website: www.glenmorangie.com

History:
1843 – William Mathesen, formerly part-owner of Balblair Distillery, and brother John apply for a license for a farm distillery called Morangie, which is rebuilt by them. Production took place here in 1738, and possibly since 1703.

1849 – Production starts in November.

1880 – Exports to foreign destinations such as Rome and San Francisco commence.

1887 – The distillery is rebuilt and Glenmorangie Distillery Company Ltd is formed.

1918 – 40% of the distillery is sold to GDCL's largest customer, Macdonald & Muir Ltd and 60 % to the whisky dealer Durham. Macdonald & Muir takes over Durham's share by the late thirties.

1931 – The distillery closes due to the depression and prohibition in the US.

1936 – Production restarts in November.

1980 – Number of stills increases from two to four and own maltings ceases.

1990 – The number of stills is doubled to eight.

1994 – A visitor centre opens. September sees the launch of Glenmorangie Port Wood Finish which marks the start of a number of different wood finishes.

1995 – Glenmorangie's Tain I'Hermitage (Rhone wine) is launched

Glenmorangie is a distillery in a period of change, something which began last year with the complete restructuring of the range of whiskies. Hopes for the future are high for this company which just a few years ago was riding on a reputation of old merits. There are many planned changes leading to expansion and several have already materialised. In order to increase capacity with two million litres a year, two new stills are being installed and new warehouses built. Even the visitor centre is on the to-do list and will be restyled. One person who will not take part in these changes is the Distillery Manager Graham Eunson. He explained in spring that he will leave the company after ten years and manage the born-again Glenglassaugh distillery instead. Their new manager is Andy MacDonald who has previously worked for Diageo.

Other changes were announced when the head office would move from Broxburn to Edinburgh and the huge bottling plant at Broxburn would be sold to Diageo; all to be realised within two years. One of the reasons is that Glenmorangie now has decided to withdraw from the blended Scotch segment of the market to focus on single malts instead. The only brands of blended Scotch which will remain within the company are Bailie Nicol Jarvie and Martin's.

Before expansion is completed the distillery was equipped with a full lauter mash tun, six stainless steel washbacks and four pairs of stills. The stills have the tallest necks in all Scotland and the still room is perhaps the most impressive in Scotland - rather like entering a church! The spirit is matured mainly in bourbon casks.

Since the restructuring of last year the core range consists of *Original* (the former 10 year old), *18 years old* and *25 years old*. The wood finishes which a decade ago became the characteristic attribute have been reduced to three; *Quinta Ruban* (port), *Nectar D´Or* (Sauternes) and *Lasanta* (sherry). They are all non chill-filtered and bottled at 46% instead of the earlier 43%.

Apart from the range mentioned above, there have been several limited editions throughout the years. One of the more recent was *Artisan Cask*, where wood management, i.e. selecting the perfect wood for the casks was in focus. This expression had a follower this year in the shape of *Astar*. Another new release for autumn 2008 was the *Glenmorangie Signet* where Bill Lumsden, by using roasted barley and chocolate malt, has created a special character. Chocolate malt is normally used to produce porter and stout.

History (continued):

1996 – Two different wood finishes are launched, Madeira and Sherry. Glenmorangie plc is formed.

1997 – A museum opens.

2001 – A limited edition of a cask strength port wood finish is released in July, Cote de Beaune Wood Finish is launched in September and Three Cask (ex-Bourbon, charred oak and ex-Rioja) is launched in October for Sainsbury's.

2002 – A Sauternes finish, a 20 year Glenmorangie with two and a half years in Sauternes casks, is launched.

2003 – Burgundy Wood Finish is launched in July and a limited edition of cask strength Madeira-matured (i. e. not just finished) in August.

2004 – Glenmorangie buys the Scotch Malt Whisky Society which has 27,000 members worldwide. The Macdonald family decides to sell Glenmorangie plc (including the distilleries Glenmorangie, Glen Moray and Ardbeg). Bidding is frantic and the buyer is Moët Hennessy (owned by Diageo and LVMH) at £300 million. A new version of Glenmorangie Tain l'Hermitage (28 years) is released and Glenmorangie Artisan Cask is launched in November.

2005 – A 30 year old is launched.

2007 – The entire range gets a complete makeover with 15 and 30 year olds being discontinued and the rest are given new names as well as new packaging.

2008 – An expansion of production capacity is started. Astar and Signet are launched.

Glenmorangie Original

DR – Rounded honey and light tangerine on the nose, much weightier on the palate, with vanilla, honey, oranges and lemons nudging alongside some tannins and soft peat, all coming together in a rich and warming finish.

DS – Pear drops, floral and buttery on the stunning nose. The palate is slightly spicy and zesty with some fruitiness and the finish is short but very moreish.

Signet

Astar

Original (10 years old)

Nectar D´Or

Lasanta

Quinta Ruban

Glen Moray

Owner:
The Glenmorangie Co
(Moët Hennessy)

Region/district:
Speyside

Founded: 1897
Status: Active (vc)
Capacity: 2 000 000 litres

Address: Bruceland Road, Elgin,
Morayshire IV30 1YE

Tel: 01343 542577
website: www.glenmoray.com

History:

1897 – West Brewery, dated 1828, is reconstructed as Glen Moray Distillery.

1910 – The distillery closes.

1912 – The distillery reopens, but soon closes again.

1920 – Financial troubles force the distillery to be put up for sale. Buyer is Macdonald & Muir.

1923 – Production restarts.

1932 – No whisky is produced this year.

1958 – A reconstruction takes place and the floor maltings are replaced by a Saladin box.

1978 – Own maltings are terminated.

1979 – The number of stills is increased from two to four.

1992 – Two old stills are replaced by new.

1996 – Macdonald & Muir Ltd changes name to Glenmorangie plc.

1999 – Three wood finishes are introduced - Chardonnay (no age) and Chenin Blanc (12 and 16 years respectively).

2004 – Louis Vuitton Moët Hennessy buys Glenmorangie plc for £300 million. A new visitor centre is inaugurated and 276 bottles of Glen Moray 1986 cask strength are released. A 20 and a 30 year old are released late in the year. Wood finishing ceases.

2005 – The Fifth Chapter (Manager's Choice from Graham Coull) is released.

2006 – Two vintages, 1963 and 1964, and a new Manager's Choice from Graham Coull are released.

2007 – The second edition of Mountain Oak is released.

2008 – The distillery is put up for sale.

Glen Moray 12 year old

DR – Maltesers and soft vanilla ice cream on the nose, full and rich sweet malt, a touch of vanilla and hints of tannin on the palate and a pleasant and pleasing finish.

DS – Soft fruits and vanilla on the nose. Light and sweet on the palate – strawberry essence. A short and sweet finish.

Glenmorangie Co´s decision to withdraw from the blended Scotch market, announced in July, had immediate consequences for one of the other distilleries in the group; Glen Moray. Most of its production has gone to blended whisky and with the new direction there is no place for it in Glenmorangie Co. Glen Moray was put up for sale and, as we write, Whyte & Mackay seem to be the hottest candidate to become new owner. Glen Moray was launched as a single malt already in the early 1960s. In 1999 the owners made a change in the maturation strategy when they began to do a finish in white wine casks (Chardonnay and Chenin Blanc). This stopped in 2004 despite sales figures having increased 150% during these years.

Glen Moray, which operates at full capacity, i e 2 million litres annually, has one stainless steel mash tun, five stainless steel wash-backs and two pairs of stills. A minor part of the maturation takes place in nine dunnage warehouses and one palletized warehouse holding some 50,000 casks. The rest is tankered away to Broxburn for filling and maturation.

A new feature was presented at the visitor centre in summer 2008 when a "Bottle Your Own" service is introduced where visitors get the chance to fill a bottle from the cask. The core range consists of *Classic*, *12 years old* and *16 years old*. The Classic is actually 8 years old and that is what is stated on the bottles exported to for instance USA. In Europe though it is presented without an age statement. Limited editions include *Signature*, a first fill bourbon from 1989, *20* and *30 years old* as well as several *vintages*. This year´s *Manager´s Choice* is a single sherry cask from 1995. Last year manager Graham Coull chose *Mountain Oak - The Final Release* from 1991 as his special bottling. It is a combination of both charred and toasted casks. Recent independent bottlings are definitely rare but there is a 16 year old from 1991 released by Douglas Laing.

1995 Manager´s Choice

Glen Ord

Owner:		Region/district:
Diageo		Northern Highlands

Founded:	Status:	Capacity:
1838	Active (vc)	5 000 000 litres

Address: Muir of Ord, Ross-shire IV6 7UJ

Tel:	website:
01463 872004 (vc)	www.malts.com

History:

1838 – Thomas Mackenzie founds the distillery and licenses it to Ord Distillery Co. (Robert Johnstone and Donald MacLennan).

1847 – Robert Johnstone, by now single owner of Ord Distillery Co., becomes bankrupt and the distillery is put up for sale.

1855 – Alexander MacLennan and Thomas McGregor buy the distillery.

1870 – Alexander MacLennan dies and the distillery is taken over by his widow who eventually marries the banker Alexander Mackenzie.

1877 – Alexander Mackenzie leases the distillery.

1878 – Alexander Mackenzie builds a new still house and barely manages to start production before a fire destroys it.

1882 – Mackenzie registers the name Glenoran to be used for whisky from Glen Ord.

1896 – Alexander Mackenzie dies and the distillery is sold to the blending company James Watson & Co. for £15,800.

1923 – John Jabez Watson, James Watson's son and the only remaining family member, dies and the distillery is sold to John Dewar & Sons. The name is changed from Glen Oran to Glen Ord.

1925 – Dewar's joins Distillers Company Limited.

1930 – Glen Ord is transferred to Scottish Malt Distillers (SMD).

1961 – Substantial renovation takes place; floor maltings is abandoned in favour of Saladin box.

1966 – The two stills are increased to six.

1968 – To augment the Saladin box a drum maltings is built.

1983 – Malting in the Saladin box ceases.

1988 – A visitor centre is opened.

2002 – A 12 year old is launched.

2003 – A limited-edition cask strength, 28 years, is launched.

2004 – A 25 year old is launched.

2005 – A 30 year old is launched as a Special Release from Diageo.

2006 – A 12 year old Singleton of Glen Ord is launched.

Singleton of Glen Ord

DR – Red fruits and blackcurrant, mince pies, red apple and sherry on the nose, enjoyable taste of apple, prune and cinnamon, and a delightful and more-ish finish.

DS – Sweet pine and resin with eucalyptus on the nose. Sweet in the mouth with some fruitiness and lots of oak especially in the long, sherried finish.

Glen Ord is situated in the fertile Black Isle, north of Inverness. Surrounded by barley fields it is perhaps not surprising that adjacent to the distillery lies the large maltings of Glen Ord. With a capacity of 36,000 tonnes per year it produces malt for several other Diageo distilleries. The distillery used floor maltings until 1961 when it was replaced by Saladin boxes (similar to Tamdhu ten years earlier). The Saladin boxes supplied malt for the distillery until 1984 but already in 1968 the large drum malting with 18 drums was built. Neighbours have been complaining for years about the odour coming from the maltings, especially when peated malt is made. Diageo is therefore to build a 45 metres tall chimney at a cost of £1m. The distillery itself is equipped with a cast iron lauter mash tun, eight washbacks made of Oregon pine and three pairs of stills.

There are five dunnage warehouses with a capacity of 15,000 casks. Since autumn 2007 the distillery is working a seven-day week with 17 mashes which means 4.4 million litres per year. Glen Ord is known as a clean and smooth whisky, the reason according to the distillery being the long fermentation time (75 hours) and the large stills with a lot of copper contact.

There have been two official bottlings in the core range since 2006 - the *12 year old* and *Singleton of Glen Ord*, the latter made for the Asian market. Those of us living outside Asia should invest in the 12 year old as it will be gone forever once the existing stock is exhausted. Outside Asia, Glen Ord is available in the distillery's own shop. The Singleton is a 50/50 mix of sherry and bourbon casks while the 12 year old contains 90% bourbon-matured malt. Several limited old bottlings (*25, 28* and *30 year old*) have also been released the last couple of years.

Independent bottlings of Glen Ord are rarely encountered but two of the latest came from Douglas Laing and Cadenheads, both from 1996.

The Singleton of Glen Ord

Glenrothes

Owner:
The Edrington Group

Region/district:
Speyside

Founded: **Status:**
1878 Active

Capacity:
5 600 000 litres

Address: Rothes, Morayshire AB38 7AA

Tel:
01340 872300

website:
www.glenrotheswhisky.com

History:
1878 – James Stuart & Co., licensees of Macallan since 1868, begins planning a new distillery in Rothes. Robert Dick and William Grant, both from Caledonian Bank and the lawyer John Cruickshank are partners in the company. Stuart has financial problems so Dick, Grant and Cruickshank terminate the partnership and form William Grant & Co. while James Stuart focuses on Macallan. William Grant & Co. takes over the building of the distillery in Rothes.

1879 – Production starts in May.

1884 – The distillery changes name to Glenrothes-Glenlivet.

1887 – William Grant & Co. joins forces with Islay Distillery Co. (owners of Bunnahabhain Distillery) and forms Highland Distillers Company.

1897 – A fire ravages the distillery in December.

1898 – Capacity doubles.

1903 – An explosion causes substantial damage.

1922 – A fire breaks out in one of the warehouses.

1963 – Expansion from four to six stills.

1980 – Expansion from six to eight stills.

1989 – Expansion from eight to ten stills.

1999 – Edrington and William Grant & Sons buy Highland Distillers.

2002 – Four single cask malts from 1966 and 1967 are launched.

2005 – A 30 year old is launched together with Select Reserve and Vintage 1985.

2006 – 1994 and 1975 Vintage are launched.

2007 – A 25 year old is released as a duty free item.

2008 – 1978 Vintage and Robur Reserve are launched.

Glenrothes Select Reserve

DR – On the nose, oranges dominating a fruit bowl of flavours that includes berries among the citrus. The palate is wonderfully rounded and complete, a masterclass in fruit, wood and spice balance, and the finish is a total joy, perfectly weighted and balanced.

DS – Rich malt and ripe fruit flavours on the nose. The palate is again rich with added spice and orange peel in syrup. A warming finish with subtle spices.

Sales of Glenrothes have more than quadrupled thanks to renowned, London-based wine merchants Berry Brothers & Rudd (BBR) who are licensed to tap official bottlings of the Edrington-owned Glenrothes.

Glenrothes has become known to the whisky community as a vintage-based distillery but this has not always been the case. In 1987, Christopher Berry Green, chairman of Berry Bros & Rudd who owned the Cutty Sark blend, suggested to Highland Distilleries that Glenrothes, the signature malt of Cutty Sark, should be launched as a single malt in order to create a link between the blend and its spiritual home. A 12 year old appeared on the market but drowned quickly amongst all other 12 year olds. BBR, having experience from the wine trade in working with vintages, proposed that the same should be done with the single malt and in 1993 the first vintage Glenrothes was released.

Glenrothes is currently producing at 90% of its capacity which translates into 5 million litres a year. The distillery is equipped with a stainless steel semilauter mash tun. Ten washbacks made of Oregon pine are in one room whilst an adjacent modern tun room houses eight new stainless steel washbacks. The still house has five pairs of stills, the last pair added in 1989. The spirit is stored in twelve dunnage and four racked warehouses on site.

The core expression of Glenrothes is the *Select Reserve* without age statement. A vast number of vintages have been released with the latest being a *1978 Vintage* launched in January 2008. In October 2007 a *25 year old* duty free exclusive was released and then in autumn 2008 yet another bottling reserved for the travel retail market was launched, *The Glenrothes Robur Reserve*. The name comes from the Spanish Oak (Quercus robur) first fill sherry casks used for maturation. Several independent bottlers have released Glenrothes. More recent bottlings include a Duncan Taylor from 1968, a 13 year old from 1995 by Signatory and a 16 year old from 1991 by Ian MacLeod.

1978 Vintage

Glen Scotia

Owner: Loch Lomond Distillery Co

Region/district: Campbeltown

Founded: 1832　**Status:** Active　**Capacity:** 750 000 litres

Address: High Street, Campbeltown, Argyll PA28 6DS

Tel: 01586 552288　**website:** www.lochlomonddistillery.com

History:

1832 – The family Galbraith founds Scotia Distillery (the year 1835 is mentioned by the distillery themselves on their labels).

1895 – The distillery is sold to Stewart Galbraith.

1919 – Sold to West Highland Malt Distillers.

1924 – West Highland Malt Distillers goes bankrupt and one of their Directors, Duncan MacCallum, buys the distillery.

1928 – The distillery closes.

1930 – Duncan MacCallum commits suicide and the Bloch brothers take over.

1933 – Production restarts.

1954 – Hiram Walker takes over.

1955 – A. Gillies & Co. becomes new owners.

1970 – A. Gillies & Co. becomes part of Amalgated Distillers Products.

1979–82 – Reconstruction takes place.

1984 – The distillery closes.

1989 – Amalgated Distillers Products is taken over by Gibson International and production restarts.

1994 – Glen Catrine Bonded Warehouse Ltd takes over and the distillery is mothballed.

1999 – Production restarts from 5th May through J. A. Mitchell & Co., owners of Springbank.

2000 – Loch Lomond Distillers runs operations with its own staff from May onwards.

2005 – A 12 year old is released.

2006 – A peated version from 1999 is released.

Glen Scotia 12 year old

DR – The nose is of rich fudge and butter, the palate sliced apricot, walnut and fudge, with a medium finish touched with sweet spice.

DS – An oily nose with some fruitiness and malt. Mild sweetness with a big hit of maltiness – spiky mouthfeel. A warming, if lacklustre, finish.

Photo: © 2005 www.thewhiskystore.de

Campbeltown, once the most important whisky town in Scotland and a proud, independent whisky region along with Highlands, Lowlands and Islay, has seen its distilleries reduced to three - Springbank, Glengyle and Glen Scotia. Currently only the latter is in production as the owners of the two others have, somewhat surprisingly, decided to let production rest until early 2009.

One cannot accuse the owners of Glen Scotia of running a showpiece distillery in Campbeltown. The distillery, hidden away between modern high-rise buildings is nowadays rather run-down and in need of investment. The latest major reconstruction was in the early eighties before the current owner took over. Currently the distillery is running at 15% of the capacity which translates into 100,000 litres per year. The work is carried out by only two men, Hector Gatt who is retired from Springbank and James Grogan who has been stillman at Glen Scotia for many years.

The equipment at the distillery consists of a traditional cast iron mash tun, six washbacks and one pair of stills. The washbacks are special in that they are made of Corten steel and Glen Scotia is probably the last distillery in Scotland to use this material.

Glen Scotia single malt is usually unpeated but peated spirit (30 ppm) has been produced since 1999. The first bottling of this version (1999/6 years old) was released in 2006 in the owner´s Distillery Select selection and more releases followed in spring 2007. Single casks of the unpeated version have also been released in the same series.

A new, official bottling was released in 2005 when the 14 and 8 year olds were replaced by a *12 year old*. Older versions include a *17 year old* and an occasional vintage. Whisky from Glen Scotia is also a part of the 8 year old vatted malt Glen Gyle. This brand was registered by Loch Lomond Distillers in 1995 and this is the reason why Glengyle distillery in Campbeltown call their whisky Kilkerran. Independent bottlings are rare; two of the most recent are a 15 year old from 1992 by Douglas Laing and a 32 year old from 1975 released by Ian MacLeod.

12 years old

Glen Spey

Owner: Diageo

Region/district: Speyside

Founded: 1878

Status: Active

Capacity: 1 390 000 litres

Address: Rothes, Morayshire AB38 7AU

Tel: 01340 831215

website: www.malts.com

History:

1878 – James Stuart & Co. founds the distillery which becomes known by the name Mill of Rothes.

1886 – James Stuart buys Macallan.

1887 – W. & A. Gilbey buys the distillery for £11 000 thus becoming the first English company to buy a Scottish malt distillery.

1920 – A fire breaks out.

1962 – W. & A. Gilbey combines forces with United Wine Traders and forms International Distillers & Vintners (IDV).

1970 – The stills are increased from two to four.

1972 – IDV is bought by Watney Mann who are then acquired by Grand Metropolitan.

1997 – Guiness and Grand Metropolitan merge to form Diageo.

2001 – A 12 year old is launched in the Flora & Fauna series.

Glen Spey 12 year old

DR – Delicate and floral on the nose, a complex mix of flavours on the palate with orange, citrus fruits, honey, vanilla and cinnamon in the mix.

DS – A fresh, minty and herbal nose – icing sugar. The palate is malty with lots of heathery sweetness. A tongue tingling finish with a fennel aftertaste.

There are four active distilleries in the town of Rothes and Glen Spey is definitely the least known among them. Glen Grant has belonged to the top four Scotch whisky distilleries for decades, Glenrothes has been transformed from a whisky known mainly by connoisseurs to a global brand in strong expansion and Speyburn is the eighth best selling single malt in the United States. Glen Spey on the other hand was from the very beginning a distillery producing malt whisky destined to become a part of blended Scotch.

The distillery is situated in the middle of the town at the foot of the hill where the ruins of Castle Rothes is to be found. This was the home of the Leslie family (Earl of Rothes) for four hundred years until 1662 when it was destroyed in a fire. Only a fragment of the outer walls remain on site, but many of the stones were used for building houses in Rothes.

Those with a technical interest in whisky distilling should take note of some features. First, the distillery has two pairs of stills where the spirit stills are equipped with purifiers. The stills are also operated at a lower pressure than usual (4 pounds per square inch instead of 8psi) so there is no need to ever use the release valves on the stills. Second, a special type of semi lauter mash tun was installed in the renovation of 1970. When it was used in other distilleries it was known as the Glen Spey mash tun.

Glen Spey is mainly found as a component in different versions of J & B. There are no other official bottlings apart from the *12 year old Flora & Fauna*.

Independent bottlings are quite rare. Among the most recent are two released in 2008 by Ian MacLeod; a 16 year old from 1992 and a 15 year old from 1993. Cadenheads have also been involved with Glen Spey releasing a 13 year old from 1995.

Flora & Fauna 12 years old

Glentauchers

Owner:
Chivas Brothers
(Pernod Ricard)

Region/district:
Speyside

Founded: **Status:**
1897 Active

Capacity:
3 400 000 litres

Address: Glentauchers, Keith,
Banffshire AB55 6YL

Tel:
01542 860272

website:
-

History:
1897 – James Buchanan and W. P. Lowrie, a whisky merchant from Glasgow, found the distillery. A company named Glentauchers Distillery Co. is also formed at the same time.

1898 – Production starts.

1902 – Buchanan offers to buy out Lowrie who is in financial difficulties.

1906 – James Buchanan & Co. takes over the whole distillery and acquires an 80% share in W. P. Lowrie & Co.

1915 – James Buchanan & Co. merges with Dewars.

1923-25 – Mashing house and maltings are rebuilt.

1925 – Buchanan-Dewars joins Distillers Company Limited (DCL).

1930 – Glentauchers is transferred to Scottish Malt Distillers (SMD).

1965 – The number of stills is increased from two to six.

1969 – Floor maltings is decommissioned.

1985 – DCL mothballs the distillery.

1989 – United Distillers (formerly DCL) sells the distillery to Caledonian Malt Whisky Distillers, a subsidiary of Allied Distillers.

1992 – Production recommences in August.

2000 – A 15 year old Glentauchers is released.

2005 – Chivas Brothers (Pernod Ricard) become new owners through the acquisition of Allied Domecq.

Glentauchers 1990 Gordon & MacPhail

DR – Deep plum and sherry on the nose, then cocoa and blackcurrant. The palate is soft, with plum, raisin and green banana, and the finish is banana and date cake.

DS – Malt and sherry dominate the nose with burnt sugar. Sweet and fruity at first (plums) followed by strong sherry flavours – balanced. Sweet, elegant finish.

Chivas Brothers owns 13 malt whisky distilleries in Scotland that are currently producing. Of these 13, nine have official bottlings. The four remaining are Allt-a-Bhainne and Braeval which are frequently used by independent bottler Aberko in releases of different Deerstalker single malts, Miltonduff which Gordon & MacPhail regularly bottle as 10 year old and finally Glentauchers. The latter distillery has unfortunately been completely overshadowed when it comes to bottlings of single malt, which does not mean that the distillery lacks significance. On the contrary, it has an impressive production capacity of almost 3,5 million litres and the whisky is an important part of Ballantine's and, to some extent, also Chivas Regal.

The owners have recently invested quite a lot of money in the distillery which was closed during part of 2006 for an upgrade of the stillhouse, then in summer 2007 the old cast iron mash tun was replaced. Today the distillery is equipped with a stainless steel mash tun, six washbacks made of European larch and three pairs of stills. The spirit is filled on bourbon casks and part of them mature in the two racked warehouses on site holding a total of 6,000 casks while the rest is taken to Chivas central warehouses in Keith by road tanker.

An official *15 year old* was released by Allied Domecq some years ago but has been difficult to obtain recently. Independent bottlings are more available. A few years ago four expressions, all from 1990, appeared from Duncan Taylor (Whisky Galore), Gordon & MacPhail, James MacArthur and Wilson & Morgan (the latter rum-finished). The most recent ones are an 18 year old from 1989 by Blackadder, a 15 year old from 1992 by Ian MacLeod and a 1990 released by Duncan Taylor.

*Gordon & MacPhail
Glentauchers 1990*

Glenturret

Owner: The Edrington Group	**Region/district:** Eastern Highlands

Founded: 1775	**Status:** Active (vc)	**Capacity:** 340 000 litres

Address: The Hosh, Crieff, Perthshire PH7 4HA

Tel: 01764 656565

website: www.thefamousgrouse.com

History:

1775 – Whisky smugglers establish a small illicit farm distillery named Hosh Distillery.

1818 – John Drummond is licensee, until 1837.

1826 – A distillery in the vicinity is named Glenturret, but is decommissioned before 1852.

1852 – John McCallum is licensee until 1874.

1875 – Hosh Distillery takes over the name Glenturret Distillery and is managed by Thomas Stewart.

1903 – Mitchell Bros Ltd takes over.

1921 – Production ceases and the buildings are used for whisky storage only.

1929 – Mitchell Bros Ltd is liquidated, the distillery dismantled and the facilities are used as storage for agricultural needs.

1957 – James Fairlie buys the distillery and re-equips it.

1959 – Production restarts.

1981 – Remy-Cointreau buys the distillery and invests in a visitor centre.

1990 – Highland Distillers takes over.

1999 – Edrington and William Grant & Sons buys Highland Distillers for £601 million. The purchasing company, 1887 Company, is a joint venture between Edrington (70%) and William Grant (30%).

2002 – The Famous Grouse Experience, a visitor centre costing £2.5 million, is inaugurated.

2003 – A 10 year old Glenturret replaces the 12 year old as the distillery's standard release.

2007 – Three new single casks are released.

Glenturret 10 year old

DR – Full and rich honeyed nose, oily and fruity palate with some appealing rootsy savouriness. Something of the farmyard about it. Charming finish.

DS – An oily and malty nose with herbal notes. The palate is gentle but sweet and fruity and this continues into the aftertaste which is short but delicate.

Glenturret distillery in Crieff, Perthshire is also the home of "The Famous Grouse Experience" – the distillery visitor centre which attracts most people of any of the visitor centres and is one of Scotland's most popular tourist destinations. The Famous Grouse is one of the most sold blended whiskies in the world but according to the staff at the visitor centre it is still the Glenturret 10 year old that is the best-seller in the shop. The "Experience" was expanded in 2007 with a chance for groups to take part in special, tutored, nosing and tasting of The Famous Grouse malt range in a specially built sample room within Warehouse No. 9.

In 2007 The Famous Grouse blended Scotch showed strength and sales increased by 7% to 37 million bottles. The Famous Grouse blended malt on the other hand, suddenly experienced a drop by nearly 30% from 2006 to 2007. This was caused by a significant reduction in the main market Taiwan. Another reason was the increased competition from other producers who now see the potential in the blended malt category.

Founded in 1775 Glenturret is considered by many the oldest still active distillery in Scotland. There is one open stainless steel mash tun dressed in wood and it is perhaps the only one in Scotland where the mash is still turned manually by large wooden spades. There are also eight Douglas fir washbacks, one pair of stills and 10,500 casks maturing in six warehouses on site. Eight mashes a week result in 156,000 litres of spirit per year.

There is only one official bottling in the core range, the *10 year old*. An 8 year old that used to be produced has now been discontinued. A limited edition of three single casks were released in Spring 2007 - a *14 year old* from 1991, a *15 year old* from 1992 and a *29 year old* from 1977. Recent independent bottlings of Glenturret include a 17 year old from 1990 by Ian MacLeod and a 20 year old from 1987 released by Cadenheads.

10 years old

Highland Park distillery

Highland Park

Owner:
The Edrington Group

Region/district:
Highlands (Orkney)

Founded: **Status:**
1798   Active (vc)

Capacity:
2 500 000 litres

Address: Holm Road, Kirkwall, Orkney KW15 1SU

Tel:
01856 874619

website:
www.highlandpark.co.uk

History:
1798 – David Robertson founds the distillery. The local smuggler and businessman Magnus Eunson previously operated an illicit whisky production on this site.

1816 – John Robertson, an Excise Officer who arrested Magnus Eunson, takes over production.

1826 – Highland Park obtains a license and the distillery is taken over by Robert Borwick.

1840 – Robert's son George Borwick takes over but the distillery deteriorates.

1869 – The younger brother James Borwick inherits Highland Park and attempts to sell it as he does not consider the distillation of spirits as compatible with his priesthood.

1876 – Stuart & Mackay becomes involved and improves the business by exporting to Norway and India.

1895 – James Grant (of Glenlivet Distillery) buys Highland Park.

1898 – James Grant expands capacity from two to four stills.

1937 – Highland Distilleries buys Highland Park.

1979 – Highland Distilleries invests considerably in marketing Highland Park as single malt which increases sales markedly.

The re-packaging of the entire range in 2006 was the starting point of a process which, according to the owners, would take Highland Park into the top ten single malts in terms of sales before 2011. They have already overtaken Lagavulin with Talisker and Bowmore remaining before their goal is achieved. It could happen more quickly than anticipated as the increase between 2006 and 2007 was an impressive 30% to 1.3 million bottles. The entire process is expected to cost £18 million and deliveries to independent bottlers have been halted in order to reach target.

Equipment consists of one full-lauter mash tun, ten wooden washbacks and two pairs of stills. The whisky matures in 19 dunnage and four racked warehouses. Highland Park is one of few distilleries malting part (20%) of their barley themselves, with the balance coming from Edrington's maltings at Tamdhu and Simpson's in Berwick upon Tweed. The distillery is now at full capacity by working a seven-day week which enables 24-25 mashes per week. 60% of production is destined for the core range while the remaining 40% are earmarked for single casks and blended whisky. Recent times have seen much effort being put into the re-vamping of the distillery with the last of the two pagoda roofs being replaced in summer 2008 and a new visitor centre launched in June.

The core range of Highland Park consists of *12, 15, 18, 25* and *30 years old*. A new addition to the family came in April 2008 in the guise of a *40 year old* priced at £900. This is thus not a limited edition but a permanent member of the range. The first Travel retail exclusive was a *16 year old* in 2005 and it was complemented with a *21 year old* released in October 2007. Recent limited editions include the *third* and *fourth* editions of *Ambassador's Cask* and with a *fifth* (and possibly the last) just around the corner. There have also been a *19 year old* Queen of the South Scottish Cup Final edition and a *30 year old* celebrating the 180th anniversary of the Spectator magazine. Independent bottlings have so far been common but are likely to become rarer as Highland Park recently decided to keep the stock for their own sales. A 23 year old from 1985 by Cadenheads, a 22 year old from 1985 by Blackadder, a 17 year old from 1990 by Signatory, a 30 year old from 1978 by Douglas Laing and a Duncan Taylor 1984 have all been released recently.

History (continued):

1986 – A visitor centre, considered one of Scotland's finest, is opened.

1997 – Two new Highland Park are launched, an 18 year old and a 25 year old.

1999 – Highland Distillers are acquired by Edrington Group and William Grant & Sons.

2000 – Visit Scotland awards Highland Park "Five Star Visitor Attraction". The distillery has spent over £2 million on the visitor centre and distillery.

2005 – Highland Park 30 years old is released, first in the US and in the autumn in UK.
A 16 year old for the Duty Free market and Ambassador´s Cask 1984 are released.

2006 – The second edition of Ambassador´s Cask, a 10 year old from 1996, is released. New packaging is introduced.

2007 – The Rebus 20, a 21 year old duty free exclusive, a 38 year old and a 39 year old are released.

2008 – A 40 year old and the third and fourth editions of Ambassador´s Cask are released.

Highland Park 12 year old

DR – Honey, peat and marmalade fruit in balance on the nose, then on the palate a big mouth feel with dark chocolate, chilli, sharp barley and honey, concluding with a monster pot pouri of a finish.

DS – A sweet and smoky nose with wafts of sherry and malt. The palate is luxuriously full of sherry and delicate smoky flavours that settle into the long finish.

40 years old

16 years old

*Ambassador´s Cask
4th edition*

12 years old

18 years old

25 years old

Imperial

Owner: **Region/district:**
Chivas Brothers   Speyside
(Pernod Ricard)

Founded: **Status:**   **Capacity:**
1897   Mothballed   1 600 000 litres

Address: Carron, Morayshire AB38 7QP

Tel: **website:**
-             -

History:

1897 – Thomas Mackenzie, who already owns Dailuaine and Talisker, founds the distillery helped by architect Charles Doig. The distillery's name hints at Queen Victoria's Diamond Jubilee this year.

1898 – The distillery is inaugurated in the summer and is administered by Thomas Mackenzie's company Dailuaine-Talisker Distilleries Limited.

1899 – The Pattison whisky crash forces the distillery to close.

1916 – Imperial is bought by Distillers Company Limited (DCL), Dewar's, Johnnie Walker and W. P. Lowrie.

1919 – Production restarts.

1925 – The distillery becomes fully owned by DCL and closes again although the maltings remains active.

1955 – Imperial, now administered by Scottish Malt Distillers (SMD), reopens.

1965 – The number of stills is doubled from two to four and a Saladin box is installed for malting.

1985 – The distillery closes.

1989 – Allied Distillers buys Imperial from United Distillers and starts refurbishing.

1991 – Once again in operation.

1998 – Imperial is mothballed.

2005 – Chivas Brothers (Pernod Ricard) become new owners through the acquisition of Allied Domecq.

Imperial 1991 Gordon & MacPhail

DR – Lime starburst and honey on the nose, melon and lemon on the palate, and drying, long and salty finish.

DS – A malty, fruity, earthy nose with hints of honey and pastry. Mild and malty at first with a flood of fruit flavours. Long, fruity finish.

Looking back at previous editions of Malt Whisky Yearbook, it is risky to write that a distillery which has been mothballed for ten years is unlikely to produce whisky in the future. Allt-a-Bhainne, Braeval and Tamnavulin have all started distilling again and, perhaps the greatest surprise of them all, Glenglassaugh which was closed for more than 22 years now has new owners and will soon be up and running. So better not to say too much about Imperial. What may be said though, is that it has been closest to demolition of all the recently mentioned ones. The owners received demolition permission for the buildings from Moray Council with permission to build new housing in the grounds. Estate Agents Bell Ingram were tasked with selling the premises before everything was put on hold in 2006. Since then Chivas Brothers have been silent about the plans.

The history of Imperial has always been dramatic and has taken many turns. In over 100 years it has been out of production for 60% of the time. Even with its run-down appearance one can imagine how impressive it must have been in its heyday, situated by the River Spey with the surrounding pine forests and the large lawns which are still well-manicured to this very day.

Virtually all the distilling equipment is still in place which means one stainless steel mash tun with traditional mixing gear, six washbacks made of larch and two pairs of stills. When it was still producing it had a capacity of 1.6 million litres of alcohol. All the dunnage warehouses are now empty. An official *15 year old* was released several years ago but has been difficult to obtain recently.

Independent bottlers have begun picking up on Imperial more recently. This past year Duncan Taylor for instance, released a handful from 1990, 1994 and 1996 and there is also a 25 year old from 1982 released by Signatory.

Gordon & MacPhail Imperial 1991

Inchgower

Owner:
Diageo

Region/district:
Speyside

Founded: 1871 **Status:** Active **Capacity:** 1 990 000 litres

Address: Buckie, Banffshire AB56 5AB

Tel: 01542 836700 **website:** www.malts.com

History:
1871 – Alexander Wilson & Co. founds the distillery. Equipment from the disused Tochieneal Distillery, also owned by Alexander Wilson, is installed.

1936 – Alexander Wilson & Co. becomes bankrupt and Buckie Town Council buys the distillery and the family's home for £1,600.

1938 – The distillery is sold on to Arthur Bell & Sons for £3,000.

1966 – Capacity doubles to four stills.

1985 – Guinness acquires Arthur Bell & Sons.

1987 – United Distillers is formed by a merger between Arthur Bell & Sons and DCL.

1997 – Inchgower 1974 (22 years) is released as a Rare Malt.

2004 – Inchgower 1976 (27 years) is released as a Rare Malt.

Inchgower 14 year old

DS – Grassy and sweet at first on the nose with vanilla and cream. Soft and sweet on the palate and again creamy – quite mellow. Vanilla lingers for an age on the finish.

Inchgower, situated near the small fishing port of Buckie in the northeast, is a beautiful distillery and since it was not acquired by United Distillers until the 1980s it managed to avoid SMD's frantic reconstruction and renovation boom that hit so many distilleries in the 1960s and 1970s.

The distillery was closed for almost a year from July 2006 to June 2007 for refurbishing. A modern, closed yeast-pitching system where the yeast is added automatically into the wash backs as a slurry comprised one of new installations. There has been a veritable, quiet revolution since three years ago concerning adding of the yeast used at the distilleries. Previously Brewer's yeast was very common but it also had the characteristic of contributing to the flavour of the spirit. After 2005 Brewer's yeast was no longer for sale and everyone began using Distiller's yeast. This sort is more efficient, gives more alcohol and is therefore more economic to use. It remains to be seen if the taste of the whisky has altered at some distilleries in connection with this shift.

All malt comes from Diageo's own facility in Burghead around 20 miles further west along the coast. The distillery is equipped with a stainless steel semi lauter mash tun, six washbacks made from Oregon pine and two pairs of stills. Most of the production is matured elsewhere, but there are also 13 warehouses on site with room for 60,000 casks, a large part of which come from other distilleries within the Diageo group. The absolutely greater part of production is used for Bell's blended whisky. Aside from the official Flora & Fauna *14 years old* there have been two Rare Malt bottlings, 1974 (22 years) and 1976 (27 years). Independent bottlings are not so common. Two of the most recent are an 18 year old from Cadenheads, a 21 year old from Douglas Laing and a 1992 released by Duncan Taylor.

Flora & Fauna 14 years old

Jura

Owner:
Whyte & Mackay
(United Spirits)

Region/district:
Highlands (Jura)

Founded: 1810
Status: Active (vc)
Capacity: 2 200 000 litres

Address: Craighouse, Isle of Jura PA60 7XT

Tel: 01496 820240
website: www.isleofjura.com

History:

1810 – Archibald Campbell founds a distillery named Small Isles Distillery.

1831 – William Abercombie obtains the first licence for Isle of Jura Distillery.

1853 – Richard Campbell leases the distillery to Norman Buchanan from Glasgow.

1867 – Buchanan files for bankruptcy and J. & K. Orr takes over the distillery.

1876 – The licence is transferred to James Ferguson & Sons.

1901 – The distillery closes and Ferguson dismantles the distillery.

1960 – Charles Mackinlay & Co. embarks on reconstruction and extension of the distillery. Newly formed Scottish & Newcastle Breweries acquires Charles Mackinlay & Co.

1962 – Scottish & Newcastle forms Mackinlay-McPherson for the operation of Isle of Jura.

1963 – The first distilling after reconstruction takes place.

1978 – Stills are doubled from two to four.

1985 – Invergordon Distilleries acquires Charles Mackinlay & Co., Isle of Jura and Glenallachie from Scottish & Newcastle Breweries.

1993 – Whyte & Mackay (Fortune Brands) buys Invergordon Distillers.

1996 – Whyte & Mackay changes name to JBB (Greater Europe).

2001 – The management of JBB (Greater Europe) buys out the company from the owners Fortune Brands and changes the name to Kyndal.

2002 – Isle of Jura Superstition is launched.

2003 – Kyndal reverts back to its old name, Whyte & Mackay. Isle of Jura 1984 is launched.

2004 – Two cask strengths (15 and 30 years old) are released in limited numbers.

2006 – The 40 year old Jura is released.

2007 – United Spirits buys Whyte & Mackay. The 18 year old Delmé-Evans and an 8 year old heavily peated expression are released.

2008 – A series of four different vintages, called Elements, is released.

Jura 10 year old

DR – The nose is sweet condensed milk, the palate an intriguing mix of earthy malt and tangy spice, with a medium sweet and spice finish.

DS – Green vegetables and malty on the nose. The palate is sweet at first followed by sour dough bread flavours which continue into the lingering finish.

When United Spirits bought Whyte & Mackay in May 2007, the owner Vijay Mallya referred to Dalmore as the "flagship" in the group. It is without doubt, however, that Jura distillery has been permitted to steal some of the limelight in recent times, not least thanks to Master Blender Richard Paterson´s ability to select extraordinary casks for new releases. This stardom is quite a new experience for a distillery which had few dedicated followers until a few years ago.

Only walls remain of the first Jura distillery founded in 1810. Today's Jura is the result of two Jura Estate owners, Tony Riley-Smith and Robin Fletcher, who wished to trigger the island's local economy. They joined forces with the architect William Delmé-Evans and built a new distillery on the same site as the older one in 1963.

Jura has one semilauter mash tun, six stainless steel washbacks and two pairs of stills. The stills are extremely high, 25 1/4 feet compared to the ones at Glenmorangie which are Scotland's tallest at over 26 feet. The spirit is matured on bourbon casks mainly from Heaven Hill and Jim Beam and with 5% maturing on sherry casks. There are five racked warehouses with a total of 28,000 casks in maturation.

The core range used to consist of *10, 16, 21 years old* and *Superstition*. In September 2007 an *18 year old* was added to the range. Limited releases last year included a *40 year old*, a heavily peated (40 ppm) and the *Delmé-Evans Bottling* with a final three years on Gonzalez Byass Oloroso cask. Exciting launches continued in 2008 with a *1974 Vintage* and the *Elements* series of four different vintages - a heavily peated (*Earth*) from 1999, a bourbon matured from 1998 (*Fire*), a 15 year old Manzanilla matured from 1993 (*Air*) and finally a sherry matured from 1989 (*Water*). They were all released in quantities of between 700 and 850 bottles. Among the most recent independent bottlings are a 10 year old Tokay finish from 1997 by Ian MacLeod.

Fire (vintage 1998)

Knockando

Owner: Diageo.

Region/district: Speyside

Founded: 1898
Status: Active
Capacity: 1 290 000 litres

Address: Knockando, Morayshire AB38 7RT

Tel: 01340 882000
website: www.malts.com

History:

1898 – John Thompson founds the distillery which is administered by Knockando-Glenlivet Distillery Company. The architect is Charles Doig.

1899 – Production starts in May.

1900 – The distillery closes in March and J. Thompson & Co. takes over administration.

1904 – W. & A. Gilbey purchases the distillery for £3 500 and production restarts in October.

1962 – W. & A. Gilbey merges with United Wine Traders (including Justerini & Brooks) and forms International Distillers & Vintners (IDV).

1968 – Floor maltings is decommissioned.

1969 – The number of stills is increased from two to four.

1972 – IDV is acquired by Watney Mann who, in its turn, is taken over by Grand Metropolitan.

1978 – Justerini & Brooks launches a 12 year old Knockando.

1997 – Grand Metropolitan and Guinness merge and form Diageo; simultaneously IDV and United Distillers merge to United Distillers & Vintners.

Knockando 12 year old

DR – Beeswax, honey and gentle peat on the nose, the palate is altogether bolder, with pepper and earthy peat in evidence mixing it with very sweet crystallised barley and a sweet and rounded finish.

DS – A spirity, grassy nose which is slightly earthy. The palate is malty with date and walnut cake flavours and a hint of ginger in the spicy finish.

The start-up of Knockando distillery was trying, to say the least. Just ten months after production had begun (in 1899), the distillery had to close due to financial difficulties caused by the disastrous Pattison crash. New, solvent owners, gin producers W & A Gilbey came into the picture after five years and the production has run without any major disruptions since then. Knockando was exported as early as 1977 and is today the fifth best selling single malt brand in the Diageo portfolio, being especially strong in the French and Spanish markets. Circa 700,000 bottles per year are sold, of which 96% are exported. Knockando was closed for six months for refurbishing and opened again in late 2006. The distillery is equipped with a stainless steel semi-lauter mash tun, eight washbacks made of Oregon pine and two pairs of stills. It is matured partly in sherry casks but primarily on bourbon barrels from Jack Daniels and Makers Mark. Approximately 8% of production is sold as single malt which is stored in five warehouses on site. The rest is shipped to different distilleries in the Diageo group, mostly to Auchroisk. There is another warehouse on the premises called the Ultima Warehouse. This is where casks from 128 distilleries in Scotland are kept with samples from all of them used for the first time in 1994 when the blend J&B Ultima was presented to celebrate 500 years of Scotch whisky.

The share not destined to become single malt, goes into J&B in which Knockando has been signature malt for a long time now.

Since the 1970s, Knockando used to bottle their whisky according to vintage (similar to Glen Rothes) and without any age statement. Only in the US, where whisky age is important in marketing, were both age and year depicted on the labels. This practice has, however, now also been applied to other markets. The core range consists of a *12 year old*, an *18 year old Slow Matured*, mainly reserved for the French market and matured in sherry casks and a *21 year old Master Reserve*. Independent bottlings are virtually impossible to find. The latest release was a Duncan Taylor 1980.

1991 12 years old

Knockdhu

Owner:
Inver House Distillers
(Thai Beverages plc)

Region/district:
Speyside

Founded: 1893

Status: Active

Capacity: 900 000 litres

Address: Knock, By Huntly,
Aberdeenshire AB54 7LJ

Tel: 01466 771223

website: www.ancnoc.com

History:

1893 – Distillers Company Limited (DCL) starts construction of the distillery which is named Knockdhu. Architects are Gordon & Macbey from Elgin.

1894 – Production starts in October.

1924 – Management of the distillery is transferred to Distillers Agency.

1930 – Scottish Malt Distillers (SMD) takes over production.

1931 – The distillery closes.

1933 – The distillery opens up again.

1983 – The distillery closes in March.

1988 – Inver House buys the distillery from United Distillers.

1989 – Production restarts on 6th February.

1990 – First official bottling of Knockdhu.

1993 – First official bottling of An Cnoc, the new name to avoid confusion with Knockando.

2001 – Pacific Spirits (Great Oriole Group) purchases Inver House Distillers at a price of $85 million.

2003 – Reintroduction of An Cnoc 12 years, with new, contemporary packaging.

2004 – A 14 year old from 1990 is launched.

2005 – Two limited editions, a 30 year old from 1975 and a 14 year old from 1991 are launched.

2006 – InverHouse changes owners when International Beverage Holdings acquires Pacific Spirits UK.

2007 – anCnoc 1993 is released.

2008 – anCnoc 16 year old is released.

In 1993 the first bottle labeled anCnoc appeared from the distillery. The name change was brought in to avoid confusion with the better known Knockando single malt. Today, the roles are reversed. Knockando, owned by Diageo, has almost disappeared from the British market (but is big in Spain and France) while anCnoc has been revived in pace with Inver House releasing new, exciting expressions.

Knockdhu has one cast iron mash tun which was recently upgraded with stirring gear to a semi lauter type. There are six washbacks made of Oregon pine and one pair of stills. One racked and four dunnage warehouses can hold approximately 7,600 casks.

Like many distilleries producing un-peated malt, for the last few years Knockdhu has produced a more peaty variety (22ppm) for just a few weeks each year. It has so far been destined for use in InverHouse's blended whiskies and it remains to be seen whether a peaty Knockdhu will be launched in the future. InverHouse is owned by ThaiBev, Thailand's largest alcohol beverages producer which is in turn owned by Charoen Sirivadhanabhakdi and his family. InverHouse has obtained a prominent place in the group as the Scottish company's headquarters in Airdrie are also responsible for all markets except Asia and North America. There are also plans for Thai Bev to run its entire international marketing from Scotland which would mean that all of the sales and marketing outside Thailand would be done in Airdrie.

The core range consists of a *12 year old* since 2004, but the owner has also launched some limited editions; a *14 year old* (the latest version from 1993 and bottled in 2007) and a *30 year old* from 1975. The latest addition was a *16 year old* launched in January 2008. This is so far the only anCnoc available which has been wholly matured in American oak casks.

16 years old

An Cnoc 12 year old

DR – Complex and layered nose, with delicate peat, green fruits and pear. On the palate there's a full savoury peatiness then tingling yellow fruity follow through and fairydust finale.

DS – Grassy with a sweet toasted caramel nose. The predominant flavours are caramel sweetness and malt. A quick, sweet finish.

Lagavulin distillery

Lagavulin

Owner:
Diageo

Region/district:
Islay

Founded: 1816

Status: Active (vc)

Capacity: 2 250 000 litres

Address: Port Ellen, Islay, Argyll PA42 7DZ

Tel: 01496 302749 (vc)

website: www.malts.com

History:

1816 – John Johnston founds the distillery.

1825 – John Johnston takes over the adjacent distillery Ardmore founded in 1817 by Archibald Campbell and closed in 1821.

1835 – Production at Ardmore ceases.

1837 – Both distilleries are merged and operated under the name Lagavulin by Donald Johnston.

1852 – The brother of the wine and spirits dealer Alexander Graham, John Crawford Graham, purchases the distillery.

1867 – The distillery is acquired by James Logan Mackie & Co. and refurbishment starts.

1878 – Peter Mackie is employed.

1889 – James Logan Mackie passes away and nephew Peter Mackie inherits the distillery.

1890 – J. L. Mackie & Co. changes name to Mackie & Co. Peter Mackie launches White Horse onto the export market with Lagavulin included in the blend. White Horse blended is not available on the domestic market until 1901.

Lagavulin is a highly efficient distillery where only one person per shift is required to oversee production. For some time now, operations have been running for 24 hours, 7 days a week, which means 28 mashes per week. One of the reasons for the increased pace is that Diageo wishes to retake first place as most sold Islay whisky, a position which Lagavulin held until 1998. Since then sales have gone down by 50% while Laphroaig have increased by 50%. In addition to this, Bowmore climbed to the number two spot a few years ago, forcing Lagavulin down to third place. The 16 year old, which had been the flagship for a long time almost disappeared from the shelves for a few years. The reason for this was that a two day week was in force at Lagavulin during a large part of the 1980s and it was not until 1991 it were increased to five-day shifts.

The distillery is equipped with a stainless steel full-lauter mash tun, ten washbacks made of larch and two pairs of stills. Unusually the spirit stills are slightly larger than the wash stills. The spirit stills are filled to 95% of capacity during distillation which is very unusual. The result is that the spirit vapour's diminished contact with the copper produces a more robust spirit. Bourbon hogsheads are used almost without exception for maturation and all of the new production is stored on the mainland. There are only around 16,000 casks on Islay split between warehouses at Lagavulin, Port Ellen and Caol Ila. Not so long ago, 60% of the Lagavulin produced was used for blending (mainly White Horse) but now almost 98% is reserved for single malts.

Lagavulin was bottled at 12 years until 1989; thereafter the classic *16 year old* was introduced. Today, the core range of Lagavulin consists of *12 years old cask strength*, *16 years* and the *Pedro Ximenez sherry finish*. A limited edition of a *25 year old* was released in 2002 and a *30 year old* was launched in 2006. A new *12 year old*, matured on refill American oak casks, was released in autumn 2008 as a Special Release. A couple of months earlier the traditional limited bottling for the Feis Isle (Islay Festival) was launched, this year a *15 year old*. Last years Festival bottling, a *14 year old*, was the first single cask Lagavulin ever.

Independent bottlings are almost impossible to find. One of the latest was a 21 year old released by Murray McDavid two years ago.

History (continued):

1908 – Peter Mackie uses the old distillery buildings to build a new distillery, Malt Mill, on the site. Mackie had previously been agent for Laphroaig but the owners were not content and terminated the contract. Malt Mill was an attempt by Mackie to compete and force Laphroaig out of the market.

1924 – Peter Mackie passes away and Mackie & Co. changes name to White Horse Distillers.

1927 – White Horse Distillers becomes part of Distillers Company Limited (DCL).

1930 – The distillery is administered under Scottish Malt Distillers (SMD).

1952 – An explosive fire breaks out and causes considerable damage.

1960 – Malt Mills distillery closes and today it houses Lagavulin's visitor centre.

1974 – Floor maltings are decommisioned and malt is bought from Port Ellen instead.

1988 – Lagavulin 16 years becomes one of six Classic Malts.

1998 – A Pedro Ximenez sherry finish is launched as a Distillers Edition.

2002 – Two cask strengths (12 years and 25 years) are launched.

2006 – A 30 year old is released.

2007 – A 21 year old from 1985 and the sixth edition of the 12 year old are released.

2008 – A new 12 year old is released.

Lagavulin 12 year old

DR – A monster truck nose with rich smoke, lychee and unripe pear, with prickly smoke and banana skin notes on the palate, and a superb long dark chocolate and smoky finish.

DS – Peaty fudge and oil on the nose. Licorice root flavours flood through with hot pepper and spice. Long bitter finish with a licorice aftertaste.

30 years old

Distiller's Edition

16 years old

12 years old (seventh edition)

21 years old

Laphroaig

Owner:
Beam Global
Spirits & Wine

Region/district:
Islay

Founded:
1810

Status:
Active (vc)

Capacity:
2 700 000 litres

Address: Port Ellen, Islay, Argyll PA42 7DU

Tel:
01496 302418

website:
www.laphroaig.com

History:

1810 – Brothers Alexander and Donald Johnston found Laphroaig.

1815 – Official year of starting.

1836 – Donald buys out Alexander and takes over operations.

1837 – James and Andrew Gairdner found Ardenistiel a stone's throw from Laphroaig.

1847 – Donald Johnston is killed in an accident in the distillery when he falls into a kettle of boiling hot burnt ale. The Manager of neighbouring Lagavulin, Walter Graham, takes over.

1857 – Operation is back in the hands of the Johnston family when Donald's son Dugald takes over.

circa 1860 – Ardenistiel Distillery merges with Laphroaig.

1877 – Dugald, being without heirs, passes away and his sister Isabella, married to their cousin Alexander takes over.

1907 – Alexander Johnston dies and the distillery is inherited by his two sisters Catherine Johnston and Mrs. William Hunter (Isabella Johnston).

1908 – Ian Hunter arrives in Islay to assist his mother and aunt with the distillery.

1923 – The two stills are increased to four.

1927 – Catherine Johnston dies and Ian Hunter takes over.

1928 – Isabella Johnston dies and Ian Hunter becomes sole owner.

1950 – Ian Hunter forms D. Johnston & Company

1954 – Ian Hunter passes away and management of the distillery is taken over by Elisabeth "Bessie" Williamson, who was previously Ian Hunters PA and secretary. She becomes Director of the Board and Managing Director.

For the last seven years Laphroaig has been the best-selling of all Islay single malts and sales have increased by 50% during that time. With the growing interest in peated whisky, things are likely to continue in this manner. The owners, Fortune Brands, have also proved that they wish to put their stakes into spirits where returns are higher. The wine business was therefore sold to Constellation Brands last November. Laphroaig is one of very few distilleries with their own maltings. Four malting floors hold 7 tonnes each and together account for 15% of requirements while the rest comes from Port Ellen maltings on Islay. Previously the malt was dried for 13 hours over a peat fire followed by 18 hours using warm air. It gave malt with a phenol content of 43 ppm. Nowadays the peat fire drying is for 18 hours and the hot air for 15 hours which results in a malt of 50-55 ppm. The malt specification from Port Ellen is set to 40 ppm and the final result is 25 ppm in the finished spirit. They have a stainless steel mash tun and six wash backs also made of stainless steel. The distillery uses an unusual combination of three wash stills and four spirit stills. The last one which was installed in 1972 is twice the size of the others. 48 000 casks are maturing in three dunnage and three racked warehouses and a further 10 000 casks at Ardbeg. Laphroaig is now running more or less at full capacity; i. e. 2.6 million litres. It seems reasonable, with the increase in sales, that Laphroaig will be the first Islay distillery to follow the recent example from many mainland distilleries in expanding capacity. Not so long ago 60% went to the blending industry but that percentage has decreased significantly.

The core range of Laphroaig is a *10 year old*, *10 year old cask strength*, *Quarter Cask* and a *15 year old*. The last-mentioned will be phased out and replaced by an 18 year old in April 2009. Limited editions include the *40 year old* and, released in 2007, a *25 year old* and a *27 year old*. This year's special release launched in connection with Feis Isle was *Cairdeas*, a young whisky drawn from quarter casks with the addition of a small proportion of 17 year old. Some months later a limited version was released, *Cairdeas 30 year old* and also *Laphroaig Triple Wood* with a maturation first in ex-bourbon barrels, then in Quarter Casks and finally in European Oak.

Independent bottlings are still common. Recent releases include Blackadder 18 year old from 1990, a 17 year old from 1990 by Signatory and an 8 year old from Single Malts of Scotland.

History (continued):

1967 – Seager Evans & Company buys the distillery through Long John Distillery, having already acquired part of Laphroaig in 1962.

1968 – The number of stills is increased from four to six.

1972 – Bessie Williamson retires. Another spirit still is installed bringing the total to seven.

1975 – Whitbread & Co. buys Seager Evans (now renamed Long John International) from Schenley International.

1989 – The spirits division of Whitbread is sold to Allied Distillers.

1991 – Allied Distillers launches Caledonian Malts. Laphroaig is one of the four malts included.

1993 – A severe gale blows the pagoda roof off the kilns, but it is repaired.

1994 – HRH Prince Charles gives his Royal Warrant to Laphroaig. Friends of Laphroaig is founded.

1995 – A 10 year old cask strength is launched.

2001 – 4 000 bottles of a 40 year old, the oldest-ever Laphroaig, are released.

2002 – The legendary distillery manager Iain Henderson retires.

2004 – Quarter Cask, a 5 year old Laphroaig matured for 7 months in a quarter cask (i. e. 105 litres) is launched in a limited edition.

2005 – Fortune Brands becomes new owner.

2007 – A vintage 1980 (27 years old) and a 25 year old are released.

2008 – Cairdeas, Cairdeas 30 year old and Triple Wood are released.

Laphroaig 10 year old

DR – Salt, peat, seawood and tar in a glorious and absorbing nose, then structured and rock like barley with waves of tarry peat washing over them, then a long phenolic and peaty finish.

DS – Pungent peat, oats and seaweed on the nose. Salty and earthy on the palate with a heavy thud of medicinal flavours (muscle rub) and a long peppery finish.

Cairdeas

Vintage 1980 27 years old

10 years old

10 years old cask strength

Quarter Cask

Linkwood

Owner:
Diageo

Region/district:
Speyside

Founded: **Status:**
1821 Active

Capacity:
2 240 000 litres

Address: Elgin, Morayshire IV30 3RD

Tel: **website:**
01343 862000 www.malts.com

History:

1821 – Peter Brown founds the distillery.

1825 – Linkwood comes on stream.

1868 – Peter Brown passes away and his son William inherits the distillery.

1872 – William demolishes the distillery and builds a new one.

1874 – The new distillery is inaugurated.

1897 – Linkwood Glenlivet Distillery Company Ltd takes over operations.

1902 – Innes Cameron, a whisky trader from Elgin, joins the Board and eventually becomes the major shareholder and Director.

1932 – Innes Cameron dies and Scottish Malt Distillers takes over in 1933.

1962 – Major refurbishment takes place.

1971 – The two stills are increased by four. Technically, the four new stills belong to a new distillery sometimes referred to as Linkwood B.

1982 – Distillers Company Limited (DCL) launches their series The Ascot Malt Cellar which includes Linkwood 12 years.

1985 – Linkwood A (the two original stills) closes.

1990 – Linkwood A is in production again for a few months each year.

2002 – A 26 year old from 1975 is launched as a Rare Malt.

2005 – A 30 year old from 1974 is launched as a Rare Malt.

2008 – Three different wood finishes (all 26 year old) are released.

Linkwood 12 year old

DS – Sour fruits dominate the nose which is also buttery. The palate is cerealy and similar to new oak. The finish is short but warming.

Linkwood distillery was established in 1821, but it was only in the early 20th century that people began to discover its whisky. It was Robert Innes Cameron, who acquired it in 1902, who made Linkwood single malt's name known in the blending industry. Cameron was also owner of Benrinnes, Teaninich and Tamdhu. His hard work and meticulous efforts resulted in Linkwood och Benrinnes being among the Top Twelve blender's list. Cameron became an influential figure n the whisky industry and later became chairman of the Malt Distillers Association. He died in 1932, aged 72.

When Linkwood was refurbished in the 70s, a new stillhouse with four stills was built. This was named Linkwood B since the old stillhouse by the road with one pair of stills was still in use and hence named Linkwood A. Currently only the new still house, B, is used. The washbacks in Linkwood A are still in use, while the mash house and still house are not. Both still houses produced different styles as Linkwood A used a cast iron worm tub while Linkwood B uses condensers. When both were operating, the spirit was mixed prior to casking which is the reason why no Linkwood A exists on its own. The distillery is equipped with a cast iron mash tun, eleven washbacks made of wood (five in the new still house and six in the old) and three pairs of stills.

Most of the production goes into Johnnie Walker and White Horse. The core expression is a *12 year old Flora & Fauna* but in autumn 2008, Diageo came up with a real surprise; three new Linkwood were released and not only that - they were *26 years old*. But perhaps the biggest thrill was that they had all been finished for the last 14 years in three different types of casks - port, rum and sweet red wine. They were bottled in specially designed 50 cl bottles.

Independent bottlings are not that un-common. Blackadder recently released a 17 year old from 1989, from Cadenheads came an 18 year old from the same year and Ian MacLeod released two bottlings - one 15 year old from 1992 and an 11 year old Tokay finish from 1996.

26 years old
(red wine finish)

Loch Lomond

Owner:
Loch Lomond
Distillery Co.

Region/district:
Western Highlands

Founded: 1965
Status: Active
Capacity: 4 000 000 litres

Address: Lomond Estate, Alexabdria G83 0TL

Tel: 01389 752781
website: www.lochlomonddistillery.com

History:
1965 – The distillery is built by Littlemill Distillery Company Ltd owned by Duncan Thomas and American Barton Brands.

1966 – Production commences.

1971 – Duncan Thomas is bought out and Barton Brands reforms as Barton Distilling (Scotland) Ltd.

1984 – The distillery closes.

1985 – Glen Catrine Bonded Warehouse Ltd with Alexander Bulloch at the helm buys Loch Lomond Distillery.

1987 – The distillery resumes production.

1993 – Grain spirits are also distilled.

1997 – A fire destroys 300,000 litres of maturing whisky.

1999 – Two more stills are installed.

2005 – Inchmoan and Craiglodge are officially launched for the first time. Both are 4 years old from 2001. Inchmurrin 12 years is launched.

2006 – Inchmurrin 4 years, Croftengea 1996 (9 years) and Glen Douglas 2001 (4 years) are launched.

Loch Lomond

DS – Malt and honey on the oily nose with a whiff of mussels. The palate is briny and spicy with malty flavours – light and dry. Short finish with a seafood aftertaste.

Loch Lomond Distillery has always followed its own path which became especially obvious in spring 2008. The trade organisation Scotch Whisky Association put forward a suggestion as to how Scotch whisky should be classified and termed in the future (for more, see p 242). Five categories were identified and the discussions in the industry and among enthusiasts were stormy. It all came to a head in late spring when Loch Lomond Distillery demanded another category; single malt whisky distilled in a column still. Loch Lomond are unique in using this method in Scotland and SWA considered this as not being a traditional way to make malt whisky in Scotland while their opponents persisted that this had been practice at many distilleries in the past. It should be mentioned in this context that Loch Lomond is not a member of SWA.

Loch Lomond Distillery is a virtually self-sufficient distillery. It has its own malt distillery, grain distillery, cooperage and bottling plant (Glen Catrine Bonded Warehouse) and only lack own maltings. The equipment consists of a stainless steel full lauter mash tun and ten stainless steel washbacks. There are two normal stills with traditional swan necks and four stills with adjustable rectifying columns. This makes it possible to vary the whisky character and widen the product range further. The Coffey Still installed in 1993 contributes to Loch Lomond's uniqueness of being the only Scottish distillery producing both malt and grain whisky at the same site. Annual production at Loch Lomond is 10 million litres of grain alcohol and 2.5 million litres of malt alcohol.

Loch Lomond produces a broad range of whiskies. Currently there are eight expressions, from unpeated Glen Douglas to heavily peated Croftengea and Inchfad.

Single malt: Loch Lomond no age, Loch Lomond 21 years, Old Rhosdhu 5 years, Old Rhosdhu 1967 32 years, Inchmurrin 4 and 12 years, Inchmoan 2001 4 years, Craiglodge 2001 4 years, Croftengea 2003 4 years, Glen Douglas 2002 5 years, Inchfad 2002 5 years.

Single blended: Loch Lomond

Blended: Scots Earl **Single grain:** Loch Lomond

Inchmurrin 12 years old

Longmorn

Owner:
Chivas Brothers
(Pernod Ricard)

Region/district:
Speyside

Founded: **Status:** **Capacity:**
1894 Active 3 500 000 litres

Address: Longmorn, Morayshire IV30 8SJ

Tel: **website:**
01343 554139 -

History:

1893 – John Duff & Company, which founded Glenlossie already in 1876, starts construction. John Duff, George Thomson and Charles Shirres are involved in the company. The total cost amounts to £20,000.

1894 – First production in December.

1897 – John Duff buys out the others and founds Longmorn Distillery.

1898 – John Duff builds another distillery next to Longmorn which is called Benriach (at times aka Longmorn no. 2). Duff declares bankruptcy and the shares are sold by the bank to James R. Grant.

1970 – The distillery company is merged with The Glenlivet & Glen Grant Distilleries and Hill Thomson & Co. Ltd. Own floor maltings ceases.

1972 – The number of stills is increased from four to six.

1974 – Another two stills are added.

1978 – Seagrams takes over through The Chivas & Glenlivet Group.

1994 – Seagrams introduces The Heritage Selection. Apart from Longmorn, Glen Keith, Benriach and Strathisla are included.

2001 – Pernod Ricard buys Seagram Spirits & Wine together with Diageo and Pernod Ricard takes over the Chivas group.

2004 – A 17 year old cask strength is released.

2007 – A 16 year old is released replacing the 15 year old.

Longmorn 16 year old

DR – Cut flowers and mixed fruit on the nose, rounded and full fruit and honey with some wood and spice adding complexity, long and rich finish.

DS – Soft hints of tropical fruits and malt on the nose. Strong sherry flavours mingle with sharp fruit and malt. A long, tingling finish.

Longmorn has often been called every distiller's second favourite malt, second only to their own produce. Apparently the owners have been on the right track from the very beginning. In 1897, just four years after inception the National Guardian wrote; "it jumped into favour with buyers from the earliest day on which it was offered". The man who started it was John Duff who 20 years earlier had founded Glenlossie and three years after Longmorn next door. Duff was of an adventurous and expansive nature and also made attempts to build distilleries in South Africa and the United States, though without success. Duff was not able to enjoy the success of Longmorn for long as much of his capital was tied up in whisky stocks and the effects of the infamous Pattison crash in 1898 hit him hard. In 1909 he declared bankruptcy.

Longmorn still enjoys a solid reputation amongst blenders and it is the most important ingredient in Chivas Regal 18 years old and in the Royal Salute.

The distillery is equipped with a stainless steel traditional infusion mash tun and the wooden washbacks were replaced some years ago by eight stainless steel ones. No less than four pairs of stills in two separate stillhouses have been operating at full capacity since Pernod Ricard took over in 2002. The wash stills were some of the last in Scotland to be fired using coal (this was abandoned in 1994). It remains to be seen in a couple of years whether the character of the whisky has changed due to the alteration that was made in heating.

The 15 year old was replaced by the *16 year old* in 2007 and there is also a *17 year old cask strength* for sale at Chivas's visitor centres which was released for the first time in 2004.

Recent independent bottlings include Douglas Laing 12 years old (1995), Ian MacLeod 12 years old (1996) and Duncan Taylor 1973.

16 years old

Macallan

Owner: **Region/district:**
Edrington Group   Speyside

Founded: **Status:**   **Capacity:**
1824   Active (vc)   8 000 000 litres

Address: Easter Elchies, Craigellachie,
Morayshire AB38 9RX

Tel: **website:**
01340 871471   www.themacallan.com

History:
1824 – The distillery is licensed to Alexander Reid under the name Elchies Distillery.

1847 – Alexander Reid passes away and James Shearer Priest and James Davidson take over.

1868 – James Stuart takes over the licence. He founds Glen Spey distillery a decade later.

1896 – James Stuart buys the distillery.

1892 – Stuart sells the distillery to Roderick Kemp from Elgin who has previously worked at and been part-owner of Talisker. Kemp expands the distillery and names it Macallan-Glenlivet.

1909 – Roderick Kemp passes away and the Roderick Kemp Trust is established to secure the family's future ownership.

1965 – The number of stills is increased from six to twelve.

1966 – The trust is reformed as a private limited company.

1968 – The company is introduced on the London Stock Exchange.

1974 – The number of stills is increased to 18.

1975 – Another three stills are added, now making the total 21.

1979 – Allan Schiach, descendant of Roderick Kemp, becomes the new chairman of the board after Peter Schiach.

1980 – The name changes to Macallan and a large launch campaign takes place in the UK.

1984 – The first official 18 year old single malt is launched.

1986 – Japanese Suntory buys 25% of Macallan-Glenlivet plc stocks.

All the major single malt brands are taking up position to meet the increased demand world wide. Glenfiddich made whisky previously destined for blends available by starting up Ailsa Bay distillery, Glenlivet is expanding production capacity and Glen Grant have unveiled plans to do the same. In 2007 Macallan finally revealed plans to recommission six stills that had been dormant since the early 1980s. These stills (two wash stills and four spirit stills) are gathered in the separate old still house which has now been completely recommisioned. The two wash stills were replaced as was the bottom of the mash tun. They have also built six new Douglas fir washbacks. This means that total capacity will increase 30% to 8 million litres. The first part of the expansion of on-site warehouses which began last year has also been completed. The first two new warehouses are ready and will hold 50,000 casks.

Macallan is one of few Scottish distilleries still using the old Golden Promise barley in the production. It is grown on fields that border the road leading to the distillery. It is sometimes called the Macallan signature barley although recent years have seen only a small percentage of production using it. A new barley strain developed in cooperation with a British plant breeding company has been in trial in recent years and if results prove promising it could become an exclusive for Macallan.

With the recommissioning of the old stillhouse, Macallan now has 16 stainless steel washbacks and six wooden ones, seven wash stills and fourteen spirit stills. The wash stills are directly fired with gas, while the spirit stills are indirectly fired using steam coils. The spirit is matured in 16 dunnage and 21 racked warehouses. The distillery is now running at full capacity, equalling 8 million litres. Sales in 2007 increased by 16% to 570,000 cases which gives them third place on the top list, just after Glenlivet.

New releases in late 2007 and 2008 are the *55 year old Lalique* and *Estate Oak*, a global travel retail exclusive. For every bottle of Estate Oak sold Macallan will plant an oak tree on Macallan Estate (similar to the Woodland Estate bottlings from 2005). The current range can be divided into:

Sherry Oak: 10 and 12 years, Cask Strength (US only), 18, 25 and 30 years
Fine Oak: 8, 10, 12 15, 17, 18, 21, 25 and 30 years old.
Travel retail: Elegancia 12 years, Cask Strength 10 years, Whisky Maker's Selection, 1851 Inspiration, 40 years
Distillery exclusives: Winter Cask Selection 2006, Summer Cask Selection 2006, Woodland Estate, Estate Oak
Fine and Rare: A range of vintages from 1926 to 1976.

History (continued):

1996 – Highland Distilleries buys the remaining stocks and terminate the Kemp family's influence on Macallan. 11,000 bottles of 1874 Replica are launched.

1999 – Edrington and William Grant & Sons buys Highland Distilleries (where Edrington, Suntory and Remy-Cointreau already are shareholders) for £601 million. They form the 1887 Company which owns Highland Distilleries with 70% held by Edrington and 30% by William Grant & Sons (excepting the 25% share held by Suntory).

2000 – The first single cask from Macallan (1981) is named Exceptional 1.

2001 – A new visitor centre is opened and 1861 Replica (17,400 bottles) are introduced.

2002 – Macallan Elegancia replaces Macallan 12 years in the duty-free assortment. 1841 Replica, Exceptional II and Exceptional III, from 1980, are also launched during the year.

2003 – 1876 Replica (19,800 bottles) and Exceptional IV, single cask from 1990 (864 bottles) are launched.

2004 – Exceptional V, single cask from 1989 (858 bottles) is launched as well as Exceptional VI, single cask from 1990 (816 bottles). The Fine Oak series is launched and Macallan 18 years old takes first place in Whisky Magazine's 'Best Malts of the World'.

2005 – New expressions are Macallan Woodland Estate, Winter Edition and the 50 year old.

2006 – Fine Oak 17 years old and Vintage 1975 are launched.

2007 – 1851 Inspiration and Whisky Maker's Selection are released as a part of the Travel Retail range. 12 year old Gran Reserva is launched in Taiwan and Japan.

2008 – Estate Oak and 55 year old Lalique are released.

Macallan 10 year old Fine Oak

DR – The nose is a mix of honey, vanilla and tinned pear, the palate combines barley sugar, wholemeal biscuits and a touch of blood orange. The finish is medium and rich.

DS – Malty and rich with a honey lozenge nose. Herbal and honeyed on the palate – rich and full bodied. The finish is reminiscent of pastry and honey.

Macallan 10 year old Sherry Oak

DR – A big hit of sherry and with red berry fruit dominate the nose. The malt has a big mouth feel, with sherry, wood and spice all in the mix and plenty of rich fruit driving towards the finish.

DS – Rich fruit and sherry flavours on the sweet and luxurious nose. The palate is again rich and moreish with lots of raisiny, fruit flavours which linger on the long and heavenly finish.

Whisky Maker's Selection

Gran Reserva 12 years old

Estate Oak

10 years old

Fine Oak 17 yo

1949 vintage

Cask Strength

18 years old

25 years old

Elegancia

Macduff

Owner:
John Dewar & Sons Ltd
(Bacardi)

Region/district:
Highlands

Founded: 1962
Status: Active
Capacity: 3 200 000 litres

Address: Banff, Aberdeenshire AB45 3JT

Tel: 01261 812612
website: -

History:
1962 – The distillery is founded by Marty Dyke, George Crawford and Brodie Hepburn (who is also involved in Tullibardine and Deanston). Macduff Distillers Ltd is the name of the company.

1963 – Production starts.

1965 – The number of stills is increased from two to three.

1967 – Stills now total four.

1972 – William Lawson Distillers buys the distillery from Glendeveron Distilleries.

1980 – William Lawson is bought by Martini Rossi through the subsidiary General Beverage Corporation.

1990 – A fifth still is installed.

1992 – Bacardi buys Martini Rossi (including William Lawson) and transfers Macduff to the subsidiary John Dewar & Sons.

Glen Deveron 10 year old

DR – The nose is a mix of crisp barley, orange, hay and a trace of smoke, and on the palate an oily and fruity combination beautifully coats the mouth before giving way to a pepper, savoury and astringent finish.

DS – A malty, heathery nose with some earthy, peaty notes. Some peatiness at first, again quite earthy with rich spice. A medium, peaty finish.

Macduff is one of those distilleries built specifically to produce malt for blended Scotch. It was at the beginning of the sixties when the industry experienced a boom similar to that of the 1890s. Exports of Scotch whisky tripled between 1960 and 1971 and Brodie Hepburn, then owner of Tullibardine, saw that there was a demand for whisky to be used for blending. He collaborated with the fashionable Mayfair wine merchant Block, Grey & Block and a couple of local businessmen and built a distillery 1962 in Macduff opposite Banff on the Deveron's outflow in Banff Bay. Ten years later it was bought by William Lawson Distillers and thereby established a connection with a blended whisky which is still in force today. Being comparatively unknown, William Lawson´s blend sells 15 million bottles annually, especially in southern Europe and Mexico.

The distillery is equipped with a stainless steel semi-lauter mash tun, nine washbacks made of stainless steel and five stills. To use an even couple of stills is the most common practice, but there are a handful of distilleries which divert from this. There are only two which use a combination of two wash stills and three spirit stills; Macduff and Talisker. For maturation, a mix of sherry and bourbon casks are used. Parts of the distillery were rebuilt in 1990 and 2000 and new boilers were installed in 2007.

Macduff is the one of the five Dewar´s distilleries which sells the most single malt. 450,000 bottles a year are sold more or less exclusively abroad, mainly to France.

A bottle of single malt bearing the name Glen Deveron is an official bottling from Macduff Distillery. If the name on the label is Macduff, it is an independent bottling. The most common Glen Deveron today is a *10 year old*. Older versions of 8 and 12 year olds are also available. Recent independent bottlings include a couple of old ones from Duncan Taylor (1968 and 1969) and a 17 year old from 1991 from Single Malts of Scotland.

10 years old

Mannochmore

Owner:		Region/district:
Diageo		Speyside

Founded:	Status:	Capacity:
1971	Active	3 220 000 litres

Address: Elgin, Morayshire IV30 8SS

Tel:	website:
01343 862000	www.malts.com

History:
1971 – Scottish Malt Distillers (SMD) founds the distillery on the site of their sister distillery Glenlossie. It is managed by John Haig & Co. Ltd.

1985 – The distillery is mothballed.

1989 – In production again.

1992 – A Flora & Fauna series 12 years old becomes the first official bottling.

1997 – United Distillers launches Loch Dhu – The Black Whisky which is a 10 year old Mannochmore. A 22 year old Rare Malt from 1974 and a sherry-matured Manager´s Dram 18 years are also launched.

Mannochmore 12 year old

DS – Fresh and minty with malty notes on the nose. Sweet and again minty on the palate with fresh baked bread flavours. A hint of oak in the finish with a bready sweetness in the aftertaste.

No less than 17 of Diageo´s 27 Scottish distilleries are located in Morayshire. Most were built in the 19th century though a few were built during the 1960s and 70s when optimism in the industry was as high as it is today. Demand grew at around 9% per annum between 1965 and 1980 and when Mannochmore was built in 1971, it was decided it would be a distillery of high capacity; 3.2 million litres. The site chosen was that of the Glenlossie distillery, which was already owned by Diageo Towards the end of the seventies, the oil crisis hit the world economy hard and people started to change their drinking habits from expensive imported Scotch to cheaper domestic vodka or to wine and beer. Mannochmore managed to survive the closing of several distilleries in 1983 but was mothballed in 1985 only to be re-opened again in 1989.

The workforce used to alternate between Mannochmore and Glenlossie with each distillery being in production for half a year at a time. With the increasing demand for whisky this schedule has been abandoned with both distilleries now producing 12 months a year since 2007. Mannochmore is equipped with cast iron full lauter mashtun, eight washbacks made of larch and three pairs of stills. Both distilleries share the cask warehouses which hold 200,000 casks in total, a large part coming from other distilleries within Diageo. There is also a huge dark grains plant on site which processes draff and pot ale from 21 different distilleries. It produces no less than 1,000 tonnes of dark grains, used for feeding livestock, per week, from 2,600 tonnes of draff and 8 million litres of pot ale.

Aside from the *12 year old* a special, dark-coloured, Mannochmore named Loch Dhu was launched in 1996. It quickly became a cult whisky, especially in Denmark.

Independent bottlings are not very common. The only recent release was a 1996 from Duncan Taylor

Flora & Fauna 12 years old

Miltonduff

Owner:
Chivas Brothers
(Pernod Ricard)

Region/district:
Speyside

Founded: 1824
Status: Active
Capacity: 5 500 000 litres

Address: Miltonduff, Elgin,
Morayshire IV30 8TQ

Tel: 01343 547433
website: -

History:
1824 – Andrew Peary and Robert Bain obtain a licence for Miltonduff Distillery. It has previously operated as an illicit farm distillery called Milton Distillery but changes name when the Duff family buys the site it is operating on.

1866 – William Stuart buys the distillery.

1895 – Thomas Yool & Co. becomes new part-owners.

1936 – Thomas Yool & Co. sells the distillery to Hiram Walker Gooderham & Worts. The latter transfers administration to the newly acquired subsidiary George Ballantine & Son.

1964 – A pair of Lomond stills is installed to produce the rare Mosstowie.

1974-75 – Major reconstruction of the distillery.

1981 – The Lomond stills are decommissioned and replaced by two ordinary pot stills; the number of stills now totalling six.

1986 – Allied Lyons buys 51% of Hiram Walker.

1987 – Allied Lyons acquires the rest of Hiram Walker.

1991 – Allied Distillers follow United Distillers' example of Classic Malts and introduce Caledonian Malts where Tormore, Glendronach and Laphroaig are included in addition to Miltonduff. Tormore is later replaced by Scapa.

2005 – Chivas Brothers (Pernod Ricard) become new owners through the acquisition of Allied Domecq.

Miltonduff 10 year old (Gordon & MacPhail)
DR – Clean, honeyed and deceptively gentle on the nose, chunky malt and clean vanilla on the plate, pleasant and warming finish

DS – Sweet biscuit and pine nuts on the nose. Mildly sweet with some maltiness and again pine nuts on the palate. Sweet-ish finish with a malty aftertaste.

In 1935 the largest distiller in Canada, Hiram Walker, Gooderham & Worts bought George Ballantine & Son. The problem was that they did not have enough malt whisky to go into the blend, especially since their worst competitor in North America, Seagrams, demanded from DCL (later Diageo) that they should not deliver to any competitors. The only solution was to buy their own capacity and in the following years both Glenburgie and Miltonduff were acquired. George Robertson, the master blender of Ballantine´s at that time, eventually decided it was time to create a blended Scotch superior to all others. The 17 year old Ballantine was born the year after and was perhaps the first example of the current trend of premiumisation. The original fingerprint malts of the 17 year old, apart from Miltonduff and Glenburgie were Ardbeg, Pulteney, Scapa, Glencadam and Balblair. These were sometimes referred to as "Ballantine´s magnificent seven".

Miltonduff a few miles southwest of Elgin is a high-capacity distillery. In fact it is second only to Glenlivet in the Chivas group and with no less than 16 stainless steel washbacks and three pairs of stills it, together with Glenburgie, produces the lion´s share of malt whisky to be included in the Ballantine´s blend. An evidence of this distillery's strong position with Pernod Ricard is that the company recently moved its headquarters for Northern Division from Strathisla to Miltonduff. The group's engineering department and a dark grains plant are also housed there.

For a period of time Lomond stills were also used at Miltonduff. The malt from these stills was named Mosstowie and is still available. An official Miltonduff 15 year old was released some years ago but it has now been discontinued. Otherwise Gordon & MacPhail are more or less responsible for "official" bottlings from Miltonduff. A 10 year old and two limited editions – cask strength from 1993 and a 1968 vintage are the current ones. Other recent bottlings are a Duncan Taylor 1966 as well as an 8 year old from the same company.

Gordon & MacPhail
1993 Cask Strength

Mortlach

Owner: Diageo

Region/district: Speyside

Founded: 1823
Status: Active
Capacity: 2 910 000 litres

Address: Dufftown, Keith, Banffshire AB55 4AQ

Tel: 01340 822100
website: www.malts.com

History:

1823 – The distillery is founded by James Findlater.

1824 – Donald Macintosh and Alexander Gordon become part-owners.

1831 – The distillery is sold to John Robertson for £270.

1832 – A. & T. Gregory buys Mortlach.

1837 – James and John Grant of Aberlour become part-owners. No production takes place at Mortlach as the equipment probably is dismantled and used in building Glen Grant Distillery.

1842 – The distillery is now owned by John Alexander Gordon and the Grant brothers.

1851 – Mortlach is once again an up and running distillery after having been used as a church and a brewery for some years. The whisky is sold under the name The Real John Gordon.

1853 – George Cowie joins as part-owner with Gordon.

1867 – John Alexander Gordon dies and Cowie becomes sole owner.

1895 – George Cowie Jr. joins the company.

1897 – The number of stills is increased from three to six.

1923 – Alexander Cowie sells the distillery to John Walker & Sons.

1925 – John Walker becomes part of Distillers Company Limited (DCL).

1930 – The administration is transferred to Scottish Malt Distillers (SMD).

1964 – Major refurbishment.

1968 – Floor maltings ceases.

1996 – Mortlach 1972 (23 years) is released as a Rare Malt. The distillery is renovated at a cost of £1.5 million.

1998 – Mortlach 1978 (20 years) is released as a Rare Malt.

2004 – Mortlach 1971, a 32 year old cask strength is released.

Mortlach 16 year old

DR – Christmas cask and rich sherry nose, and a rich full plum-fruit and soft summer fruit palate. The finish is rich, full and long, with the wood making its presence felt.

DS – Heavily sherried and fruity on the nose – floral and spicy. The palate is also floral and heavy with stewed fruit flavours – visocus. Dried fruits dominate the finish.

When it comes to the official 16 year old from the owners, the Mortlach single malt has become almost impossible to find these days. Even the shelves of the visitor centre shops within the Diageo group were empty in spring 2008. One could say that the single malt has become a victim of its own success as a blending malt. It has always been highly rated among blenders and plays an important part of rapidly increasing sales of Johnnie Walker Black Label. There is uncertainty whether Diageo will offer the 16 year old again, but if so it will probably take at least 3-4 years. Mortlach has many followers around the world and in Germany one of the most dedicated fans has created an impressive website devoted to the distillery; www.mortlach.de.

The stillhouse at Mortlach is a peculiar and unique sight with six stills of various shapes and formats. Neither does the process, which probably has been in use already since 1897, resemble any other distillery's. It is usually called partial triple distillation and is a variation of the method used at Benrinnes and Springbank. The aim is to achieve a robust and flavour-rich whisky with little copper contact. A new semi-lauter mash tun, costing £1,5 million, was installed in connection with a refurbishment in 1996 and there are six washbacks made of larch. Mortlach is also one of the fairly few distilleries still using worm tubs made of larch for cooling the vapours. There are five dunnage warehouses with a total capacity of 21,000 casks while the rest is sent to central warehouses or other distilleries in the group.

The official bottling of Mortlach (Flora & Fauna) is *16 years* but in 2004 a *32 year old cask strength* from 1971 was released as a limited edition. Mortlach has always been popular with independent bottlers. Recent expressions include a 10 year old port finish from Ian MacLeod, a 14 year old (1992) from Cadenhead, a 12 year old (1994) sherry-matured from Douglas Laing and a 1957 from Gordon & MacPhail.

Flora & Fauna 16 years old

Oban

Owner:
Diageo

Region/district:
Western Highlands

Founded: **Status:** **Capacity:**
1794 Active (vc) 670 000 litres

Address: Stafford Street, Oban, Argyll PA34 5NH

Tel: **website:**
01631 572004 (vc) www.malts.com

History:
1793 – John and Hugh Stevenson found the distillery on premises previously used for brewing.

1794 – Start of operations.

1820 – Hugh Stevenson dies.

1821 – Hugh Stevenson's son Thomas, having recently returned from Buenos Aires, takes over.

1822 – Thomas Stevenson acquires the remaining shares in Oban Brewery Company.

1829 – A series of unsuccessful business investments force Thomas Stevenson into bankruptcy with debts of over £8,000. His eldest son John takes over operations at the distillery.

1830 – John buys the distillery from his father's creditors for £1,500.

1866 – Peter Cumstie buys the distillery.

1883 – Cumstie sells Oban to James Walter Higgins who refurbishes and modernizes it.

1898 – The Oban & Aultmore-Glenlivet Co. takes over with Alexander Edwards at the helm A consortium made up of John Dewar & Sons, James Buchanan & Company and White Horse Distillers is also involved in the company.

1923 – The Oban Distillery Co. owned by Buchanan-Dewar takes over.

1925 – Buchanan-Dewar becomes part of Distillers Company Limited (DCL).

1930 – Administration is transferred to Scottish Malt Distillers (SMD).

1931 – Production ceases.

1937 – In production again.

1968 – Floor maltings ceases and the distillery closes for reconstruction.

1972 – Reopening of the distillery.

1979 – Oban 12 years is on sale.

1988 – United Distillers launches Classic Malts. Oban 14 year is selected to represent Western Highlands.

1989 – A visitor centre is built.

1998 – A Distillers' Edition is launched.

2002– The, so far, oldest Oban (32 years) is launched in a limited edition of 6,000 bottles.

2004 – A 20 year old cask strength from 1984 (1,260 bottles) is released.

Oban 14 year old

DR – A mixed nose of heather, honey, pineapple and nuts, a perfectly balanced mix of grapey fruit, pineapple chunks, roast nuts and smoky undertow, and a rounded and fruity finish, drying and more-ish.

DS – A heavily perfumed nose with honey and malt notes. Soft, fruity and mildly spicy. A dry finish with a honey after-taste.

Oban is the second smallest of the Diageo distilleries with only Royal Lochnagar being smaller. It is also unusual in that it is an urban distillery. There are only a handful of such distilleries remaining, for example Glen Garioch, Springbank och Glen Rothes. Furthermore Oban is one of only nine distilleries founded in the 18th century which are still active.

The distillery is equipped with a stainless steel mash tun, four washbacks made of European larch and one pair of stills. There is also a rectangular, double worm tub built into the roof. This was the traditional way of condensing the spirit vapours, allowing the spirit to run through long, spiralling copper pipes submerged in water. The more modern way is using a condenser connected directly to the spirit where the spirit flows in a copper tube into which a number of pipes into which cooling water flows. Tube condensers tend to deliver a lighter spirit due to the massive copper contact while the spirit from a worm tub cooled distillation hints at ruggedness. However it is important to understand that other parts of the process can both compensate and enforce this. Only 14 Scottish distilleries, of which nine belong to Diageo, still use worm tubs. Another difference between both condensers is the price. A tube condenser would typically cost around £15,000 while a worm tub costs four times that amount.

Unusually enough, almost all of the production at Oban goes to single malt which might not be so strange considering the small capacity and that Oban's popularity is great by being one of the original six Classic Malts, chosen to represent the Western Highlands.

Official bottlings are a *14 year old*, a *Distiller's Edition* with a montilla fino finish and some limited editions, among them a *32 year old* and a *20 year old*. An *18 year old* was released in autumn 2008 for sale at the distillery only and on the American market.

It is virtually impossible to find independent bottlings of Oban. The latest from Cadenhead appeared in the early nineties.

14 years old

Pulteney

Owner:
Inver House Distillers
(Thai Beverages plc)

Region/district:
Northern Highlands

Founded: 1826
Status: Active (vc)
Capacity: 1 000 000 litres

Address: Huddart St, Wick, Caithness KW1 5BA

Tel: 01955 602371
website: www.oldpulteney.com

History:

1826 – James Henderson founds the distillery.

1920 – The distillery is bought by James Watson & Co.

1923 – Buchanan-Dewar takes over.

1925 – Buchanan-Dewar becomes part of Distillers Company Limited (DCL).

1930 – Production ceases.

1951 – In production again after being acquired by the solicitor Robert Cumming.

1955 – Cumming sells to James & George Stodart Ltd, a subsidiary to Hiram Walker & Sons.

1958 – The distillery is rebuilt.

1959 – The floor maltings close.

1961 – Allied Breweries buys James & George Stodart Ltd.

1981 – Allied Breweries changes name to Allied Lyons after the acquisition of J Lyons in 1978.

1994 – Allied Lyons acquires Pedro Domecq and changes name to Allied Domecq plc.

1995 – Allied Domecq sells Pulteney to Inverhouse Distillers.

1997 – Old Pulteney 12 years is launched.

2001 – Pacific Spirits (Great Oriole Group) buys Inverhouse at a price of $85 million.

2004 – A 17 year old is launched (4 200 bottles).

2005 – A 21 year old is launched (3 000 bottles).

2006 – InverHouse changes owners when International Beverage Holdings acquires Pacific Spirits UK.

Old Pulteney 12 year old

DR – Honey and lemon lozenges on the nose, sweet citrus fruits, chunky malt and some traces of sea brine on the palate, an amusing sweet and sour two step at the finish.

DS – A hint of peat with some sugary sweetness. The palate is sweet caramel and again just the slightest touch of peat smoke which eases into the gentle finish.

Pulteney is the most northerly situated distillery on the Scottish mainland and lies in Wick, a town that was once the largest herring port in Europe. More than 1,000 boats used the port there during the heyday of the herring fishing industry in the 19th century.

In the Inver House group of brands it may be Balblair and AnCnoc which have stolen attention recently but it is Old Pulteney (as the whisky produced at Pulteney distillery is called) and Speyburn which are responsible for volumes among single malts. Around 600,000 bottles of the Old Pulteney 12 year old are sold annually and almost half of them are exported.

Pulteney is a small distillery with only one pair of stills. The wash still is large (21,700 litres) with a huge ball creating added reflux. Its top is quaintly chopped off as the still apparently was too tall for the stillroom when it was installed. The spirit still (17,300 litres) is equipped with a purifier. The semi lauter mash tun is unusually enough made of cast iron and this also applies to the six washbacks but the interiors of these are lined with stainless steel. Pulteney is one of few distilleries still using a worm tub as condenser and differs from most by having it made of stainless steel.

The distillery joined the local community a few years ago engaging in a project whereby excess heat from the distillery is being used to heat 270 houses. A plant has also been built on the distillery premises where every year 30,000 tonnes of wood chip will be turned into gas to make environmentally-friendly electricity for the distillery and also the Caithness General Hospital.

The core range is a *12 year old* with limited editions of a *17 year old* and a *21 year old*. In 2007 two exclusive *23 year old* duty free bottlings were launched, one matured in sherry casks and the other in bourbon. A new limited edition since 2007 is also the *15 year old 1991 cask strength*. A 17 year old from 1990 by Cadenheads is among the most recent independent releases.

1991 15 years old

Royal Brackla

Owner:
John Dewar & Sons
(Bacardi)

Region/district:
Highlands

Founded: **Status:** **Capacity:**
1812 Active 3 900 000 litres

Address: Cawdor, Nairn, Nairnshire IV12 5QY

Tel: **website:**
01667 402002 -

History:

1812 – The distillery is founded by Captain William Fraser.

1835 – Brackla becomes the first of three distilleries allowed to use 'Royal' in the name.

1852 – Robert Fraser & Co. takes over the distillery.

1898 – The distillery is rebuilt and Royal Brackla Distillery Company Limited is founded.

1919 – John Mitchell and James Leict from Aberdeen purchase Royal Brackla.

1926 – John Bisset & Company Ltd takes over.

1943 – Scottish Malt Distillers (SMD) buys John Bisset & Company Ltd and thereby acquires Royal Brackla.

1966 – The maltings closes.

1970 – Two stills are increased to four.

1985 – The distillery is mothballed.

1991 – Production resumes.

1993 – A 10 year old Royal Brackla is launched in United Distillers' Flora & Fauna series.

1997 – UDV spends more than £2 million on improvements and refurbishing.

1998 – Bacardi–Martini buys Dewar's from Diageo.

2004 – A new 10 year old is launched.

Royal Brackla 10 year old

DR – Pineapple and citrus fruits on the nose, candy barley, melon and pleasant sweet spice on the palate, medium sweet finish with a trace of green melon.

DS – A honey-sweet nose which is sligthly scented. The palate is earthy and quite lively – slightly bitter. The finish is long and malty with a yeasty aftertaste.

Royal Brackla was the first of a total of three distilleries to receive a Royal Warrant by William IV in 1835. In those days the honour of holding a Royal Warrant was much greater than it is today and until the reign of Queen Victoria the warrant holders totalled as few as 25. At present around 800 firms hold a Royal Warrant.

The distillery, with its beautiful location between Inverness and Forres, is equipped with a stainless steel full lauter mash tun, six washbacks made of larch and two made of stainless steel and two pairs of stills. The distillery is currently running at full capacity which means 3.9 million litres per year. All of production is matured elsewhere as the warehouses at Brackla are on a long- term lease to Diageo.

Diageo thoroughly renovated Royal Brackla in the latter half of the nineties just before they sold the distillery to Bacardi. The result was a light and elegant stillhouse with a view to Cawdor Castle.

With the possible exception of Aberfeldy, Dewars do not make a lot of noise about their single malts. This goes for Royal Brackla as well. Only a few thousand cases per year are sold as single malt with the rest going into blends like Dewar's White Label. The owners are also focussing on blends now. There are plans for expansion and their headquarter at Westthorn in Glagow (where blending and bottling also takes place) was completely redeveloped during 2008 with five new warehouses and a new blend centre. Also, the company recently bought a new site at Poniel 25 miles south of Glasgow where they plan to build a new maturation and bulk centre. The first phase will be finished in early 2009 but there are plans to expand the site until 2018.

Today's core range consists of a *10 year old* and a limited edition of a *25 year old*. Several independent bottlers have shown interest in Royal Brackla. Recent examples include a 12 year old from 1995 by Douglas Laing and a 15 year old rum finish released by Cadenheads.

10 years old

Royal Lochnagar

Owner: Diageo

Region/district: Eastern Highlands

Founded: 1845

Status: Active (vc)

Capacity: 450 000 litres

Address: Crathie, Ballater, Aberdeenshire AB35 5TB

Tel: 01339 742700

website: www.malts.com

History:

1823 – James Robertson founds a distillery in Glen Feardan on the north bank of River Dee.

1826 – The distillery is burnt down by competitors but Robertson decides to establish a new distillery near the mountain Lochnagar.

1841 – This distillery is also burnt down.

1845 – A new distillery is built by John Begg, this time on the south bank of River Dee. It is named New Lochnagar. This is today considered as the official opening year of Royal Lochnagar.

1848 – Lochnagar obtains a Royal Warrant.

1882 – John Begg passes away and his son Henry Farquharson Begg inherits the distillery.

1896 – Henry Farquharson Begg dies.

1906 – The children of Henry Begg rebuild the distillery.

1916 – When Henry Begg's only son Albert dies, the distillery is sold to John Dewar & Sons.

1925 – John Dewar & Sons becomes part of Distillers Company Limited (DCL).

1930 – Administration of the distillery is transferred to Scottish Malt Distillers (SMD).

1963 – A major reconstruction takes place.

1990 – A visitor centre is built.

2004 – A 30 year old cask strength from 1974 is launched in the Rare Malts series (6,000 bottles).

2008 – A Distiller's Edition with a Moscatel finish is released.

Royal Lochnagar 12 year old

DR – Rich fruit and honey on the nose, sophisticated mix of crystal barley, chunky fruit and delicious peat base and a warming and rounded finish.

DS – Grassy, slightly minty, with a mild spiciness on the nose. Mint is also in the mouth with more mild spices on the medium body and short finish.

Royal Lochnagar is one of three distilleries allowed to use the word Royal in its name with Royal Brackla and Glenury Royal the other two. The distillery lies just a mile from Balmoral, the Queen's summer residence in Scotland and the surroundings are truly magnificent with Royal Deeside and the imposing Lochnagar Mountain to the south. The distillery itself is a reincarnation of how a typical Highland distillery should look with its well maintained granite houses. The pretty visitor centre with its well-stocked shop attracts 10,000 visitors a year, a figure that could easily be quadrupled if it had been more accessible to one of the main roads.

The distillery is equipped with an open top cast iron mash tun, three wooden washbacks (one made of Scottish larch and two of Oregon pine) and one pair of stills. The fermentation time is quite long, from 75 up to 126 hours. The lyne arms of the stills lead out to the two cast iron worm tubs outside in order to cool the spirit vapours. The whole production is filled on site with around 1,000 casks stored in the only warehouse (the former maltings) and the rest being sent to Glenlossie for maturation.

This is Diageo's smallest operating distillery with only 4 mashes per week which gives an annual production of 450,000 litres. Royal Lochnagar is also used for education and runs courses for staff and personnel working for Diageo, namely the Malt Advocate Course.

The core range consists of the *12 year old* and the more unusual expression *Selected Reserve*. This is a vatting of selected casks (half sherry and half bourbon), usually around 18-20 years of age. This expression is not produced every year but a release of 4,700 bottles appeared in 2008. Another new release was the first *Distiller's Edition* of Royal Lochnagar with a finish in Moscatel casks. There is a 15 year old single malt called Balmoral for sale at the Balmoral Castle visitor centre. This is oddly enough produced by Springbank distillery but could probably in the near future come from neighbouring Royal Lochnagar instead. Independent bottlings are rare. Two recent ones came from Douglas Laing, 21 and 23 years old.

Selected Reserve

Scapa

Owner:
Chivas Brothers
(Pernod Ricard)

Region/district:
Highlands (Orkney)

Founded: **Status:** **Capacity:**
1885 Active 1 000 000 litres

Address: Scapa, St Ola, Kirkwall,
Orkney KA15 1SE

Tel:
01856 876585

website:
www.scapamalt.com

History:

1885 – Macfarlane & Townsend founds the distillery with John Townsend at the helm.

1919 – Scapa Distillery Company Ltd takes over.

1934 – Scapa Distillery Company goes into voluntary liquidation and production ceases.

1936 – Production resumes.

1936 – Bloch Brothers Ltd (John and Sir Maurice) takes over.

1954 – Hiram Walker & Sons takes over.

1959 – A Lomond still is installed.

1978 – The distillery is modernized.

1994 – The distillery is mothballed.

1997 – Production takes place a few months each year using staff from Highland Park.

2004 – Extensive refurbishing takes place, the cost being £2.1 million. Scapa 14 years is launched. The first spirit flows in November.

2005 – Production ceases in April and phase two of the refurbishment programme starts. Chivas Brothers (Pernod Ricard) become new owners through the acquisition of Allied Domecq.

2006 – Scapa 1992 (14 years) is launched.

Scapa 14 year old

DR – The nose is relatively gentle, with grapefruit and melon and a slight sea saltiness while the palate starts with soft yellow fruit, peaks with clean barley and then finishes with a salt and sweet interplay.

DS – Icing sugar and peach skin on the nose with rosewater and cream coming through on the palate. Hints of vanilla and spice in the finish.

It was quite obvious that the former owners, Allied Domecq, saw something special in this neglected Orkney distillery. Why otherwise invest £2 million in the resurrection and renovation in 2004. By then the distillery had been mothballed for a decade except for a couple of months a year when staff from Highland Park fired up the stills. Unfortunately Allied did not have the opportunity to take part in the harvest of the seeds they sowed as Scapa distillery went to Pernod Ricard's ownership a year later. One might argue that the new owners are neglecting this Orcadian jewel since nothing much in terms of bottlings has happened there for three years. Still, due to the sporadic distillations in the past there are limited stocks and according to Pernod Ricard, they have every intention to promote Scapa as a premium malt. Rumour even has it that there could be plans to build a visitor centre at the distillery.

Scapa is unique in using a Lomond type wash still. The rectifying plates have, however, been removed and it is now being operated like an ordinary still. There are eight stainless steel washbacks, four from the 1950's and four from 1978. Scapa has probably the longest fermentation time of any distillery in Scotland, no less than 160 hours. The distillery is sited on the Lingro burn but does not take the process water from the burn. This comes from the springs of the burn and is gravity fed (not pumped) into large iron pipes for more than a kilometre. The distillery is not producing at full capacity yet but three people are distilling for three days a week and attend to the warehouses two days which gives a production of 350,000 litres per year. The Scapa range is fairly small with a *14 year old* and limited editions of a *25 year old* from 1980 and a *Vintage 1992*.

Douglas Laing have released a couple of bottlings the recent years; a 12 year old from 1995 and a 16 year old from 1991.

14 years old

Speyburn

Owner:
Inver House Distillers
(Thai Beverages plc)

Region/district:
Speyside

Founded: 1897
Status: Active
Capacity: 2 000 000 litres

Address: Rothes, Aberlour,
Morayshire AB38 7AG

Tel: 01340 831213
website: www.inverhouse.com

History:
1897 – Brothers John and Edward Hopkin and their cousin Edward Broughton found the distillery through John Hopkin & Co. They already own Tobermory. The architect is Charles Doig. Building the distillery costs £17,000 and the distillery is transferred to Speyburn-Glenlivet Distillery Company.

1916 – Distillers Company Limited (DCL) acquires John Hopkin & Co. and the distillery.

1930 – Production stops.

1934 – Productions restarts.

1962 – Speyburn is transferred to Scottish Malt Distillers (SMD).

1968 – Drum maltings closes.

1991 – Inver House Distillers buys Speyburn.

1992 – A 10 year old is launched as a replacement for the 12 year old in the Flora & Fauna series.

2001 – Pacific Spirits (Great Oriole Group) buys Inver House for $85 million.

2005 – A 25 year old Solera is released.

2006 – InverHouse changes owner when International Beverage Holdings acquires Pacific Spirits UK.

Speyburn 10 year old

DR – Sweet malt nose, then one of the sweetest and most easy-drinking of all malts, with the faintest touch of smoke in the mix. Like eating a bag of sugar.

DS – A real malt fest on the nose with grassy notes. The palate is also very malty and slightly chalky which continues onto the tingly, warming finish.

Locals can still be heard calling both the distillery and the whisky "The Gibbet" due to its proximity to Cnoc na Croiche (Hill of the Gibbet), the place where criminals were executed. Overlooked by its previous owners, at least as a single malt, Speyburn received an injection of new life when Inver House took over in 1991. They saw the potential and used their USA contacts from the time when Inver House was controlled by American owners. Barton Brands were assigned as distributors and they began importing Speyburn to the USA in 1993. Now, 15 years later, it is the sixth most sold single malt on the American market, selling 350,000 bottles per year. The owners themselves describe Speyburn as a "value for money" whisky.

The distillery is equipped with a stainless steel mash tun, six washbacks made of larch and one pair of stills using worm tubs with 104 metres long copper tubes for cooling. There are three dunnage warehouses with 5,000 casks where the spirit intended for bottling as single malt is maturing mainly in bourbon casks. The rest of the spirit is tankered away to the company's central warehouses in Airdrie.

In 1900, Speyburn was the first distillery to abandon floor malting in favour of a new method, drum malting. In the late sixties they closed the maltings and started buying ready malt but the drum maltings are still there to see, protected by Historic Scotland.

The core range consists of a *10 year old* but they have also launched a number of limited editions throughout the years. A *21 year old* of several different vintages was replaced by a *25 year old*, the most recent being from 1977. The latest, official, bottling was a *25 year old Solera* from American fino sherry and bourbon casks which was released in late 2005.

Independent bottlings, e. g. from Gordon & MacPhail occur but are not common.

10 years old

Speyside

Owner:
Speyside Distillers Co.

Region/district:
Speyside

Founded: 1976
Status: Active
Capacity: 600 000 litres

Address: Glen Tromie, Kingussie
Inverness-shire PH21 1NS

Tel: 01540 661060
website: www.speysidedistillery.co.uk

History:

1956 – George Christie buys a piece of land at Drumguish near Kingussie.

1957 – George Christie starts a grain distillery near Alloa.

1962 – The whisky blender George Christie (founder of Speyside Distillery Group in the fifties) commissions the drystone dyker Alex Fairlie to build a distillery in Drumguish.

1986 – Scowis assumes ownership.

1987 – The distillery is completed.

1990 – The distillery is on stream in December.

1993 – The first single malt, Drumguish, is launched.

1999 – Speyside 8 years is launched.

2000 – Speyside Distilleries is sold to a group of private investors including Ricky Christie, Ian Jerman and Sir James Ackroyd.

2001 – Speyside 10 years is launched.

Speyside 12 year old

DR – Rootsy damp straw nose, a sharp and clean barley delivery on the palate with an earthy peaty undertow, and a willowy, nutty savoury finish.

DS – Dried wheat with spoonfuls of honey and oatmeal on the nose. A biscuity and slightly sweet palate leading to the medium finish with honey on the aftertaste.

Speyside distillery lies just outside the small hamlet of Drumguish in the vicinity of Kingussie but is not that easy to find. The founder and former owner, George Christie, deliberately turned the sign on the distillery gate the wrong way so that it should not be seen whilst passing, obviously implying that this distillery was never meant to cater for visitors. In one sense it is a pity as it is a very charming farm-type distillery set in beautiful surroundings.

The building of the distillery was a dream come true for whisky veteran and former submarine captain George Christie. From 1956, when he bought the land, it took 34 years until the first whisky was distilled on 12 December 1990. Christie is today over ninety years old and lives just a stone's throw from his lifetimes' achievement.

The distillery operations are managed by Andrew Shand and his four co-workers. Andrew worked for several Chivas distilleries prior to coming to Speyside. The distillery is equipped with a semi lauter mash tun, four stainless steel washbacks and one pair of stills. At the moment 5-6 day weeks are in place producing 500,000 litres per year. Since December 2006 a peated spirit is produced one week per year.

Aside from the distillery at Drumguish, there is a diverse range of activities at the company's base in Rutherglen, Glasgow. Cask warehousing, a bottling plant and a blending operation are all found there. The total number of staff is 80 and they export to more than 100 countries with top markets being the US and Far East. One of their more odd accomplishments is that they produce the number one Scotch blend in Mongolia, the Yokozuna. Speyside produces three brands of single malt; *Speyside 8, 10* and *12 years* (300,000 bottles), *Drumguish* (600,000) and the quaint and almost black *Cu Dubh* (120,000 bottles). A vatted malt named *Glentromie* is also produced. The company also owns some 20 brands of blended whiskies and two ranges of single malts from other distilleries; Scott's Selection and Private Cellar.

12 years old

Springbank distillery

Springbank

Owner:
Springbank Distillers
(J & A Mitchell)

Region/district:
Campbeltown

Founded: 1828
Status: Temp. closed
Capacity: 750 000 litres

Address: Well Close, Campbeltown,
Argyll PA28 6ET

Tel: 01586 552085
website: www.springbankdistillers.com

History:

1828 – The Reid family, in-laws of the Mitchells (see below), founds the distillery as the fourteenth in Campbelltown.

1837 – The Reid family encounters financial difficulties and John and William Mitchell buy the distillery.

1897 – J. & A. Mitchell Company Ltd is founded. William Mitchell founded Glengyle in 1872 and when he and John parted ways, John Mitchell continued operating Springbank first alone and then with his son Archibald.

1926 – The depression forces the distillery to close.

1933 – The distillery is back in production.

1960 – Own maltings ceases.

1969 – J. & A. Mitchell buys the independent bottler Cadenhead.

1979 – The distillery closes.

1985 – A 10 year old Longrow is launched as an experiment.

1987 – Limited production restarts.

1989 – Production restarts.

1990 – Longrow becomes a standard label.

1992 – Springbank takes up its own maltings again.

1997 – First distillation of Hazelburn.

1998 – Springbank 12 years is launched.

1999 – Dha Mhile (7 years) is the world's first organic single malt and is released as a limited supply of 1,000 bottles.

2000 – A 10 year old is launched.

In the beginning of summer 2008, word was spread that Springbank was shutting down. Rumours abounded for a few intensive days before a press release from the owners explained that this was a temporary issue and that production would restart in early 2009. Many hard-core Springbank fans were, understandably, greatly dismayed but even Scotch Whisky Association and a few competitors quickly declared their astonishment that a distillery could be mothballed in these days of booming demand for Scotch whisky. According to the director of production, Frank McHardy, the reason for not distilling is to strike a balance between what the distillery produces and what the future sales of this maturing stock will be. Sales are planned to grow year on year but Springbank were producing more whisky than they could comfortably sell in future years. In August they took a delivery of locally grown Optic barley to be malted end of 2008. The aim is to start limited production again in early 2009. Apart from the distilling shut down, it is business as usual at the distillery.

Production methods are as traditional as can be expected from Scotland's oldest, continuously family-owned distillery. Despite its traditional image Springbank is on the cutting edge of experimentation, for example, trying out various kinds of barley. Scottish barley is malted using peat from a bog at the nearby Machrihanish and from Tomintoul in the Highlands. Springbank produces three distinctive single malts with different phenol contents in the malted barley: Springbank is distilled two and a half times (12-15ppm), Longrow is distilled twice (50-55ppm) and Hazelburn is distilled three times (unpeated).

All whisky is matured on-site in nine dunnage and two racked warehouses. There are six washbacks made of Scandinavian Larch, one wash still and two spirit stills. The wash still is unique in Scotland as it is fired by both an open oil-fire and internal steam coils. The spirit stills are heated using steam coils. Ordinary condensers are used to cool the spirit vapours except in the first of the two spirit stills where a worm tub is used.

The core range of Springbank distillery is *Springbank 10* and *15 years*, *Springbank 10 years 100 proof*, *Longrow 10* and *14 years*, *Longrow 10 years 100 proof* and *Hazelburn 8 years old*. In spring 2008 *Longrow CV* was released which is a mix of different ages (mostly 6, 10 and 14 years) and this will become a part of the core range. Limited releases of Longrow this past year were the *18 year old* and the *7 year old* with the last 18 months in *Gaja Barolo* casks. The second batch of last year's *Springbank 1997* was launched and there is also report of a *Springbank Madeira finish* due early next year.

History (continued):

2001 – Springbank 1965 'Local barley' (36 years), 741 bottles, is launched. Barley, coal, peat and water are all obtained locally.

2002 – Number one in the series Wood Expressions is a 12 year old with five years on Demerara rum casks. Next is a Longrow sherry cask (13 years). A relaunch of the 15 year old replaces the 21 year old.

2004 – J. & A. Mitchell's main owner, Hedley Wright, opens Glengyle Distillery which has been closed since March 1925. Springbank 10 years 100 proof is launched as well as Springbank Wood Expression bourbon, Longrow 14 years old, Springbank 32 years old and Springbank 14 years Port Wood.

2005 – 2 400 bottles of Springbank 21 years old take the market by surprise when they are released in March. The next batch will not appear until in 2011. The first version of Hazelburn (8 years old) is released 5th September. Longrow Tokaji Wood Expression is launched.

2006 – Longrow 10 years 100 proof, Springbank 25 years (1,200 bottles), Springbank 9 years Marsala finish, Springbank 11 years Madeira finish and a new Hazelburn 8 year old are released.

2007 – Springbank Vintage 1997 and a 16 year old rum wood are released.

2008 – The distillery closes temporarily. Three new releases of Longrow - CV, 18 year old and 7 year old Gaja Barolo.

Springbank Vintage 1997   16 years old Rum Wood   Longrow 10 years old 100 proof

Springbank 10 year old

DR – Attractive malt and a hint of pepper and sea water on the nose, yellow fruit, sweetness and an earthy underbelly on the palate, and a complex and balanced finish.

DS – Heavy stewed fruits on the nose with wafts of crab cake. Oily and viscous with heavy sherry flavours and oak. Medium finish with a strong mussel aftertaste.

Longrow CV

DR – Sooty smoke and some gentle fruits on the nose, and a big mouth feel with smoke honey and apricot syrup vying for attention.

DS – Spicy hay and malt with strong oils on the nose. Sweet peat at first followed by spicy malt flavours and a long peppery, citrusy finish.

Hazelburn 8 year old

DR – The nose is feisty, spicy and zesty, the palate is honey and lemon cough lozenges, clean and crisp and with traces of kiwifruit or guava. The finish is dry and demands another mouthful. Careful!

DS – Resin and plum skins mixed with Dundee cake on the nose. The palate is ginger and and fruitcake with Cointreau flavours leading into the citrusy finish.

Springbank 10 years old 100 proof   Longrow CV

Strathisla

Owner:
Chivas Brothers
(Pernod Ricard)

Region/district:
Speyside

Founded: **Status:**   **Capacity:**
1786   Active (vc)   2 400 000 litres

Address: Seafield Avenue, Keith,
Banffshire AB55 5BS

Tel: **website:**
01542 783044   www.maltwhiskydistilleries.com

History:
1786 – Alexander Milne and George Taylor found the distillery under the name Milltown, but soon change it to Milton.

1825 – MacDonald Ingram & Co. purchases the distillery.

1830 – William Longmore acquires the distillery.

1870 – The distillery name changes to Strathisla.

1876 – The distillery is badly damaged by fire.

1879 – Another accident strikes; a dust explosion in the malt mill.

1880 – William Longmore retires and hands operations to his son-in-law John Geddes-Brown. William Longmore & Co. is formed.

1890 – The distillery changes name to Milton.

1940 – Jay (George) Pomeroy acquires majority shares in William Longmore & Co. Pomeroy is jailed as a result of dubious business transactions and the distillery goes bankrupt in 1949.

1950 – Chivas Brothers buys the run-down distillery at a compulsory auction for £71,000 and starts restoration.

1951 – The name reverts to Strathisla.

1965 – The number of stills is increased from two to four.

1970 – A heavily peated whisky, Craigduff, is produced but production stops later.

2001 – The Chivas Group is acquired by Pernod Ricard.

Strathisla 12 year old

DR – Rich full and fruity nose with lots of barley, then barley, currants and a touch of oak, peat and pepper, concluding with a complex and intriguing finish.

DS – Fennel and cream on the nose. The palate is medium bodied with a taste of brown bread. The finish is quite long and warming.

Strathisla is not one of the four distilleries that the owners, Chivas Brothers, wish to market as a single malt. This has nothing to do with the quality of the spirit, quite the opposite. It is an excellent malt but at the same time it plays an increasingly important role in Pernod Ricard´s most important blend - Chivas Regal. Strathisla has been the heart of this blend for over half a century and with the explicit aim of retaking the top spot as the most sold premium blend (lost to Johnnie Walker Black Label a few years ago), there are no plans to market Strathisla as a single blend.

Strathisla is one of the oldest (established in 1786) and most beautiful distilleries in Scotland. There is an excellent visitor centre, Home of Chivas Regal, with a beautiful library where one can sit down and enjoy a dram.

The distillery is equipped with a stainless steel semi-lauter mash tun, ten (formerly eleven, but one has been remade into a pot ale tank) washbacks of Oregon Pine and two pairs of stills. The spirit is piped a few hundred meters to the mothballed Glen Keith distillery for filling. A small amount is then stored on-site in a dunnage and a racked warehouse. The rest is sent to different facilities in Scotland.

Strathisla is one of three distilleries in Keith, the others are Strathmill and the mothballed Glen Keith, but there are other whisky-related activities going on in the village. It is home to the vast Keith Bonds, one of three warehousing complexes in Scotland belonging to Chivas Brothers. The other two are Dalmuir and Balgray, both near Glasgow.

Pernod Ricard have only released two official bottlings - the *12 year old* and a *15 year old cask strength*. Recent independent bottlings include a 10 year old from Ian Macleod and a 1967 from Duncan Taylor.

12 years old

Strathmill

Owner: Diageo

Region/district: Speyside

Founded: 1891 **Status:** Active **Capacity:** 1 700 000 litres

Address: Keith, Banffshire AB55 5DQ

Tel: 01542 883000 **website:** www.malts.com

History:

1891 – The distillery is founded in an old mill from 1823 and is named Glenisla-Glenlivet Distillery.

1892 – The inauguration takes place in June.

1895 – The gin company W. & A. Gilbey buys the distillery for £9,500 and names it Strathmill.

1962 – W. & A. Gilbey merges with United Wine Traders (including Justerini & Brooks) and forms International Distillers & Vintners (IDV).

1968 – The number of stills is increased from two to four and purifiers are added.

1972 – IDV is bought by Watney Mann which later the same year is acquired by Grand Metropolitan.

1993 – Strathmill becomes available as a single malt for the first time since 1909 as a result of a bottling (1980) from Oddbins.

1997 – Guinness and Grand Metropolitan merge and form Diageo.

2001 – The first official bottling is a 12 year old in the Flora & Fauna series.

Strathmill 12 year old

DS – A hint of strawberries and vanilla on the sweet nose. Complex and heathery on the palate with a touch of oakiness which continues onto the finish.

The town of Keith is probably best known, in whisky circles, for Strathisla distillery though there are many good reasons to stop by at Strathmill as well. The distillery does not receive visitors, but the exterior and its situation in a lush valley by the river Isla makes it worth the effort. Two stately pagoda roofs together with a couple of beautiful, traditional dunnage warehouses (with an additional two racked) produce a true distillery atmosphere. The distillery was closed for maintenance in June 2005 but reopened in June 2006. Strathmill was one of three distilleries bought by the British gin manufacturer W & A Gilbey in 1895, (Glenspey in 1887 and Knockando in 1904 being the other two).

The distillery is equipped with a stainless steel semilauter mash tun, six stainless steel washbacks and two pairs of stills. Strathmill is one of a few select distilleries using a facility called purifier on their two pairs of stills. It is mounted between the lyne arm and the condensers and its purpose is to produce a lighter whisky. The spirit is tankered away to Auhcroisk for filling and some of the casks find their way back for storage in six on-site warehouses .

Strathmill malt whisky is gaining importance as a component in J & B blended Scotch. The only official bottling, from Diageo, appeared in 2001, and was a *12 year old* in the Flora & Fauna series. Except for the two butts (25 years old) that were bottled in 1992 to celebrate the centenary of the distillery there are no other official bottlings. There are not that many independent bottlings but Douglas Laing recently released a 30 year old as well as a younger one, 18 years old.

Flora & Fauna 12 years

Talisker

Owner: **Region/district:**
Diageo   Highlands (Skye)

Founded: **Status:**   **Visitor centre:**
1830   Active (vc)   1 940 000 litres

Address: Carbost, Isle of Skye,
Inverness-shire IV47 8SR

Tel: **website:**
01478 614308 (vc)   www.malts.com

History:
1830 – Hugh and Kenneth MacAskill, sons of the local doctor, found the distillery.

1848 – The brothers transfer the lease to North of Scotland Bank and Jack Westland from the bank runs the operations.

1854 – Kenneth MacAskill dies.

1857 – North of Scotland Bank sells the distillery to Donald MacLennan for £500.

1863 – MacLennan experiences difficulties in making operations viable and puts the distillery up for sale.

1865 – MacLennan, still working at the distillery, nominates John Anderson as agent in Glasgow.

1867 – Anderson & Co. from Glasgow takes over.

1879 – John Anderson is imprisoned after having sold non-existing casks of whisky.

1880 – New owners are now Alexander Grigor Allan and Roderick Kemp.

1892 – Kemp sells his share and buys Macallan Distillery instead.

1894 – The Talisker Distillery Ltd is founded.

1895 – Allan dies and Thomas Mackenzie, who has been his partner, takes over.

1898 – Talisker Distillery merges with Dailuaine-Glenlivet Distillers and Imperial Distillers to form Dailuaine-Talisker Distillers Company.

Talisker has always been an admired whisky. In his poem *"The Scotsman's Return from Abroad"* from 1880, Robert Louis Stevenson writes "The king o' drinks, as I conceive it, Talisker, Islay or Glenlivet". But until five-six years ago it was still in the group just below those most talked about. Then something happened; owners Diageo were determined in their mission and launched new expressions. In a world of growing interest in peated whiskies, the only distillery of Isle of Skye finally reached the top level. The only other distillery that has increased more percentage-wise among the Top 25 Single Malts is Macallan. Talisker has passed 100,000 cases sold in a year and is heading for the top ten.

Talisker obtain malt from Glen Ord with a specification of c 22 ppm. The old cast iron mash tun was replaced by a stainless steel lauter tun thus reducing the time for mashing from ten to five hours. There are six washbacks made of pine serving the unusual combination of two wash stills and three spirit stills. This is a leftover from the time when Talisker was triple distilled. The wash stills have a remarkable appearance dating back to the construction of the original stills in 1830, with their u-shaped lyne arms. Thin copper pipes under the arms lead back to the still. Another peculiarity these days is that cooling is performed with the aid of five worm tubs instead of the more common shell/tube variety. Only a small part of the produce is matured on the island (the warehouses can store 6,000 casks) while the rest is tankered and taken to the mainland for storage.

Talisker's core range consists of a *10 year old*, an *18 year old* and a *Distiller's Edition* with an amoroso sherry finish. In January 2008 *Talisker 57° North* was released. The name alludes to both the latitude of the distillery and its alcohol content. It was initially launched as a duty-free item but will eventually become the first regularly available Talisker at "full strength" (though, this is not a cask strength). Additionally, a number of *25 year old* cask strengths have been launched, the sixth and most recent in 2008. Two *20 year olds* from 1981 and 1982, one *28 year old* from 1973, *Talisker 175th Anniversary* bottling and a *30 year old* (third edition released in 2008) are all examples of limited versions.

Independent bottlings of Talisker are rare and when they do occur the names do not reveal their origin. One of the most recent is Tactical from Douglas Laing, 18 years old from 1988.

History (continued):

1916 – Thomas Mackenzie dies and the distillery is taken over by a consortium consisting of, among others, John Walker, John Dewar, W. P. Lowrie and Distillers Company Limited (DCL).

1928 – The distillery abandons triple distillation.

1930 – Administration of the distillery is transferred to Scottish Malt Distillers (SMD).

1960 – On 22nd November the distillery catches fire and substantial damage occurs.

1962 – The distillery reopens after the fire with five new identical copies of the destroyed stills.

1972 – Malting ceases and malt is now purchased from Glen Ord Central Maltings.

1988 – United Distillers introduce Classic Malts, Talisker 10 years included. A visitor centre is opened.

1998 – A new stainless steel/copper mash tun and five new worm tubs are installed. Talisker is launched as a Distillers Edition with an amoroso sherry finish.

2004 – Two new bottlings appear, an 18 year old and a 25 year old.

2005 – To celebrate the 175th birthday of the distillery, Talisker 175th Anniversary is released (60 000 bottles). The third edition of the 25 year old cask strength is released (15 600 bottles).

2006 – A 30 year old and the fourth edition of the 25 year old are released.

2007 – The second edition of the 30 year old and the fifth edition of the 25 year old are released.

2008 – Talisker 57° North, sixth edition of the 25 year old and third edition of the 30 year old are launched.

Talisker 10 year old

DR – Grilled oily fish in lemon oil, on the nose, dry salt and pepper on the palate, peat and pepper in a tastebud treat of a finish.

DS –Immediate sea-weed – peppery with a hint of sherry and citrus. Much more peat on the palate which is full bodied. Peppery finish – warming.

57° North

25 years old
6th edition

30 years old
3rd edition

10 years old

18 years old

Distiller's Edition 1992

Tamdhu

Owner: Edrington Group

Region/district: Speyside

Founded: 1896 **Status:** Active **Capacity:** 4 000 000 litres

Address: Knockando, Aberlour, Morayshire AB38 7RP

Tel: 01340 872200 **website:** -

History:
1896 – The distillery is founded by Tamdhu Distillery Company, a consortium of whisky blenders with William Grant as the main promoter. Charles Doig is the architect.

1897 – The first casks are filled in July.

1898 – Highland Distillers Company, which has several of the 1896 consortium members in managerial positions, buys Tamdhu Distillery Company.

1911 – The distillery closes.

1913 –The distillery reopens.

1928 – The distillery is mothballed.

1948 – The distillery is in full production again in July.

1950 – The floor maltings is replaced by Saladin boxes when the distillery is rebuilt.

1972 – The number of stills is increased from two to four.

1975 – Two stills augment the previous four.

1976 – Tamdhu 8 years is launched as single malt.

Tamdhu (no age statement)

DR – Something of a rollercoaster ride. Ripe fruit salad in juice and syrup on the nose, crystallised barley, fruit flavoured sherbet, sharp pepper, nuts and peat on the palate and a spicy finish.

Until 1999, Tamdhu was owned by Highland Distillers, a well respected player in the Scotch whisky business since its foundation in 1887. In fact by the end of the 1800s, when they owned Glenrothes, Bunnahabhain, Glenglassaugh and Tamdhu it was the largest group in the malt whisky trade in terms of capacity. Highland Park was purchased in 1937 followed by Macallan in 1996. Throughout the years Highland Distillers became heavily involved with respected blends like Cutty Sark and Famous Grouse which made it an interesting target for acquisition. Buyers from the other side of the Atlantic (first Seagrams then Hiram Walker) tried twice in the seventies to buy the company. Eventually Edrington (with Wm Grant) was the successful acquirer in 1999. Edrington was founded just a few years earlier as a business umbrella for Robertson & Baxter and Clyde Bonding and with that the circle closed; William Robertson, one of the founders of Robertson & Baxter, was one of the initiators of the foundation of Highland Distillers over 100 years previously.

Tamdhu is a large distillery producing 3 million litres per year although there is a capacity of 4 million. There are nine Oregon pine washbacks serving three pairs of stills and there are four dunnage and one racked warehouse on site.

Tamdhu also has maltings with a capacity enough to supply the other distilleries in the Edrington group (especially Glenrothes) with malt. It is the only distillery still using Saladin boxes (installed in 1950).

There is only one official bottling on the market today, *without age* but typically *around 8 years old*.

Recent independent bottlings include an old expression from 1968 released by Duncan Taylor and also an 11 year old from 1997 by Douglas Laing.

Gordon & MacPhail Tamdhu 8 years old

Tamnavulin

Owner:
Whyte & Mackay
(United Spirits)

Region/district:
Speyside

Founded: 1966
Status: Active
Capacity: 4 000 000 litres

Address: Tomnavoulin, Ballindalloch,
Banffshire AB3 9JA

Tel: 01807 590285
website: -

History:
1966 – Tamnavulin-Glenlivet Distillery Company, a subsidiary of Invergordon Distillers Ltd, founds Tamnavulin.

1993 – Whyte & Mackay buys Invergordon Distillers.

1995 – The distillery closes in May.

1996 – Whyte & Mackay changes name to JBB (Greater Europe).

2001 – Company management buy out operations for £208 million and rename the company Kyndal.

2003 – Kyndal changes name to Whyte & Mackay.

2007 – United Spirits buys Whyte & Mackay. Tamnavulin is opened again in July after having been mothballed for 12 years.

Tamnavulin 12 year old

DR – Wet hay, celery and cucumber on the nose and a delightful exotic fruit and citrus taste and a satisfying and pleasant finish.

DS – A honey-pot nose with nutmeg. The palate is buttery and overflowing with honey flavours. It is quite light and has a floral, honeyed after-taste.

When Tamnavulin was reopened after 12 long years without production in August 2007 it coincided with the Indian spirits tycoon Vijay Mallya buying the distillery and its owner Whyte & Mackay. However, there had been discussions for several years that the mothballed distillery should start producing again. In fact, it was distilling for six weeks in 2000 in order to maintain the stock of whisky when people came from the nearby Tomintoul distillery to produce some 400,000 litres of spirit.

In the first months after the reopening production was one million litres and in 2008, working seven days a week, the 13 people at Tamnavulin plan to distil 3.5 million litres by doing 23 mashes a week. Most of the equipment was still in place when it opened up again but in summer 2008 the three wash stills were all replaced and the three spirit stills are due for replacement next year. There is also one full-lauter mash tun and eight washbacks. All eight used to be made of the less resistant, yet cheaper, mild steel but four of them have now been replaced by stainless steel ones. Two racked warehouses (10 casks high) on site have a capacity of 34,250 casks with the oldest ones dating back to 1967. 200 casks are filled every week on site while the rest of the production is tankered to Invergordon for filling.

Tamnavulin is situated in a very scenic part of the Highlands with Glenlivet, Tomintoul and re-opened Braeval as closest neighbours. There used to be a visitor centre but it closed at the end of the nineties.

The only standard release of Tamnavulin has been a *12 year old* for quite some time now but there has been talk of some new expressions. A number of aged *Stillman's Dram* have also occured, the most recent a *30 year old*.

Gordon & MacPhail and Douglas Laing belong to independent bottlers which have released versions of Tamnavulin. An old Tamnavulin appeared in 2008 from Douglas Laing when they released a 30 year old from 1977.

12 years old

Teaninich

Owner:
Diageo

Region/district:
Northern Highlands

Founded: 1817   **Status:** Active   **Capacity:** 4 000 000 litres

Address: Alness, Ross-shire IV17 0XB

Tel: 01349 885001   **website:** www.malts.com

History:

1817 – Captain Hugh Monro, owner of the estate Teaninich, founds the distillery.

1831 – Captain Munro sells the estate to his younger brother John.

1850 – John Munro, who spends most of his time in India, leases Teaninich to the infamous Robert Pattison from Leith.

1869 – John McGilchrist Ross takes over the licence.

1895 – Munro & Cameron takes over the licence.

1898 – Munro & Cameron buys the distillery.

1904 – Robert Innes Cameron becomes sole owner of Teaninich. He has had interests in Linkwood Distillery since 1902.

1932 – Robert Innes Cameron dies.

1933 – The estate of Robert Innes Cameron sells the distillery to Distillers Company Limited (DCL).

1970 – A new distillation unit with six stills is commissioned and becomes known as the A side.

1975 – A dark grains plant is built.

1984 – The B side of the distillery is mothballed.

1985 – The A side is also mothballed.

1991 –The A side is in production again

1992 – United Distillers launches a 10 year old Teaninich in the Flora & Fauna series.

1999 – The B side is decommissioned.

2000 – A mash filter is installed.

Teaninich 10 year old

DS – A heavy, malty nose with spice and apple skin. The palate is sweet at first with some spice and a hint of smoke. A spicy finish.

In the middle of a rather unromantic industrial estate outside Alness, north of Inverness, lies one of Diageo´s more obscure distilleries, Teaninich. It is quite in contrast with another distillery in Alness, Dalmore, with its beautiful location down by Cromarthy Firth.

At one time in the seventies it was one of the largest distilleries in Scotland with a capacity of 6 million litres. This was due to a completely new distillation complex with six stills being added in 1970, bringing the total number of stills to ten. The old distillery buildings with the first four stills, were demolished in 1999 which left a very modern-looking distillery with few traces from the 19th century. All that remains of the old distillery is the receiver house which is a listed building.

Teaninich does not lack interesting features even if it is a rather unknown distillery. In 2000 this was the first – and so far the only – Scottish distillery to install a filter press instead of a mash tun. In order to operate the mash filter the malt needs to be grinded into a very fine flour with no husks, so an Asnong hammer mill instead of a traditional roller mill had to be installed. The grist spends 30 minutes in a mash conversion tank before it goes into the mash filter with its 24 plates. One mash can be done in half the time and a more efficient extraction of sugars is obtained. The technique with mash filters is common in breweries.

Except for the six stills the distillery is equipped with 10 washbacks; eight made of larch and two of stainless steel. There are no warehouses on site, instead 4-5 tankers leave the distillery each week for filling elsewhere. 19 mashes are done per week corresponding to 4.0 million litres which is more or less at capacity

Teaninich is mainly produced to be a component of Johnnie Walker blended whiskies. The only official bottling at the moment is a *10 year old* in the Flora & Fauna series.

Independent bottlings are not that common. The most recent one is a 1971 (36 years old) from Douglas Laing which was released in 2008.

The only remaining building from the old distillery

Flora & Fauna 10 years old

Tobermory

Owner:
Burn Stewart Distillers
(C L Financial)

Region/district:
Highland (Mull)

Founded: **Status:** **Capacity:**
1798 Active (vc) 1 000 000 litres

Address: Tobermory, Isle of Mull,
Argyllshire PA75 6NR

Tel: **website:**
01688 302647 www.burnstewartdistillers.com

History:
1798 – John Sinclair founds the distillery named Ledaig Distillery.

1837 – The distillery closes.

1878 – The distillery reopens.

1890 – John Hopkins & Company buys the distillery.

1916 – Distillers Company Limited (DCL) takes over John Hopkins & Company.

1930 – The distillery closes and is used as both a canteen and a power station

1972 – A shipping company in Liverpool and the sherrymaker Domecq buy the buildings and embark on refurbishment. When work is completed it is named Ledaig Distillery Ltd.

1975 – Ledaig Distillery Ltd files for bankruptcy and the distillery closes again.

1979 – The estate agent Kirkleavington Property Company of Cleckheaton buys the distillery, forms a new company, Tobermory Distillers Ltd and starts production.

1982 – No production. Some of the buildings are converted into flats and some are rented to a dairy company for cheese storage.

1989 – Production resumes.

1993 – Burn Stewart Distillers buys Tobermory for £600,000 and pays an additional £200,000 for the whisky supply.

2002 – Trinidad-based venture capitalists CL Financial buys Burn Stewart Distillers for £50m.

2005 – A 32 year old from 1972 is launched.

2007 – A Ledaig 10 year old is released.

2008 – A limited edition Tobermory 15 year old is released.

Tobermory 10 year old

DR – Barley and crystal ginger on the nose, but the palate carries this, with a nice oily mouth feel, and creamed fruits giving way to a sharper spicier conclusion.

DS – Immediately malty on the nose with a hint of brine. The palate is sweet with some honey and peppery smoke. Lavender in the long finish.

Ledaig 10 year old

DR – Peat and smoke on the nose, more fruity and malty on the palate but with a definite tarry heart, and then gristly smoke in the finish.

DS – Grass and sweet liqueur with a hint of honey on the nose. Sweet and malt and grass on the palate with a delicious waft of smoke in the finish.

Tobermory is one of the oldest distilleries in existence and the only legal distillery that has existed on the island of Mull. For Burn Stewart Distillers, owners of Tobermory, the three core brands are the two blended whiskies Scottish Leader and Black Bottle and Bunnahabhain single malt in that order. Tobermory/Ledaig sales have decreased since 2003 but the owners hope to change that trend now. The only long-term problem is that there is not much room to increase the already modest production without expanding the facilities.

The distillery, currently producing 750,000 litres a year, has a cast iron mash tun, four washbacks made of Oregon pine and two pairs of stills. The former owners sold the old warehouses which have now been converted into flats. Since then the whisky has been sent to Deanston on the mainland for filling and then to Bunnahabhain on Islay for storage. However, since early 2007 this is not entirely correct. At that time they converted part of the old No 2 Tun room into a small maturation warehouse with a capacity of 100-150 hogsheads. This is where Master Blender Ian MacMillan intends to experiment by laying down new fill Ledaig casks in order to compare maturing on Mull with that of casks that have matured on Islay for a few years. The fresh sherry butts, part of the new 15 year old Tobermory, have also spent a final year in this small warehouse.

The production is divided into two distinctive parts; Tobermory (50% of the production) is an unpeated single malt while Ledaig is a peated whisky (35 ppm malt being bought from Port Ellen). Ledaig has been launched in many different versions. The current expression of Ledaig is a *10 year old* but earlier releases included a 7 year old, a 15 year old, a 20 year old a Sherry Finish and several vintages. For many years the only official version of Tobermory was the *10 year old* but it was supplemented in 2008 by a *15 year old* limited edition.

Three recent independent bottlings of Tobermory are Duncan Taylor 1996, Douglas Laing 1994 and Cadenhead 1994. Ian MacLeod released a 10 year old Tokay finish of Ledaig.

15 years old

Tomatin

Owner: **Region/district:**
Tomatin Distillery Co   Highland
(Marubeni Europe plc)

Founded: **Status:**   **Capacity:**
1897   Active (vc)   5 000 000 litres

Address: Tomatin, Inverness-shire IV13 7YT

Tel: **website:**
01808 511444 (vc)   www.tomatin.com

History:
1897 – The Inverness businessmen behind
Tomatin Spey Distillery Company found Tomatin.

1906 – Production ceases.

1909 – Production resumes through Tomatin
Distillers Co. Ltd.

1956 – Stills are increased from two to four.

1958 – Another two stills are added.

1961 – The six stills are increased to ten.

1964 – One more still is installed.

1974 – The stills now total 23 and the maltings
closes.

1985 – The distillery company goes into
liquidation.

1986 – Two long-time customers, Takara Shuzo
Co. and Okara & Co., buy Tomatin through
Tomatin Distillery Co. Tomatin thus becomes
the first distillery to be acquired by Japanese
interests.

1997 – Tomatin Distillery Co buys J. W. Hardie
and the brand Antiquary.

1998 – Okara & Co, owners of 20% of Tomatin
Distillery, is forced to sell its share to Takara
Shuzo Co. which now is part of the Marubeni
group.

2004 – Tomatin 12 years is launched.

2005 – A 25 year old and a 1973 Vintage are
released.

2006 – An 18 year old and a 1962 Vintage are
launched.

2008 – A 30 and a 40 year old as well as several
vintages from 1975 and 1995 are released.

Tomatin 12 year old

DR – Strawberry cream and raspberry ripple
ice cream and pecan on the nose, delicate
zesty barley on the palate, with a sweet citrus
and powdery spice mix contributing to a very
welcoming finish. More-ish.

DS – A rich malty, if slightly green, nose. The
palate is sherried and creamy, rather like a
trifle. The finish is quick but is sweet and
warming.

If you travel the A9 north towards Inverness you will see Tomatin distillery to your left a few minutes after you have passed the beautiful Findhorn bridge. The Findhorn river is also sometimes used as a water supply when the local stream runs low. The distillery was founded at the end of the 19th century but it was from 1956 and the following 20 years that saw its most rapid expansion. The number of stills increased and had reached 23 by 1974. By then it was Scotland's largest distillery with a production of 12 million litres of alcohol. However it only ran at full capacity between 1975 and 1980 when it encountered financial trouble and was liquidated in 1985. Rescue came from Japan when two Japanese companies became the first to own a Scottish distillery. Today the capacity is lower with 5 million litres (actual production in 2008 is 2.6 million) as 11 of the original stills were dismantled in 2002.

The distillery is equipped with two stainless steel mash tuns, 12 stainless steel washbacks and six pairs of stills, all the same size (almost 17,000 litres). To avoid having the wash froth and rise into the condenser during distillation, distilleries will either use defoamers or monitor the process through a sight glass on the side of the wash still. At Tomatin the traditional method of having a wooden ball inside attached to a string is used. The still man will determine by the sound how high the froth has risen. There are 14 warehouses and also a cooperage with two coopers working. Normally the whisky produced by Tomatin is unpeated but since 2004 a peated spirit (12ppm) has been produced the last week every year.

The larger part of production is either sold to other companies or used for their own blended whiskies. Today's official single malt range comprise the *12 year old* (80% of sales), *18 year old* and *25 year old*. In 2008 there was a release of several vintages and older expressions – a *30 year old* and a *40 year old* and vintages from *1975, 1976, 1980, 1990* and *1995*. Independent bottler Signatory recently released a 40 year old and from Ian MacLeod came a 15 year old.

12 years old

Tomintoul

Owner:		Region/district:
Angus Dundee Distillers		Speyside
Founded:	**Status:**	**Capacity:**
1964	Active	3 300 000 litres

Address: Ballindalloch, Banffshire AB37 9AQ

Tel:	website:
01807 590274	www.tomintouldistillery.co.uk

History:

1964 –The distillery is founded by Tomintoul Distillery Ltd, which is owned by Hay & MacLeod & Co. and W. & S. Strong & Co.

1965 – On stream in July.

1973 – Scottish & Universal Investment Trust owned by the Fraser family, buys the distillery. They buy Whyte and Mackay the same year and transfer Tomintoul to that company.

1974 – The two stills are increased to four and Tomintoul 12 years is launched.

1978 – Lonhro buys Scottish & Universal Investment Trust.

1989 – Lonhro sells Whyte and Mackay to Brent Walker.

1990 – American Brands buys Whyte & Mackay.

1996 – Whyte and Mackay changes name to JBB (Greater Europe).

2000 – Angus Dundee plc buys Tomintoul.

2002 – Tomintoul 10 year is launched as the first bottling after the change of ownership.

2003 – Tomintoul 16 years is launched.

2004 – Tomintoul 27 years is launched.

2005 – A young, peated version called Old Ballantruan is launched.

2008 – 1976 Vintage and Peaty Tang are released.

Tomintoul 10 year old

DR – Toffee and fruit on the nose then an easy, pleasant rounded and sweet barley taste before a gently fading finish.

DS – A honeyed, citrus nose with malt and mint. The palate is sweet and earthy and bitter. The finish is oily and surprisingly peppery.

Tomintoul is a typical sixties distillery built with efficient production in mind rather than being a pretty sight for visiting tourists. However it is interesting to compare it with Braeval just a few miles to the south which was built around the same time and is a beautiful collection of buildings. The two distilleries share the same surrounding scenery which is among the most breathtaking in Scotland.

One mash tun and six washbacks, all made of stainless steel and two pairs of stills heated by steam kettles are now run seven days a week. This means that capacity is used to the full and the four racked warehouses which have a capacity of 75,000 casks were completed with two new warehouses in September 2007, increasing the storage capacity by 36,000 casks. The malt used for mashing is slightly peated but two weeks per year heavily peated (55 ppm) malt is used for the peated range. Interestingly, the modern distillery is built according to old tradition with the mill placed on the top making use of energy-saving gravitation.

Almost the whole production is used in different blended whiskies but as early as 1974 there was a Tomintoul single malt on the market. The core range used to consist of *10 year old, 16 year old* and a *27 year old* with the addition of the *Old Ballantruan* which appeared in autumn 2005, a peaty expression distilled in 2001. Since autumn 2007 the owners have released three new expressions. First and foremost the oldest Tomintoul, so far, a *1976 Vintage* which was released as a limited edition in January 2008. Before that, a *12 year old* with the 18 last months in Oloroso sherry butts, and *Peaty Tang* were launched. The last one is a vatting of 4-5 year old peated Tomintoul and 8 year old unpeated Tomintoul. It is bottled at 40% compared to Old Ballantruan which is bottled at 50%. Independent bottlings are unusual and with the new owners being independents themselves it seems unlikely that they will become commonplace. Adelphi Distillery 1967, which appeared in 2003, is one of the more recent.

Peaty Tang

Tormore

Owner:
Chivas Brothers
(Pernod Ricard)

Region/district:
Speyside

Founded: **Status:**
1958   Active

Capacity:
3 700 000 litres

Address: Tormore, Advie, Grantown-on-Spey,
Morayshire PH26 3LR

Tel:
01807 510244

website:
www.tormore.com

History:
1958 – Schenley International, owners of Long John, founds the distillery.

1960 – The distillery is ready for production.

1972 – The number of stills is increased from four to eight.

1975 – Schenley sells Long John and its distilleries (including Tormore) to Whitbread.

1989 – Allied Lyons (to become Allied Domecq) buys the spirits division of Whitbread.

1991 – Allied Distillers introduce Caledonian Malts where Miltonduff, Glendronach and Laphroaig are represented besides Tormore. Tormore is later replaced by Scapa.

2004 – Tormore 12 year old is launched as an official bottling.

2005 – Chivas Brothers (Pernod Ricard) becomes new owners through the acquisition of Allied Domecq.

Tormore 12 year old

DR – A perfumey and delicate smell on the nose and soft but pleasant palate with macaroni cake and toasted almond in the mix, and a soft fading finish.

DS – Heather and vanilla with some fruitiness and raisins on the nose. Sweet at first on the palate with soft, round flavours and shortbread. A light finish with some spiciness on the finish.

The construction of Tormore distillery in the late 1950s received much attention. It was the first distillery in the 20th century to be constructed from scratch (Tullibardine och Glen Keith both made use of existing buildings) and it was given an appearance that was completely unique. The interest was so great that in 1963 an 18 minute long film was made called "Story of Tormore" which describes the whole construction process. The written commentary was made by the famous author Neil Gunn and an actor played the part of the architect Sir Albert Richardson, president of the Royal Academy who died in 1964. The building, which is already B-listed, was considered so smart that a model of it was made for the exhibition at the Scotch Whisky Heritage Centre in Edinburgh.

The equipment is made up of one stainless steel lauter mash tun from Newmill Ironworks in Elgin and eight stainless steel washbacks serving four pairs of stills. All the stills are fitted with purifiers resulting in a lighter spirit. The spirit is tankered away to Keith Bonds or another Chivas Bros facilities for filling in ex-bourbon casks and part of it returns to the distillery for maturation. The distillery lies on the A95 with an excellent view of the Spey valley and is surrounded by an interesting garden with trimmed bushes. Despite this and the interesting buildings, it is still uncertain whether Tormore will step out of its anonymous role as reliable producer of malt for Chivas Bros different blended whiskies.

The official bottling is a *12 year old* introduced in 2004/05. An official *15 year old* was released several years ago but has been difficult to obtain recently. Independent bottlings of Tormore are rare and the two most recent ones, 1994 and 1996, come from Gordon & MacPhail.

12 years old

Tullibardine

Owner:
Tullibardine Distillery Ltd

Region/district:
Highlands

Founded: 1949
Status: Active (vc)
Capacity: 2 500 000 litres

Address: Blackford, Perthshire PH4 1QG

Tel: 01764 682252
website: www.tullibardine.com

History:

1949 – The architect William Delmé-Evans founds the distillery.

1953 – The distillery is sold to Brodie Hepburn.

1971 – Invergordon Distillers buys Brodie Hepburn Ltd.

1973 – The number of stills doubles from two to four.

1993 – Whyte & Mackay (owned by Fortune Brands) buys Invergordon Distillers.

1994 – Tullibardine is mothballed.

1996 – Whyte & Mackay changes name to JBB (Greater Europe).

2001 – JBB (Greater Europe) is bought out from Fortune Brands by management and changes name to Kyndal (Whyte & Mackay from 2003).

2003 – A consortium including Michael Beamish buys Tullibardine in June for £1.1 million. The distillery is in production again by December. The first official bottling from the new owners is a 10 year old from 1993.

2004 – Three new vintage malts, from 1964, 1973 and 1988 respectively, are launched. Tullibardine 1488 Shop and 1488 Café opens.

2005 – Three wood finishes from 1993, port, muscatel and marsala are launched together with a 1986 John Black selection.

2006 – Vintage 1966 (plus a special World Cup version), Sherry Wood 1993 and a new John Black selection are launched.

2007 – Five different wood finishes are released as well as a couple of single cask vintages.

2008 – A Vintage 1968 40 year old is released.

Tullibardine 1993

DR – The nose is restrained with floral, almost perfumed notes, on the palate soft and gentle malt is decorated with the most delicate spice, a bit like scented talcum powder. The finish is ordered and polite, with a peaty note right at the finish.

DS – Spicy and earthy with honey and oak on the nose. More oak and honey on the palate with a long and dry finish.

Tullibardine distillery has made an impressive journey since a consortium headed by Mike Beamish and Doug Ross acquired the distillery in 2003. As late as 2006 production was at only 120,000 litres but in 2008, it is at capacity and staff are working 24/7 producing 2.7 million litres. The balance sheets are improving and it is expected to show a full year profit by 31st May 2008. Depending on how one sees that, the timing could be perfect to sell off and that is perhaps what will happen. At least three potential buyers surfaced in summer 2008 and the company hired Swiss investment bank UBS to assess the offers. The distillery is equipped with a stainless steel mash tun, nine stainless steel washbacks (the last three installed in 2007) and two pairs of stills. Adjacent to the distillery is a huge shopping complex, Tullibardine Retail Centre with a variety of retail outlets. More than 100,000 visitors find their way there each year.

The whole current range of malts from Tullibardine builds on produce from the previous owners since the distillery was mothballed between 1995 and 2003. The owners state that the whisky from the new production will be available in 2014.

It is difficult to identify a core range of bottlings from Tullibardine. The general idea is to bottle vintages and various wood finishes. Many expressions are limited editions but vintages from 1988, 1992 and 1993 have been released in larger quantities

The first run of wood finishes from *1993* introduced in autumn 2006, continued with new bottlings of *port, marsala, sherry, moscatel, sauternes* and *rum* in 2007. Single cask vintages from *1973* and *1975* and a vatted vintage from *1988* are also a part of the special range. New expressions for 2008 are a *40 year old* from 1968 and two vatted malts released to commemorate distillery manager John Black´s 50 years in the business - one peated *10 year old* and an *8 year old* with distinctive honey notes.

1988 vintage

Closed distilleries

The following distilleries are either demolished,
closed or dismantled and the chances of any of them
producing whisky again are slim to say the least. Even so,
new bottlings are regularly released from these silent distilleries.
Most of these releases stem from independent bottlers
whom have come across casks, but some are also
bottled by the owners themselves.

Brora distillery in the 1930s

Banff

Owner: Diageo **Region:** Speyside **Founded:** 1824

Status:
Closed in 1983, partly demolished in 1985, destroyed in a fire 1991.

Bottlings:
Banff has only occurred once as an official bottling in the *Rare Malts* series when a *21 year old* from 1982 was released in 2004. Several casks have found their way to independent bottlers, among them Gordon & MacPhail, Douglas Laing, Signatory and Cadenhead. Three of the most recent are a 1971 (37 years) and 1975 (32 years), both from Douglas Laing and a 1975 from Duncan Taylor.

Brora

Owner: Diageo **Region:** N Highlands **Founded:** 1819

Status:
Closed in 1983.

Bottlings:
A *30 year old* was released for the first time in 2002 and a new variety has appeared annually since then. In autumn 2008 a 25 year old was released by Diageo. Douglas Laing is known among the independents for some exceptional Broras. They released two a couple of years ago: a 23 year old from 1982 and a 22 year old from 1983. Quite recent independent bottlings include a Signatory, a Duncan Taylor and one from Ian MacLeod - all distilled in 1981.

Coleburn

Owner: Diageo **Region:** Speyside **Founded:** 1897

Status:
Closed in 1985, dismantled in 1996.

Bottlings:
Coleburn has appeared in the *Rare Malts* series once, a *21 year old* from 1979 released in 2000. This is the only existing official bottling available. Independent bottlings have also become extremely rare; a 34 year old from Douglas Laing and a 20 year old from Gordon & MacPhail appeared in 2002. After that it took until 2006 when Signatory released a 36 year old from 1970, matured in a wine treated puncheon.

Convalmore

Owner: Diageo **Region:** Speyside **Founded:** 1894

Status:
Closed in 1985, dismantled and buildings sold to William Grant in 1990.

Bottlings:
Diageo kept the rights to issue bottlings of Convalmore when the distillery was sold but have not taken advantage of this to a great extent. The first bottling was a *Rare Malts 24 years* from 1978 that appeared in 2003 and the second, a *28 year old Special Release*, that was launched in 2005. Independent bottlings are rare. Among the latest are a 23 year old from 1984 by Gordon & MacPhail and a 32 year old from 1975 by Douglas Laing.

Dallas Dhu

Owner: Diageo
Region: Speyside
Founded: 1898

Status:
Closed in 1983, sold to Historic Scotland in 1986 who now runs it as a museum.

Bottlings:
Apart from two releases in the *Rare Malts* series, the owners have released three bottlings for Historic Scotland in recent years. The first one was in 1998, followed by Centenerary 15 years old (1999) to commemorate the 100th anniversary of the first distilling and Millenium 25 years old (1999). Independent bottlings include Duncan Taylor 1981 and Douglas Laing 1970 (37 years) and 1971 (36 years).

Glen Albyn

Owner: Diageo
Region: N Highlands
Founded: 1844

Status:
Closed in 1983, demolished in 1986.

Bottlings:
With the exception of a 10 year old from the 1970s which is reported to have been sold in Italy, there are no official bottlings except a *Rare Malt 1975* (26 years) which turned up in 2002. Independent bottlings are definitely rare. Gordon & MacPhail has released two, 1966 and 1975, both bottled in 2005. There is also a Duncan Taylor 1979, a Douglas Laing 30 year old and quite recently a Blackadder 1974 (33 years).

Glen Esk

Owner: Diageo
Region: E Highlands
Founded: 1897

Status:
Closed in 1985, dismantled in 1996, now used as maltings.

Bottlings:
It is extremely difficult to find official bottlings. Diageo has released *Hillside* as a *Rare Malt* on three occasions, the last one in 1997. There has also been a *24 year old Glenesk*. It was released in 1993 to celebrate the 25th anniversary of Glenesk maltings.
Independent bottlings have become rare. Among the more recent ones is a 26 year old Duncan Taylor from 1981.

Glenlochy

Owner: Diageo
Region: W Highlands
Founded: 1898

Status:
Closed in 1983, demolished in 1992 except for the kiln and the malt barn.

Bottlings:
Official bottlings have occurred twice in the *Rare Malts* series (released *1995* and *1996*). Douglas Laing (Old Malt Cask) released a 49 year old in 2003 and that same year Gordon & McPhail (Rare Old) released a 37 year old. More recent independents come from Signatory and Duncan Taylor, both 24 years old and bottled in 2005.

Glen Mhor

Owner: Diageo
Region: N Highlands
Founded: 1892

Status:
Closed in 1983, demolished in 1986.

Bottlings:
The only official bottlings of Glen Mhor are a couple of *Rare Malts, 22 years old* from *1979* and *28 years old* from *1976*.
Independent bottlings have become increasingly rare. The most recent are Gordon & MacPhail 1979 (released 2004), Duncan Taylor 1975 (released 2007) and finally a 32 year old from 1975 released by Douglas Laing.

Glenury Royal

Owner: Diageo
Region: E Highlands
Founded: 1825

Status:
Closed in 1983 and later demolished.

Bottlings:
A couple of spectacular official bottlings have been released in recent years - a *50 year old* in 2003, a *36 year old* in 2005 and again in 2007, a *36 year old* distilled in 1970. In addition to them, Glenury Royal occurred three times in the Rare Malts series.
Independent bottlings are few. Among recent ones are a 34 year old from 1973 by Blackadder and, from Duncan Taylor, a 1984 bottled in 2005, 2006 and 2007.

Photo: © 2005 www.thewhiskystore.de

Photo: © 2005 www.thewhiskystore.de

Littlemill

Owner: Loch Lomond Distillery Co.
Region: Lowlands
Founded: 1772

Status:
Closed in 1992, dismantled in 1996, later demolished.

Bottlings:
The official bottling of Littlemill has recently been changed to *12 years old*. The bottle also has a new design, shared with the new 12 year olds from Glen Scotia and Loch Lomond (Inchmurrin). Recent independent bottlings include a 17 year old from 1990 released by Cadenhead and a Douglas Laing 1991 16 years old. An odd variety was also produced at Littlemill. Dunglas, distilled in 1967, was released by The Whisky Exchange in 2003.

Lochside

Owner: Chivas Brothers
Region: E Highlands
Founded: 1957

Status:
Closed in 1992, demolished in 2005.

Bottlings:
Official bottlings of Lochside have occurred but they are virtually impossible to get hold of.
Independent bottlings are also rare. Some of the most recent are Blackadder 26 years old from 1981 and a 40 year old from 1966 by Signatory. Douglas Laing has also released an unusual version of Lochside - a single grain from 1963 (42 years).

Millburn

Owner: Diageo **Region:** N Highlands **Founded:** 1807

Status:
Closed in 1985, dismantled in 1988.

Bottlings:
A couple of *Rare Malts* have been released by Diageo (the most recent and last in 2005, *35 years old*).
Independent bottlings are increasingly rare to encounter. Some of the most recent ones are Cadenhead 1974 (31 years), Douglas Laing 1969 (36 years), Signatory 1979 (26 years) and Blackadder 1974 (33 years).

North Port

Owner: Diageo **Region:** E Highlands **Founded:** 1820

Status:
Closed in 1983, demolished in 1993.

Bottlings:
The names North Port and Brechin are used interchangeably on the whisky labels.
The first two official bottlings of North Port were released as *Rare Malts; 1971* (*23 years old*) and *1979* (*20 years old*). It was therefore an opportunity to rejoice when a *28 year old* Brechin appeared in 2005 as a Special Release.
Independent bottlings include Signatory 1975 (29 years) and Duncan Taylor (Rarest of the Rare) 1981 (24 and 25 years respectively).

Pittyvaich

Owner: Diageo **Region:** Speyside **Founded:** 1974

Status:
Closed in 1993, demolished in 2002.

Bottlings:
The only official bottling of Pittyvaich is the *12 year old Flora & Fauna*. Independent bottlings are becoming rarer. Example of recent ones are Gordon & MacPhail 1993, Duncan Taylor 1979 and a 12 year old from 1995 released by Douglas Laing.

Port Ellen

Owner: Diageo **Region:** Islay **Founded:** 1825

Status:
Closed in 1983, dismantled in the 1990´s.

Bottlings:
In 2001 the owners began releasing one official bottling a year in when a *22 year old cask strength* was launched. This years release (the eighth) was a 29 year old from 1978.
Port Ellen is a favourite with independent bottlers. Recent ones include Ian MacLeod 1982 (26 years), Douglas Laing 1983 (24 years), Signatory 1982 (25 years) and a 1982 from Berry Brothers.

Rosebank

Owner: Diageo
Region: Lowlands
Founded: 1798

Status:
Closed in 1993. Buildings sold to British Waterways and Westpoint Homes. Most of the equipment still in place.

Bottlings:
There have been a number of official bottlings in the *Rare Malts* series and a *Flora & Fauna 12 years* can still be found. In 2007 a *25 year old*, distilled in 1981, appeared in the Special Release series. Several independent bottlers have also shown their interest in Rosebank. Among the latest are Single Malts of Scotland, Gordon & MacPhail, Blackadder and Cadenheads - all from 1991 and 16 years old. There is also an 1990, 18 year old from Ian MacLeod.

St Magdalene

Owner: Diageo
Region: Lowlands
Founded: 1795

Status:
Closed in 1983, most of the buildings converted into flats in the mid 1990´s

Bottlings:
St. Magdalene was never a prominent malt with blenders, but it aged very well on its own. A *19 year Rare Malt* from 1979 has been praised by many. Diageo have released four bottlings the last couple of years, three as *Rare Malts* and a *30 year old Linlithgow* from 1973.
The whisky can be difficult to obtain but a 25 year old from 1982 by Douglas Laing and a 1982 Linlithgow from Single Malts of Scotland were recently released.

Ben Wyvis

Owner: Whyte & Mackay
Region: N Highlands
Founded: 1965

Status: Closed in 1977, later dismantled.

Bottlings:
Ben Wyvis is highly sought after among collectors of rare single malts. The latest release was an official bottling of a 37 year old in 2002.

Inverleven

Owner: Chivas Brothers
Region: Lowlands
Founded: 1938

Status: Closed in 1991, later partly demolished.

Bottlings:
There are no official bottlings, but recent releases from independent bottlers include a Duncan Taylor 1979 and a 30 year old from 1977 by Signatory.

Glen Flagler / Killyloch

Owner: Inver House Distillers
Region: Lowlands
Founded: 1964

Status: Killyloch closed in 1975 and Glen Flagler in 1985.

Bottlings:
Both are major rarities. Signatory launched two Glen Flagler in the mid 1990s and Inver House released a Glen Flagler 1973 and a Killyloch 1967, both in 2003.

Kinclaith

Owner: Whitbread/Long John
Region: Lowlands
Founded: 1957

Status: Closed and dismantled in 1975, later demolished.

Bottlings:
There are no official bottlings. Two of the most recent and perhaps final bottlings were distilled in 1969 and released by Signatory and Duncan Taylor.

Glenugie

Owner: Whitbread/Long John
Region: E Highlands
Founded: 1831

Status: Closed in 1983, dismantled later.

Bottlings:
No official bottling of Glenugie exists but independent bottlings occur. Among recent ones are a Duncan Taylor from 1981 and a 1982 (26 years) by Douglas Laing.

Ladyburn

Owner: William Grant & Sons
Region: Lowlands
Founded: 1966

Status: Closed in 1975, dismantled in 1976.

Bottlings:
Two official and a couple of independent bottlings have been released since 2000, the most recent one being a Signatory 1975 and a Duncan Taylor 1973.

The really new ones!

Daftmill

Owner:	Region/district:	
Cuthbert family	Lowlands	
Founded:	**Status:**	**Capacity:**
2005	Active	c 65 000 litres
Address:	**Tel:**	**website:**
By Cupar, Fife KY15 5RF	01337 830303	www.daftmill.com

Permission was granted in 2003 for a steading at Daftmill Farmhouse in Fife to be converted into a distillery. Contrary to most other new distilleries selling shares in their enterprise, Hazel and Francis Cuthbert together with Francis´ brother Ian, have quietly established the distillery. The license to distil was granted on St Andrews Day 2005 and the first distillation was on 16 December that same year. It is run as a typical farmhouse distillery. The barley is grown on the farm and malted without peat at commercial maltsters. Equipment consists of a semi-lauter mash tun, two stainless steel washbacks and one pair of stills with slightly ascending lyne arms. The spirit is matured on the farm on bourbon casks from Heaven Hill and 14,000 litres were produced the first year.

The establishment of Daftmill increased the number of Lowland distilleries from three to four (and with Ailsa Bay, there are now five). Even though there will be legal whisky in the barrels by December 2008, there are no plans to release any bottlings until 2010 at the earliest. Daftmill Farm is not just about whisky. Besides distilling, the Cuthberts also grow potatoes and have a fine herd of beef cattle. Distilling has been irregular recently as taking care of the rest of the business on the farm (which is what at the moment is bringing in the money) takes its time.

Ailsa Bay

Owner:	Region/district:	
William Grant & Sons	Lowlands	
Founded:	**Status:**	**Capacity:**
2007	Active	5 000 000 litres
Address:		**Tel:**
Girvan, Ayrshire KA26 9PT		01465 713091

Girvan in Aysrhire is one of seven Scottish grain distilleries and has a capacity of 60 million litres. There is also a gin still, a cooperage and warehouses with 1.3 million barrels in maturation. During 1968 to 1975 there was also malt whisky production through Ladyburn distillery. Since September 2007, malt whisky is again produced at Girvan at the new Ailsa Bay distillery. With four pairs of stills and a capacity of 5 million litres, it is already one of the biggest distilleries in Scotland. A unique feature is the octangular spirit safe which sits between the two rows of stills. Each side corresponds to one specific still. Another feature is the preheater for the wash. This is in common use in Cognac, where wine heaters let steam pass through the wine tank for the next distillation in order to save heat and make the distillation faster. A similar technique is used here and the wash comes into the still preheated at 60° C. The spirit produced here is destined to become a part of Wm Grant´s blended whiskies.

Photo: © Erkin Tuzmuhamedov

Kilchoman

Owner:		Region/district:
Kilchoman Distillery Co.		Islay

Founded:	Status:	Capacity:
2005	Active (vc)	90 000 litres

Address:
Rockside farm, Bruichladdich, Islay PA49 7UT

Tel:	website:
01496 850011	www.kilchomandistillery.com

When Kilchoman Distillery was inaugurated on 3rd June 2005 it was the first distillery to open on Islay since Malt Mill opened on Lagavulin Distillery's premises in 1908. Entrepreneur Anthony Wills, with a background in the wine industry, presented his idea of a new distillery on Islay to the farmer Mark French. Mark and his wife Rohaise operated the Rockside Farm and had already started the transformation from traditional farming when Wills courted them in 2002. The previous year, for example, they had launched a gourmet range of smoked beef and lamb under the Islay Fine Food label, so the idea of a distillery fitted well with their plans of refining local produce. The new partners started on the distillery project in 2002 and three years later the distillery was ready.

To reach Kilchoman, turn to the west a couple of miles north of Bruichladdich. A narrow road winds its way through a rather solitary landscape until you reach the farm, situated a stone's throw from the open Atlantic with Canada on the other side. Kilchoman is the westernmost distillery in Scotland. It is a typical farm distillery with

the whole of the production carried out on site. The barley is grown at Rockside Farm, malted, distilled, matured and eventually bottled at the distillery. The equipment consists of a mash tun, four stainless steel wash backs (two of them installed in 2007), a wash still (2 700 litres charge) and a spirit still (1 500 litres charge). The average fermentation time is 100 hours. Floor malting that take care of 40% of requirements is used while the rest is purchased from Port Ellen. The in-house malt has a phenol specification of 25-30 ppm while the Port Ellen malt has the same specification as Ardbeg. Maturation takes place in their own dunnage warehouse with a capacity of 600 casks. When it is filled plans are to store some at Bruichladdich Distillery. Kilchoman produces around 95,000 litres per year (around 630 bourbon barrels and 40 sherry butts) which is more or less full capacity.

The first distillation took place in late 2005 and they plan to launch a 5 year old in 2010, gradually increasing the range with 8, 10 and 12 year olds. However there is a possibility that there will be a first, limited bottling already in late 2008 or early 2009 of a 3 year old. Wills is uncertain whether he will launch wood finishes, but is working with four variables to create different expressions; sherry- or bourbon-matured and own malt or Port Ellen-malt. The bottles based on Port Ellen malt will have the name Kilchoman on the label whereas the bottles containing whisky made from their own malted barley will be called Kilchoman 100% Islay. There is also a visitor centre with a café and a shop and around 10 000 visitors a year are already attracted to the distillery.

Glengyle

Owner:
Mitchell's Glengyle Ltd

Region/district:
Campbeltown

Founded: **Status:** **Capacity**
2004 Temp. closed 750 000 litres

Address:
85 Longrow, Campbeltown, Argyll PA28 6EX

Tel: **website:**
01586 552009 www.kilkerran.com

Glengyle Distillery was the first distillery to open in the new millennium and the first to open in Campbeltown for 125 years though its heritage is ancient. Glengyle was founded by William Mitchell in 1872. Mitchell owned Springbank with his brother John for some years before the two brothers went separate ways. Glengyle closed in 1925.

Nearly 80 years later Hedley Wright, owner of Springbank and great great nephew of William Mitchell, founded a new company, acquired the run-down buildings and embarked on painstaking renovations. Stills were bought from the closed Ben Wyvis Distillery in 2002 and were rebuilt to increase the reflux. The stills had only been used for a few years before Ben Wyvis closed and the copper is therefore quite thick, even if they were built in the early sixties. The wash still has a capacity of 18 000 litres and the spirit still 11 000 litres. Spirit safe and spirit receivers also came from Ben Wyvis and a left-over malt mill

from Craigellachie's expansion was purchased and installed. A new semi-lauter mash tun and four washbacks made of larch were installed and the new Glengyle was finally inaugurated on 25th March 2004.

The owners are now working on a five-year plan where new warehouses and a bottling plant will be constructed and in ten years' time the distillery will also have their own maltings. Today the malt is brought over from neighbouring Springbank whose staff also run operations. Two months' work at Glengyle suffices the annual requirement which is at 60 000 litres. The spirit is filled on a variety of different casks; sherry, bourbon, Madeira, Marsala and Port. There is currently no distillation taking place at Glengyle due to the temporary production stop at Springbank distillery which was announced by the owners in summer 2008.

A big celebratory party was held in Campbeltown 5th May 2007 when the first spirit from Glengyle turned 3 years old and legally became whisky. A small cask was placed in the Tasting Room for visitors to enjoy the first Kilkerran - three years old and port matured. The name Kilkerran is used for the whisky as Glengyle was already in use for a vatted malt produced by Loch Lomond Distillers. It will take some time until the next occasion; the owners are planning to release a limited amount of an 8 year old in 2012, 2013, 2014 and 2015. The standard Kilkerran 12 years will be released first in 2016. For those who do not wish to wait that long, a new Mitchell's blended whisky which contains some whisky from Glengyle is available for sale.

Distilleries per owner

c = closed, d = demolished, mb = mothballed, dm = dismantled

Diageo
Auchroisk
Banff (d)
Benrinnes
Blair Athol
Brora (c)
Bushmills
Caol Ila
Cardhu
Clynelish
Coleburn (dm)
Convalmore (dm)
Cragganmore
Dailuaine
Dallas Dhu (c)
Dalwhinnie
Dufftown
Glen Albyn (d)
Glendullan
Glen Elgin
Glenesk (dm)
Glenkinchie
Glenlochy (d)
Glenlossie
Glen Mhor (d)
Glen Ord
Glen Spey
Glenury Royal (d)
Inchgower
Knockando
Lagavulin
Linkwood
Mannochmore
Millburn (dm)
Mortlach
North Port (d)
Oban
Pittyvaich (d)
Port Ellen (dm)
Rosebank (c)
Royal Lochnagar
St Magdalene (dm)
Strathmill
Talisker
Teaninich

Pernod Ricard
Aberlour
Allt-a-Bhainne
Braeval
Caperdonich (mb)
Glenallachie
Glenburgie
Glen Keith (mb)
Glenlivet
Glentauchers
Imperial (c)
Inverleven (d)
Lochside (d)
Longmorn

Miltonduff
Scapa
Strathisla
Tormore

Edrington Group
Glenrothes
Glenturret
Highland Park
Macallan
Tamdhu

Inver House (Thai Beverage)
Balblair
Balmenach
Glen Flagler (d)
Knockdhu
Pulteney
Speyburn

John Dewar & Sons (Bacardi)
Aberfeldy
Aultmore
Craigellachie
Macduff
Royal Brackla

Whyte & Mackay (United Spirits)
Dalmore
Fettercairn
Jura
Tamnavulin

William Grant & Sons
Ailsa Bay
Balvenie
Glenfiddich
Kininvie
Ladyburn (dm)

Glenmorangie Co.
(Moët Hennessy)
Ardbeg
Glenmorangie
Glen Moray

Morrison Bowmore (Suntory)
Auchentoshan
Bowmore
Glen Garioch

Burn Stewart Distillers
(CL Financial)
Bunnahabhain
Deanston
Tobermory

Loch Lomond Distillers
Glen Scotia
Littlemill (d)
Loch Lomond

Angus Dundee Distillers
Glencadam
Tomintoul

Long John Whitbread
Glenugie (dm)
Kinclaith (d)

J & A Mitchell
Glengyle
Springbank

Beam Global Spirits & Wine
Ardmore
Laphroaig

Benriach Distillery Co.
Benriach
Glendronach

Campari Group
Glen Grant

Isle of Arran Distillers
Arran

**Signatory Vintage
Scotch Whisky Co.**
Edradour

Ian Macleod Distillers
Glengoyne

Tomatin Distillery Co.
(Marubeni Europe plc)
Tomatin

J & G Grant
Glenfarclas

Bruichladdich Distillery Co.
(Murray McDavid)
Bruichladdich

**Co-ordinated
Development Services**
Bladnoch

Gordon & MacPhail
Benromach

**Glenglassaugh Distillery Co Ltd
(Scaent Group)**
Glenglassaugh

Ben Nevis Distillery Ltd (Nikka)
Ben Nevis

Tullibardine Distillery Ltd
Tullibardine

Speyside Distillers Co.
Speyside

Cooley Distillery plc
Cooley
Kilbeggan

Kilchoman Distillery Co.
Kilchoman

Cuthbert family
Daftmill

Single malts from Japan

Miyagikyo Distillery

On the following pages we present ten Japanese whisky distilleries. Eight of them are producing at the moment (with Chichibu being the last to come on stream), one was demolished four years ago (Hanyu) and a third has been mothballed for the last decade (Shinshu). There are other whisky ventures emerging, for example Monde Shuzou, a winemaker established in 1952 which has produced and sold a couple of blended whiskies for some time. Quite recently a single malt, distilled in 1983 at Monde Shuzou, was released by a Japanese independent bottler and it may well be that we will see more releases, maybe even official ones, from this producer. Chris Bunting of *nonjatta.blogspot.com* (the best source to Japanese whiskies on the internet), identifies at least eight or nine other companies that could be on the verge of stepping in to produce malt whisky and he calls them "Ji-whisky" operations, a Japanese term for micro- or boutique distilleries.

It is a fact that malt whiskies from Japan continue to reap the fruits of success since last year. The array of malt whiskies is not as impressive as in Scotland but the top whiskies are convincing. In the latest World Whisky Awards 2008, arranged by Whisky Magazine, Yoichi 1987 20 years old was voted the Best Single Malt Whisky and Hibiki 30 year old from Suntory won Best Blended Whisky. That should suffice as an argument fore the most sceptical to give malt whiskies from Japan a chance.

The contents on the following pages is based on Hideo Yamaoka´s texts from Malt Whisky Yearbook 2008 with updates for news. It is our intention to present an expanded section on Japanese whisky in the next edition of the Yearbook. Until then we can recommend Chris Bunting´s blog to keep abreast with latest developments and not least the first book devoted solely to Japanese whisky, the recently published *Japanese Whisky - facts, figures and taste* by Ulf Buxrud. Read more on page 262.

Chichibu

Owner: Ichiro Akuto   **Founded:** 2008   **Capacity:** ?

Malt whisky range:
none

Eight years after the first Chichibu distillery or Hanyu as it is often called, had to close, the grandson of the founder, Ichiro Akuto, opened the first new whisky distillery in Japan since 1973. In spring 2008 he started distilling at his Chichibu distillery two hours northwest of Tokyo. According to tradition and in order to bring fortune to the future distillery, before building started last summer, a local Shinto priest visited the site in order to conduct a Jichinsau ground breaking ceremony.

Ichiro Akuto uses two types of malt for the production, one imported from Germany and one from England but his goal is to become self-sustaining in the future and he has even found a source for peat in the vicinity. The distillery is equipped with a mash tun, five washbacks made of Japanese oak and one pair of stills made by Forsyth´s in Scotland. Until the whisky from his own production is ready to sell, Akuto will continue through his company Venture Whisky, to sell his renowned "Card" series of single cask whiskies bottled from the stock of the demolished Hanyu distillery.

Eigashima

Owner: Eigashima Shuzo   **Founded:** 1919   **Capacity:** ?

Malt whisky range:
none

Eigashima Shuzo is a maker of sake and shochu. They had produced spirits-based drinks from 1919, and full-scale whisky production began in 1984 when they built the current distillery. It is located in Akashi near Kobe in Hyogo Prefecture.

Japanese microdistillery whiskies were very popular in Japan in the early 1980s, keeping the Eigashima Distillery in operation around the clock. However, the shochu boom of the mid 1980s, the revision of Japan's Liquor Tax Law in 1989 and the decline in prices of imports took their toll and demand dropped and continues at a low level. They now produce malt whisky only once a year.

The average length of maturation is 4 years. The maturation warehouses are beside the sea and it is very hot in the summer. Annual loss to the angels' share is from 7 to 8 %. All the malt whisky produced goes to their blend, "White Oak", in which it is mixed with no age grain spirit from the USA or their own shochu.

Most of the malt whisky is matured in sherry hogsheads which previously held Scotch malt whisky,

but they also have peaty malt whisky which has been aging in several sherry butts for over 10 years. It is possible that this may be released as a single cask bottling in the future.

Fuji-Gotemba

Owner: Kirin Brewery
Founded: 1973
Capacity: 12 000 000 litres (incl grain whisky)

Malt whisky range:
Fuji-Gotemba Single Malt 18 year old, Fuji-Sanroku Single Malt 18 year old, Fuji-Gotemba Single Cask 10 year old.

Fuji-Gotemba Distillery, in Shizuoka Prefecture near Mt. Fuji, released six versions of Single Cask Whisky Fuji-Gotemba 10 year old in 2007. They are the first single cask whiskies released by Fuji-Gotemba Distillery. Four are available only at the distillery while the other two are sold online. The ABVs are around 43-46% but they are all cask strength. The ABV at the time of cask filling is around 50.5%. Almost all the casks used by Fuji-Gotemba are barrels.

Fuji-Gotemba is one of the few distilleries in the world which not only has malt whisky stills but also grain whisky stills, a bottling plant and a cooperage. It was founded by Kirin-Seagram in 1973. Kirin-Seagram was a joint venture of Kirin Brewery Company Ltd. (Japan), JE Seagam Company Ltd. (USA) and Chivas Brothers (UK). The premium blend "Evermore", versions of which had been released every year from 1999 to 2005, used to contain the same vatted malt as that used in Chivas Regal, but

matured in Japan and blended with malt and grain whisky produced at Fuji-Gotemba.

Kirin Brewery became the sole owner of Fuji-Gotemba in 2002, and Kirin Brewery acquired Mercian including its Karuizawa Distillery in 2007. However, Kirin currently has no plans to release a blend using malt whisky from both Fuji-Gotemba and Karuizawa.

Hakushu

Owner: Suntory
Founded: 1973
Capacity: 3 000 000 litres

Malt whisky range:
Hakushu Single Malt 10, 12, 18 and 25 year old.

The concept of the Hakushu distillery facilities is harmony with nature. The distillery is known as the "Forest Distillery" because it was constructed within a dense green forest covering the foothills of Mt. Kaikomagatake in Yamanashi Prefecture.

In 1981 on the same grounds, a new distillery, Hakushu East, was built, and only that distillery is currently working. The old distillery (referred to as Hakushu West) is now sometimes used for concerts. Although the original lantern-shaped pot stills of Hakushu East were smaller than those of Hakushu West, some have been replaced with even smaller pot stills. Hakushu East has a wide variety of pot stills enabling it to produce many different styles of spirit. There are pot stills with different sizes and shapes, different lyne arm configurations and both direct-fired and indirect-heated stills.The wash from the No.1 wash still goes to the No.1 and No.2 spirit stills. Only the No.2 spirit still is heated by steam coils while the rest are direct fired using gas. The No.3 wash still has a square worm tub while all the other stills have shell-and-tube condensers.

Some of Hakushu's malt whiskies are filtered after maturation using bamboo charcoal giving it a rounded character. These are used in the blended whisky, "Zen", which is said to go well with Japanese food.

Hanyu

Owner:	Founded:	Capacity:
Toa Shuzo	1941	Dismantled

Malt whisky range:
Ichiro´s Malt 15 and 20 year old, Ichiro´s Malt Vintage 1988, Ichiro´s Malt Card Series (single casks distilled from 1985 to 2000)

Toa Shuzo, a maker of sake and shochu, built Hanyu distillery in Saitama Prefecture in 1946 and began full-scale whisky distillation in 1983. However, the company was sold and the new owner demolished the distillery in 2004. They also planned to discard about 400 casks of malt whisky left in storage but Ichiro Akuto, the grandson of the original founder of Toa Shuzo, arranged to have the casks transferred to Sasanokawa Shuzo, a sake maker in Fukushima Prefecture which once had made whisky and which had an empty warehouse.

Akuto established "Venture Whisky" in 2004 and began to release Hanyu single cask bottlings under the name Ichiro's Malt in 2005. Ichiro's Malt 1988 with the "King of Diamonds" label won top honors in the Japanese whisky tasting in "Whisky Magazine" in 2006. In the same tasting in 2007, the "King of Spades" label bottling was awarded top honors and the "Ace of Hearts" and "Two of Clubs" (finished in Japanese oak) were runners up. A couple of Akuto´s most recent bottlings are "Seven of Clubs", aged 8 years and finished in a refill American oak hogshead and "Two of Diamonds", 17 years old with a finish in a bourbon barrel.

During spring 2008 Akuto started distilling at his new distillery at Chichibu Midorigaoka in Saitama Prefecture. Read more under Chichibu on page 205.

Karuizawa

Owner:	Founded:	Capacity:
Mercian (Kirin Brewery)	1955	150 000 litres

Malt whisky range:
Karuizawa 15 and 17 year old, Karuizawa Wine Cask 12 year old, Karuizawa Vintage (1982, 1988 and most recently 1986, bottled in 2008).

Karuizawa Distillery, located in the mountain resort town of Karuizawa, and its parent company, Mercian, were acquired by Kirin Holdings in September 2007. Going forward, cooperation between Kirin's Fuji-Gotemba Distillery and Karuizawa Distillery is expected.

Karuizawa's stillhouse has two wash stills of the same size and two spirit stills, but only one of the spirit stills is used for malt whisky. The other is used to make marc brandy by distilling once more pomace wine already distilled a first time at Mercian Katsunuma Winery. The capacity of each pot still is only 4,000 litres. The malt whisky is matured mainly in sherry casks. All the casks are stored in racked warehouses. There is also one new racked warehouse which is unique because the movement of casks on the racks is automated.

Karuizawa uses only Golden Promise barley imported from the UK. Ichiro Akuto (see entry on Hanyu) bought a cask from Karuizawa and released the bottling as Ichiro's Choice in 2006, labeled as "Peated Golden Promise".

In 2007, Karuizawa Wine Cask 12yo was released to commemorate the 12th anniversary of the museum which is on the site of the distillery. It was sold in the distillery shop and sold out quickly. Also in 2007, four single cask bottlings were sold in Europe, two for the UK and two for Germany.

Miyagikyo

Owner: Nikka
Founded: 1969
Capacity: 5 000 000 litres

Malt whisky range:
Miyagikyo Single Malt 10, 12 and 15 year old, Miyagikyo Single Cask 1987.

Miyagikyo Distillery is also known as Sendai Distillery, and in the 80s and 90s it was sold under the brand Sendai Single Malt. After the acquisition of Nikka by Asahi Brewery in 2001, disitribution was expanded to cover all of Japan and it was renamed Miyagikyo.

When the distillery was built in 1969, two pairs of pot stills were installed. The capacity of the wash stills is 15,500 litres and that of the spirit stills is 12,500 litres. In 1976, two more pairs of stills were installed with the capacity of the wash stills being 25,500 litres and that of the spirit stills 18,500 litres. The malt is flowery and fruity. This is said to be due partly to the fact that the pot stills have boil balls and the lyne arms are slanted slightly upwards. All the stills are steam-heated and use shell-and-tube condensers.

Miyagikyo also has Coffey stills, which are now rare even in Scotland. They were moved from the Nishinomiya distillery in 1999. Sometimes they are used to distill wash which is made using only malted barley. After aging, this is blended with

"regular" Miyagikyo malt whisky, distilled twice in pot stills. Whisky made this way is bottled as the inexpensive "All Malt" for general sale and as "The Kokubucho" which is available only at the distillery.

Shinshu

Owner: Hombo Shuzo
Founded: 1960
Capacity: Mothballed

Malt whisky range:
Komogatake 10 year old, Komogatake Single Cask 1986 and 1989, Mars Malt Gallery 1985, 1988 and 1991.

Hombo Shuzo, a maker of shochu, built the Yamanashi Distillery in 1960, moved it to Miyata in 1980 and renamed it Shinshu. The brand name of the whisky is Mars. Production was stopped around 10 years ago and there are currently no plans to restart production. Only some 100 casks of malt whisky are still left. There is a distillery tour and a few limited single cask bottlings are available only at the distillery shop.

Hombo Shuzo also has a shochu distillery, Kagoshima Distillery, where they did trial production of peated malt whisky from 1982 to 1984. The capacity of the pot stills was only 500 litres each. Maltage 8 year old is pure malt whisky whose components are this peated malt and the malt from Shinshu Distillery.

Kiichiro Iwai designed the pot stills of Shinshu Distillery. He was at one time the boss of Masataka Taketsuru, the founder of Nikka, when they worked at the Japanese sake maker, Settsu Shuzo, before Taketsuru went to Scotland to study whisky production. When Taketsuru returned to Japan,

he showed Iwai his "Taketsuru Report" about whisky production in Scotland. The neck shape of the pot still is a straight head like that of Yoichi, which Taketsuru started.

Mars Single Cask Komagatake 1986 & 1988 were awarded silver medals at the IWSC in 2007.

Yoichi

Owner:	Founded:	Capacity:
Nikka	1934	5 000 000 litres

Malt whisky range:
Single Malt Yoichi 10, 12, 15 and 20 year old, Nikka Single Cask 1987, 1988.

Yoichi, (also known as Hokkaido Distillery) is on the island of Hokkaido and is the most northern of Japan's distilleries. It was founded in 1934 by Masataka Taketsuru, who had previously studied whisky production in Scotland and supervised the startup of Yamazaki, Japan's first whisky distillery, when he worked for Kotobukiya (later to become Suntory).

Yoichi has developed its own production technique by using first fill and refill bew wood American oak casks (i.e. not previously seasoned with other spirits or wines). Yoichi chars the new casks to lover the amount of the woody pencil-shavingslike flavour that is imparted to the whisky by the new wood.

First fill new wood casks have been used for several notable single cask bottlings of Yoichi, including the bottling that received the highest rating in Whisky Magazine's 2001 "Best of the Best" blind tasting. This cask had been charred, but Yoichi began to char the casks only from around the mid 1980s. Until then, the casks had been toasted or just smoked. Not only Suntory but also Nikka has some Japanese oak (mizunara) casks laid down, but no Japanese oak single cask bottlings have yet been released for general sale by Nikka.

In 2008, Yoichi 1987 20 years was awarded Best Single Malt Whisky in the World Whisky Awards arranged by Whisky Magazine.

Yoichi is the only malt whisky distillery in the world to have direct coal-fired stills. The last distillery in Scotland to have coal-fired stills, Glendronach, switched to steam heating in 2005.

Yamazaki

Owner:	Founded:	Capacity:
Suntory	1923	3 500 000 litres

Malt whisky range:
Yamazaki 10, 12, 18, 25, 35 and 50 year old.

An important component of the standard bottlings of Yamazaki single malt is that the spirit has matured in Japanese oak (mizunara) casks. Suntory tried this technique during the post World War II years when there was a shortage of sherry casks. However, they found that the casks leaked more easily than casks made from white oak because Japanese oak has less tyloses.

The Japanese oak casks were stored deep inside the warehouses and forgotten as sherry casks became more available. However, when these Japanese oak casks were checked many years later, the whisky was found to have acquired a unique oriental flavor reminiscent of sandalwood. Suntory now considers this to be an essential part of the flavor profile of the standard bottlings of Yamazaki single malt and of the Hibiki blends.

Yamazaki has wooden washbacks and six pairs of stills and three of the pairs were replaced with new stills in 2006. The shape of the new stills are all different. The necks of the No.1 stills are straight and the lyne arm of the wash still is slanted downward, resulting in a spirit with a lot of body. Each No. 2 still has a boil ball resulting in a more elegant spirit. The necks of the No. 4 pair of stills are wide and straight resulting in a well-balanced spirit. All the new wash stills are direct-fired.

New releases in Europe in autumn 2008 were Cask of Yamazaki 1993, a heavily peated single cask and Cask of Yamazaki 1990, sherry-matured.

Distilleries
around the globe

*Malt whisky distilling has long since stopped
being just a Scottish concern. Follow us on an exciting journey
to distilleries from all corners of the world.*

Great Southern Distilling Company, Western Australia

The international world of whisky is filled with people who simply refuse to believe that God is not always on the side of those who are trying to build a distillery. There are many pitfalls along the way (read Gavin Smith's excellent article on pp 26-39) and there are many examples of delayed or abandoned projects. As an example, more has been written about *Blackwood distillery* in the Shetlands without a single stone ever having been laid to its foundations, than about other distilleries which have produced whisky for decades.

But there are also those who have succeeded; the people at *Mackmyra* in Sweden have metamorphosed from a group of enthusiasts into highly professional distillers and their success inspires others. This year we can report on the second Swedish distillery that started distilling in May and at least five other projects in the country have reached different stages of development.

Another enthusiast is to be found in Australia, in Tasmania, where Keith Batt of *Nant distillery* filled his first cask in April this year. Interestingly, the distillery has decided to handle all stages of the process themselves, including growing and malting the barley (like *Kilchoman* on Islay). Again, inspiration from another entrepreneur, Bill Lark who started whisky production in Australia a couple of decades ago, played a large part in getting started at Nant.

The number of craft distilleries has exploded in the US and some of them also include malt whisky in their ranges. *Dry Fly Distilling* produced their first batch of malt whisky in January 2008 and in Virginia, Englishman Chris Allwood plans to start *Eades distillery* in spring 2009. Another waiting its turn is Chris Weld of *Berkshire Mountain Distillers* in Maine who already produces rum, gin, vodka and bourbon and will go into malt whisky in the autumn. Nick Quint, who is running *Yahara Bay Distillers* in Wisconsin, currently distilling vodka and gin, is also planning to introduce malt whisky.

Remaining in North America we can report that ground has been broken for the third Canadian malt whisky distillery, also being the second on Vancouver Island, this summer, namely *Shelter Point distillery*, with partners Jay Oddleifson and Andrew Currie (who took part in starting Arran distillery in Scotland). They calculate on producing in early 2009.

We are also excited about reports we have received concerning Russia's first malt whisky distillery, *Kizlyarskoye*, in the Republic of Dagestan. Apparently it has already been distilling for a couple of years because its first three year old whisky was presented at a conference in 2007. The whisky is still not for sale but will probably be on the market around the end of 2008.

Meanwhile, in Germany, Austria and especially in Switzerland, small distilleries continue to surprise whisky drinkers with their high quality produce (read more in Dominic Roskrow's feature on pp 64-73). Disappointingly, their products rarely find their way outside the country, which applies to too many of the distilleries covered on the following pages. But there are hopes of improvement; alert importers have begun to sniff out the quality whisky which is often on offer. The largest retailer in France, *Maison du Whisky*, has for example adopted American *Clear Creek Distillery* and *Tuthilltown Spirits* with the purpose of distributing their whisky within the whole of the EU.

So keep an eye open the next time you visit your whisky shop - there just may be a couple of bottles from Sweden or Russia next to the Glenmorangie and Bowmore!

EUROPE

Austria

DISTILLERY: Waldviertler Roggenhof,
Roggenreith
FOUNDED: 1995
OWNER/MANAGER: Johann & Monika Haider
www.roggenhof.at

In the small village of Roggenreith in northern
Austria, Johann and Monika Haider have been
distilling whisky since 1995. In 2005 they opened
up a Whisky Experience World with guided tours, a
video show, whisky tasting and exhibitions. In 2008
a theme garden was opened, showing the four
elements of whisky - fire, water, earth and air.
Roggenhof was the first whisky distillery in Austria
and the first year 1,000 litres were distilled. The
quantity increased every year and reached 30,000
litres in 2006.

The new make is filled on to casks made of the
local Manhartsberger oak adding a slight vanilla
flavour and left to mature for three years. When the
casks are used a second time, the whisky matures for
five years. They use the casks a third time, but only
after dismantling, shaving and charring them before
filling. Spirit on third fill casks is expected to mature
for 12-18 years. Storage capacity is 56,000 litres at
the moment, but will double in 2009 when a new
warehouse is built. Two single malts are available:
Gersten Malzwhisky J. H. (light malt) and Gersten
Malzwhisky J. H. Karamell (dark, roasted malt).

DISTILLERY: Wolfram Ortner Destillerie,
Bad Kleinkirchheim
FOUNDED: 1990
OWNER/MANAGER: Wolfram Ortner
www.wob.at

Fruit brandies of all kinds are Wolfram Ortner´s main
produce as well as cigars, coffee and other luxuries.
For the last few years he has also been producing
malt whisky. New oak of different kinds (Limousin,
Alolier, Nevers, Vosges and American) is used for
the maturation process. His first single malt, WOB
DÖ MALT Vergin began selling in 2001 and a new
product line, in which Ortner mixes his whisky with
other distillates such as orange/muscatel, is called
WOB Marriage.

DISTILLERY: Destillerie Weutz,
St. Nikolai im Sausal
FOUNDED: 2002
OWNER/MANAGER: Michael & Brigitte Weutz
www.weutz.at

This family distillery, initially producing schnapps

and liqueur from fruits and berries is situated in
Steiermark in the south of Austria. In 2004 Michael
Weutz started cooperation with the brewer Michael
Löscher and since then Weutz has added whisky to
its produce based on the wash from the brewery.
The business grew quickly and in 2006 the distillery
moved to a bigger location. Since 2004, more than 10
different malt whiskies have been produced. Some of
them are produced in the traditional Scottish style;
Hot Stone, St.Nikolaus and the peated Black Peat.
Others are more unorthodox, for example Green
Panther, in which 5% pumpkin seeds are added to
the mash, and Franziska based on elderflower. Apart
from barley wheat, corn and spelt are also used for
some expressions.

Annual production is currently at approximately
14,000 litres and for maturation casks made of
French Limousin and Alliere oak are used. So far the
whisky is only available for purchase in Austria.

DISTILLERY: Reisetbauer, Axberg
FOUNDED: 1994 (whisky since 1995)
OWNER/MANAGER: Julia & Hans Resisetbauer
www.reisetbauer.at

A family-owned farm distillery near to Linz in
northern Austria. Specialised in brandies and
schnapps made of fruit but has included single
malt whisky in its range since 1995. The distillery is
equipped with five 350 litre stills. All stills are heated
using hot water rather than steam which according
to Hans Reisetbauer allows for a more delicate and
gentle distillation. Some 20,000 litres of pure alcohol
destined for whiskymaking are produced annually
with local barley used to make the malt. The malt
is dried without the use of peat due to Austrian
health regulations as phenols are believed to be
carcinogenic. Casks are sourced locally from the best
Austrian wineproducers. The whisky is filled the same
day the winecasks have been emptied in order to
save aromas from oxidation and to avoid the use of
SO_2.

The current range includes a 7 year old single malt
which is a vatting of whiskies aged in casks that have
previously contained Chardonnay and Trockenbeeren-

Some of the first expressions from Destillerie Weutz

auslese. There is also a 10 year old cask strength aged exclusively in Trockenbeerenauslese and in 2008 the first ever Austrian 12-year old whisky with a maturation in ex ice-wine barrels was released.

Belgium

DISTILLERY: The Owl Distillery, Grâce Hollogne
FOUNDED: 1997
OWNER/MANAGER: Etienne Bouillon (manager), Luc Foubert and Pierre Roberti
www.belgianwhisky.com
www.thebelgianowl.com

Last year, Belgium's first single malt was finally bottled. The first casks were filled on 29th October 2004 and in late October 2007 Etienne Bouillon released his first 400 bottles of 'The Belgian Owl' as the whisky was named. At the same time the distillery, formerly known as PUR.E. Distillerie changed its name to The Owl Distillery. The next bottling came in June 2008 but was exclusively reserved by customers. The first bottling to be available in shops will be the third bottling and will be available around November 2008. Bouillon expects to produce c 24,000 bottles a year thereafter.

Every step of production (including malting) is carried out at the distillery near Liege and maturation takes place in first fill bourbon casks from Kentucky. Since the distillery started in 2004, bottles of the spirit from The Owl Distillery have been for sale and even if it has not been whisky in the legal sense this has given the consumers an opportunity to sample the development of the produce at different steps of aging.

DISTILLERY: Brouwerij Het Anker, Mechelen
FOUNDED: 1369 (whisky since 2003)
OWNER/MANAGER: Charles Leclef
www.hetanker.be

Gouden Carolus from Het Anker became the third Belgian malt whisky to reach the market after The Belgian Owl and Goldlys when it was released in January 2008. The brewery itself is one of the oldest in Belgium and has been in the ownership of the current family since 1873. In common with many other breweries worldwide the whisky is a sidetrack where the wash intended for beer production is distilled into whisky. The Gouden Carolus Single Malt is four years old and its first edition was 2,500 bottles.

Czech Rebublic

DISTILLERY: Gold Cock Distillery
FOUNDED: 1877
OWNER/MANAGER: Rudolf Jelinek a.s
www.rjelinek.cz

The distilling of Gold Cock whisky started already in 1877. Gold Cock was originally a malt whisky made from abundunt local barley. Now it is produced in two versions – a 3 year old blended whisky and a 12 year old malt. Production was stopped for a while but after the brand and distillery were acquired by R. Jelinek a.s, the leading Czech producer of plum brandy, the whisky began life anew. The malt whisky is double distilled in 500 litre traditional pot-stills. The new owner has created a small whisky museum which is also home to the club Friends of Gold Cock Whisky with private vaults, where any enthusiast can store his bottlings of Gold Cock.

Etienne Bouillon, Luc Foubert and Pierre Roberti of The Owl Distillery

Gold Cock - currently the only distillery in the Czech Republic

Denmark

DISTILLERY: Stauning Whisky, Stauning
FOUNDED: 2006
OWNER/MANAGER:
www.stauningwhisky.dk

Nine gentlemen on the Danish west coast with a passion for whisky have become the nation's first whisky entrepreneurs. What started as a hobby project in summer 2006, aiming at producing 100 litres a year, turned into plans for full-scale whisky production after Jim Murray tasted the first spirit and said it reminded him of an Ardbeg from the seventies. So far they have been using their "pilot" stills (400 and 200 litres) brought in from Spain , though new and larger stills (1,000 and 600 litres respectively) have been ordered and the conversion of an acquired estate to a distillery is in progress. Production is planned to begin in autumn 2008. Stauning has its own malting floor and local peat will be used for one of two expressions, the heavily peated. The second version will be lighter and unpeated but there will also be room for experimentation with special, limited editions. At the moment 30 litre casks made of new Limousin oak for maturation are used. The annual production is planned to start at roughly 7,000 litres, which will subsequently be expanded.

DISTILLERY: Braunstein, Køge
FOUNDED: 2005 (whisky since 2007)
OWNER/MANAGER: Michael & Claus Braunstein
www.braunstein.dk

Denmark's first micro distillery was built in an already existing brewery in Køge, just south of Copenhagen. The distillation process is special as the spirit is distilled only once and a column still is used. The purpose of this, according to the owners Michael and Claus Braunstein, is to produce an extremely clean spirit. The Braunstein brothers filled their first spirit on a 225 litres ex-Oloroso sherry cask in March 2007 and for the second edition in December 2007 they used a 190-litres ex-bourbon cask. The first bottlings can be expected in two years. Beer and different kinds of schnapps are also produced here.

DISTILLERY: Ørbæk Bryggeri, Ørbæk
FOUNDED: 1997 (whisky since 2007)
OWNER/MANAGER: Niels and Nicolai Rømer
www.oerbaek-bryggeri.nu

The combination microbrewery and microdistillery is apparently a fruitful one and not that surprising as an existing brewery can easily produce the wash which is required in the distillation process to make whisky. This was also the idea of Niels Rømer and his son Nicolai who have run Ørbæk Brewery since 1997 on the Danish island of Fyn. The whisky, in common with their beer, will be ecological and two different expressions are planned for release in 2010 - Isle of Fionia and the peated Fionia Smoked Whisky. It is matured on ex bourbon barrels from Jack Daniels and ex sherry casks. Within five years the estimated yearly production will amount to 10-20,000 bottles.

England

DISTILLERY: St. George´s Distillery, Roudham, Norfolk
FOUNDED: 2006
OWNER/MANAGER: The English Whisky Co.
www.englishwhisky.co.uk

This distillery near Thetford in Norfolk produced its first run on 12th December 2006 and thus became the

The future bottle of Stauning Whisky

St George´s Distillery in Norfolk

first English malt whisky distillery for over a hundred years (not counting annual distillations of 400 litres which St Austell Brewery and The Cornish Cyder Farm have done since 2003). St. George's Distillery was started by father and son, James and Andrew Nelstrop. Fortunately, they managed to interest Iain Henderson in the project. Iain, fomerly of Laphroaig and most recently of Edradour, is a highly esteemed person in the whisky industry. Iain was succeeded as distillery manager in July 2007 by ex-brewer David Fitt. The distillery is equipped with a stainless steel semi lauter mash tun and three stainless steel wash-backs. There is one pair of stills, the wash still with a capacity of 2,800 litres and the spirit still of 1,800 litre capacity. They use mainly first fill bourbon barrels for maturation which are stored in a dunnage warehouse on site but they have also filled the odd sherry, madeira and port casks. Non-peated malt is bought from Crisp Malting Group and peated malt from Simpson's Malt in Berwick upon Tweed. Around 60% of production is unpeated and the rest is peated.

Production is close to 100,000 litres per year and the owners expect to make a first release of 100,000 bottles of an unpeated version in December 2009. A limited release of a heavily peated expression is to follow. There are only two people involved with the production while another ten run the visitors centre which opened in summer of 2007.

DISTILLERY: The Cornish Cyder Farm,
Penhallow, Cornwall
FOUNDED: 2003 (whisky production)
OWNER/MANAGER: David Healy
www.thecornishcyderfarm.co.uk

At the Cornish Cyder Farm, 80,000 gallons of apple juice is pressed each year. Most of it becomes cider

but c 10,000 gallons is made into wine and fruit juices. A distillery was opened quite recently in 2000 in which cider is distilled to apple brandy in a pot still. They then became the first distillery in Cornwall for 300 years. There is only one small (1,200 litres) still in use although the brandy is double distilled and then matured on oak casks.

Four years ago Cornish Cyder Farm together with St Austell Brewery attempted to produce whisky. Wash from the brewery was distilled on the farm resulting in 400 litres of spirit. This seemingly one-off attempt has become an annual occurence. There are no plans for bottling in the next few years but those who have tested the latest new make claim it is much improved compared to the first trials.

Finland

DISTILLERY: Teerenpeli, Lahti
FOUNDED: 2002
OWNER/MANAGER: Anssi Pyysing
www.teerenpeli.com

The first Teerenpeli Single Malt was sold as a three-year old in late 2005, though solely at the owners' restaurant in Lahti. Now, two years later, the first bottles of a 5 year old are sold in one of the state owned ALKO-shops in Helsinki. Anssi Pyysing also sells both a 4 year old and a 5 year old at his five restaurants in Finland. The next release, probably in spring 2009, will be a 6 year old which will be launched in larger quantities. Teerenpeli uses locally obtained lightly peated malt and the whisky matures in ex sherry and ex bourbon casks. 7,500 bottles are produced annually.

Stillroom at St George's Distillery

The stills at Teerenpeli

France _____

DISTILLERY: Glann ar Mor, Pleubian, Bretagne
FOUNDED: 1999
OWNER/MANAGER: Jean Donnay
www.glannarmor.com

Glann ar Mor distillery in Brittany ("Glann ar Mor" means literally "By the Sea" in Breton language) is now in regular production since 12 June 2005. In fact the first whisky from Glann ar Mor was distilled already in 1999 as a trial and 99 bottles were released in 2004 and named Taol Esa. Two expressions are being distilled, a peated (35-40 ppm) and an unpeated and the first cask of the unpeated version was bottled in October 2008. If you wish to try the peated version (which will have another name in order to differentiate it from the unpeated one) you will have to wait one more year (autumn 2009). Jean Donnay makes his whisky in the old style using wooden wash backs, direct heating of the two stills and condensing the vapours in worm tubs rather than using shell and tube condenser. Ex-bourbon casks and first fill Sauternes barriques are used for maturation and the distillery occasionally offers a limited number of "en primeur" casks (55 litres) of the latter.

Apart from the Glann ar Mor venture, Jean Donnay has also specialised in double maturation Single Malts. The "Celtique Connexion" range includes whiskies originally distilled and matured in Scotland, then further matured at the company's seaside warehouse. The casks used for this are from Sauternes, Vin de Paille du Jura, Armagnac, Champagne and Coteau du Layon amongst others. The company has just opened its new premises, including in particular a larger warehouse and a visitor centre, and situated a couple of miles away from the distillery's location, still by the seaside. The whiskies can be found at www.tregorwhisky.com

DISTILLERY: Distillerie Guillon, Louvois, Champagne
FOUNDED: 1997
OWNER/MANAGER: Thierry Guillon
www.whisky-guillon.com

Thierry Guillon, originally a wine man, decided in 1997 to begin distilling whisky. Not perhaps a novel idea if it was not for the fact that the distillery is located in the heart of the Champagne district. But besides champagne this area is also known as a major barley producer in France. In fact several Scots maltsters buy barley from this region. Guillon distills some 80,000 bottles per year and often uses slightly peated malt in production. The range of single malts is quite large and one in particular, Guillon No. 1, has a rather interesting maturation process. It is a five year old matured in a new oak cask the first year, a whisky barrel the second year, then white wine, red wine and finally the last year in a port pipe. Apart from single malts there is also a blend in the range, Le Premium Blend, consisting of 50% malt and 50% grain whisky and a whisky liqueur.

DISTILLERY: Distillerie Warenghem, Lannion, Bretagne
FOUNDED: 1990
OWNER/MANAGER: Warenghem
www.distillerie-warenghem.com

Leon Warenghem founded the distillery already at the beginning of the 20th century but Armorik, the first malt whisky, was not distilled until 1994 and released in 1999. A blended whisky with 25% share of malt, Whisky Breton W. B. is also produced at Warenghem. Armorik is available in several European countries and is also exported to Japan.

DISTILLERY: Distillerie Bertrand, Uberach, Alsace
FOUNDED: 1874 (whisky since 2002)
OWNER/MANAGER: Affiliate of Wolfberger
www.distillerie-bertrand.com

Distillerie Bertrand is an independent affiliate of Wolfberger, the large wine and eaux-de-vie producer. The manager, Jean Metzger, gets his malt from a local brewer and then distils it in Holstein type stills. Two different types of whisky are produced. One is a single malt at 42,2%, non chill-filtered and with maturation in both new barrels and in barrels which have previously contained the fortified wine Banyuls. The other is a single cask at 43,8% matured only in Banyuls barrels. The first bottles, aged 4 years, were

Uberach Single Cask and Armorik Single Malt

released in late 2006 and whilst the annual production is 20,000 bottles, 5,000 bottles are currently sold per year. Jean Metzger is now planning for yet another release in late 2008 - Single Cask Collection which is a limited edition from six different Banyuls barrels. The interesting point is that he replaces the evaporated part (angel´s share) by continuously filling up with water during the maturation process.

At the moment the whisky is only sold in France but American importers have already shown an interest. The whisky, Uberach Single Malt Alsace Whisky, gets its name from the village.

Germany _____

DISTILLERY: Slyrs Destillerie, Schliersee
FOUNDED: 1928 (whisky sinve 1999)
OWNER/MANAGER: Florian Stetter
www.slyrs.de

Lantenhammer Destillerie in Schliersee, Bavaria was founded in 1928 and was producing mainly brandy until 1999 when whisky came into the picture and in 2003 Slyrs Destillerie was founded. The malt, smoked with beech, comes from locally grown grain and the spirit is distilled twice at low temperatures in the 1,500 litres stills. Maturation takes place in charred 225-litres casks of new American White Oak from Missouri. The un-chillfiltered whisky is called Slyrs after the original name of the surrounding area, Schliers, and the first single malt was Vintage 1999, which was released in 2002 in 6,000 bottles.

The next vintage (2003) appeared in 2006 in 10,000 bottles and all the 30,000 bottles of the 2008 release sold out on pre-orders before its release in May. Beginning 2008 they will also be selling the whisky in the distillery shop. Every year 3,000-5,000 bottles are kept for later release. Florian Stetter has plans for a 12 year old in 2015. A new distillery, dedicated exclusively to whisky production, opened in July 2007. The whisky is available in Germany, Switzerland and Denmark.

DISTILLERY: Whisky-Destillerie Blaue Maus, Eggolsheim-Neuses
FOUNDED: 1980
OWNER/MANAGER: Robert Fleischmann
www.fleischmann-whisky.de

This is the oldest single malt whisky distillery in Bavaria and it celebrated its 25th anniversary in February 2008. The first distillate, never released on the market, was made in 1983. It took 15 years until the first whisky, Glen Mouse 1986, appeared. Fleischmann uses unpeated malt and the whisky matures for around eight years in casks of fresh German oak. All whisky from Blaue Maus are single cask and there are currently five single malts; Blaue Maus, Spinnaker, Krottentaler, Schwarzer Pirat and Grüner Hund. According to Mr. Fleischmann the difference between them is in the malt mixture variation which he uses. A new expression was introduced quite recently; Austrasier which is the first grain whisky from the distillery. In 2006 a new distillery was built solely for whisky production while mostly new types of malt will be produced in the older distillery.

Florian Stetter, Slyrs distillery

Robert Fleischmann, Whisky-Destillerie Blaue Maus

DISTILLERY: Brennerei Höhler, Aarbergen
FOUNDED: 1895 (whisky since 2001)
OWNER/MANAGER: Holger Höhler
www.brennerei-hoehler.de

The main produce from this distillery in Hessen consists of different distillates from fruit and berries as well as liqueurs. The first whisky, a bourbon variety based on over 50% maize, was distilled in 2001 and released in 2004. Since then Holger Höhler has experimented with different types of grain (rye, barley, spelt and oat). There was a limited release of a single malt in July 2007. Until recently all casks were made from Sessart oak with a storage capacity of between 30 and 75 litres. In spring 2007 Höhler started filling 225 litres barriques. He aims to increase production and eventually launch older whisky. The whisky is marketed under the name Whesskey, i. e. whisky from Hessen.

DISTILLERY: Hammerschmiede, Zorge
FOUNDED: 1984 (whisky since 2002)
OWNER/MANAGER: Karl-Theodor and
                                  Alexander Buchholz
www.hammerschmiede.de

As far as we know this is the only whisky producer in the Harz region. In common with many other small whisky producers on mainland Europe, Hammerschmiede´s main products are liqueurs, bitters and spirits from fruit, berries and herbs. But since 2002 a small portion of production (5%) consists of malt whisky. They buy their unpeated malt in Germany and mature the spirit in a variety of casks - German oak, sherry, cognac, port, marsala, malaga and madeira casks and also Dornfelder barriques (German

red wine). The first distillation took place in late 2002 and the first 278 bottles were released in early 2006 under the name Glan Iarran. A month later a bourbon-matured malt called Glan Taint was launched. Since the release in summer 2007 all whisky is named Glen Els after the small river Elsbach which flows past the premises. The Buchholz´s have several casks in bond and the latest bottling took place in July 2008 (Single Amoroso Sherry Cask). The next casks, two sherry casks and one marsala cask, will be ready for bottling at the beginning of 2009. So far the whisky has been matured for 3-4 years but older expressions can be expected in the future. In 2007 a new warehouse was opened in a nearby village. The building used to be a blacksmith´s, built between 1250 and 1270. More than 150 casks are maturing there, and in 2010 the first bottlings from this site will be released.

The Netherlands ——————

DISTILLERY: Us Heit Distillery, Bolsward
FOUNDED: 2002
OWNER/MANAGER: Aart van der Linde
www.usheitdistillery.nl

This is one of many examples where a beer brewery also holds a whisky distillery. Frysk Hynder, as the whisky is called, is the first Dutch whisky, making its debut in 2005 at 3 years of age. Their barley is grown in surrounding Friesland and is malted at

Maturing casks at Hammerschmiede distillery

Frysk Hynder from Us Heit distillery

the distillery. Some 10,000 bottles are produced annually and the whisky is matured on various casks - sherry, bourbon, red wine, port and cognac, each contributing its special character to each bottling. Information on the beer from Us Heit can be found at www.bierbrouwerij-usheit.nl.

DISTILLERY: Zuidam Distillers, Baarle Nassau
FOUNDED: 1974 (whisky since 1998)
OWNER/MANAGER: Zuidam family
www.zuidam-distillers.com

Zuidam Distillers was started in 1974 as a traditional family distillery producing liqueurs, genever, gin and vodka. The first attempts to distill malt whisky took place in 1998 but according to one of the owners, Patrick van Zuidam the result is not fit for bottling. Instead the first release is from the 2002 production and it was bottled in February 2007 as a 5 year old. The whisky is double distilled in pot stills made by Kothe & Holstein in Germany. There will be three varieties of malt whisky - unpeated, lightly peated and peated. The first release, called Millstone, is unpeated. Other whiskies include rye whisky and grain whisky. At the moment 20,000 litres per year are produced.

DISTILLERY: Vallei distilleerderij, Leusden
FOUNDED: 2002 (officially opened 2004)
OWNER/MANAGER: Bert Burger
www.valleibieren.nl

This is the latest addition to Dutch whisky distilleries. Bert Burger buys barley from a local farmer but apart from that he is very much in control of the whole process from malting to bottling. The whisky is double distilled in pot stills and he produces some 2,500 litres per year. The first trials were in 2002 but in 2004 the distillery was officially opened. After

a while Burger started bottling his two year old spirit as Valley single malt spirit in 40 ml bottles for customers to try. Finally on 1 December 2007 the first bottles of single malt whisky reached the market as a three year old. Other products include whisky liquor and two kinds of beer.

Russia

DISTILLERY: Kizlyarskoye, Mirny, Kizlyar, Republic of Dagestan
FOUNDED: 2003
OWNER/MANAGER: Nauchno-Proizvodstvenoye Predpriyatie Whisky Rossii

In 1948 a winery called Kizlyarski was founded on the outskirts of Kizlyar in Dagestan. Most of the wines are sold locally but some brandy is produced which has become fairly well-known in other parts of Russia.

In 2003 a group of enthusiasts led by Alibek Irazi-hanov, current CEO and distillery manager, ventured into an experiment in the field of whisky. After visiting Inverhouse operations in Scotland and studying the scientific side and economics of the situation they were ready to start pilot samples. Today the equipment consists of four copper pot stills (5000 litres each) and a stainless steel column still. Capacity is 3000 litres of malt whisky per day and 6000 litres of grain whisky. The spirit is matured on American oak as well as Russian oak from Maikop. The first sample of the whisky, a 3 year old malt, was presented at a conference in Krasnodar in 2007. The company's product has not yet been certified, so it is not available for sale but limited sales of Kizkyarskoye malt whisky, Kizlyarskoye grain whisky and Kizlyarsoye blended whisky are planned for the end of 2008.

Millstone, Zuidam Distillers and Valley Single Malt, Vallei distillery

Whisky from Kizlyarskoye distillery in Dagestan

So far production has been very scarce – not more than one month in 2007. Most of the time the stills are used for distillation of brandy. No official volumes of maturing whiskies are disclosed, nor is it clear when the company will start a consistent regular whisky distillation. But the company receives state support and is listed in prospective Dagestan state plan of Wine and Vineyards development, so it should be just a matter of time for all bureaucratic issues to be resolved.

Sweden

DISTILLERY: Mackmyra Svensk Whisky, Valbo
FOUNDED: 1999
OWNER/MANAGER: Mackmyra Svensk Whisky AB
www.mackmyra.se

The people at Mackmyra seem to be doing everything right. They launched Preludium, their first series of six limited releases, one after the other in 2006/2007 just to whet the appetite of whisky enthusiasts. They all sold out in record time and, perhaps even more important, were awarded good ratings, at least for whiskies of such a young age. They managed to be the most talked about of all the malt whisky distilleries outside Scotland and they did a great job attending whisky fairs both in Sweden and in the rest of Europe. On top of that the balance sheets closed in 2007 with a decent profit even though the company was only established a few years ago.

Mackmyra is based on two basic recipes; one resulting in fruity and elegant whisky, the other being more peaty. The peatiness does not stem from peat, but from juniper wood and bog moss. The Preludium expressions, all released in volumes between 4000 and 12000 bottles, used casks both from the pilot distillery, which operated 1999-2002, and from the current distillery which started in 2002. The first "real"launch was in June 2008 - The First Edition (Den Första Utgåvan). It is still a fairly young whisky and 95% bourbon casks and 5% casks made from Swedish oak have been used. Circa 45% of the mix is stored in 100 litre casks. In total, 40,000 bottles were released in June of which 30,000 went to the domestic, Swedish market. More bottles will be released in October.

The casks for The First Edition have all matured at a depth of 50 meter in the Archean rock in an abandoned mine in the north of Sweden. Mackmyra has another three storage sites; an island in the archipelago of Stockholm, on the west coast and at a castle in the southernmost part of Sweden.

DISTILLERY: Spirit of Hven, Ven
FOUNDED: 2007
OWNER/MANAGER: Backafallsbyn AB
(The family Engdahl Molin)
www.hven.com

The second Swedish distillery to come on stream after Mackmyra was Spirit of Hven, a distillery situated on the island of Ven right between Sweden and Denmark.

The distillery had its official inauguration May 7th 2008, but the project started already back in 2001.

Mackmyra distillery and their First Edition

Already then it was an old dream of the proprietor Henric Molin. Henric and his wife Anja took over the hotel and restaurant Backafallsbyn in 1997, making whisky their niche and the whisky bar has grown to be one of the best in the area. This led the family to want to create their own variety. Henric, being a chemist by education, took on the challenge and after many years hard work everything is now finally in place and whisky is flowing in the spirit safe. The equipment consists of one mash tun, six wash backs, one wash still (2,000 litres) and one spirit still (1,500 litres). The malt is imported as grist from Scotland but the owners hope to have their own maltings and mill in the future when they are also hoping to be able to use local barley grown on the island. The plans are to produce three different types of malt whisky - unpeated, lightly peated and heavily peated, the latter at around 80 ppm.

A long fermentation time of 90-120 hours is used in order to achieve a more fully flavoured product with high citric notes and a nutty character. The wood policy is also significant; Spirit of Hven distillery handles all its wood itself from the forest to the final product, which means that cutting, toasting, charring and priming are under the control of the distillery. To finance the distillery until the whisky is ready for the market, somewhere around 2012, the distillery makes other spirits such as an Organic Vodka, an organically distilled Gin and a variety of Rhum made from sugar beets.

Switzerland _____

DISTILLERY: Whisky Castle, Elfingen, Aargau
FOUNDED: 2002
OWNER/MANAGER: Ruedi Käser
www.whisky-castle.com

The first whisky from this distillery in Elfingen in the north of Switzerland reached the market in 2004. It was a single malt under the name Castle Hill. Recent new bottlings include a cask strength (64,5%) which has matured on Hungarian oak, a Doublewood with a maturation on both a cask made of chestnut and a cask which previously contained Scotch whisky and, finally, a Dinkelwhisky. A new distillery was built in 2005 and commissioned in 2006 and the annual production has now increased from 5,000 to 10,000 bottles. The whisky is matured in Hungarian and American ex-bourbon and ex-sherry casks and can be bought in Germany, The Netherlands and Austria apart from in Switzerland. The whisky production is centred around several different expressions based on barley, rye and spelt while the Käser's main production comprises some 70 different kinds of schnapps based on fruit and berries. Ruedi Käser has constructed a complete visitor's experience including a restaurant and a shop.

DISTILLERY: Spezialitätenbrennerei Zürcher, Port, Bern
FOUNDED: 1954 (whisky from 2000)
OWNER/MANAGER: Daniel & Ursula Zürcher

This distillery was founded already in 1954 by Willi Zürcher. However the first in the family to distil whisky was Heinz Zürcher in 2000 who released the first 1,000 bottles of Lakeland single malt in 2003. It was time for the third generation, Daniel and Ursula Zürcher, to take over in 2004. They continued their uncle's work with whisky and launched a second release in 2006. The main focus of the distillery is specialising in various distillates of fruit and calvados, cognac, armagnac, grappa, vodka and rum. Whisky will always be a sideline according to Daniel Zürcher. The good news is that new bottlings will take place annually in the future. One barrel of Lakeland

The still room at Spirit of Hven

Ice Label, matured in ice

222

single malt was bottled 18 June 2008 and the next bottling is planned for July 2009. The wash for the whisky is bought from a brewery in Interlaken and maturation takes place in oloroso sherry casks.

The cooperation with the Rugenbräu brewery has developed in recent years in that Zürcher sometimes distil the wash and then send back the new make to the brewery for it to be filled to casks to mature. Two expressions from Rugenbräu were released March 2008 - Swiss Highland Single Malt Interlaken (46% and released for the first time in 2007) and brand new Swiss Highland Single Malt Ice Label (58,8%). The latter is an interesting novelty. It was filled in an Oloroso sherry cask and then matured for almost 4 years at 3,454 metres altitude in the ice of Jungfraujoch with a constant temperature of minus 4 degrees Celsius. A total of 859 bottles of this rare whisky have been released.

DISTILLERY: Whisky Brennerei Holle,
Lauwil, Baselland
FOUNDED: 1999 (for whisky distillation)
OWNER/MANAGER: The Bader family.
www.swiss-whisky.ch, www.single-malt.ch

Since WW1 Switzerland has had a law forbidding the use of staple food such as potatoes and grain for making alcohol. On 1st July 1999 this was abolished and the spirit streamed through the stills of Holle the very same day making it the first Swiss producer of malt whisky. The whisky is stored on French oak casks, which have been used for white wine (Chardonnay) or red wine (Pinot Noir). There are currently circa 100 casks in the warehouse. Most bottlings are four years old and contain 42% alcohol. A five year old has also been released, which has had three years on Pinot Noir casks followed by two years on Chardonnay casks. Other expressions include a peated version and a cask strength Chardonnay-matured one.

The latest release was an Easter bottling in Spring 2008, having had 6 years on two different casks - American Oak bourbon and French Oak which previously had contained Chardonnay. Bader also recently released what he calls a dessert whisky from a white wine cask as well as his first single grain whisky. Annual production amounts to roughly 30 000 bottles. The main production of the distillery consists of schnapps distilled from a variety of fruit.

DISTILLERY: Maison Les Vignettes - Swhisky,
Ardon, Tessin
FOUNDED: 2000
OWNER/MANAGER: Alex Delaloye
www.swhisky.ch

The first malt distillation by this distillery in Ardon took place in 2001 and 4 000 bottles are produced annually. There have been four different single malts in the range since beginning of production; Annouim, Gwenwed (matured in Syrah casks), Abred (a peaty variety) and Keugant (cask strength 56%). Another four expressions were added in 2006;

Challenge, Celtica, Skipper (a peated version) and finally Triad, older than the others and finished in a Vosne Romanée cask. New bottlings for 2007 were Swhisky Must 1825 (six years old and the oldest version so far) and Swhisky Must Grand Cru, matured in a Red Meursault cask.

DISTILLERY: Brennerei Hagen,
Hüttwilen, Thurgau
FOUNDED: 1999
OWNER/MANAGER: Ueli Hagen

A triple distilled malt whisky is since a few years produced by Ueli Hagen in the small village of Hüttwilen in the northernmost part of Switzerland. The spirit is matured in bourbon barrels and the first produce was sold in 2002 as a three year old. Ueli Hagen produces mainly schnapps and absinth and distills around 300 bottles of malt whisky a year, a number he expects to double. He has recently been experimenting. Four years ago when he was building a new cow shed, he found a 1700 year old oak tree in the ground so he put pieces of the oak into a maturing barrel of spirit and he says it gives the whisky a slightly peated touch.

DISTILLERY: Burgdorfer Gasthausbrauerei,
Burgdorf, Bern
FOUNDED: 1999
OWNER/MANAGER: Thomas Gerber
www.burgdorferbier.ch

The Burgdorfer Single Malt Whisky is an excellent example of the kind of cross-fertilization that more and more breweries are choosing. When a wash is made for beer brewing, it is an excellent opportunity to use the batch (without adding hops) to distil spirit which can be made into whisky. The first whisky from Burgdorfer was released as a five year old in 2006 and it is sold using a kind of subscription system. The customer pays 50 swiss francs for a 50 cl bottle and receives it 5 years later. They produce around 300 bottles annually and this year will start taking orders for a 10 year old.

Wales

DISTILLERY: Penderyn Distillery, Penderyn
FOUNDED: 2000
OWNER/MANAGER: Welsh Whisky Company Ltd
www.welsh-whisky.co.uk

In 1998 four private individuals started The Welsh Whisky Company. Equipment was in place two years later and distilling began on 14th September 2000. A new type of still, developed by David Faraday for Penderyn distillery, differs from the Scottish and Irish procedures in that the whole process from wash to new make takes place in one single still. But that is not the sole difference. Every distillery in Scotland is required by law to do the mashing and fermenting on site. At Penderyn though, the wash is bought from a regional beer brewer, S.A. Brain & Co, and is transported to the distillery on a weekly basis. The normal procedure at a brewery is to boil the wash to clear it from any lactic acid which can make it appear cloudy. This was a problem for Penderyn as lactic acid creates a second fermentation which is beneficial in a whisky context and adds more taste. Penderyn has solved this by pumping the wash to a heated tank where lactic acid is added before distillation is commenced.

The first single malt was launched on St. David's Day 1st March 2004. 60,000 bottles were produced the first year and the target is 100,000 bottles. The core expression is matured on ex bourbon barrels and then finished on Madeira casks. Several special bottlings have also been launched, among them Oloroso and a Softly Peated version.

A new expression for 2008 is Penderyn Sherrywood, a limited edition of 10,000 bottles matured in Oloroso casks.

A visitor centre originally planned for autumn 2007 was officially opened by HRH The Prince of Wales in June 2008 at a total cost of £850,000.

In common with many other newly started whisky distilleries, Penderyn has been financially dependent on other produce until the first whisky became available on the market. Brecon Five Vodka, Brecon Dry Gin and Merlyn Welsh Cream Liqueur can be mentioned among these.

NORTH AMERICA

USA _____

DISTILLERY: Clear Creek Distillery, Portland, Oregon
FOUNDED: 1985
OWNER/MANAGER: Stephen McCarthy
www.clearcreekdistillery.com

Steve McCarthy in Oregon was one of the first to produce malt whiskey in USA and his three year old single malt has earned a reputation as a high-quality whiskey fully comparable to the best Scotch whiskies. Like many other small distilleries, Clear Creek started by distilling eau de vie from fruit, especially pears, and then expanded the product line into whiskey.

Penderyn Single Malt, McCarthy's Oregon Single Malt and Stranahan's Colorado Whiskey

Clear Creek began making whiskey in 1996 and the first bottles were on the market three years later. There is only one expression at the moment, McCarthy´s Oregon Single Malt 3 years old. Steve has hoped for a long time to launch an 8 year old, but so far it has simply not been possible to save adequate quantities due to high demand.

The whiskey reminds much of Islay and the malt is purchased direct from Islay with a phenol specification of 30-40 ppm. It is then made into wash at the Widmer Brothers brewery in Portland and distilled in Holstein pot stills. Maturation takes place in ex-sherry butts with a finish in new Oregon White Oak hogsheads.

Steve has doubled the production of whiskey every year since 2004 which does, however, not seem to be enough to satisfy demand. The usual procedure is one release in March and one in August with both of them selling out quickly and 2008 was no exception. Steve has expanded the number of pot stills to four this year to try and catch up with demand. Unlike many of the single malts from the USA, McCarthy´s Oregon Single Malt is available in several European countries. Steve has recently strengthened his cooperation with Maison du Whisky in Paris, and this will be the centre for expansion in Europe.

rather than being pumped through a pipe from the previous brewery.

The barrels (American White Oak) come from World Cooperage of Lebanon, Missouri. Stranahans used only the one pot still until spring 2006 when another still (made wash still) was installed while the old became the spirit still.

US Federal law requires that any whiskey to be designated "Straight" as in Straight Rocky Mountain Whiskey must be aged in new, charred, American White Oak barrels, for a minimum of two years. There are also additional processes a producer must follow to have his whiskey designated "straight". The first three barrels were bottled in April 2006 and currently the bottle ten barrel batches.

Recently they have also made a port finish and two different wine finishes (among them a Cabernet Franc from Creekside Cellars Winery). These releases, named "Snowflakes", will be extremely limited according to owner and manager Jess Graber and the launch date is not yet set.

The production at Stranahans is averaging six barrels a week which is equivalent to 60,000 bottles a year. From exclusively selling locally in Colorado, the whiskey can now be found in 26 states and also in Amsterdam and Tokyo.

DISTILLERY: Stranahans Whiskey Distillery,
Denver, Colorado
FOUNDED: 2003
OWNER/MANAGER: Jess Graber,
George Stranahan et al.
www.stranahans.com

The first whiskey distillery in Colorado used to get its wash from the neighbour, Flying Dog Brewery. This has now changed and the wash is produced by Oskar Blues Brewery in their brand new facility in Longmont Colorado. This means that the wash is now trucked in weekly via a food grade tanker

DISTILLERY: Triple Eight Distillery,
Nantucket, Massachusetts
FOUNDED: 2000
OWNER/MANAGER: Cisco Brewers
www.ciscobrewers.com

This is the first North American distillery situated on an island; Nantucket Island, Massachusetts. In 1995 Cisco Brewers was established and five years later it was expanded with Triple Eight Distillery. The base of the whiskey production is of course wash from the brewery where Maris Otter barley is used. The first distillation took place as long ago as 2000 and

Triple Eight release party 8th August 2008 with Jay Harman holding the first bottle of Notch under the supervision of Jim Murray

enthusiasts have been expecting a bottling to appear any time for the last couple of years. Finally, the first 888 bottles (5 barrels) were released on 8 August 2008 as an 8 year old. To keep in line, the price of these first bottles is $888. The whiskey is named Notch (as in "not Scotch"). There are currently 115 barrels in their warehouse. Annual production is approximately 5,000 bottles and the storage is on ex bourbon casks from Brown Forman (Woodford Reserve) and finished in French Oak.

The Nantucket facility consists of brewery, winery and distillery. The parent company, Cisco Brewers, produces Whales Tale Pale Ale and they use a similar mash for producing the Notch. Triple Eight also produces vodka and rum that is already on the market. Whiskey production was moved to a new distillery in May 2007.

DISTILLERY: Tuthilltown Spirits,
Gardiner, New York
FOUNDED: 2003
OWNER/MANAGER: Ralph Erenzo & Brian Lee
www.tuthilltown.com

This is the first artisan distillery in the state of New York since Prohibition. Just 80 miles from New York City, Ralph Erenzo and Brian Lee in conjunction with three employees produce bourbon, malt whiskey, rye whiskey, rum and Heart of the Hudson vodka distilled from apples. Ralph Erenzo bought the 18th century property in 2002 with the aim of turning it into a camping ground, but neighbours objected. A change in the law in New York State made it possible to start an artisan distillery; paying just $1,450 for a license Erenzo changed direction and started distilling instead.

The first spirit launched were various expressions of bourbon. The Hudson Baby Bourbon is produced with 100% corn while Hudson Four Grain Bourbon uses corn, rye, wheat and malted barley. The same malted barley is also now used for the Hudson Single

Malt Whiskey. It is aged in new, charred American oak and the casks are very small – 3-14 gallons per cask. The first products came onto the shelves in 2006 and are currently selling in Hudson Valley and New York City though there are plans to start selling in California too. The European distributor is La Maison du Whisky in Paris.

DISTILLERY: Eades Distillery,
Lovingston, Virginia
FOUNDED: 2008
OWNER/MANAGER: The Virginia Distillers Co.
(Chris Allwood, Joe Hungate, Brian Gray)
www.eadeswhisky.com

A new malt whisky distillery is now being built in Nelson County, Virginia. It entails investments of $5 million and will bring job opportunities for almost 20 people when production starts in spring 2009. All equipment has been made in Scotland by Northern Fabricators; a 2 tonnes mash tun, a 10,000 litre wash still and an 8,000 litre spirit still. Unlike most other new distilleries currently being built, the malting of barley will actually be done on site. The barley will be grown locally and they are cooperating with Virginia Tech University to test around 8 strains to find the best variety.

Initial production volumes are expected to be around 2,500 200 litre barrels per year and the spirit will mature in Bourbon barrels, Port pipes and wine barrels from local wineries. It will take five years before the first bottlings of matured whisky are for sale but this does not mean that own branded whisky will not be sold until then. The owners have created a series of vatted malt whiskies called "Eades Anticipation Series". In association with Jim McEwan of Bruichladdich, single malts from various Scottish producers have been selected. The idea was to select two different malts for each bottling, marry them and then let them have a second maturation in wine

Hudson Single Malt from Tuthilltown Spirits

Eades Anticipation Series

barrels. The three expressions released so far are Eades Highland a combination of Ben Nevis (85%) and Clynelish (15%), Eades Speyside with Longmorn (50%) and Glen Moray (50%) and finally Eades Islay where Bowmore (60%) and Caol Ila (40%) have been married. The company calls this technique Double Malts.

DISTILLERY: Edgefield Distillery,
            Troutdale, Oregon
FOUNDED: 1998
OWNER/MANAGER: Mike and Brian McMenamin
www.mcmenamins.com

Brothers Mike and Brian McMenamin started their first pub in Portland, Oregon in 1983. It has now expanded to a chain of more than 40 pubs and hotels in Oregon and Washington. Over 20 of the pubs have adjoining microbreweries (the first opened in 1985). Their first and so far only distillery opened in 1998 at their huge Edgefield property in Troutdale and their first whiskey, Hogshead Whiskey (46%), was bottled in 2002. Annual production used to be 3,000 bottles but a second wash-back has now been added making it possible to do four mashes a month which has increased yearly outcome to around 10,000 litres. In the past, ex-bourbon casks were used for maturation but now only charred, new American white oak barrels are used. Hogshead Whiskey is the top seller (3,600 bottles in 2007) but brandy and gin are also produced and new products in the pipeline are Absinthe, Pear Brandy, London Dry Gin (to complement their Dutch-style Gin) and possibly rum. A planned second distillery is on hold waiting for building permits to be approved.

DISTILLERY: Nashoba Valley Winery,
            Bolton, Massachusetts
FOUNDED: 1978 (whiskey since 2003)
OWNER/MANAGER: Richard Pelletier
www.nashobawinery.com

Nashoba Valley Winery lies in the heart of Massachusetts' apple country just 40 minutes from Boston. The winery, founded in 1978 by Jack Partridge, has been owned since 1995 by Richard Pelletier who, prior to this made his living in construction and real estate development. This place is mainly about wines and they have earned a solid reputation for their products made from both fruit and grapes. In recent years the facilities have expanded with a brewery producing ten different kinds of ales and lagers, and Massachusetts first distillery which holds a farmers-distiller license. Here he produces a wide range of spirits including vodka, brandy and grappa.

Since 2001 malt whiskey is also distilled. The malt is imported from England, France and Canada and the wash is of course produced in his own brewery. The whiskey is matured in a combination of ex-bourbon barrels and American and French oak casks which previously have contained wine from the estate. Richard Pelletier produces around 9,000 bottles per year and a first release is planned for 2009.

DISTILLERY: St. George Distillery,
            Alameda, California
FOUNDED: 1984
OWNER/MANAGER: Jörg Rupf/Lance Winters
www.stgeorgespirits.com

The distillery is situated in a hangar at Alameda Point, the old naval air station on the San Fransisco

Edgefield Distillery

Nashoba Winery

Bay. It was founded by Jörg Rupf, an immigrant from Germany who came to California in 1982 with a Holstein pot in tow. Several generations of his ancestors had preceded him by being distillers of eau de vie and Rupf became one of the forerunners when it came to craft distilling in America. After a while, Lance Winters joined him and today he is Distiller as well as co-owner.

The main produce is based on eau de vie, from locally grown fruit, and vodka under the brand name Hangar One. Whiskey production was picked up in 1996 and the first single malt appeared on the market in 1999. Some of the malt used has been dried with alder and beech but is non-peated. Maturation is on bourbon barrels (80%), French oak (15%) or port pipes (5%). St. George Single Malt used to be sold as three years old, but nowadays comes to the market as a blend of whiskeys aged from 4 to 12 years. Another spirit was added in late 2007 when St. George became the first distillery, since the ban in 1912 to sell Absinthe in the US.

Lance Winters, who used to be a nuclear engineer, is a man fond of experimenting with flavours. Douglas Fir pine needles and wasabi are some of the flavours he has used for vodka. It did not then come as a surprise when he and two companions started another enterprise in 2006, Qi Spirits. They produce liqueurs using tea and the first two releases were Qi Black with Lapsang Souchong Tea, and Qi White, with White tea. The distillation of Qi Spirits is also carried out at St. George distillery.

DISTILLERY: Charbay Winery & Distillery,
St. Helena, California
FOUNDED: 1983
OWNER/MANAGER: Miles and Marko Karakasevic
www.charbay.com

Charbay has a wide range of products; vodka, grappa, pastis, rum, port and since 1999 also malt whiskey. The only bottling so far is Double-Barrel Release One from 2002, cask strength and non-chill filtered. There were only 840 bottles and the price tag of $325 may seem off-putting. Maturation takes place in newly charred American white oak barrels. A speciality of Charbay is the addition of dried hops to the wash before distillation. Another single malt (43%) may be released at the more modest price of $85 but there is no indication of when at the moment.

DISTILLERY: Copper Fox Distillery,
Sperryville, Virginia
FOUNDED: 2000
OWNER/MANAGER: Rick Wasmund
www.copperfox.biz

Copper Fox Distillery was founded in 2000 by Rick Wasmund using the premises and license of an old, existing distillery. The first whiskey, Copper Fox Whiskey was made in cooperation with the distillery which they were about to buy but after a disagreement over the contract, the project came to a halt. In 2005 they moved to another site, built a new distillery and began distilling in January 2006.

Rick Wasmund started by working for 6 weeks at Bowmore distillery on Islay to learn the trade and he has become one of the most unorthodox producers of single malt. The malted barley is dried using smoke from selected fruitwood but variations of that concept are also used in other places, for example Sweden and New Zeeland. It is the maturation process that Rick takes one step further thereby differing from common practice. In every barrel of new make spirit, he adds plenty of hand chipped and toasted chips of apple and cherry trees and oak wood.

Adding to the flavour, Wasmund also believes that this procedure drastically speeds up the time necessary for maturation. In fact he bottles his Wasmund´s Single Malt after just four months in the barrel. Every batch ranging from 250 to 1,500 bottles tastes a little different and the distillery is now producing around 2,500 bottles every month. Twenty different batches have been launched up to the summer of 2008. At the moment the Wasmund´s Single Malt can be found in Virginia, Washington DC, Maryland, New Jersey, Illinois, Florida and California among others.

DISTILLERY: High Plains Distillery,
Atchison, Kansas
FOUNDED: 2004
OWNER/MANAGER: Seth Fox
www.highplainsinc.com

Former process engineer Seth Fox is mainly known for his Most Wanted Vodka of which he sells over 13,000 cases a year in Kansas, Missouri and Texas. The product range was expanded in late 2006 to include also a Most Wanted Kansas Whiskey (reminiscent of a Canadian whisky) and Kansas bourbon whiskey. Fox continued in 2007 to produce his first single malt whiskey made from malted barley. He also produced both a wheat and a rye whiskey as well as rum and tequila. The two stills were bought second-hand from Surrey in England. When High Plains opened, it was the first legal distillery in Kansas since 1880. Despite its success, Seth Fox and his wife Dorcie run operations with just the help of two part-timers.

DISTILLERY: Woodstone Creek Distillery,
Cincinnati, Ohio
FOUNDED: 1999
OWNER/MANAGER: Donald Outterson
www.woodstonecreek.com

Woodstone Creek is Ohio's first licensed micro-distillery. Don Outterson opened a farm winery in Lebanon, Ohio in 1999 and relocated to the present facilities in 2003. Malt whiskey was already produced in 1999. The malted barley is imported from Scotland (actually from Don´s ancestral home, Berwick-Upon-Tweed) and port and sherry casks of own production are used for maturation. Bottling has been delayed with the owners hoping for a change in Ohio state law, allowing sales of whiskey directly to the public from the distillery premises. In the beginning of 2008 there were signals that the legislation would indeed change during the year and the Outtersons, who had been participating in the process, were making preparations in anticipation. Labels were approved and a special bottling of a peated version was presented at American Distillers Conference in April where it received favourable reviews. The first commercial bottling was available in summer 2008 and there was an unpeated version available as well. As Don has another full-time job he only distills at weekends and production will not increase until he is able to fully concentrate on the distillery. Apart from wine and whiskey, Woodstone Creek produces bourbon, brandy, rum and vodka. The capacity for single malts in the future is planned to be 10 barrels per year.

DISTILLERY: St. James Spirits, Irwindale, California
FOUNDED: 1995
OWNER/MANAGER: Jim Busuttil
www.saintjamesspirits.com

Peregrine Rock is the name of the three year old single malt Jim Busuttil produces in Irwindale, east of Los Angeles. The malt comes from Baird Malts in the UK and is medium peated. Heavy charred new American oak barrels, but also ex bourbon barrels from Jim Beam and Jack Daniels are used.

DISTILLERY: Dry Fly Distilling, Spokane, Washington
FOUNDED: 2007
OWNER/MANAGER: Don Poffenroth & Kent Fleischmann
www.dryflydistilling.com

Dry Fly Distilling began distilling as late as autumn 2007 and then became the first grain distillery to open in Washington since Prohibition. The two founders share a mutual interest; dry fly fishing, hence the name of the distillery. To ensure a positive cash flow from the start, in common with many other distilleries, vodka and gin was produced and was already on the shelves in October 2007. The first batch of Malt whisky was distilled on 4th January 2008 and the owners expect to make 200-300 cases of malt whisky annually (total production being estimated at 5,000 cases). Don and Kent are aiming at releasing a 4 year old for their first single malt, which should be at the beginning of 2012 but they will start looking after two years to monitor maturation.

Canada _____

DISTILLERY: Glenora Distillery, Glenville, Nova Scotia
FOUNDED: 1990
OWNER/MANAGER: Lauchie MacLean
www.glenoradistillery.com

Glenora, situated in Nova Scotia, was the first malt whisky distillery in Canada. The start-up was difficult as funds dried up a couple of times and production stopped on several occasions. Lauchie MacLean took over in 1994 and operations became more stable. The first launch of own produce came in 2000 but a whisky called Kenloch had been sold before that. This was a 5-year old vatting of some of Glenora's own malt whisky and whisky from Bowmore distillery on Islay. The first own expression, a 10 year old, came in September 2000 and was named Glen Breton. Until now there have been eight releases. Around 35,000 bottles of Glen Breton are produced every year.

A new expression, Glen Breton Ice (10 years old), the world's first single malt aged in an ice wine barrel was launched in November 2006. Interest was massive and another release came onto the market in spring 2007. This expression will apparently become a permanent member of the product range. Glenora's whisky has not been easy to obtain outside Canada, but exports currently go to countries such as USA, Poland, Sweden, Switzerland, Spain and Singapore.

Since 2001 Glenora has been locked in a legal fight with Scotch Whisky Association over the name of Glen Breton. The opinion of SWA is that the use of the word Glen is misleading and confusing for the customer and will make many believe that they are

Future bottle from Dry Fly Distilling and Glen Breton Ice from Glenora

actually buying a Scotch whisky. The distillery, on the other hand, states that Glen is an established geographical name in this part of Canada. In 2007 the Trademarks Opposition Board in Ottawa ruled in favour of the distillery's right to continue to sell the whisky under the name Glen Breton. SWA appealed and won in April 2008 when a Federal Court reversed the previous ruling.

DISTILLERY: Winchester Cellars,
British Columbia, Canada
FOUNDED: 2002 (whisky since 2007)
OWNER/MANAGER: Ken Winchester
www.winchestercellars.com

Ken Winchester has been a winemaker since 1983 when he started in a garage in Montreal. Eventually he moved to San Fransisco to work as a publisher but decided to become a full-time winemaker north of Santa Barbara where he built up Winchester Vineyards. Back in Canada since 2002, he has now established himself as a winemaker on Vancouver Island where he has also recently opened the first licensed distillery on the island.

The inspiration for whisky-making came from spending some time at Bruichladdich in 2006 and initially he will bring in malted barley (both unpeated and lightly peated) from Scotland. Later on he intends to use barley grown on Vancouver Island.

The wash is made to specification by local microbreweries. The copper still is made by Muller in Germany and the spirit will be matured mainly in refill bourbon barrels but also on wine casks. The first distillation took place in summer 2007 and Ken expects to produce around 6,000 bottles per year.

Bakey Hill Cask Strength, Lark Distiller's Selection and Hellyer's Road Original

AUSTRALIA & NEW ZEALAND

Australia

DISTILLERY: Lark Distillery, Hobart, Tasmania
FOUNDED: 1992
OWNER/MANAGER: Bill Lark
www.larkdistillery.com.au

One can consider Bill Lark the father of the modern whisky distilling we see today in Australia. In 1992 he was the first person to take out a distillation license in Tasmania for 153 years.

The original establishment was in Kingston but moved to Hobart in 2001. In common with many other small distilleries, Lark looked for alternative products to secure liquidity whilst the whisky was maturing. Lark Briol (replacing the old Tasmanian Bush Liqueur) based on Tasmanian Pepperberry, Pepperberry Vodka (triple distilled) and Apple Schnapps deserve mentioning as examples of these.

On the whisky side the Single Cask Malt Whisky at 40% has been the main product but Bill Lark has also recently released a Distillers Selection at 46% and a Cask Strength at 58%, both of which are also single cask. The range is completed by a malt whisky liqueur called Slainte and a Pure Malt Spirit at 45%. All of the products from Lark Distillery are now also Kosher Certified by Kosher Australia.

In 2006 a new distillery was constructed on a farm at Mt Pleasant, 15 minutes from Hobart. The farm grows barley for Cascade brewery and at the moment it is from there Lark distillery gets its malt. However, their intention is to set up their own floor maltings within two years thereby enabling them to produce everything themselves from barley field to bottle at one site. And that is not all - in January 2007 they purchased the cooperage that makes the barrels and they have also secured their own peat bog at Brown Marsh. All in all, they are now very much in control of the whole chain.

The whisky is double-distilled in a 1,800-litres wash still and a 600-litres spirit still and then matured in 100-litre "quarter casks". The current production is 10-12 barrels per month. According to Bill Lark, four or five years in those small casks are equivalent to 10 years in Scotland. Bill Lark is also planning for a break-through on the export market with shipments to the UK and USA. The "old site" down in Hobart by the waterfront is now a showcase for the Lark whisky with a shop, café and a whisky bar with over 100 different single malts.

DISTILLERY: Hellyers Road Distillery,
Burnie, Tasmania
FOUNDED: 1999
OWNER/MANAGER: Betta Milk Co-op/
Laurie House
www.hellyersroaddistillery.com.au

Hellyer's Road Distillery is the largest single malt whisky distillery in Australia and although they have been producing since 1999, they have not been on the market for more than two years. Despite this short period of time, they have established contacts in both Asia and the US in order to export their whisky which is currently sold only in Tasmania, mainland Australia and, more recently, Hong Kong. The capacity allows for 500 casks per year to be produced but they also have 2,500 200-litres casks in bond. The Tasmanian barley is malted at Cascade Brewery in Hobart and peat from Scotland is used for the peated expressions. Maturation takes place in ex bourbon casks.

A visitor centre and a website were set up in 2006 and a number of expressions were released for the first time. There are now three varieties of Hellyers Road Single Malt Whisky in the range: Original, Slightly Peated and Peated. There is also the premium expression Hellyers Road Distillers Choice which is only available to visitors who take the guided tour at the distillery. A special version, The Southern Fire, reserved for the export market is planned but has not yet been released.

This distillery was previously known as Whisky Tasmania but when the first bottles were released the name was changed to Hellyers Road Distillery after Henry Hellyer, one of the first European explorers to set foot in Tasmania. Founder and owner of the distillery is, perhaps surprisingly, Betta Milk Co-operative Ltd. Founded in 1956, it is a farmer-owned dairy enterprise which decided to diversify its product range in the late 20th century by getting into the whisky business.

DISTILLERY: Bakery Hill Distillery, North Balwyn, Victoria
FOUNDED: 1998
OWNER/MANAGER: David Baker
www.bakeryhilldistillery.com.au

2008 has been an exciting time for the Bakery Hill Distillery. With the completion and successful commissioning of the brewery it now has total control of all the processes from milling the grain to bottling the matured spirit. Production levels have subsequently been increased and David Baker is eagerly awaiting the maturation of the first barrels of Bakery Hill's very own production.

The first spirit at Bakery Hill distillery was produced in 2000 and the first single malt was launched in autumn 2003. Three different versions are available - Classic and Peated (both matured in ex bourbon casks) and Double Wood (ex bourbon and French oak). As Classic and Peated also are available as cask strength bottlings, they can be considered two more varieties. The whisky is double-distilled in a copper pot still. All unpeated malt comes from an Australian maltster while the malt for the peated version is imported from the UK.

Sales have picked up momentum and David has now been forced to limit the number of bottles available to each customer. The peated cask strength and the Double Wood are especially popular.

With the Bakery Hill Distillery being situated about 25 km inland in the Southern portion of Australia, the climate is very different to that of Scotland. The overall ambient temperatures are much higher while the air mass is much drier. These factors influence the rate of flavour development and ultimate whisky character and David Baker is constantly experimenting with a wide variety of oak to find the optimal path.

Bakery Hill Distillery

Patrick Maguire (left) and Paul Monks from Tasmania Distillery

DISTILLERY: Tasmania Distillery,
Cambridge, Tasmania
FOUNDED: 1996
OWNER/MANAGER: Patrick Maguire
www.tasmaniadistillery.com

The whisky we see bottled today from Tasmania Distillery is what chief distiller Patrick Maguire describes as their "second generation whisky". With that term he wishes to point out the differences in quality between the whisky produced in the late nineties and the whisky the new owners distilled at the beginning of the 21st century. A third group of owners, led by Patrick Maguire, took over in November 2003 after the distillery had been mothballed for two years. Annual production amounts to 120 200-litres casks of non chill-filtered whisky which is matured in American oak bourbon casks and French oak port barrels.

The brand has been completely re-packaged recently and the range is made up of Sullivan's Cove cask strength (60%) matured in either bourbon casks or port casks and Sullivan's Cove Double Cask (40%) which is a marriage of port and bourbon casks. Following a number of awards, the rest of the world has now started to take an interest in the whisky and it is available in Sweden, Denmark, Holland, Korea, Singapore, Taiwan, Hong-Kong and China. A special version distilled at Tasmania Distillery in 2000 was released in March 2008 as Trapper's Hut by whisky enthusiasts who bought some casks from the distillery.

DISTILLERY: Nant Distillery, Bothwell, Tasmania
FOUNDED: 2007
OWNER/MANAGER: Keith Batt
www.nantdistillery.com.au

Many of the new malt whisky projects popping up all over the world have sprung from already existing brewing and/or distilling facilities. Nant distillery

in Bothwell in the Central Highlands of Tasmania is something quite different. Queensland businessman Keith Batt bought the property in 2004 and has since renovated the homestead and rebuilt it into a distillery. The first distillation took place on 5 April 2008. Keith´s initial idea was to manage the whole production process on site. Barley has been grown on the estate since 1821 and continues to this day. At the homestead there was also a 180 year old water driven flour mill which is now used for grinding the barley into grist. Peat from nearby bogs will also be used in the malting process. The distillery is equipped with an 1800 litres wash still and a 600 litres spirit still. For maturation Keith will be using quarter casks (100 litres) previously used for port and sherry. Tasmanian veteran distiller Bill Lark has been consulted to ensure the quality of the production and the first bottling is expected in 2011. The capacity of the distillery will be about 300 100-litres barrels per year.

Visitors are welcome to Nant distillery for a guided tour and there is also an excellent whisky bar in the Atrium Lounge.

DISTILLERY: Great Southern Distilling Company,
Albany, Western Australia
FOUNDED: 2004
OWNER/MANAGER: Great Southern Distilling Company Pty Ltd/Cameron Syme
www.distillery.com.au

This is the only whisky distillery in the western part of Australia. It was built in Albany on the southwestern tip of Australia in 2004 with whisky production commencing in late 2005. Throughout the initial years production of whisky, vodka and gin took place in a set of sheds on the outskirts of Albany. A move was made in October 2007 to a new, custom-built distillery with a visitor centre on Princess Royal Harbour.

Keith Batt, owner of Nant Distillery, and the stillroom

Production takes place in pot stills (one wash still of 1,900 litres and one spirit still of 580 litres) and a 600 litre copper pot antique gin still has also been installed. For maturation a mix of ex bourbon and ex brandy barrels are used as well as new and reshaved/charred American Oak and French Oak casks. Great Southern Vodkas and Gin have been available for sale since October 2006. The first expression of the malt whisky, called Limeburners, was released in April 2008, the second appearing a couple of months later. Both releases were single casks (or single barrels) and non-chillfiltered. There are plans for other varieties including a peated version, using peat from local peat bogs. The first peated expression went into barrel in August 2008.

The owner, Cameron Syme, a commercial lawyer by profession, is a qualified distiller who learnt to distil malt whisky in distilleries in Tasmania and Scotland but the day-to-day distillery production is managed by Tony Browne, a Scotsman with 13 years experience of making malt whisky at various Scottish distilleries and Juergen Schluidi a German qualified Master Distiller with 16 years experience.

DISTILLERY: Overeem Distillery, Blackmans Bay, Tasmania
FOUNDED: 2007
OWNER/MANAGER: Casey Overeem

This distillery in Tasmania came on stream in 2007. By summer 2007 four barrels (100 litres) had been

Limeburners - the first single malt release from Great Southern Distilling Company

produced and the distillery will continue to produce at least two barrels per month. The omnipresent Bill Lark (see Lark distillery) has also assisted here. He produces the wash for Overeem and is also supplying the barrels from their own cooperage. The two stills at Overeem (wash still of 1 800 litres and spirit still of 600 litres) were made by the Hobart still maker Knapp-Lewer.

New Zealand_____

DISTILLERY: New Zealand Malt Whisky Co, Queenstown, South Island
FOUNDED: 2000 (distillery prob. in 2009)
OWNER/MANAGER: Warren Preston
www.nzmaltwhisky.co.nz
www.milfordwhisky.co.nz

Warren Preston comes from one of New Zealand's most well-known wine-making families. When he saw the enormous export successes the country made in wines, he started to become interested in achieving something similar for whisky. In 2001 he bought the entire stock of single malt and blended whisky from decommissioned Wilsons Willowbank Distillery in Dunedin. This distillery was founded by local businessmen in 1969 and was later owned by Seagram International. It stopped producing in 1997 and was dismantled in 2000. The supplies Preston acquired consisted of, among other things, 400 casks of single malt whisky including production dating back to 1987. Before he bought it, the whisky was sold under the name Lammerlaw but Preston renamed it Milford. There have been 10, 12, 15, 18 and a 20 year export bottlings, with a 21 year old cask strength bottling to take place later in 2008. The casks containing Milford whisky are maturing at Preston´s 125 year old grain store located in Oamaru which is a small town on the East Coast of the South Island.

Securing the stock from this closed distillery was just a step along the way for Warren Preston. His long-term objective was to establish a whisky distillery at a highland property near Queenstown at Nevis Bluff on the Kawaru River. He was granted a 5 year consent in 2007 from the local authorities to build a boutique distillery. Preston is currently looking for investors so as to commence the distillery in 2009. The idea is to initially produce 300,000 litres a year which would make it the largest distillery in this part of the world. The whisky will be made from New Zealand barley with different peating levels and some of the maturation will be in French Oak wine casks seasoned with New Zealand wine.

ASIA

India

DISTILLERY: Amrut Distilleries Ltd., Bangalore
FOUNDED: 1948
OWNER/MANAGER: Jagdale Group
www.amrutdistilleries.com
www.amrutwhisky.co.uk

Amrut was the first (and so far the only) Indian distillery with serious aspirations of establishing itself on the European market. Their first single malt (matured 3-4 years) became available in the UK at the end of 2004 and can now be found, among other countries, in the Netherlands, Sweden, France, Germany and Italy. When Amrut has become firmly established on the European market, the expansion is anticipated to continue in the USA and Far East.

The main part of its malt production, commenced in the mid-eighties, is used for their blended whiskies. The malt is produced in Jaipur and Delhi from grain grown in Punjab and Rajasthan. Distilling takes place at Amrut in Bangalore and the water is brought by lorry from a well 15 miles outside the town. The casks are mainly ex Bourbon of American oak. The rather harsh climate during maturation gives an angel's share of between 12 and 15%. This means that a storage period of longer than four years is practically impossible.

Rakshit N. Jagdale, grandson of the founder, consolidated the marketing of Amrut Single Malt in Scotland when he studied at the University of Newcastle upon Tyne. Step one included establishing the brand at as many Indian restaurants as possible in Glasgow, the curry capital of Britain. The target, according to Amrut, is to sell 10,000 cases within four years mainly through the UK's 20,000 Indian restaurants. An Amrut cask strength was released in 2006 and in 2008 it was followed up by a peated cask strength (62,8%).

The whisky is named after the nectar that, according to Hindu mythology, is drunk by the gods.

DISTILLERY: McDowell's, Ponda, Goa
FOUNDED: 1988 (malt whisky)
OWNER/MANAGER: UB Group
www.clubmcdowell.com

McDowell's has been part of the United Breweries Group since 1951 when the company was acquired by Vittal Mallya. Other companies in the group are Herbertsons, Triumph Distillers & Vintners and, since 2005, Shaw Wallace. The group, now owned by the son of the founder, Vijay Mallya, is number three in the world after Diageo and Pernod Ricard. Scottish & Newcastle acquired a share in the brewery division of United Breweries in 2005. The UB Group does not deal exclusively in spirits but also media and pharmaceuticals and operates Kingfisher Airline. The major brands in the group are huge sales-wise. Bagpiper blended whisky is the world's best-selling whisky with 13 million cases sold in 2007. That same year Johnnie Walker Red Label and Black Label sold roughly 15 million cases together. McDowell's No 1 is one of the fastest growing whiskies in the world. It sold 9 million cases in 2007 compared to 2,5 million 10 years ago and is on the way to becoming the largest selling whisky in India. The group now sells 66 million cases each year of their 140 different brands; of which 16 sell in quantities exceeding more than 1 million cases per year. Single malt sales are of course negligible compared to these figures. McDowell's Single Malt (3-4 years) is made at the distillery in Ponda (Goa) and sells some 20 000 cases each year.

In 2007 United Spirits Limited acquired the Scottish whiskymaker Whyte & Mackay (with, inter alia, Whyte & Mackay blend and Dalmore, Jura and Fettercairn distilleries) for £595m.

Pakistan

DISTILLERY: Murree Brewery Ltd., Rawalpindi
FOUNDED: 1860
OWNER/MANAGER: Bhandara family
www.murreebrewery.com

It may seem an impossible mission to produce alcoholic beverages in a muslim country. As many as 97% of the population are excluded as consumers due to their religion. This leaves the Christian and Hindu communities. However, the ingenuity of many muslim Pakistanis is great and the company claims that 99% of their customers are Muslim.

The owner of Murree Brewery and ex-member of the Pakistan National Assembly, Minoo Bhandara died 15 June 2008 barely 70 years old. Whilst on a visit to China he met with a car accident and was seriously injured. He was flown back to Rawalpindi where he later died of his injuries. Minoo Bhandara was succeeded as Chief Executive by his son Isphanyar Bhandara.

Murree Brewery in Rawalpindi, started as a beer brewery supplying the British Army. The assortment was completed with whisky, gin, rum, vodka and brandy. Three single malts have been available for some time; 3, 8 and 12 years respectively.

In 2005 an 18 year old single malt was launched and the following year their oldest expression so far, a 20 year old, reached the market. There are also a number of blended whiskies such as Vat No. 1, Lion and Dew of Himalaya.

Company sources mention a supply of half a million litres of whisky in underground storage. The brewery makes their own malt (using both floor maltings and Saladin box).

Unlike the beer, sold in Indian restaurants in the UK via a Belgian brewery under the slogan "Have a Murree with your curry", the whisky is not available outside Pakistan.

Turkey

DISTILLERY: Tekel (Mey Corporation), Ankara
FOUNDED: 1930 (whisky since 1963)
OWNER/MANAGER: Texas Paficic Group (TPG)
www.mey.com.tr

Both production and sales of tobacco and alcohol in Turkey have been administered by the national company Tekel, which also has a salt division. A change in legislation in 2001 opened a window for privatization and the wine and spirits division was sold to four companies Nurol, Limak, Özaltin and Tütsab in 2004 for $292 million. They formed a holding company, Mey Industry & Trade to market and distribute the products but kept the company name Tekel. In 2006 Mey Corporation was sold to the American Texas Pacific Group for $900 million. There is a large range of beverages, mainly consisting of wine and raki, but vodka, gin, 'cognac' and whisky are also included. The company has produced a whisky named Ankara Turk Viskisi since 1963. It can probably not be called a single malt as it is reported to contain a portion of malted rye and rice mixed with malted barley. The whisky is aged for three years on oak casks.

AFRICA

South Africa

DISTILLERY: James Sedgwick Distillery, Wellington, Western Cape
FOUNDED: 1886 (whisky production 1990)
OWNER/MANAGER: Distell Group Ltd.
www.distell.co.za

James Sedgwick Distillery initially produced brandy but converted to whisky in 1990. The first trials with malt whisky had already started in 1985 at Robertson & Buxton Distillery in Stellenbosch. When the latter closed, all production was transferred to James Sedgwick. 6,000 bottles of Three Ships 10 year single malt was released for the first time in autumn 2003. The line of blended whiskies is larger: Three Ships Original, Three Ships 5 years, Three Ships Bourbon Cask Finish, Harrier and Knights which all amount to 7,000,000 bottles a year. The interest in Scotch whisky has virtually exploded in South Africa during recent years. The sales of Scotch whisky in the country have increased by 9% giving it 9th position in the world market in terms of value and 5th position in terms of volume.

The whisky is matured on ex bourbon and ex sherry casks and a small share of own malt production goes into the blends. No further bottlings of single malt have been made since 2003. The whisky in the warehouses destined for single malt bottling has now reached eight years of age. The final decision on what age to release the next bottles has not yet been made though Manager Andy Watts says, "the maturation of the next single malt is being carefully monitored and further exciting projects are planned for the coming year."

DISTILLERY: Drayman´s Distillery, Silverton, Pretoria
FOUNDED: 2006
OWNER/MANAGER: Moritz Kallmeyer
www.draymans.com

Being a full-time beer brewer since 1997, Moritz Kallmeyer decided it was time to take the next step and begin distilling malt whisky in July 2006. Until now production has been small (one cask of 225 litres a month) but operations have now been expanded to two pot stills.

Kallmeyer calculates a first release in February 2010 of about 4,000 bottles. This version will be unpeated, distilled exclusively from South African dry-land barley malt from the Swartland area.It will be aged exclusively in used red wine barrels (Pinotage and Cabernet) being of European oak origin.

Kallmeyer is also planning a peated version but since he has been unable to find a supplier of peated malt in South Africa, he has now decided to build a small kiln of his own and will be using Canadian peat to smoke it.

The distillery already sells whisky. It is bought from Scotland, blended and solera-matured at Drayman's, being sold in 5 litre miniature barrels.

Drayman´s Distillery

The Whisky Year That Was

Scotch whisky continue breaking records

Scotch whisky has enjoyed a terrific surge during the past couple of years and inevitably, the market must be getting nearer a point where sales at least increase at a slower rate but 2007 was definitely not the year that happened. Instead we saw new records being broken and more markets evolving.

Scotch whisky exports rose by 14% compared to 2006 and reached £2,818m, the highest ever value beating a previous high of last year's £2,478m.

In terms of volume, a new record high was set with shipments reaching the equivalent of 1,135 million bottles, an increase by 8% compared to the previous year. The picture, if broken down into malt and blends is as follows (note that bulk shipments are not included):

Bottled Malt - export
Value: +11% to £454m
Volume: -5% to 72m bottles

Bottled Blended Scotch - export
Value: +15% to £2.22bn
Volume: +15% to 874m bottles

The decrease for Bottled Malt (-5%) is surprising but probably just temporary. Figures for the first quarter of 2008 show a surge by 21% in that same segment.

If we look at the different markets it is probably USA that gives most joy to the whisky producers. It is the most important export market for Scotch in terms of value but many had fears that the recent economic slowdown would affect sales. The volume actually did decrease by 5% but instead the Americans bought more expensive brands, thus the value of the export went up by 5% and is now worth £419m. In Asia, Taiwan can be a bit of a roller coaster and we have seen figures doubling or being halved in just a year. In 2007 the value of the export went down by 23%. Singapore on the other hand showed an impressive increase of 84%. Part of the reason behind this figure though is that Singapore serves as a hub for re-exports to, for example, China. Another market in Asia which was a cause for celebration was India which, due to a tariff reform with lower duties, increased by as much as 36%.

In Africa, South Africa continued to show strength with an increase of 9% and the country is now firmly settled amongst the top 10 export markets for Scotch. In Europe, finally, some figures raised more than one eyebrow. Usually considered a mature market with small movements the EU increased totally by 27%. Germany increased by 62% but the situation is the same there as with Singapore, since Germany re-exports to Central and Eastern Europe. Spain was also a reason for celebration; with the exception of 2003 this market had been going down since 2000 but suddenly the volume increased by 38% and the value by 57%. This means that France was overtaken as the second important market in terms of value, after USA. Looking at volumes though, France is still the largest market.

It is clearly evident from the first four months of 2008 that the success of single malt is a continuing trend. Total exports rose by 22% compared to January-April 2007. Some EU countries in particular have noted considerable increases in exports, namely Spain (165%), Italy (65%) and Germany (62%).

Total export of bottled blends increased with a more subtle 2% in which EU saw a 14% increase while all other markets fell by 5%.

If we look at malt and blend together there are some markets, particularly in Asia, which have begun with a negative trend in 2008; China (-19%), Hong Kong (-13%) and Thailand (-11%). The winners are to be found notably in eastern Europe, where countries like Poland, Romania and the Czech Republic have advanced.

The big players

Diageo
As usual Diageo presented a convincing report for the year ending in June 2008.
Net sales increased by 8% from £7,481m to £8,090m and profits increased by 3% from £2,159m to £2,226m. Johnnie Walker's success continues and the brand grew in net sales by 12% and now sells over £1 billion in a year. The other big Scotch brand in the portfolio, J&B is now making strides after the successful "Start a Party Campaign". Sales increased with a total of 9% during the year. South America remains a strong market for Scotch and efforts in Eastern Europe and Russia are starting to be reflected on the balance sheet. Operating profit fell by 12% in Asia Pacific which may seem strange but can be explained by Diageo being without an import license for more than half the year. Their licence had been revoked by the authorities after Diageo used unlicensed wholesalers. It was not reinstated until February 2008.

Even if CEO Paul Walsh believes in a continued growth for Diageo, he advocates caution due to the more challenging economic trends that could lie ahead.

Pernod Ricard
Pernod Ricard announced a weaker year than the previous when summing up the fiscal year ending 30th June 2008. Sales did, however, increase but only by 2.3% to €6,589 million. It is unclear what that means for the profit at the time of writing. The preliminary results were published a little later than usual due to the aqcuisition of Swedish Vin & Spirt earlier in the year. It is, however, obvious that premiumisation is the key to growth. The 15 strategic brands were responsible for a 5% volume increase and 11% value increase. Among these are e. g. Glenlivet (+14%), Chivas (+11%) and Ballantine's (+11%). The Asian market increased and China (+29%) and India (+39%) were responsible for 2/3 of the growth. All major Western European markets increased, excepting Italy, but greatest success occured in the East; Russia for example increased by 38%.

United Spirits
United Spirits Limited (part of the Indian UB Group) took their first steps into the Scotch whisky market when they bought Whyte & Mackay last year, thereby also becoming the world's number 3 spirits producer after Diageo and Pernod Ricard. In the fiscal year of 2007/2008 (ending 31 March) the net income rose by 16% to R31,663m whereas the profit before tax decreased from R6,216m to R5,004m. United Spirits also reports that the total number of sold cases went up from 66,4 million to 73,9 million.

Looking at Whyte & Mackay separately, the new owners managed to turn a loss of £1,2m to a profit of £13m. During the year, the two most important single malt brands of Whyte & Mackay, Dalmore and Jura, were both introduced in India and the company also revealed plans to launch a low-cost Whyte & Mackay for that market. The domestic version will be bottled in India but the original Whyte & Mackay bottled in Scotland will still be sold separately.

United Spirits, headed by the charismatic owner Vijay Mallya, has so far shown great success but like its rivals it is affected by raised commodity prices. Higher prices of molasses, the base of Indian whisky as barley is in Scotch, affects United Spirits. The increase in price is caused by lower sugar production and a growing demand for ethanol. Recent rumours mention an interest from both Diageo and Bacardi in buying a small share of United Spirits to get a foothold on the Indian market.

Edrington
The Edrington Group increased sales by 4.9% to £291,5m in the year to March 2008 and the profit increased by almost 10% to £75,6m. Sales of The Famous Grouse blended range increased by 7% to 37 million bottles. The malt range of Famous Grouse on the other hand backed considerably from 2,1 million bottles sold during 2006 to 1,5 million in 2007.

Pierre Pringuet, Pernod Ricard´s CEO from November

According to Edrington the reason is that demand from the most important market, Taiwan has decreased considerably and competition increased markedly in the vatted malt segment.

In contrast, Highland Park, was subject for rejoicing with an increase of over 20%. Almost 1,3 million bottles were sold in total and the brand is heading for the top 10. Macallan is also increasing steadily and has also expanded production capacity with 30% during 2008.

Outside of the whisky business, the company made an investment in the rum business by acquiring 61% of Brugal, the fastest growing golden rum in international markets. Despite these good figures, Edrington is cautious for the coming year. Financial climate and raised prices of commodities, they say, can slow growth in the near future.

Morrison Bowmore

Morrison Bowmore (owner of Bowmore, Auchentoshan and Glen Garioch distilleries) managed to transform a good result in 2006 into a brilliant result in 2007. The turnover rose by 22% to £38,4m while pre-tax profits came in at £3,2m, an increase of 19%. The incremental transformation from the low-margin blend market to the more lucrative single malt market which was started in 2006 has of course contributed to the good results.

Inver House

The company really turned around compared to the previous year when the result was marred by big investments in a couple of the brands, particularly Old Pulteney and Balblair. In 2007 they could report an increased profit by 108% to £3.8m and sales were up by 52% to £57.8m. Speyburn single malt continued to be successful in the US market and is the 6th best selling single malt there. Another brand in the portfolio, Old Pulteney, performed very well in the UK increasing sales there by 24% and the aim is for it to be placed in the top 10 UK malts by 2009.

Fortune Brands

The American company with its headquarter in Deerfield, Illinois is active in three different areas; Home & Hardware, Golf and Spirits. The latter is contained within subsidiary Beam Global Spirits & Wine with major spirits brands such as Jim Beam, Maker's Mark, Canadian Club, Courvoisier and, in Scotch, Teacher's and Laphroaig. In order to focus on spirits where the returns are higher, the company sold off its wine business to Constellation Brands in late 2007.

The full year report for 2007 was a disappointment with operating income reduced by 5% to $1,376m. Total sales on the other hand increased by 0,5% to $8,563m. The greatest disappointment was found in the business areas Golf and especially Home & Hardware where profit fell by 28%. Spirits performed much better with a total increase of profits by 16%. Spirit brands are responsible for 30% of the groups' total turn-over but generates more than half of Fortune Brands' total income.

Bob Kunze-Concewitz, CEO Gruppo Campari

Gruppo Campari

The owners of Glen Grant, Italian Davide Campari-Milano could look back at a good year in 2007. Annual net profits increased by 6.9% to €125.2m. Sales increased by 2.7% to €957.5m but if one only looks at the spirit portfolio, which amounts to 72% of the group's turn-over, sales increased by 4.6%. The reason for this, compared to last year, less spectacular profit and sales is that both Glen Grant and the two blended whisky brands Old Smuggler and Braemar were acquired in 2006. The whisky was the driving force also in 2007 with an increase in sales of 22.2%.

LVMH

Louis Vuitton Moët Hennessy, the owner of Glenmorangie, Ardbeg and (when writing this book at least) Glen Moray show roughly the same pace of increase as in the previous year. Total turn-over (all business groups) increased by 8% to €16,481m while Wines & Spirits rose 13% to €3,226m. Total profits for the whole group increased by 12% to €3,555m, in which Wine & Spirits were responsible for an increase of 10% to €1,058m.

Nothing is mentioned in the abbreviated annual report about the brands in Scotland. Focus is instead on Moët & Chandon champagne and Hennessy cognac. The company also went into the Chinese domestic market when they acquired a 55% stake in Wen Jun Spirits, a Chinese producer of premium white spirits.

The big brands

Glenfiddich still lies far ahead of everyone else on the global sales list. During 2007, 11.1 million bottles were sold, which means that every seventh bottle of single malt sold in the world is Glenfiddich. The goal is to reach the ideal figure of 1 million 9-litres cases sold in a year during 2008. But this does not mean that number two and three show poor sales. On the contrary, *Glenlivet* (613,000 cases) and *Macallan* (570,000 cases) have both increased their market shares considerably during 2007. Last years' number four, *Glen Grant* (312,000 cases), is however still trying to reach its former levels. The decrease is continuing and during 2007 this brand was overtaken by both *Glenmorangie* and *Johnnie Walker Green* (vatted malt). The top six malt whisky brands are responsible for almost half of all Scotch malt whisky sold.

As usual, when it comes to blended whiskies, *Johnnie Walker Red Label* is the most sold in the world. On the other hand we have a new number two, *Ballantine´s*, which thereby has pushed down *J&B* which is losing market shares despite increased volumes. Another brand that has overtaken J&B is *Johnnie Walker Black Label* at third place which continues to increase strongly. If its pace is maintained, there will be two Johnnie Walkers in the top spots of the world list next year. The success of Black Label continues to increase the lead to the arch rival over most sold premium Scotch, *Chivas Regal*. The latter which increased so much in the early 21st century is now losing market shares for the second consecutive year. *Famous Grouse* managed to become the most sold Scotch in the UK in 2006. Happiness was short though, as *Bell's* had resumed the top spot the year after, following unprecedented sales.

Clouds on the horizon

British government raises whisky duties

The UK tax on spirits has been frozen since 1991 but when Chancellor Alistair Darling delivered his first budget in March it included an increased duty corresponding to 59p per bottle. One might think that the whisky producers should have been satisfied having had the same tax for more than a decade, but that is not the case. On the contrary, they have struggled for many years to lower the tax in order to compete more favourably with wine and beer; it is a matter of fact that the national drink of Scotland is taxed considerably higher than for example imported wines. After the latest rise, the duty charged on one unit of alcohol is 20.9 p for beer, 24.3 p for wine and 29.9 p for whisky. Tax is now no less than 75% of the cost of every bottle of whisky and it does not stop there; Darling announced that the tax is set to increase even more - by 2% over the rate of inflation for every year until 2013.

According to Alistair Darling, the purpose of raising the tax was partly to mitigate increased alcohol consumption, partly to finance increased support to families on low income and pensioners. Of course, the Scotch Whisky Association reacted strongly. Gavin Hewitt, the chief executive of SWA said; "Scottish distillers are astonished by the Chancellor´s announcement. The government's own figures show that any duty increase on whisky is likely to reduce revenue at a time when public finances are tight."

The tax increase strikes the distilleries at a time when they are already struggling with increasing raw material (barley, crude oil and gas) prices. The whisky industry employs 65,000 people and is responsible for 67% of the value of Scotland´s food and drink exports.

Rising commodity prices worries distilleries

For the past couple of years sales of Scotch whisky has continuously broken new records. Emerging markets like the BRIC nations (Brazil, Russia, India and China) fill an important niche for producers when changed alcohol habits and slower economies damage sales in established markets. But even if sales increase, there are clouds on the horizon when it comes to higher commodity prices.

A malt whisky is made of three ingredients - water, barley and yeast but it could also be said that the production process is made up of three key components, namely barley, oil or gas and wood. When looking only at the distillation process, raw materials and fuel stand for 65% of costs whilst the remaining share is of labour and overhead costs. When the cost of one of the components suddenly rises it quickly affects the bottom line of profit and loss account. When the price of all three commodities begins increasing at an uncontrollable level, worries are justified and this is where the industry finds itself now.

In February 2006 a tonne of malted barley cost around £240. A year later it was £350 and a few months into 2008 the price had risen to £400 and looks like it will continue to rise. This problem is greatest for small distilleries which cannot make use of the discounts used by large producers but may have to pay upwards of an additional £100 per tonne.

The increasing oil and gas price is another major concern and the problem with higher oil prices is not only that is effects the costs for the whisky producers but it also effects the economy in those markets where they will be selling their whisky. A recession caused by high oil prices may cause drinkers to abandon imported whisky favouring locally produced spirits instead. The Brent crude oil price has doubled from June 2007 to June 2008.

The last of the three key components is wood, i. e. the casks for maturing the spirit. It has become increasingly difficult to source new casks and when found, the price is substantial. This can lead to re-using casks more frequently than before and there is a growing concern that spirit is occasionally filled on casks of poorer quality today compared to a few years ago. If this is correct we will experience a discouraging result in a few years when the finished whisky starts appearing on the markets.

Increasing oil prices is only one of the problems the whisky industry will have to face

How do these increasing prices affect us as consumers? The whisky producers have seen reduced margins the last few years due to rising costs. At the same time, price of Scotch whisky has been pretty stable but in 2006 they started rising and rose more rapidly in 2007. It is evident that the whisky companies now feel that they must increasingly compensate for the diminishing margins.

The challenge is to get consumers to pay more for the same brand they usually buy. There has been speculation whether this is a reason for some whisky companies to replace their 10 year old core expressions with a 12 year old. The increased marginal costs for the extra two years are comparatively modest, while it may be easier to obtain customer acceptance for a greater increase in price.

Changes in ownership

Glendronach

Pernod Ricard's intentions concerning Glendronach distillery, situated outside Huntly, have been pondered over for several years. It already owns several Speyside distilleries, three of which are heavily marketed as brands of their own - Glenlivet, Aberlour and Longmorn. The capacity of Glendronach (1.3m litres) is also much smaller than the others and the distillery would probably find its niche within a smaller company. Therefore it was no surprise to anyone when Pernod Ricard in August 2008 announced that the distillery had been sold to the owners of BenRiach distillery headed by Billy Walker. The financial magnitude of the deal is thought to lie at approximately £15m. The sale of Glendronach is probably one of several steps in the restructuring of Pernod Ricard's business and ownership, perhaps in part due to its acquisition of Swedish Vin & Sprit with Absolut Vodka earlier in 2008.

Billy Walker raises his glass to celebrate the purchase of Glendronach

Glen Moray

Glenmorangie Company announced in July that they would sell the Broxburn bottling plant to Diageo. Broxburn is the site of the company headquarters. It will continue to operate from the Broxburn site for another two years until a new state-of-the-art facility has been built in the Lothians area. At the same time the Glenmorangie head office will move to Edinburgh. The underlying reasons are that Glenmorangie is now redefining its business and are exiting the blended Scotch market to concentrate on single malts. Since most of the produce at the Glen Moray distillery in Elgin is destined for blended whisky, the distillery has been put up for sale. It is not clear at the time of writing who will take over Glen Moray but it is not likely that Diageo, Pernod Ricard, William Grant or Edrington are candidates. A company which probably is more interested could be Whyte & Mackay.

Tullibardine

The Tullibardine owners were able to celebrate their first year of profits after some tough years since acquisition in 2003. It was therefore quite surprising when rumours were circulating that the distillery was up for sale. The company´s Director Michael Beamish expressed it like this; "There´s no reason to sell the business, but anything is for sale at the right price." At least three possible buyers have shown interest so in order to assess potential takeover offers, the company hired Swiss investment bank UBS.

Glen Barclay, Director of Legal Affairs at the Scotch Whisky Association

New categories for Scotch whisky

One of the big topics of discussion among whisky producers this past year has been the increasing financial crisis, not least in the important American market. Other causes for concern have been increased commodity prices and the increase of duty on spirits in the UK. But the issue that has involved both producers and consumers to the greatest extent has without doubt been the changes to Scotch whisky legislation and especially the new sales categories that have been proposed.

There is actually a whole package of changes which Scotch Whisky Association (SWA) has put forward to the government to decide upon. The general idea is to strengthen the definitions of Scotch Whisky to protect the term against an anticipated dilution. One of the proposed regulations is that Scotch whisky should be wholly matured in Scotland. This means that Scotch whisky cannot be exported in wooden casks. The rules are even stricter when it comes to single malts; they must be both bottled and labelled before they can be exported. For those companies that export whisky in bulk to be bottled abroad today, this means a considerable restriction. Most agree that many of the proposals are important and pointing in the right direction to strengthen the global identity of Scotch whisky.

But the greatest and most stormy debate is the proposed five categories of Scotch whisky which SWA advocate;

Single Malt Scotch whisky
whisky made from malted barley in pot stills at a single distillery

Blended Malt Scotch whisky
a blend of whisky made from malted barley in pot stills from two or more distilleries

Single Grain Scotch whisky
whisky made from different cereals including malted barley at a single distillery

Blended Grain Scotch whisky
a blend of whisky made from different cereals including malted barley from two or more distilleries

Blended Scotch whisky
a blend of malt whisky and grain whisky.

The second category - Blended Malt Scotch Whisky is the one which has caused most uproar. For many years it has been called Vatted Malt and SWA now claims that it is a confusing term, especially for younger consumers, and that Blended in combination with Malt describes exactly what it is all about.

The many opponents to the suggestion uphold that, on the other hand, using the term Blended places this variety of malt whisky in the same category as Blended Scotch which by most whisky drinkers is considered a simpler whisky. In many peoples' minds it would even entail a poor and inferior whisky. But that is not all. According to the proposed regulations, one is not allowed to label a whisky with the name of a distillery if it is not produced at that distillery. On the other hand, nothing is said as to whether the name of a distillery where the whisky was produced has to appear on the label. Consequently, this could mean that for a certain blended (vatted) malt one does not have to state the names of all the distilleries which contributed; if so desired, just one name would do.

The critics are of the opinion that this sets the scene for a new Cardhu situation. A couple of years ago, Diageo decided to suddenly turn their single malt Cardhu into a vatted malt with whisky from other distilleries as well, though keeping the name Cardhu on the label. The reason was that Cardhu single malt had become so popular that demand outstripped supply. According to many, the risk is that the consumer can be falsely led to believe that he has bought single malt when there only is a name of a distillery on the label even if it says Blended Malt beneath the name

The whole debate has been further seasoned by the fact that SWA is dominated by the big groups in the business, such as Diageo, Pernod Ricard, Wm Grant, Edrington etc while most of the smaller producers such as Springbank, Loch Lomond and Bruichladdich are not members (by their own choice, it should be noted). SWA represents 95% of the industry capacity and 60% is controlled by the two largest - Diageo and Pernod Ricard. The opinion among independents is that SWA's actions mainly are driven to favour the big companies.

A petition against the new proposal, initiated by John Glaser from Compass Box Whisky, was circulated on the internet and had more than 1000 named signatures and has been delivered to the Department Environment Food and Rural Affairs (DEFRA).

The debate took an unexpected turn in early June when Loch Lomond Distillers (not a member of the SWA) suggested a sixth category be added. Loch Lomond Distillers is the only distillery in Scotland equipped with both pot stills and a column still. The latter is mainly used for distilling grain whisky but Loch Lomond have also made single malt whisky in the same still and so argues that the sixth category should be Single Malt Scotch Whisky distilled in a column still. SWAs stance is that this category is not required as it is not a traditional way of making malt whisky. Protests came from many quarters, pointing out that distillation of malt whisky in column stills took place a hundred years ago.

Changing of the Guards

Many were taken by surprise when *Graham Eunson*, Distillery Manager at Glenmorangie announced that he would leave the company to become manager at Glenglassaugh. This came at a time when Glenmorangie finally had regained its previous high profile. Continuous campaigns with discounted Glenmorangie being sold in super markets and a dearth of new, exciting bottlings had given the distillery a dull reputation.

Eunson's challenge will of course be to take part in the restart of a distillery that has been mothballed for 22 years. *Andy MacDonald* became the new manager at Glenmorangie. He had previously worked for Diageo, most recently at the Benrinnes and Dailuaine distilleries.

Diageo´s CEO *Paul Walsh* was appointed chairman of The Scotch Whisky Association in January 2008. He replaced *Richard Burrows* from Pernod Ricard. Burrows had been on the board of SWA for six years; as chairman for the last two.

Distillery Manager *Ronnie Learmond* retired in the spring after 27 years at Auchentoshan distillery. He was succeeded by the present Master Blender for Morrison Bowmore, the only 33 years old *Iain McCallum*.

Kate Wright, who many readers have most likely met at different whisky festivals over the years, has left Springbank. Her new position since August is Sales & Marketing Executive at Glenfarclas distillery where she will initially focus on the French and Spanish markets.

Kate Wright, now with Glenfarclas

New, revived and planned distilleries

In 2005 Allt-a-bhainne restarted production, two years later Tamnavulin came on stream again and this year, yet another two mothballed distilleries were resurrected.

First *Braeval*, sister distillery of Allt-a-bhainne and one of the distilleries which Pernod Ricard mothballed in 2002 shortly after they had taken over Chivas Brothers. Braeval, placed in a remote part of the Highlands, was built in 1973 and is a highly efficient distillery with a capacity to produce four million litres of spirit a year. In order to start distilling again a new boiler was installed and upgrades of still venting and control systems were put into place. Production re-started in July.

The other revived distillery came as more of a surprise. The odds were not especially high that *Glenglassaugh*, which had been dormant since 1986, ever would become active again but in March the owner, Edrington, announced that the distillery had been sold for £5m to a Dutch company, the Scaent Group which until now has mostly been active in the energy and telecommunication sectors. Production will begin at the end of 2008 and there are also plans for a number of releases from existing stocks. A visitor centre will also be built and will probably open during the second quarter of 2009.

And if the ressurection of Glenglassaugh took us by surprise, what can one say about the plans for *Annandale distillery* in Dumfries? This distillery was mothballed in 1919 and finally closed in 1921! Most of the buildings, including the pagoda roof, are still there but the equipment is of course long gone. The site was bought by Professor David Thomson and his wife from a local farmer and the budget for the project is fixed at £4.5m. Both Historic Scotland and the Scottish Government have contributed and the legendary Dr. Jim Swan has been employed as consultant. It is still not clear when this Lowland distillery will be ready to produce again.

At the other end of the scale, size-wise, is the newest distillery in Scotland to start producing malt whisky, namely *Ailsa Bay*. Plans to build a new malt distillery next to their grain distillery complex in Girvan were announced by William Grant & Sons last year. Building finished in record time and in October the first sprit was distilled in the eight stills. The distillery has an impressive capacity of five million litres and the whisky produced is intended for the company´s blended whiskies. The last time malt whisky was produced at Girvan was back in 1975 when Ladyburn distillery closed.

An even larger distillery will come on stream next year when Diageo´s *Roseisle distillery* in Moray will be finished. The buildings will comprise 3,000m² where 14 stills will have a capacity of 10m litres per year. The construction has required 1,000 tonnes of steel and 1,000 tonnes of concrete. Diageo reports that the building is on target and they plan to commision the plant in January 2009 and be operating by spring. In common with Ailsa Bay, the whisky produced at Roseisle will become part of Diageo´s different blended whiskies, especially Johnnie Walker. Diageo`s total whisky output will increase by 10% with the new distillery.

Mark Tayburn, a businessman from the Isle of Lewis, applied for a building permission last summer for theb construction of a distillery near Uig. A year later, *Abhainn Dearg distillery* (Red River in gaelic) is running and Tayburn plans to produce 10,000 litres this year and increase to 25,000 litres next year. This is the first legal distillery on Lewis for more than 200 years.

A lot of other distillery projects are in planning phases and it remains to be seen how many will finally be realised. In the Lowlands, a company called *Falkirk Distillery Company* has applied for detailed planning permission to build a distillery in Falkirk. As many readers undoubtedly already know, Falkirk is also home of the now closed Rosebank distillery. Since most of the equipment is still in place (particularly the stills) at the old distillery, the question remains as to whether the new Falkirk Distillery Co intends to buy the equipment and create a "new" Rosebank.

Investments

Macallan
Last year Edrington announced that it had submitted plans to the authorities for a "multi-million pound" project to build new warehouses and an operations building adjacent to the existing site. So far, the first two warehouses, which together hold 50,000 casks, were commissioned in September 2008.
Macallan also announced that £5 million would

One of the 14 pot stills installed at Roseisle distillery in summer 2008

Photo: © Diageo

be invested to revive the old stillhouse which was last used in the early 1980s. It has now been recommissoned which means that there are now another six stills (two wash stills and four spirit stills) in production. Two of the old wash stills were replaced and they also built six new Douglas fir wash backs as well as replacing the bottom of the mash tun. Capacity has now increased by 30%.

Glenlivet
The Glenlivet has enjoyed a terrific growth in the last few years and in 2006 a major milestone was reached when over 500,000 cases were sold. The owners expect the success to continue and have therefore decided to increase capacity at the distillery. In March Glenlivet submitted plans to the Moray Council to install six new stills, one mash tun and eight new washbacks. An old malt barn will be upgraded to a stillhouse and with the added equipment Glenlivet should reach Glenfiddich's level in terms of capacity, i. e. around 10 million litres.

Bushmills
Another distillery with big plans is Bushmills. The goal is to sell 1 million cases by 2012 and in order to reach that £6m have been invested in a new mash tun last year and, for this year, a new still (the 10th) and another warehouse.

The new wash still is installed at Glenkinchie

Glenmorangie

It seems that the owners of Glenmorangie, LVMH had reached a watershed when it came to managing the company which was acquired back in 2004. The image of the Glenmorangie brand had become rather tarnished by frequent selling of the whisky at discounted prices in supermarkets. That did not suit the LVMH range of more luxury-inclined merchandise. A decision was made to phase withdrawal from bottling and sale of blended Scotch whisky and to instead concentrate on the higher priced single malts. The only brands of blended Scotch which will remain within the company are Bailie Nicol Jarvie and Martin´s.

In connection with this strategy it was decided to sell Glen Moray distillery, the bottling plant in Broxburn and move the head office to Edinburgh. The two remaining distilleries, Glenmorangie and Ardbeg, will receive a well-deserved facelift. At Glenmorangie, two more stills have been added to the existing ten, new warehouses are being built and the visitor centre restyled. The production capacity will rise from 4 million litres to 6 million. Ardbeg is also to receive a facelift to the visitor centre as well as new warehousing facilities. The total cost of these changes will be a staggering £45m.

Balvenie

Like several other distilleries, Balvenie invested in increased capacity this past

Old traditions kept alive when coppersmith Dennis McBain sweetens the new stills at Balvenie with Juniper.

year. In February, two new stills were installed (one wash still and one spirit still) which means that there are now five wash stills and six spirit stills in place. Another five washbacks, made of stainless steel rather than of Douglas fir like the previous ones, were also included in the expansion. Total capacity is now 6.2m litres.

Glenkinchie

In March it was time to replace the wash still at Glenkinchie. This was not an easy task as it is one of the largest stills in the industry (30,963 litres). Additionally, parts of the roof had to be dismantled in order to install it. The still was made by Diageo´s own coppersmiths in Alloa and it took six weeks to manufacture.

Green investments

Diageo´s new distillery at Roseisle will be using the ultimate in recycling technology. The aim is that approximately two thirds of energy requirements will be covered by renewable sources, amongst them by-products from the spirit-making process. Pot ale is normally used for cattle feed but at Roseisle it will pass through a three-step process which will produce clean water which will then be used for steeping at Diageo´s nearby Burghead Maltings.

Diageo are also making other environmental investments in already existing distilleries. In a program which will cost £65m, carbon emissions are to be reduced by 56,000 tonnes at Scotland´s biggest distillery, Cameronbridge in Fife. The new facility will recover 98% of steam and 80% of electrical power which will of course reduce both water and energy comsumption.

But it is not only the large dragons that are investing in environmentally beneficial improvements. Independent bottler Duncan Taylor, which is about to build their first distillery in Huntly, spares no expense when it comes to reducing the effects on the environment in the process of whisky making. Their goal is, in fact, to build the first "carbon-neutral" distillery in Scotland by planning to use a woodchip/biomass process and space heating and rain water harvesting. This is of course more expensive than if they constructed an ordinary distillery and the total investment is in the region of £3.5m.

On the other side of Scotland, on Islay, Mark Reynier of Bruichladdich is building a new distillery on an old site, Port Charlotte. Similarly to Euan Shand he aims to create a "green" distillery with a zero carbon footprint. He has begun well as most of the equipment has been brought in from the closed Inverleven distillery in 2003 so there is no need to buy more new equipment.

In March, the Combination of Rothes Distillers (CoRD) - which comprises Edrington, Chivas Brothers, Glen Grant, Inver House, Diageo and BenRiach distilling groups - announced plans for a combined heat and power plant fuelled by biomass at Rothes. The site would be built within the existing dark grains plant. The idea is to generate electricity using distillery by-products such as draff and pot ale. The consortium hope to be able to generate 7,2 MW per year which is enough electricity to power 9,000 homes.

Euan Shand, owner of the independent bottler Duncan Taylor, outside the Granary where the new distillery will be built

Selection of this year's Vintage Glenfiddich; (left to right) David Stewart, Jimmy Bradley, Erkin Touzmohamedov, Gavin D Smith and Walter Schobert

Bottling grapevine
(see pp 252-255 for a detailed listing)

Ardbeg fans all over the world were blessed with the *new 10 year old*. It symbolised Ardbeg Very Young reaching its destination after a journey which started some years ago. But the first 10 year old produced during Glenmorangie's ownership actually appeared a few months earlier in the guise of the limited *Rennaisance*. *Arran* came of age and released their *first 12 year old* as well as a handful of new wood finishes and *Balblair* replaced one of their popular vintages with a new - *Vintage 1975*. In order to celebrate Master Distiller David Stewart's 45 years in the business, *Balvenie* released *a 12 year old called Signature*. In autumn they followed up with a *17 year old rum cask finish*. Neighbouring *Glenfiddich* followed their tradition of releasing a new *Vintage* in October, a sherry cask from *1977*. Remember *Glenmorangie's* Artisan Cask a while ago? Well, it now has a follower in the form of *Astar* and the key word is still wood management, i. e. carefully selected wood for the casks. The oldest ever *Tomintoul* was launched – a *1976 Vintage* and for peat lovers, *Peaty Tang*. *Glenrothes* marked the end of an era when they launched the last of the 1970's vintage, a *1978*. Gerry Tosh, Brand Ambassador for *Highland Park*, was also busy and has selected two new releases of *Ambassador's Cask* but managed to top that with the *40 year old* which is not a one-off but will become a permanent member of the range. The people at Bruichladdich were busier than ever (which does not say a little!) when they launched no less than 21 new bottlings from June to November. Amongst the highlights were the first

expression of heavily peated *Octomore* (5 years old) and *Bruichladdich 2001*, the first Bruichladdich from their own production. Gordon & MacPhail continue to release odd bottlings from their *Benromach* distillery. A couple of years ago it was Organic, the first fully certified organic single malt, this year they have concentrated more on what comes into the whisky from the beginning and not what is added in the form of finishing on various casks. *Origins Batch 1* is the first of a series and was made entirely of Golden Promise barley. The people down at *Bladnoch* had reason to celebrate when they released the first of their own production - *three six year olds* (sherry- and bourbon-matured respectively as well as a slightly peated). From *Springbank* came the second batch of the much appreciated *Vintage 1997* but it was otherwise the year of *Longrow* with three new expressions - *CV, 18 year old and the 7 year old Gaja Barolo* finish. Official bottlings of *Glenburgie* are

Hazelwood Reserve (Kininvie single malt) - one of the rarest releases this year

rare but this year saw the release of a *15 year old cask strength* which will be sold at the Chivas visitor centres only. *Auchentoshan* metamorphosised when the rather dull, old bottles were replaced by contemporary packing but there were also new releases in the shape of an *18 year old* and the *bourbon-matured Classic. Tomatin* made a magnificent effort and released a *30 year old* as well as a *40 year old* in addition to a *number of vintages*. The people of *Isle of Jura* created a series of four limited releases called *Elements*, all different vintages with a different maturation. Last year saw the release from *Glenfarclas* of no less than 43 different vintages which were named *Family Casks* and this all became particularly impressive when it turns out that it was an uninterrupted series from 1952 to 1994. Some of these are now sold out and this year new casks from some of the years were released. New expressions are usually not expected from *Tobermory* but 2008 was an exception as a *15 year old* was released, having been matured both on the mainland as well as on Mull. Finally, *17 year old Hazelwood Reserve,* the first official bottling of Kininvie (except for a very limited release in August 2006) was launched at Heathrow's Terminal 5 in February.

Will Scotland and India reach an understanding?

For several years, there has been a battle between Scotch Whisky Association and the Indian government concerning the import tariffs that the Indians impose on Scotch whisky. The highest duty levels were more than 500%, at least until last summer when the central government in Delhi decided to reduce it to 150%. The only problem was that the Indian Constitution allows for each of the 28 states to decide on taxes on imported goods even if they are encouraged to abide by the government's proposals. Local authorities in both Mumbai and Delhi suggested considerably higher duty than the central government but after lobbying, the proposals were withdrawn.

Even so, the current 150% tax is much higher than the corresponding tarifs in, for example, China (10%) and Brazil (20%) and the SWA have therefore tried to persuade India to reduce the trade barriers between the two countries even further via the World Trade Organisation (WTO). The problem is that India considers the EU to have set up obstacles by not allowing Indian whisky be called whisky as it is made from molasses and not grain. Hopes were nonetheless high within SWA that the WTO talks in Geneva at the end of July would lead to a step forward in this issue, but hopes were once again dashed as talks ended without any results.

India ranks 20th when it comes to exports of Scotch whisky but the potential for increasing, with reduced taxes, is much higher. If domestic whisky is included, India has the largest consumption in the world.

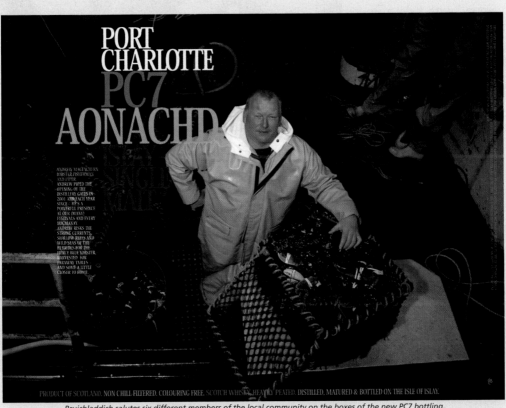

Bruichladdich salutes six different members of the local community on the boxes of the new PC7 bottling. Here, Andrew MacEachern, lobster fisherman and piper

Whisky Awards

Naturally the whisky world has its share of competitions and awards and hardly a week goes by without accolades being given to a certain producer, bottling or whisky personality. There is, however, a handful of occasions where whisky is celebrated which has a greater impact than all other competitions. This year we have focused on some of the winners of the Icons of Whisky 2008, where Whisky Magazine through an independent panel focuses the spotlight on some well deserved profiles every year.

Distiller of the Year
InverHouse Distillers

InverHouse Distillers were awarded for their particularly bold relaunch of Balblair single malt - one of their core brands. From being a whisky with an age statement, it went on to become several vintages revamped with new and inspiring packaging. But there are other gems in the company's range, for example anCnoc and Old Pulteney.

Karen Walker, Marketing Manager of InverHouse

Ambassador of the Year
Ronnie Cox

Ronnie Cox is a familiar face to many visitors at whisky fairs around the world and has preached the Scotch whisky gospel to thousands of people over the years. His darling is Glenrothes - at this moment one of the fastest growing malts in the world. Ronnie has been a part of the whisky industry for three decades and is also a Master Keeper of the Quaich.

Retailer of the Year multiple outlets

Ian Bankier in front of the Whisky Shop in Paternoster, London

The Whisky Shop

After many years as an executive in the production side of the business, in 2004 Ian Bankier decided to try his luck at selling the products. That was when he bought the rather anonymous Whisky Shop company and since then he has profiled and vitalised the enterprise into the largest specialist retailer of whiskies in the UK with 13 outlets. No less than five new Whisky Shops were opened just last year and simultaneously their own special assortment of selected malt whiskies called Glenkeir Treasures was launched.

Lifetime Achievement Award
John Ramsay

A Master Blender yet a very humble man, John Ramsay has been in the whisky business since 1966. Today he is in charge of Edrington´s range which includes top blended whiskies such as Famous Grouse and Cutty Sark and also famous single malts like Glenrothes and Highland Park. He is responsible for the quality of the almost 60 million sold bottles a year.

More Winners

Innovator of the Year - The Glenmorangie Company

Visitor Attraction of the Year - Maker´s Mark

Retailer of the Year Single Outlet - LeNell´s, New York

Restaurant of the Year - Boisdale, London

Bar of the Year
Bombay High, Mumbai - The Grill, Aberdeen
Desha´s Restaurant and Bar, Lexington

Other competitions

Malt Advocate Whisky Awards
www.maltadvocate.com

Malt Maniacs Awards
www.maltmaniacs.org

International Wine and Spirit Competition
www.iwsc.net

San Francisco World Spirits Competition
www.sfspiritscomp.com

Independent Bottlers

*The independent bottlers play an important role
in the whisky business. With their innovative bottlings, they increase
the diversity. Single malts from distilleries where the owners' themselves decide
not to bottle also get a chance through the independents.
The following are a selection of the major companies.*

Douglas Laing & Co
www.douglaslaing.com
Established in 1948 by Douglas Laing and today run by his two sons, Fred and Stewart. One of their most talked about ranges is The Old Malt Cask, introduced in 1998 and which contains many rare and old bottlings. More than 100 different expressions can be found regularly in this range where bottlings are diluted to 50%. Some malts are released in an even more exclusive range - The Old and Rare Selection, offered at cask strength. A third range is called McGibbon´s Provenance, often aged around 10-12 years, almost always diluted to 46%. Sometimes some very old (over 40 years) and rare single grains are released in the Clan Denny range.
Chill filtration and colouring is banned at Douglas Laing.

Fred and Stewart Laing - owners of Douglas Laing & Co

Murray McDavid
www.murray-mcdavid.com
Established in 1995 by Mark Reynier (who later bought Bruichladdich distillery on Islay), Gordon Wright and Simon Coughlin. Murray McDavid has three to four releases a year averaging 25 expressions per time. The range is highly selective and all casks are chosen by Jim McEwan who has more than 40 years experience in the whisky industry
Unlike most independent bottlers, their bottlings are vattings of four or five casks (same age) at 46% without chill-filtration or tinting. The range can be divided into three categories: – the Mission Range (unusual aged stock), the Celtic Heartlands range (old stock from 60s and 70s) and the Murray McDavid range. The majority of bottles have been enhanced by a second maturation on casks that have previously held various wines.

Gordon & MacPhail
www.gordonandmacphail.com
Established in 1895 they still occupy the same premises in Elgin. Apart from being an independent bottler, they operate a legendary store in Elgin and own their own distillery, Benromach, since 1993. The company is owned by the Urquhart family.
There is a wide variety of bottlings, for example Connoisseurs Choice, Private Collection, Macphail´s Collection and Pride of the Regions. Many of the bottlings have been diluted to 40%, 43% or 46% but the series Cask Strength obviously, as the name implies, contains bottlings straight from the cask. Another range called Rare Old consists of unusually old single malts, quite often from closed distilleries as well.

Berry Bros. & Rudd
www.bbr.com
Britain´s oldest wine and spirit merchant, founded in 1698. They have been selling their own world famous blend Cutty Sark since 1923. Berry Brothers had been

offering their customers private bottlings of malt whisky for years but it was not until 2002 that they launched Berry's Own Selection of single malt whiskies. Under the supervision of Spirits Manager Doug McIvor, some 30 expressions are offered every year. They usually bottle at 46% but also offer expressions bottled at cask strength..

Signatory Vintage Scotch Whisky

Founded in 1998 by Andrew and Brian Symington, Signatory lists at least 50 single malts at any one occasion. The most widely distributed range is Cask Strength Collection which sometimes contains spectacular bottlings from distilleries which have long since disappeared. Another range is The Unchillfiltered Collection bottled at 46%. Andrew Symington bought Edradour Distillery from Pernod Ricard in 2002.

Duncan Taylor
www.dtcscotch.com

Duncan Taylor & Co was founded in Glasgow in 1938 and in 2001 Euan Shand bought the company and operations were moved to Huntly. The company bottles around 200 expressions per annum. The range includes Rarest of the Rare (single cask, cask strength whiskies of great age from demolished distilleries), Duncan Taylor Collection (single cask, cask strength malts and grains aged 17-42 years), NC2 (mainly single casks, 12-17 years, non chill-filtered at 46%), Battlehill (younger malts at 43%), Lonach (vattings of two casks from same distillery of the same age to bring them up to a natural strength of over 40%) and Big Smoke (Islay whiskies at 40% and 60%). Duncan Taylor has obtained planning permission to build a new distillery in Huntly and the idea is to make it the first carbon-neutral distillery in Scotland.

Caperdonich 37 years from Duncan Taylor's Lonach range

Sukhinder Singh - owner of The Whisky Exchange

Speciality Drinks
www.thewhiskyexchange.com

Sukhinder Singh, known by most from his two very well-stocked shops in London, The Whisky Exchange, is behind this company. Since 2005 he is also a bottler of malt whiskies operating under the brand name The Single Malts of Scotland. He has around 50 bottlings on offer at any time, either as single casks or batches bottled either at cask strength or at 46%

Blackadder International
www.blackadder.nu

Blackadder is owned by Robin Tucek, together with John Lamond the author of the classic The Malt Whisky File. Apart from the Blackadder and Blackadder Raw cask, there are also a number of other ranges - Aberdeen Distillers, Clydesdale Original and Caledonian Connections. All bottlings are single cask and in the case of Raw Casks they are also completely unfiltered. Most of the bottlings are diluted to 43-45% but there are also cask strength expressions on offer. Around 100 different bottlings are launched each year.

William Cadenhead & Co.
www.wmcadenhead.com

Established in 1842 and owned by J & A Mitchell (who has also owns Springbank) since 1972. The single malts from Cadenheads are never chill-filtered or coloured. When it comes to whisky, they work essentially with three different ranges; Authentic Collection (cask strength), Original Collection (diluted to 46%) and Chairman's Stock (older and rarer whiskies).

New bottlings

It is virtually impossible to list all new bottlings during a year,
there are simply too many and sometimes it is difficult to find information on them.
In this list we have selected more than 450 that were released from late 2007 until autumn 2008.
All bottlings (except for certain official ones) are listed with year of distillation, age,
finish or special maturation (if applicable), alcohol strength and bottler.
Read more about the major independent bottlers on pages 250-251.

Aberlour

	18	43,0%	OB
	31		OB
1995		46,0%	DT
1986	21	50,0%	DL
1990	17	50,0%	DL
1996	12	46,0%	DL
1989	18	46,0%	CAD
1990	17	59,7%	BA

Allt a Bhainne

1996	11	46,0%	DL
1992	15	55,9%	CAD

An Cnoc

	16	46,0%	OB

Ardbeg

	10	46,0%	OB
	Corryvreckan	57,2%	OB
	10 Rennaisance	55,9%	OB
	Blasda	40,0%	OB
	10 Mor (4.5 l)	46,0%	OB
2000	7	62,6%	SD
1993	14	46,0%	CAD
1994	14	58,3%	CAD

Ardmore

1993	13	56,8%	SD

Arran

	Sassicaia	55,0%	OB
	Madeira	55,0%	OB
	Moscatel	55,0%	OB
	St Emilion	55,0%	OB
	12	46,0%	OB
Robert Burns 1998		40,0%	OB
1998	Bourbon Cask	58,0%	OB
1995	11	50,0%	DL
1998	9	46,0%	DL
1996	11	56,5%	CAD

Auchentoshan

	18	55,8%	OB

1957	50	49,1%	OB
	Classic	40,0%	OB
1988 Bordeaux finish		52,4%	OB
1999		46,0%	DT
1990	17	50,0%	DL
1990	18	57,3%	CAD

Auchroisk

1975	33	47,2%	DL
1989	18	60,9%	BA

Aultmore

1997	11	57,5%	CAD
1989	18	50,4%	BA

Balblair

1975		46,0%	OB
1986 duty free		46,0%	OB
	1985 France	55,1%	OB
1990	17	50,0%	DL
1990	18	46,0%	CAD

Balmenach

1990	18	46,0%	IM
1989	19	52,4%	CAD
1990	17	52,9%	BA

Balvenie

Signature 12		40,0%	OB
Balvenie Rose 16 Port		53,4%	OB
	17 Rum	43,0%	OB
1976		53,8%	OB

Banff

1975		45,7%	DT
1971	37	53,0%	DL
1975	32	44,2%	DL

Ben Nevis

1992	14	46,0%	OB
1990		46,0%	DT
1996	11	46,0%	DL
1996	11	60,1%	AD

Benriach

Maderensis 13yo		46,0%	OB
	12	46,0%	OB
	16 Sauternes	46,0%	OB
1976	32	50,3%	OB
1977	31 Moscatel	54,9%	OB
1977	31	51,3%	OB
1978	30 Moscatel	50,0%	OB
1979	28 lt. peated	51,2%	OB
1984	23 Tawny Port	52,4%	OB
1988	19 New Wood	53,6%	OB
1991	16 Claret	52,8%	OB
1994	14 New Wood	54,0%	OB
1996		46,0%	DT
1990	18	50,0%	DL
1996	11	46,0%	DL
1993	14	43,0%	IM
1984	23	54,2%	SD

Benrinnes

1996	11 Tokay	46,0%	IM
1996	12	57,8%	CAD

Benromach

1999 Origins Batch 1		50,0%	OB
	7 Marsala	45,0%	OB
1999	Clipper Lat 53	53,0%	OB
1999	Clipper Lat 55	55,0%	OB
2000	Clipper Lat 57	57,0%	OB
2002	Peat Smoke	46,0%	OB

Bladnoch

	6 Bourbon	57,3%	OB
	6 Sherry	56,9%	OB
	6 Lt peated	58,5%	OB
1992	15	50,0%	DL
1992	15	53,5%	CAD

Blair Athol

1989	18	50,0%	DL
1995	12	46,0%	DL

Bowmore

1964	43 White	42,8%	OB
1992	16 Bordeaux	53,5%	OB

OB = Official bottling from the owner, AD = Adelphi Distillery, BA = Blackadder, BB = Berry Brothers, CAD = Cadenhead, DL = Douglas Laing, DR = Dewar Rattray, DT = Duncan Taylor, GM = Gordon & MacPhail, IM = Ian MacLeod, MM = Murray McDavid, SIG = Signatory, SD = Speciality Drinks

252

1982		55,8%	DT
1987		52,4%	DT
1998		46,0%	DT
1983	25	50,0%	DL
1989	18	50,0%	DL
1992	15	50,0%	DL
1998	9	46,0%	DL
1992	15	46,0%	CAD

Braeval

1995	13	46,0%	IM

Brora

	25	56,3%	OB
1981		54,5%	DT
1981	26	57,1%	SIG
1981	26	46,0%	IM

Bruichladdich

Rocks	46,0%	OB
Peat	46,0%	OB
Waves	46,0%	OB
2001 Bruichladdich	46,0%	OB
1984 Golder Still	46,0%	OB
15 Links Torrey Pines	46,0%	OB
15 Links Birkdale	46,0%	OB
15 Links Valhala	46,0%	OB
1998 Manzanilla	46,0%	OB
1998 Oloroso	46,0%	OB
18 sec ed	46,0%	OB
21	46,0%	OB
16	46,0%	OB
16 Ch Lafite	46,0%	OB
16 Ch Margaux	46,0%	OB
16 Ch Latour	46,0%	OB
16 Ch Y´quem	46,0%	OB
16 Ch Haut B.	46,0%	OB
16 Ch Lafleur	46,0%	OB
2001 PC7	61,0%	OB
5 Octomore	64,5%	OB
1988	46,0%	BB
1988 20	50,0%	DL
1993 14	50,0%	DL
1989 19	50,0%	IM

Bunnahabhain

1970		40,3%	DT
1996	11	50,0%	DL
1999	8	46,0%	DL
1994	13	46,0%	IM
1990	18	46,0%	IM
1979	28	46,0%	SD

Caol Ila

	8 Highland	54,2%	OB
1981		53,8%	DT
1992		46,0%	DT
1975	32	58,4%	SIG
	9	46,0%	DL
1990	17	50,0%	DL
1995	12	50,0%	DL
1998	10	43,0%	IM
1993	15	50,0%	IM
1984	24	48,0%	IM
1992	17	57,9%	SD
1998	9	60,7%	SD
1991	17	46,0%	CAD
1995	12	60,8%	BA
1982	25	57,9%	AD
1984	23	57,3%	AD

Caperdonich

1968		56,0%	DT
1969		44,7%	DT
1970		43,3%	DT
1967	40	42,9%	DL
1973	34	41,5%	DL
1996	11	46,0%	DL
1980	27	56,8%	CAD
1968	37 Madeira	46,2%	MM

Clynelish

1993		46,0%	DT
1971	36	44,6%	DL
1996	11	46,0%	DL
1990	17	46,0%	IM
1991	17	46,0%	IM
1992	15	46,0%	SD
1972	35	53,7%	SD
1992	15	56,4%	CAD
1993	14	57,0%	AD

Convalmore

1975	32	50,0%	DL
1984	23	43,0%	GM

Cragganmore

1993		46,0%	DT
1985	22	56,7%	SD
1993	15	60,0%	CAD
1993	15	59,1%	AD

Craigellachie

1994		56,4%	BB
1996	11	46,0%	DL

Dailuaine

1973	34	50,0%	DL
1996	11 Tokay	43,0%	IM

Dallas Dhu

1981		55,8%	DT
1970	37	50,0%	DL
1971	36	50,0%	DL

Dalmore

Grand Reserva		40,0%	OB
	15	40,0%	OB
1974		42,0%	OB
1263 King Alexander III		40,0%	OB
1990		56,9%	DT
1995	12	46,0%	IM
1990	17	59,7%	AD

Dufftown

1988	19	53,5%	CAD

Edradour

Ballechin Port		46,0%	OB
1997	10 Sauternes	58,1%	OB
1996	11 Rum	57,7%	OB
1994	14	55,8%	OB

Glen Albyn

1974	33	58,9%	BA

Glenallachie

1995		46,0%	DT

Glenburgie

1992	15	58,8%	OB
1996		46,0%	DT

Glencadam

	10	46,0%	OB
	15	46,0%	OB

Glencraig

1976	30	49,6%	SIG

Glendullan

1996		46,0%	DT

Glen Elgin

	16	58,5%	OB
1991	16	50,0%	DL
1991	16	55,1%	AD

Glenesk

1981		56,9%	DT

Glenfarclas

Family Casks,			
11 different vintages			OB
1990	18	54,2%	CAD

Glenfiddich

Vintage 1977		OB

Glen Garioch

1988		55,5%	DT
1989		53,3%	DT
1995	12	46,0%	DL
1990	17	55,8%	AD

Glenglassaugh
1973 34 52,0% DR

Glengoyne
16 Shiraz 48,0% OB
40 OB

Glen Grant
1969		52,3%	DT
1970		51,5%	DT
1972		53,4%	DT
1974		53,8%	DT
1976	31	58,6%	DL
1978	30	45,9%	DL
1985	22	50,0%	DL
1996	11	46,0%	DL
1973	34	54,7%	SD
1993	14	56,2%	CAD
1985	22	62,1%	AD

Glen Keith
1995 13 43,0% IM

Glenlivet
1968		50,6%	DT
1970		51,0%	DT
1971		46,0%	BB
1988	19 Port	56,7%	CAD
1978	29	52,1%	AD

Glenlochy
1980 25 55,3% SIG
1980 27 54,8% DT

Glenlossie
1993 14 Port 57,6% CAD
1988 20 53,9% BA

Glen Mhor
1975 43,5% DT
1975 32 44,1% DL

Glenmorangie
Astar 57,1% OB
Signet 46,0% OB

Glen Moray
1995 Man. Choice 59,6% OB
1991 16 50,0% DL
1992 15 Sauternes 57,9% CAD
1995 13 53,7% BA

Glen Ord
1996 12 46,0% DL
1996 12 58,2% CAD

Glenrothes
1978 43,0% OB

	25	43,0%	OB
1968		53,3%	DT
1969		43,1%	DT
1995	13	61,6%	SIG
1996	11	46,0%	DL
1991	16	46,0%	IM
1991	17	57,7%	CAD
1990	17	46,0%	CAD
1989	19	58,3%	CAD
2000	8	58,0%	AD

Glen Scotia
1992 15 50,0% DL
1975 32 46,0% IM

Glenspey
1992 16 50,0% IM
1993 15 46,0% IM
1995 13 58,8% CAD

Glentauchers
1990 57,6% DT
1992 15 43,0% IM
1989 18 48,7% BA

Glenturret
1990 17 43,0% IM
1987 20 51,6% CAD

Glenugie
1982 26 58,0% DL

Glenury Royal
1984 49,3% DT
1973 34 47,4% BA

Highland Park
1974 Amb. Cask No. 3	44,8%	OB
1979 Amb. Cask No. 4	56,1%	OB
40	48,3%	OB
19 Q of the S	48,1%	OB
1984	50,9%	DT
1986	55,7%	DT
1997	46,0%	DT
1990 17	56,5%	SIG
1978 30	50,0%	DL
1996 11	50,0%	DL
1985 23	50,1%	CAD
1985 22	56,0%	BA
1967 35	40,1%	MM

Imperial
	9	43,0%	DT
1990		53,9%	DT
1994		46,0%	DT
1996		46,0%	DT
1982	25	55,7%	SIG

Inchgower
1992 46,0% DT
1986 21 50,0% DL
1989 18 57,6% CAD

Inverleven
1978 45,5% DT
1979 57,0% DT
1977 30 49,2% SIG

Jura
1974		53,0%	OB
1999	Earth	46,0%	OB
1998	Fire	46,0%	OB
1993	Air	46,0%	OB
1989	Water	50,0%	OB
1996	11	43,0%	IM
1997	10 Tokay	46,0%	IM
1992	15	55,4%	SD
1992	15	53,4%	CAD

Kinclaith
1963 32 40,0% GM

Knockando
1986 21 43,0% OB
1980 49,1% DT

Ladyburn
1973 42,4% DT

Lagavulin
12 56,4% OB
1993 15 Feis Isle 52,9% OB
1984 21 42,0% MM

Laphroaig
	Cairdeas	55,0%	OB
	30 Cairdeas	42,3%	OB
	Triple Wood	48,0%	OB
1990	17	56,3%	SIG
1990		55,6%	BB
	8	46,0%	DL
1989	18	50,0%	DL
1992	15	50,0%	DL
1994	13	50,0%	DL
1999	8	57,6%	SD
1990	18	56,3%	BA
1990	18	56,6%	DR

Ledaig
1997 10 Tokay 46,0% IM
1997 11 57,7% CAD

Linkwood
1981 26 Port 56,9% OB
1981 26 Rum 54,5% OB
1981 26 Red wine 55,5% OB
1996 11 Tokay 46,0% IM

1992	15	46,0%	IM
1988	19	56,9%	SD
1989	18	55,4%	CAD

Linlithgow
1982	25	46,0%	SD

Littlemill
1991	16	50,0%	DL
1990	17	60,1%	CAD

Lochside
1966	40	54,4%	SIG
1981	26	55,8%	BA

Longmorn
1973		46,9%	DT
1995	12	46,0%	DL
1996	11	46,0%	DL
1996	12	43,0%	IM
1990	18	46,0%	CAD

Longrow
	CV	46,0%	OB
	18	46,0%	OB
	7 Gaja Barolo	55,8%	OB

Macallan
Estate Oak		40,0%	OB
	55 Lalique	40,1%	OB
1969		40,4%	DT
1988		53,3%	DT
1989		48,7%	DT
1990		53,3%	DT
1978	28	52,0%	DL
1987	20	54,4%	DL
1989	19	50,0%	DL
1977	30	53,2%	DL
1989	19	54,4%	CAD
1992	15	61,8%	BA
1969	36 Marsanne	41,0%	MM

Macduff
1968		45,2%	DT
1969		40,3%	DT
1990	17	50,0%	DL
1991	17	46,0%	SD

Mannochmore
1996		46,0%	DT

Millburn
1974	33	55,1%	BA

Miltonduff
	8	43,0%	DT
1966		40,0%	DT
1999		46,0%	DT
1990	17	50,0%	DL

Mortlach
1993		46,0%	DT
1991		56,4%	BB
1992	15	50,0%	DL
1988	19	57,6%	CAD
1990	17	57,5%	AD

Mosstowie
1975		48,5%	DT
1979	28	49,9%	SIG

Oban
	18	43,0%	OB

Pittyvaich
1979		54,0%	DT
1995	12	46,0%	DL

Port Ellen
1978	29	55,3%	OB
1981	27 Feis Isle	56,6%	OB
1982	25	59,3%	SIG
1982		46,0%	BB
1979	27	50,0%	DL
1982	25	57,7%	DL
1983	24	46,0%	DL
1982	26	57,6%	IM
1982	25	60,4%	DR

Pulteney
1990	17	54,2%	CAD

Rosebank
1991		43,0%	GM
1990	18	48,0%	IM
1991	16	55,2%	SD
1991	16	55,7%	CAD

Royal Brackla
1995	12	46,0%	DL
1992	15 Rum	57,3%	CAD
1994	13	58,2%	BA

Royal Lochnagar
Distiller's Ediition		40,0%	OB
1984	23	50,0%	DL
1986	21	53,1%	DL

St Magdalene
1982	25	50,0%	DL
1982	25	61,8%	BA

Scapa
1995	12	46,0%	DL

Springbank
1997	11 Batch 2	54,9%	OB
1970	37	53,9%	SIG

1989	18	50,0%	DL
1996	11	50,0%	DL
1995	12	55,7%	BA

Strathisla
1967		47,0%	DT
1968		43,7%	DT
1998	10	43,0%	IM
1987	21 Port	57,1%	CAD
1967	38 Grenache	43,6%	MM

Strathmill
1977	30	50,0%	DL
1989	18	50,0%	DL
1976	31	44,8%	AD

Talisker
	25	54,2%	OB
	30	49,5%	OB

Tamdhu
1968		40,0%	DT
1997	11	46,0%	DL

Tamnavulin
1977	30	50,0%	DL

Teaninich
1971	36	50,0%	DL

Tobermory
	15	46,3%	OB
1995		46,0%	DT
1996		46,0%	DT
1994	13	50,0%	DL
1994	13	59,6%	CAD

Tomatin
	30		OB
	40		OB
1975			OB
1976			
1980			OB
1990			OB
1995			OB
1965		52,1%	DT
1967	40	51,8%	SIG
1975	31	50,0%	DL
1992	15	46,0%	IM
1990	17	59,1%	BA

Tomintoul
Peaty Tang		40,0%	OB
1976		40,0%	OB
	12 Oloroso	40,0%	OB

Tullibardine
1968	40		OB

Whisky Shops

AUSTRIA

Potstill
Strozzigasse 37
1080 Wien
Phone: +43 (0)676 965 89 36
www.potstill.org
Austria's premier whisky shop with over 1100 kinds of which c 900 are malts, including some real rarities. Arranges tastings and seminars and ships to several European countries. On-line ordering.

BELGIUM

Whiskycorner
Kraaistraat 18
3530 Houthalen
Phone: +32 (0)89 386233
www.whiskycorner.be
A very large selection of single malts, no less than 1100 different! Also other whiskies, calvados and grappas. The site is in both French and English. Mail ordering, but not on-line. Shipping worldwide.

Jurgen´s Whiskyhuis
Gaverland 70
9620 Zottegem
Phone: +32 (0)9 336 51 06
www.whiskyhuis.be
An absolutely huge assortment of more than 2,000 different single malts with 700 in stock and the rest delivered within the week. It has an odd assortment, such as 40 different grain whiskies and 120 bourbons. There is also online mail order with shipments worldwide.

DENMARK

Juul´s Vin & Spiritus
Værnedamsvej 15
1819 Frederiksberg
Phone: +45 33 31 13 29
www.juuls.dk
A very large range of wines, fortified wines and spirits. Around 500 single malts. Also a good selection of drinking glasses. On-line ordering. Shipping outside Denmark (except for Scandinavian countries).

Cadenheads Whisky & Lifestyle
Vestergade 21
5000 Odense C
Phone: +45 66 139 505
www.whiskyandlifestyle.com
A whisky specialist with a very good range, not least of Cadenhead's bottlings (c 100 different). Also a

nice range of champagnes, cognacs and rums. Arranges whisky and beer tastings. On-line ordering. Shipping to a few countries outside Denmark.

Whiskyhouse.dk
Peter Bangs Vej 74
2000 Frederiksberg
Phone: +45 38 878 670
www.whiskyhouse.dk
A large range of spirits and beers including c 400 kinds of whisky. Arranges recurrent tastings. On-line ordering.

ENGLAND

The Whisky Exchange (2 shops)
Unit 7, Space Business Park
Abbey Road, Park Royal
London NW10 7SU
Phone: +44 (0)208 838 9388

The Whisky Exchange
Vinopolis, 1 Bank End
London SE1 9BU
Phone: +44 (0)207 403 8688
www.thewhiskyexchange.com
This is a great whisky shop established in 1999 and owned by Sukhinder Singh. Started off as a mail order business which was run from a showroom in Hanwell, but since some years back there is also an excellent shop at Vinopolis in downtown London. The assortment is huge with well over 1 000 single malts to choose from. Some very rare single malts which can hardly be found anywhere else are offered much thanks to Singh's great interest for antique whisky. There are also other types of whisky and cognac, calvados, grappa, rum etc. On-line ordering and ships all over the world.

The Whisky Shop
(See also Scotland, The Whisky Shop)
Unit 1.09 MetroCentre
Red Mall
Gateshead NE11 9YG
Phone: +44 (0)191 460 3777

11 Coppergate Walk
York YO1 9NT
Phone: +44 (0)1904 640300

510 Brompton Walk
Lakeside Shopping Centre
Grays, Essex RM20 2ZL
Phone: +44 (0)1708 866255

7 Turl Street
Oxford OX1 3DQ
Phone: +44 (0)1865 202279

3 Swan Lane
Norwich NR2 1HZ
Phone: +44 (0)1603 618284

7 Queens Head Passage
Paternoster
London EC4M 7DY
Phone: +44 (0)207 329 5117
www.whiskyshop.com
The first shop opened in 1992 in Edinburgh and this is now the United Kingdom's largest specialist retailer of whiskies with 13 outlets.
A large product range with over 700 kinds, including 400 malt whiskies and 140 miniature bottles, as well as accessories and books. The own range 'Glenkeir Treasures' is a special assortment of selected malt whiskies. On-line ordering and shipping all over the world except to the USA.

Royal Mile Whiskies
3 Bloomsbury Street
London WC1B 3QE
Phone: +44 (0)20 7436 4763
www.royalmilewhiskies.com
The London branch of Royal Mile Whiskies. See also Scotland, Royal Mile Whiskies.

Berry Bros. & Rudd
3 St James´ Street
London SW1A 1EG
Phone: +44 (0)870 900 4300
www.bbr.com/whisky
A legendary shop that has been situated in the same place since 1698. One of the world's most reputable wine shops but with an exclusive selection of malt whiskies. There are also shops in Dublin and Hong Kong specialising primarily in fine wines. Mail order for wine only.

The Wright Wine and Whisky Company
The Old Smithy, Raikes Road, Skipton
North Yorkshire BD23 1NP
Phone: +44 (0)1756 700886
www.wineandwhisky.co.uk
A very good selection of over 500 different single malts to choose from. There is also a range of bourbons, blends and Irish whiskeys. 900 different wines are likely to impress the visitor. There is a mail service, but not on-line. Deliveries within UK.

Whiskys.co.uk
The Square, Stamford Bridge
York YO4 11AG
Phone: +44 (0)1759 371356
www.whiskys.co.uk
Good assortment with more than 600 different whiskies. Also has a nice range of armagnac, rum, calvados etc. On-line ordering, ships outside of the UK.

Mainly Malts
3-4 The Courtyard, Bawtry
Doncaster DN10 6JG
Phone: +44 (0)1302 714 700
www.whisky-malts-shop.com
A good range with c 350 different
whiskies of which 260 are single malts.
Arranges tastings and seminars. On-line
ordering with shipping also outside
the UK.

Nickolls & Perks
37 Lower High Street, Stourbridge
West Midlands DY8 1TA
Phone: +44 (0)1384 394518
www.nickollsandperks.co.uk
A company dating back to 1797. Mostly
known as wine merchants but also has
a good range of whiskies with c 300
different kinds including 200 single
malts. On-line ordering with shipping
also outside of UK.

The Wine Shop (2 shops)
22 Russell Street, Leek
Staffordshire ST13 5JF
Phone: +44 (0)1538 382408

56 Lawton Street, Congleton
Cheshire CW12 1RS
Phone: +44 (0)1260 295 415
www.wineandwhisky.com
In addition to wine there is a good
range of c 300 whiskies and also
calvados, cognacs, rums, continental
beer etc. They also stock a range
of their own single malt bottlings
under the name of 'The Queen of the
Moorlands'. Mailorders can be made by
telephone or email for UK delivery.

The Lincoln Whisky Shop
87 Bailgate
Lincoln LN1 3AR
Phone: +44 (0)1522 537834
www.lincolnwhiskyshop.co.uk
Mainly specialising in whisky with more
than 400 different whiskies but also
500 spirits and liqueurs and some 100
wines. Mailorder only within UK.

Milroys of Soho
3 Greek Street
London W1D 4NX
Phone: +44 (0)20 7437 2385
www.milroys.co.uk
A classic whisky shop in Soho founded
by John Milroy in 1964 but now owned
by the retail wine merchant Jeroboams
Group. A very good range with over
700 malts and a wide selection of
whiskies from around the world.
Supplementing this are selected fine
wines. Tastings are arranged in the
tasting cellar in the shop. On-line
ordering for shipping within the UK.
If contacted directly they can ship to
other countries as well.

The Covent Garden Whisky Shop
3 Russell Street, Covent Garden
London WC2B 5JD
Phone: +44 (0)20 7379 4640
www.coventgardenwhiskyshop.co.uk

One in a chain of shops owned by
independent bottlers Cadenhead. Sells
Cadenhead's product range and c 200
other whiskies. Ordering via email or
telephone.

The Vintage House
42 Old Compton Street
London W1D 4LR
Phone: +44 (0)20 7437 5112
www.sohowhisky.com
A huge range of over 1400 kinds of
malt whisky. Many are rare or unusual
and attract collectors. Supplementing
this is also a selection of fine wines.
On-line ordering with shipping only
within the UK.

The Wee Dram
5 Portland Square, Bakewell
Derbyshire DE45 1HA
Phone: +44 (0)1629 812235
www.weedram.co.uk
Large range of Scotch single malts (c
350) with whiskies from other parts of
the world and a good range of whisky
books. Run 'The Wee Drammers Whisky
Club' with tastings and seminars. On-
line ordering.

Whisky On-line
Units 1-3 Concorde House, Charnley
Road, Blackpool, Lancashire FY1 4PE
Phone: +44 (0)1253 620376
www.whisky-online.com
A good selection of whisky and also
cognac, rum, port etc. On-line ordering
with shipping all over the world. They
also arrange recurrent tastings

Constantine Stores
30 Fore Street
Constantine, Falmouth
Cornwall TR11 5AB
Phone: +44 (0)1326 340226
www.drinkfinder.co.uk
The shop was established in 1957
and seven years ago it started web
mailorder. It is a full-range wine and
spirits dealer with a good selection of
whiskies from the whole world (around
800 different, of which 600 are single
malts). Worldwide shipping except for
USA and Canada.

FRANCE

La Maison du Whisky (2 shops)
20 rue d'Anjou
75008 Paris
Phone: +33 (0)1 42 65 03 16

47 rue Jean Chatel
97400 Saint-Denis
Phone: +33 (0)2 62 21 31 19
www.whisky.fr
France's largest whisky specialist with
over 1000 whiskies in stock. Also a
number of own-bottled single malts.
Two shops and on-line ordering. Ships
to some 20 countries.

GERMANY

Celtic Whisk(e)y & Versand
Otto Steudel
Bulmannstrasse 26
90459 Nürnberg
Phone: +49 (0)911 450974-30
www.whisky.de/celtic
A very impressive single malt range
with well over 1000 different single
malts and a good selection from other
parts of the world. On-line ordering
with shipping also outside Germany.

SCOMA - Scotch Malt Whisky GmbH
Am Bullhamm 17
26441 Jever
Phone: +49 (0)4461 912237
www.scoma.de
Very large range of c 750 Scottish malts
and many from other countries. Holds
regular seminars and tastings. The
excellent, monthly whisky newsletter
SCOMA News is produced and can be
downloaded as a pdf-file from the
website. On-line ordering.

The Whisky Store
Am Grundwassersee 4
82402 Seeshaupt
Phone: +49 (0)8801-23 17
www.thewhiskystore.com
A very large range comprising c 700
kinds of whisky of which 550 are malts.
Also sells whisky liqueurs, books and
accessories. The website is a veritable
goldmine of information about the
whisky business and especially so
when it comes to photographs of
distilleries. There are 7500 photos of
168 distilleries. On-line ordering.

Cadenhead´s Whisky Market
Luxemburger Strasse 257
50939 Köln
Phone: +49 (0)221-2831834
www.cadenhead.de
This first Cadenhead shop outside of
the UK was established in 2001. Good
range of malt whiskies (c 350 different
kinds) with emphasis on Cadenhead's
own bottlings. Other products include
wine, cognac and rum etc. Arranges
recurring tastings and also has an on-
line shop.

Cadenhead´s Whisky Market
Fasanenstrasse 4
10623 Berlin-Charlottenburg
Phone: +49 (0)30-30831444
www.cadenhead-berlin.de
Cadenhead's second German shop.
Good product range with c 350
different kinds of malt with emphasis
on Cadenhead's own bottlings as well
as wine, cognac and rum etc. Arranges
recurrent tastings.

Malts and More
Hosegstieg 11
22880 Wedel
Phone: +49 (0)40-23620770
www.maltsandmore.de
Very large assortment with over 500

different single malts from Scotland.
Islay whiskies are well represented.
Also a small selection of cognac, rum
etc. Only on-line orders.

Whiskywizard.de
Christian Jaudt
Schulstrasse 57
66540 Neunkirchen
Phone: +49 (0)6858-699507
www.whiskywizard.de
Large assortment of single malt (over
500) and other spirits. Only orders on-
line, shipping also outside Germany.

Whisky-Doris
Germanenstrasse 38
14612 Falkensee
Phone: +49 (0)3322-219784
www.whisky-doris.de
Large range of over 300 whiskies
and also sells own special bottlings.
Orders via email. Shipping also outside
Germany.

Finlays Whisky Shop
Köpperner Strasse 109
61273 Wehrheim-Saalburgsiedlung
Phone: +49 (0)6081 - 58 67 15
www.finlayswhiskyshop.de
Whisky specialists with a large range
of around 700 single malts. Finlays
also work as the importer to Germany
of Douglas Laing, James MacArthur
and Wilson & Morgan. There is an
impressive listing of 700 bottlings of
Port Ellen on the website. Shop in
Wehrheim as well as on-line orders.

Weinquelle Lühmann
Lübeckerstrasse 145
22087 Hamburg
Phone: +49 (0)40-25 63 91
www.weinquelle.com
A very impressive selection of both
wines and spirits in this shop. Among
over 1000 different whiskies of which
850 are malt whiskies. In addition
there are 2500 kinds of wine and other
spirits, including an impressive range
of rums. General information about
whisky on the site, part of which is in
English. On-line ordering with shipping
also possible outside Germany.

Liquids
Heerstrasse 350
50169 Kerpen-Brüggen
Phone: +49 (0)2237-975491
www.liquids-and-more.de
A good range (over 200 single malts)
and a fine assortment of whiskies
from other countries. Also books and
accessories. On-line ordering.

The Whisky-Corner
Reichertsfeld 2
92278 Illschwang
Phone: +49 (0)9666-951213
www.whisky-corner.de
A small shop but large on mail order.
A very large assortment of over 1200
whiskies. Also sells blended and
American whiskies. The website is very

informative with features on, among
others, whisky-making, tasting and
independent bottlers. On-line ordering.

World Wide Spirits
Hauptstrasse 12
84576 Teising
Phone: +49 (0)8633 50 87 93
www.worldwidespirits.de
A nice range of c 500 whiskies with
some rarities from the twenties. Also
large selection (c 1000) of other spirits.
On-line ordering.

Banneke
Kreuzeskirchstr. 37
45127 Essen
Phone: +49 (0)201 247710
www.banneke.de
Very impressive assortment of 4500
different kinds of spirit and wine. Good
range of malt whiskies (c 400) and
rum (c 200). On-line ordering and will
deliver outside of Germany.

WhiskyKoch
Weinbergstrasse 2
64285 Darmstadt
Phone: +49 (0152) 29 51 75 72
www.whiskykoch.de
The English chef, Christopher Pepper,
and his wife Marion opened up this
interesting combination of a whisky
shop and a restaurant end of 2007. The
shop has a nice selection of single malts
as well as other Scottish products and
the restaurant has specialised in whisky
dinners and tastings.

Whisk(e)y Shop Tara
Rindermarkt 16
80331 München
Phone: +49 (0)89-26 51 18
www.whiskyversand.de
Whisky specialists with a very broad
range of, for example, 800 different
single malts. On-line ordering.

Mara Malt-Rarities
Roland Puhl & Co. GbR
Cahenslystr. 14
65549 Limburg
Phone: +49 (0)6431-41176
Phone: +49 (0)6432-508690
www.maltwhisky-mara.com
Probably the main experts on rare
whisky offering over 1000 kinds. Also
arranges tastings. Mail orders by fax or
phone. Shipping also outside Germany.

Single Malt Collection
(Glen Fahrn Germany GmbH)
Hauptstraße 38
79801 Hohentengen a. H.
Phone: +49 (0)77 42 -857 222
www.whisky-wagner.de
A very large range of Scottish single
malts (c 600). Newsletter. On-line
ordering. Shipping also outside
Germany.

Kierzek
Weitlingstrasse 17
10317 Berlin
Phone: +49 (0)30 525 11 08
www.kierzek-berlin.de

This shop in Berlin was established
already in 1910. There are over 400
different whiskies in stock (of which
250 are single malts). In the product
range 50 kinds of rum and 450 wines
from all over the world are found
among other products. The owner
is also one of the organisers of the
whisky festival „Cöpenicker Whisky
Herbst" in Berlin. Mail order is
available within Germany.

Whisky & Cigars
Sophienstrasse 8-9
10178 Berlin-Mitte
Phone: +49 (0)30 2820376
www.whisky-cigars.de
Over 1000 kinds of whisky and a large
selection of cigars from all over the
world. Tastings are arranged. No mail
order.

House of Whisky
Ackerbeeke 6
31683 Obernkirchen
Phone: +49 (0)5724-399420
www.houseofwhisky.de
Aside from over 500 different malts
also sells a large range of other spirits
(including over 100 kinds of rum).
On-line ordering with shipping also
outside Germany.

Whiskyscheune
Alte Bornstrasse 4
61250 Usingen-Eschbach
Phone: +49 (0)6081-582642
www.whiskyscheune.de
Large selection with c 400 Scottish
malts in addition to whiskies from
other countries. Only mail order.

Whiskyworld
Ziegelfeld 6
94481 Grafenau / Haus i. Wald
Phone: +49 (0)8555-406 320
www.whiskyworld.de
A good assortment of c 450 whiskies
including more than 200 malts. Also
has a good range of wines, other
spirits, cigars and books. On-line
ordering, shipping to Germany, Austria,
Switzerland and Liechtenstein.

Whisky Spirits
Wallstraße 23
60594 Frankfurt
Phone: +49 (0)69-96 20 06 43

Berlinerstrasse 39
60311 Frankfurt
Phone: +49 (0)69-36 70 33 44
www.whiskyspirits.de
Large assortment of over 500 whiskies.
Tastings with different themes. No
on-line mail order but goods can be
sent home.

Dudelsack (4 shops)
Treibgasse 6
63739 Aschaffenburg
Phone: +49 (0)6021-219654
www.dudelsack.com
One of four in a chain with the
three other outlets in Limburg,

Mainz and Frankfurt. All shops hold recurring whisky seminars. The whisky wholesaler Whisky Max is included in the chain.

Kirschgarten 4, 55116 Mainz
Phone: +49 (0)6131-3297518
www.whisky-selection.de
Large assortment of more than 300 kinds of Scottish single malts. On-line ordering.

Bischofsplatz 1, 65549 Limburg
Phone: +49 (0)6431-590388
www.dudelsack-limburg.de

My Whisky Frankfurt
Textorstrasse 2-4 , 60594 Frankfurt a.M.
Phone: +49 (0)69-60607524

Casa Verde
Ährenweg 14
79258 Hartheim
Phone: +49 (0)7633 101856
www.casa-ver.de
A shop with a good selection of more than 500 whiskies and 100 grappas. There is also a tasting-room and arranged tastings through its own whisky club. Orders via email.

Grandwhisky
Saint-Priest Strasse 14 A
63165 Mühlheim
Shop: Bahnhofstrasse 60, Mühlheim
Phone: +49 (0)6108-8240987
www.grandwhisky.de
Has a good selection of Irish whiskeys as well as Scottish. Arranges tastings and has useful information on a number of distilleries on the website. On-line ordering.

Wine, Spirits & Cigars
(Whiskypack Spirituosenhandel)
Schnakenberg 15-19
31608 Marklohe/Lemke
Phone: +49 (0)5021-888150
www.whiskypack.de
Has a nice selection of cigars in addition to whisky, wines and spirits. On-line ordering.

World Wide Whisky
Eisenacher Strasse 64
10823 Berlin-Schöneberg
Phone: +49 (0)30-7845010
www.world-wide-whisky.de
A shop combined with a pub. Arranges tastings and seminars. Has a large number of rarities. Orders can be made via email.

IRELAND

Celtic Whiskey Shop
27-28 Dawson Street
Dublin 2
Phone: +353 (0)1 675 9744
www.celticwhiskeyshop.com
More than 60 kinds of Irish whiskeys but also a good selection of Scotch. Also sells wines and other spirits. On-line ordering with shipping all over the world.

THE NETHERLANDS

Whiskyslijterij De Koning
Hinthamereinde 41
5211 PM 's Hertogenbosch
Phone: +31 (0)73-6143547
www.whiskykoning.nl
An enormous assortment with more than 1400 kinds of whisky including c 800 single malts. Also whisky-related items like decanters, books etc. Arranges recurring tastings. The site is in Dutch and English. On-line ordering. Shipping all over the world.

Whisky- en Wijnhandel Verhaar
Planetenbaan 2a
3721 LA Bilthoven
Phone: +31 (0)30-228 44 18
www.whiskyshop.nl
A wide selection of wines and spirits with no fewer than 1300 whiskies of which 1000 come from Scotland. Email orders.

Wijnhandel van Zuylen
Loosduinse Hoofdplein 201
2553 CP Loosduinen (Den Haag)
Phone: +31 (0)70-397 1400
www.whiskyvanzuylen.nl
Excellent range of whiskies (c 500) and wines. Email orders with shipping to some ten European countries.

Wijnwinkel-Slijterij
Ton Overmars
Hoofddorpplein 11
1059 CV Amsterdam
Phone: +31 (0)20-615 71 42
www.tonovermars.nl
A very large assortment of wines, spirits and beer which includes more than 400 single malts. Arranges recurring tastings. Orders via email with shipping to ten European countries.

Van Wees - Whiskyworld.nl
Leusderweg 260
3817 KH Amersfoort
Phone: +31 (0)33-461 53 19
www.whiskyworld.nl
A very large range of 1000 whiskies including over 500 single malts. On-line ordering.

Cadenhead
Rozengracht 232
1016 SZ Amsterdam
Phone: +31 (0)20-3306287
www.cadenhead.nl
Specialises in Cadenhead's bottlings (c 200 different) but also a good range of another 300 whiskies. Arranges recurrent tastings. On-line ordering.

Le Cellier Amsterdam
Spuistraat 116
1012 VA Amsterdam
Phone: +31 (0)20-638 65 73
www.lecellier.nl
A wide range of spirits, not least vodkas, wines and fortified wines. 200 single malts.

NEW ZEALAND

Whisky Galore
797 Colombo Street
Christchurch 8013
Phone: +64 (3) 377 6824
www.whiskygalore.co.nz
The best whisky shop in New Zealand with 550 different whiskies, approximately 350 which are single malts. The owner Michael Fraser Milne, has also founded The Whisky Guild which has, as one of its aims, to produce exclusive single cask bottlings for members. There is also online mail-order shipping within New Zealand.

POLAND

George Ballantine´s
Krucza str 47 A, Warsaw
Phone: +48 22 625 48 32

Pulawska str 22, Warsaw
Phone: +48 22 542 86 22
www.sklep-ballantines.pl
These two shops have the biggest assortment in Poland with more than 360 different single malts. Apart from whisky there is a full range of spirits and wines from all over the world. Recurrent tastings are arranged and mail-orders are dispatched. The owners of the shops, Tudor House, also import whiskies for other vendors in Poland.

PORTUGAL

Whisky & Co
Rua Visconde de Seabra 12-A
1700-370 Lisboa
Phone: +351 217 933 314
www.whiskyco.com
Established in 2001 this is the foremost whisky shop in Portugal with more than 800 different whiskies and also a Whisky Museum with more than 10.000 bottles on display.

RUSSIA

Whisky World Shop
9, Tverskoy Boulevard
123104 Moscow
Phone: +7 495 787 9150
www.whiskyworld.ru
This shop was opened in 2003 in the centre of Moscow, close to the Kremlin. The assortment is huge with more than 1,000 different single malts, mainly from independent bottlers. It also stocks a selection of rare and old whiskies bought at auctions and private collectors and a blended Scotch under their own label, Glen Clyde. The range is supplemented with a nice range of cognac, armagnac, calvados, grappa and wines. Tastings are arranged but no mail order is available due to Russian law.

SCOTLAND

Gordon & MacPhail
58 - 60 South Street, Elgin
Moray IV30 1JY
Phone: +44 (0)1343 545110
www.gordonandmacphail.com
A legendary shop that opened already
in 1895 in Elgin. The owners are
perhaps the most well-known among
independent bottlers. The shop stocks
more than 800 bottlings of whisky
and more than 600 wines and there is
also a delicatessen counter with high-
quality grocery products. Tastings can
be arranged in the shop and there are
shipping services both within the UK
and overseas. The shop was refurbished
two years ago and now attracts visitors
from all over the world.

Royal Mile Whiskies (2 shops)
379 High Street, The Royal Mile
Edinburgh EH1 1PW
Phone: +44 (0)131 2253383

3 Bloomsbury Street
London WC1B 3QE
Phone: +44 (0)20 7436 4763
www.royalmilewhiskies.com
Royal Mile Whiskies is one of the most
well-known whisky retailers in the
UK. It was established in Edinburgh in
1991. There is also a shop in London
since 2002 and a cigar shop close to
the Edinburgh shop. The whisky range
is outstanding with many difficult to
find elsewhere and they are skilled in
finding odd types, such as grain whisky
and Japanese whiskies. They have the
most comprehensive commercial site
regarding information on regions,
distilleries, production, tasting etc.
Royal Mile Whiskies also arranges
'Whisky Fringe' in Edinburgh, a two-
day whisky festival which takes place
annually in mid August. On-line
ordering with worldwide shipping.

The Whisky Shop
(See also England, The Whisky Shop)
Buchanan Galleries
220 Buchanan Street
Glasgow G1 2GF
Phone: +44 (0)141 331 0022

17 Bridge Street
Inverness IV1 1HD
Phone: +44 (0)1463 710525

11 Main Street
Callander FK17 8DU
Phone: +44 (0)1877 331936

93 High Street
Fort William PH33 6DG
Phone: +44 (0)1397 706164

Station Road
Oban PA34 4NU
Phone: +44 (0)1631 564409

28 Victoria Street
Edinburgh EH1 2JW
Phone: +44 (0)131 225 4666

Unit 23
Princes Mall
Edinburgh EH1 1BQ
Phone: +44 (0)131 558 7563

www.whiskyshop.com
The first shop opened in 1992 in
Edinburgh and this is now the United
Kingdom's largest specialist retailer
of whiskies with 13 outlets. A large
product range with over 700 kinds,
including 400 malt whiskies and 140
miniature bottles, as well as accessories
and books. The own range 'Glenkeir
Treasures' is a special assortment
of selected malt whiskies. On-line
ordering and shipping all over the
world except to the USA.

Loch Fyne Whiskies
Inveraray
Argyll PA32 8UD
Phone: +44 (0)1499 302 219
www.lfw.co.uk
This is a legendary shop in western
Scotland with an equally legendary
owner, Richard Joynson. Joynson is
known as a person with a high degree
of integrity who does not mince his
words on whisky matters and also
has a solid knowledge of whisky.
Loch Fyne Whiskies are devoted to
selling only whisky and whisky-related
items. The range of malt whiskies is
large and they have their own house
blend, the prize-awarded Loch Fyne,
as well as their 'The Loch Fyne Whisky
Liqueur'. There is also a range of house
malts called 'The Inverarity'. Loch
Fyne Whiskies also publish the highly
readable 'Scotch Whisky Review' which
previously was produced by Joynson
but now has authorities such as Charles
MacLean and Dave Broom on the staff.
Also on-line ordering with worldwide
shipping.

Duncan Taylor's "Whiskies of Scotland"
Gordon Street, Huntly
Aberdeenshire,
Phone: +44 (0)1466 794055
www.dtcscotch.com
Duncan Taylor is one of Scotland's
largest independent bottlers and has
quite recently opened a new shop in
Huntly which sells videos, books and
DVDs on whisky as well as the whole
Duncan Taylor range.

Parker's Whisky
27 Low Street, Banff AB45 1AU
Phone: +44 (0)1261 812353
www.parkerswhisky.co.uk
Dedicated malt whisky specialist with
a very nice range of more than 500
malt whiskies. On-line ordering with
worldwide shipping.

The Whisky Shop Dufftown
1 Fife Street, Dufftown, Keith
Moray AB55 4AL
Phone: +44 (0)1340 821097
www.whiskyshopdufftown.co.uk
Whisky specialist in Dufftown in the
heart of Speyside, wellknown to
many of the Speyside festival visitors.
More than 200 single malts as well as
other kinds of whisky. Also arranges
tastings as well as special events during
the Festivals. On-line ordering with
worldwide shipping.

The Scotch Whisky Experience
354 Castlehill, Royal Mile
Edinburgh
Phone: +44 (0)131 220 0441
www.whisky-heritage.co.uk
The Scotch Whisky Heritage Centre is
of course a must for whisky devotees
visiting Edinburgh. This is a unique,
interactive visitor centre dedicated
to the history of Scotch whisky. You
can join a tour and discover all the
aspects of whisky making. The Model
Distillery and the Whisky Barrel Ride
are among the highlights. This five-
star visitor attraction, which receives c
250 000 visitors a year, has an excellent
whisky shop with almost 300 different
whiskies in stock. The shop is open
to the general public and not only to
those who have taken the whisky tour.
Do not miss the award-winning Amber
Restaurant with its whisky advisor
who advises guests when they wish to
choose whisky to go with the food.
The ingredients are mainly from
Scotland and whisky is sometimes used
in the cooking.

**Cadenhead's Campbeltown Whisky
shop (Eaglesome)**
7 Bolgam Street
Campbeltown
Argyll PA28 6HZ
Phone: +44 (0)1586 551710
www.wmcadenhead.com
One in a chain of shops owned by
independent bottlers Cadenhead.
Sells Cadenhead's products and other
whiskies with a good range of, for
example, Springbank. On-line ordering.

Cadenheads Whisky Shop
172 Canongate, Royal Mile
Edinburgh EH8 8BN
Phone: +44 (0)131 556 5864
www.wmcadenhead.com
The oldest shop in a chain owned by
independent bottlers Cadenhead. Sells
Cadenhead's product range and a good
selection of other whiskies and spirits.
Arranges recurrent tastings. On-line
ordering.

Robbie's Drams
3 Sandgate, Ayr
South Ayrshire KA7 1BG
Phone: +44 (0)1292 262 135
www.robbiesdrams.co.uk
A whisky specialist with a very good
on-line shop as well. Large selection
with almost 600 kinds of Scotch malt
whisky and another 200 whiskies,
including a well-developed assortment
of Japanese malts.

Single Malts Direct
36 Gordon Street
Huntly AB54 8EQ
Phone: +44 (0)845 6066145
www.singlemaltsdirect.com
Very good assortment including an exciting range of own bottlings. Good selection of whisky literature. Emphasis on on-line orders, shipping worldwide.

Luvian's Bottle Shop (2 shops)
93 Bonnygate, Cupar
Fife KY15 4LG
Phone: +44 (0)1334 654 820

66 Market Street, St Andrews
Fife KY16 9NT
Phone: +44 (0)1334 477752
www.luvians.com
Wine and whisky merchant with a very nice selection of more than 600 malt whiskies.

The Maltman
(S. R. & E. Barron (Dyce) Ltd.)
119 Victoria Street, Dyce
Aberdeen AB21 7BJ
Phone: +44 (0)1224 722208
www.maltman.co.uk
Specialises in malt whiskies from Scotland. A good range with almost 400 kinds, including a 'Collector's Corner' with some very rare malts. There is a mail order service, but not on-line. Only shipping within the UK.

Spirit of Galloway
191 King Street
Castle Douglas DG7 1DZ
Phone: +44(0)1556 504654
www.drambusters.com
This new branch of TB Watsons displays a selection of 400 malt whiskies, along with a wide choice of other spirits and liqueurs from around the world.

Robert Graham Ltd (2 shops)
194 Rose Street
Edinburgh EH2 4AZ
Phone: +44 (0)131 226 1874

Finlay House
10-14 West Nile Street
Glasgow G1 2PP
Phone: +44 (0)141 248 7283
www.whisky-cigars.co.uk
A company with its traditions established already in 1874 specialising in Scotch whisky and cigars. They have a nice assortment of malt whiskies (c 100) and their range of cigars is impressive – no less than 160 Cuban cigars and 175 non-Cuban. On-line ordering with shipping all over the world in addition to shops in Edinburgh and Glasgow.

Angel's Share Whisky
9 Friars Street
Stirling
Stirlingshire FK8 1HA
Phone: +44 (0)1786 451 620
www.angelsshare-whisky.com
A newly established shop which is dedicated to whisky with around 350 single malts in the range, some

of which are very rare. There is also mailorder but currently only delivers within the UK

Whisky Castle
Main Street
Tomintoul
Aberdeenshire AB37 9EX
Phone: +44 (0)1807 580 213
www.whiskycastle.co.uk
A classical whisky specialist situated in the heart of malt whisky country. With over 500 single malts, the specialisation is in independent bottlings. There is also a mail order shipping worldwide with the exception of USA.

John Scott & Miller
15-19 Bridge Street, Kirkwall
Orkney KW15 1HR
Phone: +44 (0)1856 873146
www.jsmorkney.co.uk
The best whisky shop in the Orkneys. A very large range of whisky from all over the world and, naturally, a special selection from Orkneys' two distilleries Highland Park and Scapa. There is also a range of Havana, Dominican Republic and Dutch cigars.

Drinkon
Allanhill, Grange Road
St Andrews, Fife KY16 8LJ
Phone: +44 (0)1334 477333
www.drinkon.com
A large assortment of wine, whisky, armagnac, cognac and other spirits and liqueurs with c 200 single malts to choose from. On-line orders only and shipping within the UK.

Scotch Malt Whisky Society
www.smws.com
A society with more than 20 000 members worldwide. They are specialised in own bottlings of single casks and release between 150 and 200 bottlings a year. Orders on-line for members only. Shipping only within UK (see www.smws.com for addresses to national branches of SMWS).

SWITZERLAND

P. Ullrich AG
Schneidergasse 27
4051 Basel
Phone: +41 (0)61 338 90 91
Another two shops in Basel:
Laufenstrasse 16
Unt. Rebgasse 18
www.ullrich.ch
A very large range of wines, spirits, beers, accessories and books. Over 800 kinds of whisky with almost 600 single malt. On-line ordering. Deliveries mainly within Switzerland.

Eddie's Whiskies
Dorfgasse 27
8810 Horgen
Phone: +41 (0)43 244 63 00
www.eddies.ch

A whisky specialist with emphasis on single malts (more than 500 different). Arranges tastings.

World of Whisky
Via dim Lej 6
7500 St. Moritz
Phone: +41 (0)81 852 33 77
www.world-of-whisky.ch
This is a legendary shop situated in the Hotel Waldhaus Am See which has an even more legendary whisky bar, the Devil's Place. It was created by one man, Claudio Bernasconi, owner of the hotel and a whisky aficionado. With over 2,500 different whiskies, the bar even appears in the Guinness Book of Records. The shop which is run by Christian Lauper, stocks almost 1,000 different whiskies and apart from whisky there is a good range of other spirits such as rum, cognac and armagnac. There is also a World of Whisky Malt Club and mail order.

Glen Fahrn
Fahrnstrasse 39
9402 Mörschwil
Phone: +41 (0)71 860 09 87
www.glenfahrn.com
A wide range of spirits, fortified wines and champagnes. A large selection of whisky, with over 600 from Scotland. On-line ordering. Ships within Switzerland and to adjacent countries.

Monnier
Büetigenstrasse 30
2557 Studen
Phone: +41 (0)32 373 43 53
www.whiskytime.ch
A large range of whisky including 600 single malts. Also grappas and champagnes. On-line ordering. Shipping mainly within Switzerland.

Scot & Scotch
Wohllebgasse 7
8001 Zürich
Phone: +41 (0)1 211 90 60
www.scotandscotch.ch
A Whisky specialist with a great selection including c 560 single malts. Mail orders, but no on-line ordering. Current pricelist can be obtained through email.

Angels Share Shop
Unterdorfstrasse 15
5036 Oberentfelden
Phone: +41 (0)62 724 83 74
www.angelsshare.ch
A combined restaurant, lounge and whisky shop. More than 400 different kinds of whisky as well as a good range of cigars. Scores extra points for short information and photos of all distilleries (also non-Scottish ones). On-line ordering.

New Books We Enjoyed

It seems that last year´s *The Legend of Laphroaig* by Hans Offringa started a trend in portraying single distilleries. Gavin D Smith for example, made an excellent presentation of another of Islay´s large distilleries this year with his *Ardbeg: A Peaty Provenance*

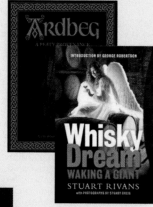

(216 pages) and *Whisky Dream: Waking a Giant* (224 pages) by Stuart Rivans and Stuart Greig was also published. This tells the story of one man, Mark Reynier and his passionate dream of resurrecting two distilleries, Bruichladddich and Port Charlotte. From Sweden comes the second book by Ulf Buxrud who saw great

success with his Rare Malts a few years ago. Ulf has now turned towards the east with his *Japanese Whisky - facts, figures and taste* (160 pages) which is a much-longed for insight into Japanese whisky production. Charles MacLean is the editor of the very handy and comprehensive *Eye Witness Companion to Whisky* (288 pages) and Dominic Roskrow has written the perfect guide for the beginner - *Whiskies* (192 pages) in the Collin´s "Need to know" series. Finally a whisky book from Russia appeared, *World Whisky Guide* (362 pages) by Erkin Tuzmuhamedov - the foremost whisky writer in Russia and who is also the editor of the only whisky magazine in the country.

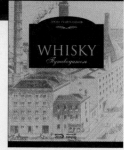

Ardbeg: A Peaty Provenance
ISBN 978-0955414565

Whisky Dream: Waking a Giant
ISBN 978-1841586816

Japanese Whisky - facts, figures and taste
ISBN 978-9163320934

Eyewitness Companion to Whisky
ISBN 978-1405328142

Whiskies (Collins Need to Know)
ISBN 978-0007261642

World Whisky Guide
ISBN 462-0000260127

Recommended Magazines

Malt Advocate
www.maltadvocate.com

Whisky Magazine
www.whiskymag.com

Whisky Time
www.whiskytime-magazin.com

Der Whisky-Botschafter
www.whiskybotschafter.com

Whisky Watch
www.whiskywatch.de

Allt om Whisky
www.alltomwhisky.nu

New Websites To Watch

blog.maltadvocate.com

This blog, also known as *What Does John Know*, was started a year ago by John Hansell, the founder and editor of the famous whisky magazine *Malt Advocate*. John has long since been considerably better positioned than most of us through his unique network, knowing anyone who is anyone in the whisky business. He often takes advantage of this being the first with breaking news concerning new bottlings or take-overs of companies.

www.spiritofislay.net

OK, this is not a new website about whisky. It has been around for some years now but since we for some reason have not mentioned it in previous editions of the Yearbook (even though we visit it regularly) we list it under this header. Gordon Homer has created the ultimate site about whiskies from Islay but there is also much to be learned about the island itself. His recurring column is titled *Whiff of Peat Smoke* but there is also a forum and a chat room.

www.caskstrength.net

Joel and Neil deliver tasting notes - maybe not an original theme these days but the notes are well written and recently they have started adding reports from trips and interviews with people in the business. There is a good potential here for the future.

www.scotchchix.com

This site is rather unusual in that it is a blog run by two women! According to them "it is time for women to claim Scotch as their own drink." As with most other blogs there is a wealth of tasting notes, but it really shines with the headline *The saga of the scotch chix*. These essays are so well-written and to the point that you really don´t care if it covers which glasses are the best to enjoy malt whisky or which whisky the characters in *Sex and the City* would order if they weren´t drinking Cosmos.

www.thewhiskychannel.com

Ian Buxton, well-known whisky writer, whisky consultant, publisher and director of *World Whiskies Conference* has mysteriously been able to find time to establish thewhiskychannel.com as well - a gateway to just about anything whisky related. Ian Buxton is also the administrator of the whisky version of Wikipedia - *Whiskipedia* at www.whiskipedia.org.

Some of Our Old Favourites

www.maltmadness.com
Our all-time favourite with something for everyone. Managed by malt maniac Johannes van den Heuvel.

www.maltmaniacs.org
A bunch of knowledgeable whisky lovers dissect, debate, attack and praise the varying phenomena of the whisky world.

www.nonjatta.blogspot.com
A blog by Chris Bunting with a wealth of interesting information on Japanese whisky as well as Japanese culture.

www.thescotchblog.com
Still the best whiskyblog! Kevin Erskine has managed to keep the quality at the highest level.

drwhisky.blogspot.com
Sam Simmons delivers tasting notes that include exciting stories and reflections about distilleries, people and events.

www.whiskycast.com
The best whisky-related podcast on the internet and one that sets the standard for podcasts in other genres as well.

www.whisky-news.com
Apart from daily news, this site contains tasting notes, distillery portraits, lists of retailers, whisky clubs, events etc.

www.onlymalts.com
Norway's best whisky site with features on distilleries, whisky production, whisky history and a discussion forum.

www.whiskyforum.se
Swedish whisky forum with more than 1,800 enthusiasts. Excellent debate as well as more than 2,000 tasting notes.

www.whisky-pages.com
Top class whisky site with features, directories, tasting notes, book reviews, whisky news, glossary and a forum.

www.whiskynyt.dk
A Danish whisky site with emphasis on an active members' forum. Updated news on whisky is also presented.

www.whiskymag.com
The official website of the printed 'Whisky Magazine'. A very active whisky forum with over 3000 registered members.

www.thewhiskystore.de
German whisky dealer with more than 7 500 photos of 168 distilleries on the site.

www.whisky.de
German site managed by Dr. Clemens Dillman, author of '*W wie Whisky*' who also produces the newsletter Whisky Flash.

www.whisky-distilleries.info
A great site that is absolutely packed with information about distilleries as well as history and recent bottlings.

www.whiskyguiden.se
An excellent Swedish site with thorough descriptions of most distilleries as well as continuously updated whisky news.

www.whiskyfun.com
Serge Valentin, one of the Malt Maniacs, is almost always first with well written tasting notes on new releases.

www.peatfreak.com
Jeroen Kloppenburg has created this whisky site with features, tasting notes and hundreds of relevant whisky links.

Statistics

The following pages cover statistics and forecasts on production, sales, exports, consumption and capacity. The pages have been made possible thanks to kind cooperation from mainly three sources - The Scotch Whisky Industry Review, Scotch Whisky Association and Euromonitor International.

The Scotch Whisky Industry Review 2008

is written and compiled by Alan S Gray,

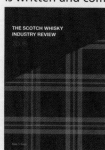

Sutherlands Edinburgh. It is now in its 31st consecutive year and provides a wealth of unique business critical information on the Scotch Whisky Industry on 284 pages.
Copies (£425 in the UK and £450 overseas) can be obtained from Sutherlands Edinburgh, 61 Dublin Street, Edinburgh EH3 6NL. (Telephone 0131 565 2020). Details also on the website **www.sutherlands-ed.com**

Scotch Whisky Association (SWA)

is the trade association for the Scotch Whisky industry. Its members account for more than 95% of production and sales of Scotch Whisky. Their main objective is to promote, protect and represent the interests of the whisky industry in Scotland and around the world. They also produce a plethora of statistical material covering production and sales of Scotch whisky. More information can be found on **www.scotch-whisky.org.uk**

Euromonitor International

is the world's leading independent provider of business intelligence on industries, countries and consumers. Founded in 1972, it is a privately owned company with offices in London, Chicago, Singapore, Shanghai and Vilnius. In this edition of the Yearbook, they gave us their kind permission to use the exciting whisk(e)y forecast that you can see on the next page. More information on **www.euromonitor.com**

Whisk(e)y forecast (volume & value) by region and sector 2007-2012

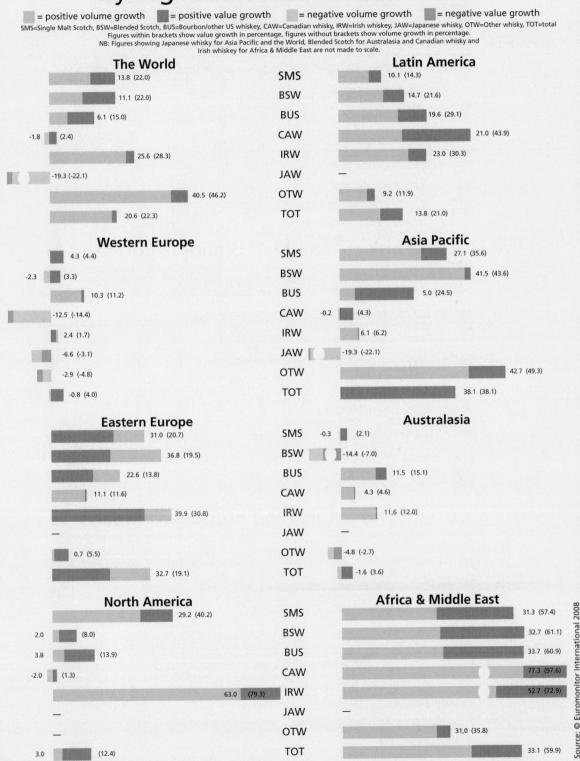

= positive volume growth = positive value growth = negative volume growth = negative value growth

SMS=Single Malt Scotch, BSW=Blended Scotch, BUS=Bourbon/other US whiskey, CAW=Canadian whisky, IRW=Irish whiskey, JAW=Japanese whisky, OTW=Other whisky, TOT=total
Figures within brackets show value growth in percentage, figures without brackets show volume growth in percentage.
NB: Figures showing Japanese whisky for Asia Pacific and the World, Blended Scotch for Australasia and Canadian whisky and
Irish whiskey for Africa & Middle East are not made to scale.

The World

SMS	13.8 (22.0)
BSW	11.1 (22.0)
BUS	6.1 (15.0)
CAW	-1.8 (2.4)
IRW	25.6 (28.3)
JAW	-19.3 (-22.1)
OTW	40.5 (46.2)
TOT	20.6 (22.3)

Latin America

SMS	10.1 (14.3)
BSW	14.7 (21.6)
BUS	19.6 (29.1)
CAW	21.0 (43.9)
IRW	23.0 (30.3)
JAW	—
OTW	9.2 (11.9)
TOT	13.8 (21.0)

Western Europe

SMS	4.3 (4.4)
BSW	-2.3 (3.3)
BUS	10.3 (11.2)
CAW	-12.5 (-14.4)
IRW	2.4 (1.7)
JAW	-6.6 (-3.1)
OTW	-2.9 (-4.8)
TOT	-0.8 (4.0)

Asia Pacific

SMS	27.1 (35.6)
BSW	41.5 (43.6)
BUS	5.0 (24.5)
CAW	-0.2 (4.3)
IRW	6.1 (6.2)
JAW	-19.3 (-22.1)
OTW	42.7 (49.3)
TOT	38.1 (38.1)

Eastern Europe

SMS	31.0 (20.7)
BSW	36.8 (19.5)
BUS	22.6 (13.8)
CAW	11.1 (11.6)
IRW	39.9 (30.8)
JAW	—
OTW	0.7 (5.5)
TOT	32.7 (19.1)

Australasia

SMS	-0.3 (2.1)
BSW	-14.4 (-7.0)
BUS	11.5 (15.1)
CAW	4.3 (4.6)
IRW	11.6 (12.0)
JAW	—
OTW	-4.8 (-2.7)
TOT	-1.6 (3.6)

North America

SMS	29.2 (40.2)
BSW	2.0 (8.0)
BUS	3.8 (13.9)
CAW	-2.0 (1.3)
IRW	63.0 (79.3)
JAW	—
OTW	—
TOT	3.0 (12.4)

Africa & Middle East

SMS	31.3 (57.4)
BSW	32.7 (61.1)
BUS	33.7 (60.9)
CAW	77.3 (97.6)
IRW	52.7 (72.9)
JAW	—
OTW	31,0 (35.8)
TOT	33.1 (59.9)

Source: © Euromonitor International 2008

Top five Scotch Whisky Single Malt brands UK sales %

Brand	Year	%
Glenfiddich	2007	13,6
	2006	15,0
	2005	14,5
Glenmorangie	2007	11,9
	2006	12,8
	2005	14,0
The Glenlivet	2007	5,7
	2006	5,1
	2005	3,8
Laphroaig	2007	5,7
	2006	4,9
	2005	5,0
The Macallan	2007	4,8
	2006	4,8
	2005	4,6

Top five Scotch Whisky Single Malt brands export sales %

Brand	Year	%
Glenfiddich	2007	14,5
	2006	12,9
	2005	14,8
The Glenlivet	2007	10,1
	2006	8,2
	2005	8,7
The Macallan	2007	9,5
	2006	7,6
	2005	8,7
Glen Grant	2007	5,6
	2006	6,7
	2005	7,6
Cardhu	2007	4,5
	2006	4,6
	2005	5,7

Top five Scotch Whisky Single Malt brands world sales %

Brand	Year	%
Glenfiddich	2007	14,4
	2006	13,1
	2005	14,8
The Glenlivet	2007	9,5
	2006	7,8
	2005	7,9
The Macallan	2007	8,9
	2006	7,2
	2005	8,0
Glenmorangie	2007	5,1
	2006	5,0
	2005	5,9
Glen Grant	2007	4,8
	2006	5,8
	2005	6,4

Source: The Scotch Whisky Industry Review 2008
(Sutherlands Edinburgh)

Top five Scotch Whisky Blended brands UK sales %

Bell's	2007	15,9
	2006	13,8
	2005	13,8
Famous Grouse	2007	14,2
	2006	13,9
	2005	13,7
Teacher's	2007	7,6
	2006	6,3
	2005	6,3
Grant's	2007	5,5
	2006	6,5
	2005	6,0
High Commissioner	2007	5,3
	2006	4,4
	2005	4,1

Top five Scotch Whisky Blended brands export sales %

J W Red	2007	11,4
	2006	10,7
	2005	10,4
Ballantine's	2007	6,6
	2006	6,6
	2005	7,0
JW Black	2007	6,5
	2006	5,7
	2005	5,4
J & B Rare	2007	6,3
	2006	6,8
	2005	7,4
Grant's	2007	5,0
	2006	5,0
	2005	4,9

Top five Scotch Whisky Blended brands world sales %

J W Red	2007	10,4
	2006	9,7
	2005	9,3
Ballantine's	2007	6,1
	2006	6,0
	2005	6,3
J W Black	2007	6,0
	2006	5,3
	2005	5,0
J & B	2007	5,8
	2006	6,2
	2005	6,6
Grant's	2007	5,1
	2006	5,1
	2005	5,0

Source: The Scotch Whisky Industry Review 2008
(Sutherlands Edinburgh)

World Consumption of Scotch Whisky

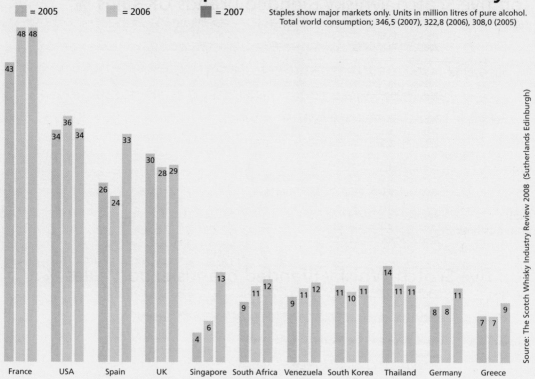

= 2005   = 2006   = 2007

Staples show major markets only. Units in million litres of pure alcohol.
Total world consumption; 346,5 (2007), 322,8 (2006), 308,0 (2005)

Source: The Scotch Whisky Industry Review 2008 (Sutherlands Edinburgh)

France: 43, 48, 48
USA: 34, 36, 34
Spain: 26, 24, 33
UK: 30, 28, 29
Singapore: 4, 6, 13
South Africa: 9, 11, 12
Venezuela: 9, 11, 12
South Korea: 11, 10, 11
Thailand: 14, 11, 11
Germany: 8, 8, 11
Greece: 7, 7, 9

Exports of Scotch Whisky

= volume in million litres of alcohol   = value in £ million (inflation adjusted)

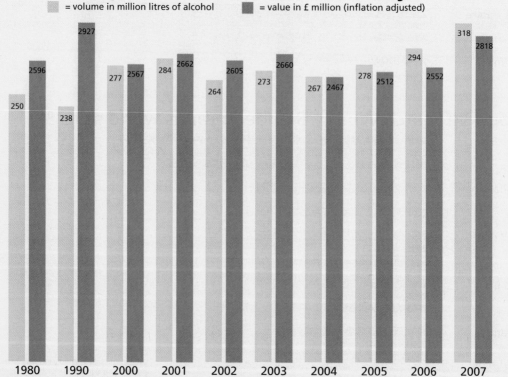

1980: 250, 2596
1990: 238, 2927
2000: 277, 2567
2001: 284, 2662
2002: 264, 2605
2003: 273, 2660
2004: 267, 2467
2005: 278, 2512
2006: 294, 2552
2007: 318, 2818

Source: Scotch Whisky Association and Office for National Statistics

Distillery Capacity

Litres of pure alcohol, Scottish, active distilleries only
* the figures for these distilleries are based on ongoing or planned extension (please note that Diageo's Roseisle distillery will go straight to the top of the list (10m litres) when operational in spring 2009)

Glenfiddich	10 000 000	Glen Elgin	1 830 000	Scapa	1 000 000
Glenlivet*	10 000 000	Balmenach	1 800 000	Tobermory	1 000 000
Macallan*	8 000 000	Auchentoshan	1 750 000	Knockdhu	900 000
Balvenie	6 200 000	Glenkinchie	1 750 000	Arran	750 000
Glenmorangie*	6 000 000	Strathmill	1 700 000	Glengyle	750 000
Glen Grant	5 900 000	Cragganmore	1 520 000	Glen Scotia	750 000
Glenrothes	5 600 000	Bruichladdich	1 500 000	Springbank	750 000
Miltonduff	5 500 000	Glencadam	1 400 000	Oban	670 000
Ardmore	5 100 000	Glenspey	1 390 000	Speyside	600 000
Ailsa Bay	5 000 000	Balblair	1 330 000	Benromach	500 000
Glen Ord	5 000 000	Glendronach	1 300 000	Royal Lochnagar	450 000
Tomatin	5 000 000	Knockando	1 290 000	Glenturret	340 000
Allt-a-Bhainne	4 500 000	Glengoyne	1 100 000	Bladnoch	100 000
Kininvie	4 400 000	Ardbeg	1 000 000	Daftmill	100 000
Clynelish	4 200 000	Glen Garioch	1 000 000	Edradour	90 000
Glenburgie	4 200 000	Glenglassaugh	1 000 000	Kilchoman	90 000
Dalmore	4 200 000	Pulteney	1 000 000		
Dufftown	4 120 000				
Tamnavulin	4 000 000				
Tamdhu	4 000 000				
Loch Lomond	4 000 000				
Teaninich	4 000 000				
Royal Brackla	3 900 000				
Braeval	3 800 000				
Tormore	3 700 000				
Caol Ila	3 650 000				
Craigellachie	3 600 000				
Auchroisk	3 580 000				
Aberfeldy	3 500 000				
Aberlour	3 500 000				
Longmorn	3 500 000				
Glentauchers	3 400 000				
Dailuaine	3 370 000				
Glendullan	3 360 000				
Tomintoul	3 300 000				
Mannochmore	3 220 000				
Macduff	3 200 000				
Deanston	3 000 000				
Glenfarclas	3 000 000				
Glenallachie	3 000 000				
Mortlach	2 910 000				
Aultmore	2 900 000				
Benriach	2 800 000				
Laphroaig	2 700 000				
Benrinnes	2 540 000				
Bunnahabhain	2 500 000				
Tullibardine	2 500 000				
Highland Park	2 500 000				
Strathisla	2 400 000				
Cardhu	2 390 000				
Fettercairn	2 300 000				
Lagavulin	2 250 000				
Linkwood	2 240 000				
Dalwhinnie	2 200 000				
Jura	2 200 000				
Glenlossie	2 140 000				
Speyburn	2 000 000				
Ben Nevis	2 000 000				
Bowmore	2 000 000				
Glen Moray	2 000 000				
Inchgower	1 990 000				
Blair Athol	1 940 000				
Talisker	1 940 000				

Summary of Malt Distillery Capacity by Category

Category	Litres of alcohol	% of Industry	Average capacity
Speyside (45)	162 090 000	60,9	3 602 000
Islands (6)	9 390 000	3,5	1 565 000
Rest of the Highlands (29)	68 220 000	25,6	2 352 000
Islay (8)	15 690 000	5,9	1 961 000
Lowlands (5)	8 700 000	3,3	1 740 000
Campbeltown (3)	2 250 000	0,8	750 000
Total (96)	**266 340 000**	**100**	**2 774 000**

Summary of Malt Distillery Capacity by Owner

Owner (number of distilleries)	Litres of alcohol	% of Industry
Diageo (27)	68 000 000	25,5
Pernod Ricard (12)	48 500 000	18,2
William Grant (4)	25 600 000	9,6
Edrington Group (5)	20 440 000	7,7
Bacardi (John Dewar & Sons) (5)	17 100 000	6,4
Whyte and Mackay (4)	12 700 000	4,8
Moët Hennessy (Glenmorangie) (3)	9 000 000	3,3
Beam Global (2)	7 800 000	2,9
Pacific Spirits (Inver House) (5)	7 030 000	2,6
C L Financial (Burn Stewart) (3)	6 500 000	2,4
Campari (Glen Grant) (1)	5 900 000	2,2
Tomatin Distillery Co (1)	5 000 000	1,9
Suntory (Morrison Bowmore) (3)	4 750 000	1,8
Loch Lomond Distillers (2)	4 750 000	1,8
Angus Dundee (2)	4 700 000	1,8
Benriach Distillery Co (2)	4 100 000	1,5
J & G Grant (1)	3 000 000	1,1
Tullibardine Distillery Ltd (1)	2 500 000	0,9
Nikka (Ben Nevis Distillery) (1)	2 000 000	0,8
Bruichladdich Distillery Co (1)	1 500 000	0,6
J & A Mitchell (2)	1 500 000	0,6
Ian Macleod Distillers (Glengoyne) (1)	1 100 000	less than 0,5
Scaent Group (Glenglassaugh) (1)	1 000 000	- " -
Isle of Arran Distillers (1)	750 000	- " -
Speyside Distillers Co (1)	600 000	- " -
Gordon & MacPhail (Benromach) (1)	500 000	- " -
Co-ordinated Developm. (Bladnoch) (1)	100 000	- " -
Francis Cuthbert (Daftmill) (1)	100 000	- " -
Kilchoman Distillery Co (1)	90 000	- " -
Signatory Vintage (Edradour) (1)	90 000	- " -

Do you want to find out more in detail where the different distilleries are situated? We suggest that you pay a visit to a new, excellent website - www.maltmaps.com. There you will find not only Scottish distilleries but all the other distilleries presented in Malt Whisky Yearbook.

Shetland

ORKNEY ISLANDS

Wick

Isle of Lewis

NORTH HIGHLANDS

SKYE

Kyle of Lockalsh

Inverness

SPEYSIDE

Aberdeen

Loch Ness

CENTRAL HIGHLANDS

Fort William

EAST HIGHLANDS

WEST HIGHLANDS

MULL

Oban

Pitlochry

Dundee

Loch Tay

Loch Lomond

Perth

St. Andrews

JURA

Stirling

Glasgow

Edinburgh

ISLAY

ARRAN

Campbeltown

Ayr

THE LOWLANDS

Dumfries

Stranraer

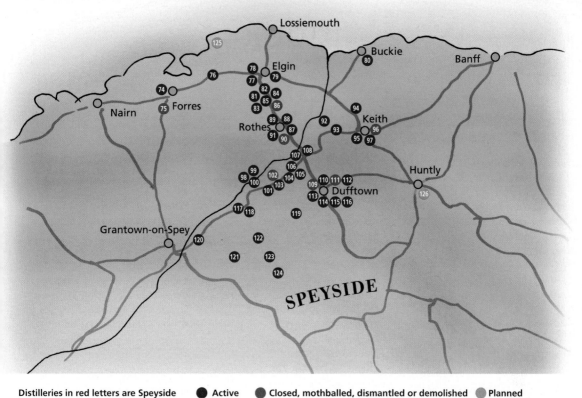

Lossiemouth

Buckie

Banff

Elgin

Nairn

Forres

Rothes

Keith

Huntly

Dufftown

Grantown-on-Spey

SPEYSIDE

Distilleries in red letters are Speyside ● **Active** ● **Closed, mothballed, dismantled or demolished** ● **Planned**

Index

Bold figures refer to the main entry in the distillery directory.

Index

Bold figures refer to the main entry in the distillery directory.

Index

Bold figures refer to the main entry in the distillery directory.